Debates in Primary Education

This powerful text encourages both pre-service and established teachers, as well as teacher educators, to engage with contemporary debates in primary education. Promoting a critical approach, the chapters explore a wide range of key themes including the importance of values in primary education and the imperative for a curriculum which embraces the whole range of available subjects. At the same time, the chapters are underpinned by a belief that children should be at the heart of all the decisions we make and that primary education should inspire a love of learning, for life.

The book aims to support practitioners to make informed judgements and feel confident to argue their point of view with deeper theoretical knowledge and understanding, thus increasing teacher agency and confidence in responding to complex educational and social dilemmas such as literacy levels and rising mental health concerns. Chapters encompass both the macro aspects of primary education and more specialised debates on key topics such as reading, mathematics, languages, early years education and the use of technology.

With annotated further reading and reflective questions, this key text is essential reading for all those wanting to develop a better understanding of the issues that shape their practice, including student teachers at both undergraduate and postgraduate level, practising teachers engaged in continuing professional development and teacher educators.

Virginia Bower is currently a Senior Lecturer at Canterbury Christ Church University and an Associate Lecturer with The Open University.

Debates in Subject Teaching
Series edited by Susan Capel

Each title in the Debates in Subject Teaching series presents high-quality material, specially commissioned to stimulate teachers engaged in initial teacher education, continuing professional development and Master's level study to think more deeply about their practice, and link research and evidence to what they have observed in schools. By providing up-to-date, comprehensive coverage, the books in the series support teachers in reaching their own informed judgements, enabling them to discuss and argue their point of view with deeper theoretical knowledge and understanding.

Debates in Geography Education, 2nd edition
Edited by Mark Jones and David Lambert

Debates in Computing and ICT Education
Edited by Sarah Younie and Pete Bradshaw

Debates in Physical Education, 2nd edition
Edited by Susan Capel and Richard Blair

Debates in English Teaching, 2nd edition
Edited by Jon Davison and Caroline Daly

Debates in Mathematics Education, 2nd edition
Edited by Gwen Ineson and Hilary Povey

Debates in Primary Education
Edited by Virginia Bower

For more information about this series, please visit: https://www.routledge.com/Debates-in-Subject-Teaching/book-series/DIST

Debates in Primary Education

Edited by Virginia Bower

Routledge
Taylor & Francis Group
LONDON AND NEW YORK

First published 2021
by Routledge
2 Park Square, Milton Park, Abingdon, Oxon OX14 4RN

and by Routledge
52 Vanderbilt Avenue, New York, NY 10017

Routledge is an imprint of the Taylor & Francis Group, an informa business

British Library Cataloguing-in-Publication Data
A catalogue record for this book is available from the British Library

Library of Congress Cataloging-in-Publication Data
Names: Bower, Virginia, editor.
Title: Debates in primary education / Edited by Virginia Bower.
Description: Abingdon, Oxon; New York, NY: Routledge, 2021. | Series: Debates in subject teaching | Includes bibliographical references and index.
Identifiers: LCCN 2020019622 (print) | LCCN 2020019623 (ebook) | ISBN 9780367548841 (hardback) | ISBN 9780367548865 (paperback) | ISBN 9781003091028 (ebook)
Subjects: LCSH: Education, Primary–Aims and objectives. | Primary school teachers–Training of. | Primary school teachers–In-service training.
Classification: LCC LB1513 .D43 2021 (print) | LCC LB1513 (ebook) | DDC 372–dc23
LC record available at https://lccn.loc.gov/2020019622
LC ebook record available at https://lccn.loc.gov/2020019623

ISBN: 978-0-367-54884-1 (hbk)
ISBN: 978-0-367-54886-5 (pbk)
ISBN: 978-1-003-09102-8 (ebk)

Typeset in Galliard
by Deanta Global Publishing Services, Chennai, India

Printed in the United Kingdom
by Henry Ling Limited

Contents

Illustrations

Figures

Tables

Contributors

Rebecca Austin is a Senior Lecturer at Canterbury Christ Church University. She works with students across initial teacher education, Master's and doctoral programmes. She has written books to support students working on research projects and undertaking assignments. Her interest lies in the ways in which student teachers come to their beliefs and values in relation to teaching – particularly the teaching of Primary English.

Jonathan Barnes is a Visiting Senior Research Fellow at Canterbury Christ Church University and a National Teaching Fellow. In a career spanning 47 years he has taught in Asia and Africa and in primary and secondary schools in England. He was head of a primary school throughout the 1990s and a university tutor until 2017. He writes on a values-led curriculum that connects academic subjects and the lives of young people. His books *Cross-Curricular Learning 3–14* and *Applying Cross-Curricular Approaches Creatively* are widely used in teacher education. He currently works with refugees and migrants in schools.

Andy Bloor is a Senior Lecturer at the University of Derby, a Fellow of the Higher Education Academy and a Fellow of the Royal Society of Arts. He is Programme Lead for the International Postgraduate Certificate in Education (iPGCE) and teaches across undergraduate and postgraduate SEND programmes and Initial Teacher Education courses. His research field is specifically looking at the language we use to describe inclusion and children with SEND. He has undertaken this research in the UK and US and hopes to extend it out to Europe in the next year. Before this, Andy was ITE Lead in SEND at Canterbury Christ Church University, where he worked on a World Bank–funded project supporting teacher educators in Palestine. This work was awarded the THE International Impact Award in 2018.

Virginia Bower is currently a Senior Lecturer at Canterbury Christ Church University and an Associate Lecturer with The Open University. Virginia has worked as a primary school teacher and senior leader before moving into higher education, and her research interests are poetry, pedagogy and practice in Primary English and supporting children with English as an Additional

Language. Her publications include *Developing Early Literacy: 0 to Eight*, London: SAGE (2014) and *Supporting Pupils with EAL in the Primary Classroom*, OU Press (2017).

Catherine Carden is a Senior Lecturer and Faculty Director of Learning and Teaching in the Faculty of Education at Canterbury Christ Church University. She is also a Senior Fellow of the Higher Education Academy and a Founding Fellow of the Chartered College of Teaching. She has taught in a range of educational settings and phases and held a variety of leadership positions both within Higher Education and school. She is also a Chair of Governors and contributes to a range of educational publications, conferences and teacher development programmes. Catherine's research and writing focuses broadly on educational leadership and the wider landscape of education and educational issues linked to policy and practice. Catherine was awarded a University Teaching Fellowship in 2015 for her innovative approaches to learning and teaching.

Teresa Cremin is a Professor of Education (Literacy) at The Open University. Teresa undertakes research and consultancy in the UK and abroad. Her sociocultural research focuses on volitional reading and writing, teachers' literate identities and practices and creative pedagogies. Teresa has written and edited nearly 30 books, including *Learning to Teach in the Primary School* (with Cathy Burnett, Ed., 4th edition, Routledge 2018), and she edits the accompanying series focused on Teaching Creatively across the primary curriculum. Her forthcoming text is *Children Reading for Pleasure in the Digital Age* (with Natalia Kucirkova, Sage, 2020).

Gina Donaldson is a Senior Lecturer at Canterbury Christ Church University, specialising in primary mathematics. Before this she has had extensive experience as a primary school teacher. Her interests are in teaching for mastery of mathematics, the role of the mathematics specialist teacher and teachers' mathematical subject knowledge.

Wendy Garner is a Senior Lecturer and Senior University Teaching Fellow within the Faculty of Education and Children's Services at the University of Chester. She has published extensively in the area of primary geography and also in relation to learning and teaching more generally. Wendy is also research active and currently undertaking a PhD.

Lee Hazeldine is a Research Fellow and Senior Lecturer in Education at Canterbury Christ Church University. He has a PhD in Philosophy and has over twenty years' experience working in education. Lee has previously worked as a learning consultant, providing guidance on effective teaching practice to a variety of educational professionals. He has published on a variety of subjects and has particular expertise in technology-based learning.

Leigh Hoath is a Senior Lecturer in Science Education at Leeds Trinity University. Her doctorate focussed on developing an effective pedagogy for teaching in the outdoor setting. She is editor of the Association for Science Education's journal *Primary Science*, a PSQM hub leader and regular writer and contributor at conferences within the UK and internationally.

Andrew Lambirth is a Professor of Education in The Faculty of Education and Health at The University of Greenwich, London. Andrew has published widely in the field of the teaching of Literacy and English, including: *Creativity and Writing: Developing Voice and Verve in the Classroom* (2005, Routledge) with Grainger and Goouch; *Understanding Reading and the Teaching of Phonics: Critical Perspectives* (2007, Open University); *Literacy on the Left: Reform and Revolution* (2007, Bloomsbury); *Understanding Reading and the Teaching of Phonics: Critical Perspectives* (2007, Open University) with Goouch; *Teaching Early Reading and Phonics: Creative Approaches to Early Literacy* (2011, Sage) with Goouch; *Making Poetry Matter* (2013, Bloomsbury) with Dymoke and Wilson.

Julia Lawrence is a Senior Lecturer in Education at the University of Hull. Julia has written on a number of subjects relating to primary education including physical education, mentoring, reflective practice and becoming a teacher educator.

Zoe Lewis is a Senior Lecturer in Early Years in the Department of Childhood, Youth and Community at Birmingham City University. Zoe worked as an early years teacher and leader while undertaking her Master's research, which explored assessment practices in Reception classes. She is currently studying for an EdD in Early Childhood Education where her research seeks to understand the role of the social and material environment in young children's creativity.

Rhiannon Love is a Senior Lecturer in the Institute of Education at the University of Winchester, where she is the Route Leader for the PGCE in Secondary Religious Education and Curriculum Lead for Primary RE and Philosophy for Children (P4C). Rhiannon has written on a number of subjects relating to P4C and primary education including links with RE, SMSC and wellbeing. She is currently completing her doctorate, which is exploring Student Teacher Identity, Performativity, Social Justice and Philosophy for Children.

Imran Mogra has worked with pupils of all age groups. He has published articles on various subjects and issues. He has written *Jumpstart RE* (Routledge, 2018) to enhance the teaching of Religious Education in primary schools and *Islam: A Guide for Teachers* (SAGE, 2020) to support subject knowledge of Islam. Imran is a Senior Lecturer in professional studies and RE on several programmes in the Department of Early Years and Primary Education at Birmingham City University.

Louise Pagden is the Co-Director of the Institute of Education, University of Winchester and is jointly responsible for the strategic and operational direction of the department. She has taught across initial teacher education programmes and postgraduate research courses. Louise's research interests lie in sociolinguistics, language and literacy, as well as education for forced migrants. Prior to working in higher education, Louise was a primary languages consultant and primary teacher in Hampshire.

Tony Pickford is a Visiting Lecturer in Education at the University of Chester. He is an active writer and researcher in the areas of primary history, primary geography and primary computing. His most recent research project explored the use of process drama in the teaching of prehistory.

Alistair Richardson is a Senior Lecturer at the University of Winchester, where he leads the Professional Doctorate and Master's in Social Research in Education programmes. He teaches mainly on initial teacher education courses, specialising in Religious Education and PSHE+C. His research interest is in teaching sensitive issues, specifically Holocaust Education – focusing on how young people emotionally engage with the topic of the Holocaust and the impact this has on their learning.

Hermione Ruck Keene is a Senior Lecturer in Creative Curriculum and Primary Education at Oxford Brookes University, where she teaches on BA Primary Education and Education Studies and PGCE programmes. Her school teaching career focused on primary music education and she has continued to research and write in this area since commencing her university career, with a particular interest in musical identity, participation and lifelong learning.

Vanessa Sawyer is a Senior Lecturer in Early Years/Primary Education and PGCE Primary Provider Lead Coordinator at Leeds Trinity University. Vanessa leads on Early Years Pedagogy and Enhancing the Curriculum modules and teaches both the undergraduate and postgraduate students. She has taught in four primary schools in both Leeds and Bradford and was an Assistant Headteacher and Early Years moderator for the Bradford district. Vanessa is currently working on her Master's in Education research study, exploring students' perceptions of staff and students working in collaboration.

Megan Stephenson is a Senior Lecturer in English and PGCE Primary Phase Coordinator for Primary Education at Leeds Trinity University. She leads the English team and teaches both the undergraduate and postgraduate students. She has taught in six primary schools in Leeds and Bradford over the last 22 years where she has led both the Reading Recovery and phonics teaching; including the training of staff within the local education authority. Megan has contributed to a number of books focusing on the value of a creative learning environment in order to develop a love of learning. She has presented at National Conferences in the UK on her approach to developing 'Inspirational Teacher Education', and is currently writing for a publication identifying the benefits of vocabulary-rich early years settings.

Paula Stone is a Senior Lecturer at Canterbury Christ Church University. Her thesis, entitled 'Confronting myself: An auto/biographical exploration of the impact of class and education on the formation of self and identity' is illustrative of her research interests; auto/biographical and ethnographical research, class, education, and self and identity. Paula has worked within Initial Teacher Education with student teachers for the past 12 years and has a particular passion for encouraging teachers and student teachers to see that research-informed practice and research-engaged practice are an integral part of their professional identity.

Introduction to the series

This book, *Debates in Primary Education*, is one of a series of books entitled Debates in Subject Teaching, many of which are now in their second and third editions. The series has been designed to engage with a wide range of debates related to subject teaching. Unquestionably, debates vary among the subjects, but may include, for example, issues that are related to:

- the definition, purpose and aims of the subject;
- the curriculum and content of the subject;
- subject pedagogy;
- the development of the subject and its future in the twenty-first century;
- the relationship between the subject and broader educational aims and objectives in society, and the philosophy and sociology of education.

The outcome of these debates might, for example, support the justification for the subject; be addressed in the classroom through the teaching of the subject and/or impact on initial teacher education and continuing professional development (CPD) in the subject.

Likewise, debates change within subjects over time. Consequently, each book presents key debates that subject teachers should understand, reflect on and engage in at the time it was written (and subsequent editions of the book are likely to include debates about different issues, as well as revisiting some enduring debates in the subject). Chapters have been designed to highlight major questions, and to consider the evidence from research and practice in order to find possible answers. Some subject books or chapters offer at least one solution or a view of the ways forward, whereas others provide alternative views and leave readers to identify their own solution or view of the ways forward. It is anticipated that readers will want to pursue the issues raised; hence, chapters include questions for further debate and suggestions for further reading. Debates covered in the series provide the basis for discussion in university subject seminars and meetings between professionals in school departmental meetings and in the context of CPD courses. The topics are also appropriate for consideration in assignments or classroom-based research. The books have been written for all those with a professional interest in the subject, including student teachers learning to teach the subject in primary schools; newly qualified teachers; teachers undertaking study at Master's level; teachers with a subject coordination or leadership role and those preparing for such responsibility; as well as school-based mentors, university tutors and advisers of the aforementioned groups.

Because of the range of issues covered, each subject book is an edited collection. Editors have commissioned new writing from experts on particular issues for debate, which, collectively, represent many different perspectives on a subject and the teaching of the subject. Readers should not expect a book in this series to: cover all aspects of a debate, cover the entire range of debates in a subject, offer a completely unified view of the subject/teaching of the subject, deal with each debate discretely. Part of what each book in this series offers to readers is the opportunity to explore the interrelationships between positions in debates and, indeed, among the debates themselves, by identifying the overlapping concerns and competing arguments that are woven through the text. Many initiatives in teaching continue to originate from central government, and, as a result, teachers have decreasing control of content, pedagogy and assessment strategies. It is strongly felt that for teaching to remain properly a vocation and a profession, teachers must be invited to be part of a creative and critical dialogue about teaching and learning, and should be encouraged to reflect, criticise, problem-solve and innovate. This series is intended to provide teachers with a stimulus for democratic involvement in the development of the discourse of teaching.

Susan Capel
March 2019

Introduction

This text aims to engage readers with key debates in Primary Education. It is suitable for those undertaking teacher education programmes; qualified practitioners and senior leaders working in settings where the education of young children is the primary goal; as well as for those working in initial teacher education. Chapters encompass both the macro aspects of Primary Education such as aims and values, curriculum and pedagogy; as well as more specialised debates covering areas such as reading, mathematics and the use of technology.

Successive governments, seemingly fuelled by a politically inspired desire for quick-fix remedies to complex educational and social dilemmas (for example, literacy levels, teenage disaffection and rising concerns with mental health and well-being), have become fixated on the false elixir of short-term expedient solutions. This might take the form of responding to the latest news of educational success elsewhere – systematic synthetic phonics or Singapore Maths – or grasping with almost frenetic zeal the emergent soundbites of education – rote learning, times tables, language learning from the age of five – airing them at every opportunity, before discarding them for the next fashion or fad.

It is too much of a cliché to describe the education of young children as a political football; clichés too easily skate the surface of deep chasms of ill-conceived pedagogies and practice. Primary Education might better be described as a vulnerable target, subject to the whim of those who aspire to power, who strive not for a long-term investment in the future of young people, but for immediate results and dramatic headlines. This vulnerability can, in important ways, be countered by the promotion and maintenance of a culture of integrity and open-mindedness, where discussion and debate move learning and Primary Education forward in a way that benefits both teacher and taught.

There will always be debate about how primary-aged children are best educated to equip them for the next phase of their lives and ultimately for living, working and flourishing in the modern world. These debates must, however, be underpinned by theory that has emerged from the study of learning and teaching over decades, and be grounded in the research and practice of those who have the education of the whole child at the centre of their beliefs. Children deserve memorable primary school experiences, inspired by those who believe that the concepts of teaching and learning are reciprocal and responsive to the needs of individuals. To retain these principles and to ensure that a teaching career is sustainable within an era of accountability, it is vital that key debates – where a range of perspectives are aired – are shared and discussed and permeate our everyday practice. This book aims to introduce a number of these debates and to present viewpoints both to interest and challenge the reader.

Each chapter concludes with questions to invite reflection, further reading and appropriate resources for future study. The chapters are not presented in any particular order, although the first four focus on generic aspects including the purpose of education and values. Following this, the chapters offer perspectives on different subjects and age groups and are designed to be read as part of the whole text, or selected individually at moments when they might most support or inspire you. The authors come from diverse backgrounds and experiences and it is hoped that, because of this, a range of philosophies, perspectives and debating points will emerge. A commonality, however, is the authors' commitment to placing the child at the centre of Primary Education alongside a determination to do justice to principles and practice underpinned by robust and authoritative research.

Chapter 1

The purpose of education

The purpose of primary education

Virginia Bower

Introduction

It seemed imperative, in a book debating a range of aspects of primary education, that the starting point debate the *purpose* of education; and more specifically, the purpose of *primary* education. Although opinions on this will vary, highlighting these differing viewpoints is essential in order to better understand the arguments put forward throughout the book. What we believe to be the purpose of education will depend on a substantial range of factors including our own experience of education; our philosophies; our political standpoints; and our personal and professional lives.

Only once we have a clear definition in mind can decisions be made regarding curriculum content, pedagogies to be promoted and assessment methods. The problem, of course, is that the definition for a primary school teacher might differ considerably from the definition for a politician, or for a local authority, a head teacher or other colleagues. The ensuing tensions have the potential to affect both how children learn and their experience of school; teacher agency and autonomy; and satisfaction with and retention to the profession. This does not, however, mean that different philosophies, approaches, pedagogies and practices cannot be mutually accommodating. What is important, though, is a thorough understanding of the theory and research which underpin viewpoints, so that informed decisions can be made, built on robust evidence and with the learner as the centre of the debate.

This chapter will begin by exploring three theoretical models which underpin beliefs relating to the purpose of education and, consequently, the approaches taken in terms of curriculum, pedagogy and assessment. These models are the human capital model, the rights-based model and the capabilities model, and were chosen because they encapsulate some of the challenges faced when deciding the purpose of education. It will be argued that our view of the purpose of education will inevitably be influenced – in some way – by all three theoretical models and that there are strengths and challenges with each. However, a stance will then be taken arguing that in primary education a focus on the capabilities model is more likely to offer young learners the holistic, innovative, motivational educational experience they deserve, and which they need to prepare them for an exciting but arguably unforeseeable future. Four themes are discussed, which are felt to reflect the capabilities model and which might be utilised to underpin the purpose of primary education: education for sustainable development; education to prepare learners for an uncertain future; education which promotes a critical, questioning stance; and education for lifelong learning. Before summarising, the chapter finishes with a consideration of the challenges for us all in defining a purpose and remaining true to it.

What lies behind our beliefs? Three theoretical models

Human capital model

Human capital theory is centred on the area of economic growth, whereby workers are seen as commodities. Within this, the purpose of education is seen as instrumental; preparing learners for the world of work, where their knowledge, skills and experience will benefit the economy, and therefore the focus 'is on a person's income-generating abilities' (Robeyns, 2006, p.72), as 'an educated population is a productive population' (Olaniyan and Okemakinde, 2008, p.479). An education system built on this model will promote curricula, pedagogies and assessment systems which reflect the perceived needs of society and within which measurement of ability and success takes priority. There are clear benefits to this, in that there is the potential for learners to feel motivated and inspired as they look towards their working future and their earning potential. They can see their education as contributing to both the collective and individual good. Also, if governments believe that education has the potential to raise the economic status of their country, they are likely to be more willing to invest in it.

Of course, this model also imposes severe limitations in terms of the education provided and the philosophy driving the education system, as 'it does not recognize the intrinsic importance of education, nor the personal and collective instrumental social roles of education' (Robeyns, 2006, p.74). Within a human capital approach to education, focus tends to rest on standardisation, accountability and measurable assessment. Freire (2001, p.102) warned that this leads to a loss of freedom, creativity and the desire to take risks; and a 'mass production' of the conforming individual. Freire talks about the 'fatalistic philosophy of neoliberal politics' (ibid., p.93) and how this ensures that whenever market values are threatened, human interests are abandoned.

Klees (2016) argues that it is impossible to measure the impact of education on 'society as a whole' (p.647) and that to decide to invest in particular aspects of education or specific age groups based on what is perceived as economic efficiency is to believe in a world where the rate of return is easily measurable. In other words, if this much investment is put into primary education, the result will be this. Klees (ibid., p.651) argues that the rate of return based on what people earn is not useful because it does not provide a 'complete and accurate picture of social returns and can result in a major misdirection of policy'. He goes on to say that you cannot accurately measure education's impact on earnings, as there are too many variables including health, amount and quality of schooling, gender, cognition and race. Another perspective on this is from the economist Sen (n.d., p.42), who puts forward the idea that 'a country can be very rich in conventional economic terms (i.e., in terms of the value of commodities produced per capita) and still be very poor in the achieved quality of human life'. In a later section examining the capabilities model, Sen's ideas will be further examined.

An education system based on the human capital model also needs to be well-informed in terms of what employers perceive as valuable in their workforce. The current government's focus is on a knowledge-based curriculum, with the potential to further block 'creative teaching' and lead to 'a greater emphasis on didactic approaches' (Dadds, 2001, p.44), and yet conversely, 'industry is crying out for 21st-century skills – CEOs last year put collaboration (50 per cent), honesty (27 per cent) and vision (25 per cent) ahead of knowledge (19 per cent) as essentials for success' (Heppell, 2016, no page).

You might at this point want to consider in what ways the curriculum, pedagogies and assessment systems with which you are familiar reflect elements of the human capital model.

Rights-based model

Fundamentally, the rights-based model posits that all children are entitled to an education and that 'education is not seen simply as "a good thing" to be pursued if and when there are some funds available, but rather as the right of every child, implying that any government needs to mobilize the resources needed to offer a quality education' (Robeyns, 2006, p.75). Notice here that Robeyns refers to 'quality' education, linking with Biesta's (2015, p.81) argument that 'the duty of education is to ensure that there is good education for everyone everywhere'. The human rights model is more concerned here with accessibility for all and a removal of barriers to learning, which might include finance, travel, geography, political stability and disabilities. It might be imagined that these barriers are not so relevant to countries in the developed world, but Rodriguez (2013, p.87) argues that in a 'policy context that privileges conformity and standardization over responsiveness and inclusiveness, educators confront hegemonic forces that continue to shape public education for the majority of students living in poverty or who are ethnically, linguistically, and otherwise diverse'. The barriers are therefore likely to be a reality in all settings.

A rights-based approach aims to make education accessible for all, but assessing the quality of that education is more problematic and it is possible that, in making the purpose to ensure education for all, corners might be cut in terms of teacher training and professional development and resources, leading to a prescribed perspective on what a school curriculum might consist of (Ngwaru, 2011) – which often fails to take into account diverse lives, languages and cultures. Platt (2007, p.505) describes English society as both 'class stratified' and 'discriminatory', which makes certain groups more vulnerable than others. Furthermore, 'lack of equality of opportunity, can compound the effect of the lack of equal starting positions that vex the whole meritocratic ideal' (ibid.). It is unlikely that a quality education can emerge from this, and if the education lacks quality, then learners are unlikely to be in the best position to contribute to the economy (see the human capital model), or to become flourishing, fulfilled, lifelong learners (see the capabilities model).

At this point, you might want to consider how accessible the curriculum is to all the learners in your setting. Are there any barriers to them receiving a quality education?

Capabilities model

Amartya Sen is an economist and authority in this area and believes that a capability approach 'sees human life as a set of "doings and beings" – we may call them "functionings" – and it relates the evaluation of the quality of life to the assessment of the capability to function' (n.d., p.43). Capability theory is centred on one's ability and freedom to make choices about what one wants to do and be, and of course this is highly relevant when we think about the purpose of education and what it has the potential to achieve.

The model is focused on social justice, which, it might be argued, associates it directly with the human rights model. However, in the rights-based model there is the potential – in the well-meant aim of education for all – to fail to consider barriers which face individuals or groups or for an education to be provided which is not of good and/or sufficient quality. In the capability approach, however, 'all sources of inequalities in people's opportunity sets are taken into account, hence in principle a capability analysis should always strive to account for all significant effects, even if this is a hard task' (Robeyns, 2006, p.79). In the striving for equality within the human rights model,

> Equality of resources falls short because it fails to take account of the fact that individuals need differing levels of resources if they are to come up to the same level of capability to function. They also have differing abilities to convert resources into actual functioning.
>
> (Nussbaum, 2003, p.35)

The capabilities model promotes the idea that people should be given the freedom to do what they want to do and be what they want to be (functionings), but of course they need the capabilities to achieve this. Schools have the power to provide opportunity, motivation, resources, ideas, knowledge, space, support and a nurturing environment; they also have the power to restrict all of these elements, thus reducing learners' capabilities, as 'schools and communities continue to reflect pervasive, overt and subtle power balances that related to the economic, political, and social history and context of society at every level' (Rodriguez, 2013, p.103).

One could argue that the capabilities model has strong connections with Grant's (2012) notion of the importance of 'cultivating flourishing lives', wherein learners receive an education 'that is responsive to their identity and cultural historical background' (ibid., p.911). Grant writes that the purpose of education and the job of every teacher is to cultivate 'the intellect of *every* student' (ibid., p.915, original emphasis) and that teachers should:

> hold high expectations for students, recognize the intellectual capacity of often marginalized students, provide curriculum content that is challenging and culturally responsive, and maintain ongoing reflective assessment of what they teach, how they teach, and why.
>
> (ibid.)

Here you can see the interconnectedness of a clear purpose for education and the role of the teacher, the result being learners who have the capabilities to achieve what they want to do and be. To what extent does the learning and teaching in your setting allow for this capabilities approach?

Bringing the models together

I would argue that, in a pursuit of the purpose of education, we are all influenced, to some degree, by these three theoretical models, but that it is the balance which affects curriculum design, pedagogy and statutory assessment. It would be difficult to argue against good education for all, that prepares students for their futures and which brings to them the opportunity to flourish and contribute to wider society. The issue lies in what is believed to be 'good' education, how those 'futures' are envisaged and what stands in the way of 'flourishing' lives. Biesta (2015, p.76) argues that the purpose of education is not simply 'to learn'. Instead, he posits that 'the point of education is that students learn *something*, that they learn it for a *reason*, and that they learn it *from someone*' (ibid., original emphasis). This brings us back to the three models, as these will of course influence what this 'something' is – knowledge and skills; what this 'reason' is – for work, for intellectual satisfaction, for the joy of learning; and of course who this 'someone' is – including government ministers from whom prescribed directives emerge, local authorities, head teachers, teachers, teaching assistants, classroom helpers and so on, who may all be working to different agendas.

Perhaps one way of bringing the models together is to consider what Biesta refers to as the 'domains of educational purpose'. He describes these as 'qualification, socialisation and subjectification'. Qualification relates to the 'transmission and acquisition of knowledge, skills and dispositions' (ibid., p.77) and relates directly to the English National Curriculum aims:

> The national curriculum provides pupils with an introduction to the essential knowledge they need to be educated citizens. It introduces pupils to the best that has been thought and said and helps engender an appreciation of human creativity and achievement.
>
> (DfE, 2014, no page)

Of course, the way that 'qualification' is interpreted within curricula, pedagogies and assessment systems has an impact on whether the knowledge and skills are prescribed for a narrow purpose, or whether they are designed to promote intellectual curiosity and a commitment to lifelong learning.

Biesta goes on to examine his second domain – socialisation – whereby learners are introduced to 'ways of being and doing, such as cultural, professional, political, religious traditions' (ibid.). This has clear links with Bruner's ideas on the purpose of education in terms of cultural identity:

> a failure to equip minds with the skills for understanding and feeling and acting in the cultural world is not simply scoring a pedagogical zero. It risks creating alienation, defiance, and practical incompetence. And all of these undermine the viability of a culture.
>
> (Bruner, 1999, p.43)

The problem, of course, is that the 'ways of being and doing' may well reproduce the existing social order, with its attendant inequalities and structures which restrict access to many.

Biesta's final domain is subjectification, which he describes as 'the way in which children and young people come to exist as subjects of initiative and responsibility rather than as objects of the actions of others' (Biesta, 2015, p.77). Here, the onus is on developing curious, independent learners – 'a curiosity that is critical, bold, and adventurous' (Freire, 2001, p.38) – who can be responsive to the demands of the 21st century and flexible in terms of methods, resources and conceptual thinking.

Biesta claims that seeing these three domains as interlocking and mutually dependent enables us to identify a more transparent educational purpose; to adjust to what learners need to know (whilst acknowledging that who makes decisions on this content has a significant effect); to respond to the environment within which they are living their lives; and to promote their development as unique individuals.

The purpose of primary education

This book debates issues relating to *primary* education. Now that I have discussed perspectives relating to the purpose of education more generally, this section will focus more specifically on the purpose of that phase. The discussion assumes that a capabilities approach is vital, ensuring that young children are given the opportunities to be the best that they can be; to set them up as confident, inquisitive, empowered individuals, who have been given the foundations to lead 'flourishing lives' (Grant, 2012). But to achieve this, purposes need to be clearly defined, as without these, it is not possible to design curricula, pedagogies and assessments which embed the capabilities model.

Alexander (2010), in his Cambridge Primary Review (CPR) Final Report, *Children, Their World, Their Education*, groups his aims for primary education into three:

- The individual;
- Self, others and the wider world;
- Learning, knowing and doing.

The first group – the individual – considers well-being, engagement, empowerment and autonomy. The second – self, others and the wider world – attends to respect and reciprocity; promoting interdependence and sustainability; empowering local, national and global citizenship; and celebrating community and culture. And the final group – learning, knowing and doing – consists of exploring, knowing, understanding and making sense; fostering skill; exciting the imagination; and enacting dialogue. These aims have been adopted by many primary schools in England (Alexander, 2016) and it is from these that my own four key purposes of primary education have emerged. These purposes are inevitably broad and are designed more to promote you to consider what *you* believe the purpose of primary education to be. You could then take a closer look at the CPR aims and begin to think about how purposes and aims might come together in your classroom.

I propose four key purposes for primary education:

- Education for sustainable development;
- Education to prepare learners for an uncertain future;
- Education which promotes a critical, questioning stance;
- Education for lifelong learning.

Primary education for sustainable development

Education is a key driver for sustainable development as 'behavioural change and public awareness' (Mohanty and Dash, 2018, p.2253) are crucial. Sustainable Development Goal (SDG) 4 is focused specifically on education – 'Quality Education – Ensure inclusive and equitable quality education and promote lifelong learning opportunities for all' (UNESCO, 2017, p.6). Within the learning objectives for the SDGs, it is argued that education has a duty to ensure that the thoughts and practices of learners are transformed, and to promote 'the knowledge, skills, values and attitudes that empower them to contribute to sustainable development' (ibid., p.7).

The purpose of education here is complex and demanding, particularly as we are unclear about the future challenges, both globally and locally, and it is difficult to predict what knowledge or skills are going to be most useful or powerful. However, Wade (2014) argues that employers want a workforce which is sustainably literate, as a focus on sustainable development requires the promotion of creative thinking and looking beyond current boundaries towards so far unseen possibilities. This is certainly more complex than teaching to a test and is perhaps, therefore, less palatable to those who wish to hold us accountable (Wade, 2014). However, if we look at one of the key aims highlighted in the UNESCO learning objectives (2017), there are undoubtedly ways that the primary curriculum might reflect these aims, moving forward with a clear vision and purpose:

> ESD aims at developing competencies that empower individuals to reflect on their own actions, taking into account their current and future social, cultural, economic and environmental impacts, from a local and a global perspective. Individuals should also be empowered to act in complex situations in a sustainable manner, which may require them to strike out in new directions; and to participate in socio-political processes, moving their societies towards sustainable development.
>
> (UNESCO, 2017, p.7)

A curriculum which encourages learners to engage with the local and the global; to take responsibility for their actions; and to be able to debate current issues, their historical backgrounds and the implications for the future – this would be a curriculum of which to be proud. Part of this purpose is to prepare children to go into society ready to challenge injustice and inequality, not to accept subordination (Cummins, 2001); to have the courage and language to stand up for their beliefs – beliefs which are grounded in a secure understanding of key global and local issues. This would ensure a dynamic and exciting learning experience incorporating a focus on issues surrounding the environment, the economy and society generally, alongside attention to personal life quality and personal development (Mohanty and Dash, 2018).

Primary education to prepare learners for an uncertain future

Sustainable education – open to new ideas, discussion, debate and argument – must be a better alternative to a narrow, prescribed curriculum, heavy in knowledge which may not be in any way relevant to learners in primary school settings. Bass (1997) believes that a curriculum needs to preserve what is worthwhile and learned from previous generations, whilst promoting change and innovation in response to a changing world, and although these ideas are 25 years old, there is much to be taken from them when considering the purpose of primary education. Prince highlights some of the requisites of an education suited to an uncertain future:

- Curriculum needs to be inverted, with core social-emotional competencies shaping the design of inquiry projects and the school and classroom rituals that anchor the learning climate and culture;
- Students need to be grouped in new ways to follow flexible learning pathways;

- Classrooms need to become more fluid and open, enabling new ways of structuring learning;
- School schedules need to be transformed to allow for more interdisciplinary collaboration, deep reflection and personalized learning;
- Educators' roles need to be reconfigured to focus less on content or grade specialization and more on foundational skills and practices, as well as on interdisciplinary, phenomenological or challenge-based learning.

(Prince, 2019, no page)

Much of this is in evidence in many primary classrooms, but much more could be done. This would rely, however, on a clear purpose for education and a system that trusted teachers to take risks, utilise creative assessment strategies, and be flexible in terms of curriculum content and pedagogies.

Primary education which promotes a critical, questioning stance

The extent of information that is available freely to children globally in these times, whether this is through television, access to the Internet, social media, e-books, advertising campaigns and so forth, is as comprehensive as it is bewildering. Developing a critical stance towards this data bombardment is essential, to sift out the 'wheat from the chaff' and to remain aware that what is accessed is not necessarily how things are. According to Massa (2014, p.388), critical thinking is to apply 'meaningful, self-regulatory judgment', and developing critical thinking enables learners to 'evaluate the correctness, the merit and the validity of claims or arguments' (Asari, 2014, p.2). This requires a focus on problem-solving, active learning and plenty of time to collaborate and exchange ideas, reflecting Freire's ideas that 'to teach is not *to transfer knowledge* but to create the possibilities for the production or construction of knowledge' (Freire, 2001, p.30, original emphasis), and in this way, the teacher and the student are both being formed and reformed.

If we see one of the purposes of education as providing young learners with the skills and confidence to be critical thinkers, it may be that we have to re-think 'normal' classroom practices and embrace what Faltis and Abedi (2013, p.viii) describe as 'extraordinary pedagogies' which enable us to transform the curriculum to ensure its appropriateness for children learning in 21st-century classrooms.

Primary education for lifelong learning

Ates and Alsal (2012) provide four reasons why lifelong learning should be actively promoted:

- Increase in life expectancy;
- Old-age dependency ratio;

- To maintain life quality;
- To keep in good mental and physical health.

Because we are living longer, we are often working longer, and this requires the ability to adapt to what is needed in the workforce and to be prepared constantly to update one's knowledge and understanding of different fields. This is linked closely to the second reason above, where it is acknowledged that there is an increasing old-age population in relation to the younger generation, and this has a two-fold effect. The younger members of society may have to undertake a range of jobs during their working lives, taking the place of older workers, whilst engaging with the current labour force requirements. And, alongside this, the older generation may be required to learn new skills to enable them to continue in the labour market for longer. You might reflect on these points in relation to the human capital model discussed earlier, whilst making further connections with the capabilities model in terms of quality of life; part of which is feeling that one can 'flourish' (see earlier discussion) at all stages and ages of life and being confident to engage with new ways of working, including technologies, communication and transport, whilst being mindful of sustainability issues. The fourth point – being mindful of one's physical and mental health – is vital to ensuring the success of the others.

But how does lifelong learning play a part in all of these and how can primary education promote this? Lifelong learning can be for personal fulfilment or career advancement, and it starts with the youngest learners in early years and primary settings. To experience the joy of discovery and to learn something just for the pleasure it gives are what we need to facilitate in primary classrooms. If children conclude, at a young age, that they are merely learning something so that they can regurgitate the information in a test, we are not preparing them for lifelong learning. If we think back to the capabilities model, discussed earlier, the focus is on 'what people are actually able to do and to be' (Nussbaum, 2003, p.39), and one of our key purposes for education should be to ensure children's minds are kept open to what they can do and be and to promote the idea that learning empowers, endures and enlightens.

Challenges

There are huge pressures on those who work in educational settings because the purpose of education means different things to different people. Schools are expected to attain national and international benchmarks, where the human capital model exerts its powerful influence. Teachers are expected to prepare young learners for these assessments, being aware that they may not be preparing them to be successful in the modern world or, indeed, be personally fulfilled by their learning. Because of the increased accountability and expectations for linear progression, coverage of the curriculum becomes the focus rather than learning. The emphasis shifts from responding to the needs of the children, and merely reacts to the prescribed requirements of imposed curricula (Dadds, 2001). At the same time, parental expectations regarding the purpose of education for their children might be very different and pressure is exerted from that direction. This is on top of being potentially overwhelmed by the day-to-day demands of a primary school teacher's life.

Teacher agency is therefore essential, as a curriculum is only as good as the way it is implemented or, indeed, allowed to be implemented. Teachers need to feel convinced by the purpose of education and utilise pedagogies to promote this, alongside the belief that they can make informed decisions about curriculum implementation which best reflect the learners in their classrooms. Alexander (2004, p.7) defines pedagogy as 'both the act of teaching and its attendant discourse' and writes that pedagogy in England is 'neither coherent nor systematic' (ibid., p.8). This is partly because ideology and pragmatism combine to produce an unattainable goal, particularly for teachers in their early careers, who find that the theory and understanding they meet in training fails to match up with what they experience in schools (ibid.). Alexander talks about government 'doublespeak', where, on the one hand, autonomy is promoted in relation to teaching and pedagogy; and on the other, the main focus is on tests, targets and performance-related pay – 'offering freedom while in reality maintaining control' (ibid., p.15).

To come to a decision about what you believe the purpose of education to be and to have the courage to ensure that this purpose provides the foundation for everything you do in the classroom is a duty for us all. The purpose for the young children we teach has also to be *our* purpose and be driven by the same aims: to live sustainable lives, be appreciative yet critical of modern advances, be prepared for whatever the future brings and ensure we are advocates for and models of lifelong learning.

Summary

Without a clear purpose for education and, more specifically, a clear purpose for *primary* education, it is unlikely that young learners will receive an education which allows them to lead flourishing lives. If there is no clear purpose, there is the danger of abstract notions around learning prevailing or the focus on assessment and testing becoming the tail that wags the dog (Klitmoller, 2016). A lack of purpose, or a purpose which is not underpinned by research, experience and an eye to the future, equals a lack of direction. This, in turn, leads to a dangerous susceptibility to the designs of those who seek only to promote their own values and for whom education is perceived as a tool for self-promotion and a vehicle for personal ideologies to prevail, based not on robust and rigorous research, but on narrow, elitist, privileged experiences of schools and schooling. Dadds writes that:

> Too much centralised power has generated a pedagogy in both teacher training and in schools, which is silencing enquiry and diverse critical perspectives of both teachers and children.
>
> (2001, p.43)

Having a clear purpose and a depth of understanding of what underpins teaching and learning for the 21st-century empowers us to challenge this centralised power and to demand the rights to be co-creators of curricula; to be innovators. The chapters throughout this book provide debates around key issues in primary education, and knowledge and understanding of these is empowering on its own. However, they also provide numerous examples of exciting and innovative approaches to teaching and learning, illustrating some of the purposes of education highlighted in this chapter. This will, I hope, instil a sense of hope, allowing us to embrace the challenges and make the most of the lively, receptive minds we work with each and every day. And finally, keep in mind Freire's metaphor as you develop your own purpose of education:

> the active knower, not the mind as a repository of "information", is the goal of education.
>
> (2001, p.14)

Questions for reflection

What do you believe the purpose of education to be?

How have your own life, experiences, education and workplaces influenced this belief?

How would you hope to encourage those you teach to be lifelong learners?

Further reading and resources

Alexander, R. J. (ed.) (2010) *Children, Their World, Their Education: Final Report and Recommendations of the Cambridge Primary Review*. Oxon: Routledge.

Note, this publication will give you hope. Published in 2010, 'the CPR was the most comprehensive enquiry into England's system of primary education for nearly half a century. Between 2006 and 2012, and supported by researchers from 20 other universities, the CPR's Faculty-based team assembled a vast array of evidence and published 31 interim reports' (Cambridge University, n.d.).

Freire, P. (2001) *Pedagogy of Freedom*. Oxford: Rowman and Littlefield.

This book is uplifting, yet provocative – a book not just about education but about life and learning. Freire questions our seeming endorsement of a world that accepts poverty and extreme wealth positioned side by side. You might want to consider this alongside the three models discussed in this chapter.

References

Alexander, R. J. (2004) 'Still No Pedagogy? Principle, Pragmatism and Compliance in Primary Education', *Cambridge Journal of Education*, 34(1): 7–33.

Alexander, R. J. (ed.) (2010) *Children, Their World, Their Education: Final Report and Recommendations of the Cambridge Primary Review*. Oxon: Routledge.

Alexander, R. J. (2016) 'What works and what matters: Education in spite of policy', *Primary Education: What is and What Might Be, Cambridge Primary Review Trust National Conference*, London, 18 November 2016.

Asari, R. A. (2014) 'Ideas for Developing Critical Thinking at Primary School Level', *Paper Presented at an International Seminar on Addressing Higher Order Thinking: Critical Thinking Issues in Primary Education, Islamic University of Muhammadiyah Makassar*, 12–13 April 2014. Makassar.

Ates, H. & Alsal, K. (2012) 'The Importance of Lifelong Learning Has Been Increasing', *Procedia - Social and Behavioural Sciences*, 46: 4092–4096.

Bass, R. V. (1997) 'The Purpose of Education', *The Education Forum*, 61(2): 128–132.

Biesta, G. (2015) 'What Is Education For? On Good Education, Teacher Judgement and Educational Professionalism', *European Journal of Education*, 50(1): 75–87.

Bruner, J. (1999) *The Culture of Education*. London: Harvard University Press.

Cambridge University (n.d.) *Cambridge Primary Review Trust: The National Primary Network*. Available at: https://www.educ.cam.ac.uk/networks/primaryreview/ (Accessed 02.02.20).

Cummins, J. (2001) *Language, Power and Pedagogy*. Clevedon, England; Buffalo, NY: Multilingual Matters Ltd.

Dadds, M. (2001) 'The Politics of Pedagogy Teachers and Teaching', *Teachers and Teaching*, 7(1): 43–58.

Department for Education (2014) *National Curriculum in England: Framework for Key Stages 1 to 4*. Available at: https://www.gov.uk/government/publications/national-curriculum-in-england-framework-for-key-stages-1-to-4/the-national-curriculum-in-england-framework-for-key-stages-1-to-4 (Accessed 31.01.20).

Faltis, C. & Abedi, J. (2013) 'Extraordinary Pedagogies for Working Within School Settings Serving Non-Dominant Students', *Review of Research in Education*, 37(1): vii–xi.

Freire, P. (2001) *Pedagogy of Freedom*. Oxford: Rowman and Littlefield.

Grant, C. A. (2012) 'Cultivating Flourishing Lives: A Robust Social Justice Vision of Education', *American Educational Research Journal*, 49(5): 910–934.

Heppell, S. (2016) 'Opinion: Stephen Heppell on the Importance of Arts Education', *Tate Etc.*, (37), Summer. Available at: https://www.tate.org.uk/tate-etc/issue-37-summer-2016/opinion-stephen-heppell-on-importance-arts-education (Accessed 31.01.20).

Klees, S. J. (2016) 'Human Capital and Rates of Return: Brilliant Ideas or Ideological Dead Ends?' *Comparative Education Review*, 60(4): 643–672.

Klitmøller, J. (2016) 'Educational Practice, Student Experience, and the Purpose of Education – A Critique of 'Pedagogy in Practice'', *Oxford Review of Education*, 42(6): 646–660.

Massa, S. (2014) 'The Development of Critical Thinking in Primary School: The Role of Teachers' Beliefs', *Procedia - Social and Behavioural Sciences*, 141: 387–392.

Mohanty, D. & Dash, D. (2018) 'Education for Sustainable Development: A Conceptual Model of Sustainable Education for India', *International Journal of Development and Sustainability*, 7(9): 2242–2255.

Ngwaru, J. M. (2011) 'Transforming Classroom Discourse and Pedagogy in Rural Zimbabwe Classrooms: The Place of Local Culture and Mother Tongue Use', *Language and Culture and Curriculum*, 24(3): 221–240.

Nussbaum, M. C. (2003) 'Capabilities a Fundamental Entitlements: Sen and Social Justice', *Feminist Economics*, 9(2–3): 33–59.

Olaniyan, D. A. & Okemakinde, T. (2008) 'Human Capital Theory: Implications for Educational Development', *Pakistan Journal of Social Sciences*, 5(5): 479–483.

Platt, L. (2007) 'Making Education Count: The Effects of Ethnicity and Qualifications on Intergenerational Social Class Mobility', *The Sociological Review*, 55(3): 484–508.

Prince, K. (2019) *Preparing All Learners for an Uncertain Future of Work*. Available at https://www.gettingsmart.com/2019/02/preparing-all-learners-for-an-uncertain-future-of-work/ (Accessed 31.01.20).

Robeyns, I. (2006) 'Three Models of Education: Rights, Capabilities and Human Capital', *Theory and Research in Education*, 4(1): 69–84.

Rodriguez, G. M. (2013) 'Power and Agency in Education: Exploring the Pedagogical Dimensions of Funds of Knowledge', *Review of Research in Education*, 37(1): 87–120.

Sen, A. (n.d.) 'Development as Capability Expansion', Available at: http://morgana.unimore.it/Picchio_Antonella/Sviluppo%20umano/svilupp%20umano/Sen%20development.pdf (Accessed 31.01.20).

UNESCO (2017) *Education for Sustainable Development Goals*. Paris: UNESCO.

Wade, R. (2014) 'Learning for Sustainability: The Challenges for Education Policy and Practice'. In: Atkinson, H. & Wade, R. (ed.), *The Challenges of Sustainability: Linking Politics, Education and Learning* (pp. 63–86). Bristol: Policy Press.

Chapter 2

Intimations of Utopia

Values, sustaining environments and the flourishing of children and teachers

Jonathan Barnes

Three stories shared by teachers talking about values:

> At 8 or 9 I lived in Burundi. My home was near the Sisters of Mercy. I watched them working and got to hear about Mother Teresa... At that time, I had a brother and he was in hospital, but when I went to visit him I saw that many children around him had no visitors and no food was brought to them, so I went straight home and made food and brought it to the other kids who were sick. I did this many times.
>
> (Beatrice, Rwanda)

> When I was 9 I had an opportunity to sit with a 12-year-old girl on the school bus. I felt really nervous as she was pretty good-looking. She was eating a packaged snack and was seated by the open window. When she finished, guess what she did? She folded the wrapper nicely and placed it carefully in her pocket. That single incident is the only reason that I have never littered to this day. She said nothing, wasn't showing me deliberately, she was just doing her own thing.
>
> (Chow, Malaysia)

> When I was 6 or 7 my mother was shopping with me. My mum bought me an ice lolly and I was in a busy marketplace stood by her side. While she was buying something she lost sight of me. After 10 minutes of panicking she found me beneath a railway bridge with another boy my age. The other boy was a homeless child, body and clothes tattered...we were both perched on a rock, like brothers, she watched me speaking with him, I'd lick the ice lolly then pass to him and he'd lick it...my mum says that when she saw me there she knew that I was destined to help people, to work with people and to share the things that I have.
>
> (Arji, India)

Introduction

Values matter. The stories above trace precise times and places for the birth of values.[1] Many of us use such brief, often-told narratives to explain the origin of personal principles – I call them *key-stories*. These fragments of autobiography are frequently set in our younger days (Barnes, 2012). Retelling them to ourselves and others affirms and consolidates the values that matter most to us.

Values help construct identity. They hold cultures and subcultures together and are shaped and sustained by our feelings (Damasio, 2018). Values can be selfish or altruistic. Those described as virtuous appear similar across the world. Virtuous values[2] are particularly relevant to teachers. Questions at their interviews for teacher education probe them, and daily judgements of good and bad, right, wrong, fair, unfair, true or relevant characterise what they do and say in class, corridor and playground. Having sought the values of some 2500 prospective teachers in life as a head and teacher educator, I have found that teachers are generally led to education because they want to make the world a better place. At least initially they see schooling as a route towards Utopia.[3]

Sadly, in the West these naïve ideals are swiftly challenged by education realities. Worthy personal beliefs can seem far from the realities of 21st-century teaching life. Negative, often exclusive language dominates media reports, parliamentary debate, legislation and management talk. Teachers' ideals are commonly dismissed with tolerant, patronising or pitying smiles and challenged by disaffected youngsters. The drift towards harder, polarised, one-size-fits-all, market-orientated public policy seems inexorable.

Ministerial speeches offer little support for 'idealistic' beliefs (see, for example, *Telegraph*, 2013). Indeed, English government advice on Initial Teacher Education (ITE) omits the word 'values' (DfE, 2018). The statutory ITE 'Standards' for primary schools (DfE, 2013) require commitment to only 'British' values, ignoring near-universal human values like kindness, humility, generosity, sustainability or social justice. Current education policy requires levels of accountability (for example, Javid, 2019) that counteract many values with which teachers entered the profession. I believe values-conflict and job dissatisfaction arise from the mismatch between externally imposed expectations of control, conformity and competition and the creative, constructive roles many teachers expected (Cooper Gibson Research/DfE, 2018; ATL, 2015; NEU, 2019).

Increasing numbers of teachers are leaving the profession (HC, 2018; We are Teachers, 2018). In England, one in five plan to leave in the next five years (NEU, 2019) and 30% depart within their first five (TES, 2016). They blame excessive workload (NUT, 2018), unreasonable accountability measures, shifting expectations, poor pay, lack of support, bad leadership, challenging pupil behaviour and declining opportunities for creativity (*Guardian*, 2018; NEU, 2016; Why Teach?, 2018). Teacher shortages and disaffection plus stories of parent dissatisfaction, equipment shortages, reduced budgets, isolation units, radicalism and knife- and drug-related crime confirm impressions of dystopia in schools. Such negative conditions may account for steady declines in the mental health and well-being of teachers and children (Education Support Partnership, 2018; WHO, 2016). Perceptions of 'crisis' in recruitment and retention of teachers are therefore unsurprising (*TES*, 2017; *Guardian*, 2018; *Time Magazine*, 2018). Even government briefing papers conclude that ITE and in-service support has 'given insufficient priority to teacher retention and development' (HC, 2018).

Adverse narratives powerfully and negatively influence children's lives and futures. There is hope, however. Evidence suggests that when serious attention is paid to teachers' well-being (including nurturing core personal values, helping them discover creative strengths and providing settings that promote friendships), they feel happier, more resilient and more fulfilled, and increase their capacity to give and learn (Kell, 2018). Flourishing teachers *generate similar responses in children* – bringing education closer to a kind of Utopia. Moral, fair, kind, affirmative and hopeful classrooms do exist, and examples far from 'the West' can show us where to start.

Seeking signs of Utopia outside 'the West'

Earlier study in England (Barnes, 2012) concluded that values-consistency between school and teacher was a major source of personal resilience and job satisfaction. I sought evidence of any universality in this conclusion in a new study outside the West (Barnes, 2019). Using detailed '*values-discussions*' with 16 well-established teachers in explicitly values-led primary schools in India, Rwanda, Japan and Ethiopia during 2018 and 2019, I examined relationships between teacher fulfilment, their values and the environments they created and occupied in schools.

Collecting teachers' values

Teachers were invited to write their key values on a traced outline of their hand. Samples below illustrate the care that teachers gave to this exercise.

Text box 1: Translation of a Japanese teacher's named values

Thumb: Treasure my debt of gratitude to my founder, father and mother, colleagues

Forefinger: Be a person who continues to challenge myself

Middle finger: Have the heart that wishes for children's growth

'Medicinal' finger: Have appreciation to be a part of this job

Pinkie: Passion and faith to have hope

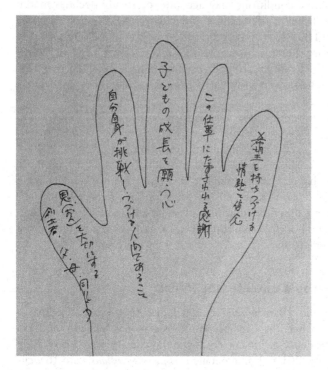

Figure 2.1 Values hands completed by teachers in Japan and India.

Text box 2: Translation of a South Indian teacher's named values

Pinkie: To love others as you love yourself, no violence, no fight anything
Ring finger: Live in happiness every moment, learning from children
Middle finger: Make others enjoy and feel happy
Index finger: To be truthful
Thumb: Equality to have good faith that all are the same

Between them, 16 teachers generated over 90 values (see Table 2.1).

These teachers' chosen values avoided the instrumentalist, target- and standards-driven philosophies dominant in their national education policies. Predominantly, their values aligned to social reconstructionist, liberal or humanist philosophies of education. Exceptions were few and consistently identified alongside values like honesty, service and humility.

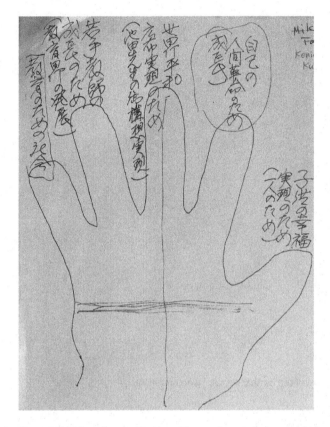

Figure 2.2 Values hands completed by teachers in Japan and India.

Becoming aware of the source of values

Most (15/16) teachers told *key-stories* to explain the birth of their values. Almost all mentioned environments, events or people from childhood (4–15 years). One, for example, said:

> I still treasure my experience at school with Mrs Yakiama in grade 3 (7-year-olds); her attitude become the basis of my own values. She praised kids and taught well, we loved her. She let me create my own play and song about a frog… This play gave me confidence. I told myself, "I can do this" – I have never forgotten it.
>
> (MM, Japan)

Others described the influence of mothers humbly responding to violent or drunken partners, generosity shown in difficult times and unexpected acts of kindness, hope or wisdom.

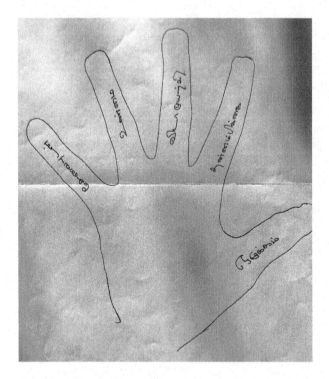

Figure 2.3 Values hands completed by teachers in Japan and India.

Past teachers and mentors were significant sources of values. Their names, from 20–30 years before, came quickly to mind. F from Rwanda described a teacher 'sooo [sic] lively and who moved all around the classroom and used great songs to interact with us, he cared so much for us...'. With tears in his eyes he sang the French song his teacher taught him. Another spoke enthusiastically of his teacher's 'trust and compassion', adding:

> if I was away for a day he would even visit my home to make sure I was okay... My cousin was often unable to pay school fees and would be sent back home, but he would say..."take the money out of my salary this month to pay the fees". ...he ensured I take part in all school activities, spotted my leadership traits, exposed me to challenges and opportunities...his personality contributes to my actions today.
>
> (IS, Rwanda)

The Japanese teachers credited their beliefs in pacifism to their school's founder, describing emotional, warm and direct interactions with him early in their lives.

Table 2.1 Teachers' values

Theme	Related value-words	Frequency	Theme	Related value-words	Frequency
love	Caring, compassion, kindness helping others, service	16/16[a]	positivity	Encouragement, self-confidence, happiness	11/16
peace	Human dignity, pacifism, hope, sanctity of life, 'refraining from terrifying deeds'	15/16	gratitude	Humility, selflessness, avoiding 'vain speech', gratitude, obedience	10/16
justice	Community, collective responsibility, fairness, equality, respect, cooperation, democracy	13/16	integrity	Reliability, constancy, accountability, courage, responsibility, trustworthiness	9/16
truth	Trust, integrity, openness, honesty, truthfulness	11/16		Communication, deference, creativity, diligence, belief, friendship	8/16 – 5/16

[a] Fractions over 16 show numbers of teachers claiming a particular value

A former 'school-refuser' described a home-education teacher so gentle and affirming that he changed his attitude. Our values-discussion concluded:

> I want to contribute to society, humanity and the happiness of others, it's a vow that I want to hold for the rest of my life. The constant question in my mind is: "To what purpose are you doing this?" The answer is that I am here to help these students grow and positively change their perspective whether they like me or hate me.
>
> (OS, Japan)

Family generated values too. SO from Osaka described how his mother raised him 'in the principle of serving others and making them happy' and his subsequent desire to find a job 'that fitted that principle'. MT from Tamil Nadu credited her father:

> because of my father only, I am sitting here. Our family background is so different from these students, they are really poor children, when they come to school they're already hungry, they don't have enough clothes and they have such a different attitude. But my father pleaded with me to accept their family background, and teach them not to use bad words and lead them to better satisfaction with life – he told me so many moral stories from the Ramayana to support this.
>
> (MT, India)

One teacher traced the emergence of a passion for science, mathematics and history to a solitary childhood following his stationmaster father to outlying communities:

> Alone, I became curious about different things. Living by the ocean I liked collecting stuff, flowers, fossils and rocks in the mountains…in another place I remember wondering at the remains of ancient arches.
>
> (SO, Japan)

Sustaining values

Many remarked on how *friendships* helped sustain their values. Indian teachers, for example, enthusiastically celebrated religious holidays with colleagues of other faiths, claiming that attending these occasions brought:

> peace and tolerance, love, mutuality, unity, diversity and tolerance, grace, love and a sense that "we worship the god in you" when we collaborate together.
>
> (TK, Tamil Nadu)

Friendship was considered essential to holistic education. ITE assessments, for example, measured trainees' ability to 'form supportive relationships and work… in productive, creative teams' and recognised their impact on mental well-being. Compassion, confidence, sharing and 'healthy competition' were integrated into all subject teaching and expected in lesson plans.

This collegiate approach was evident in conversations across schools and cultures. Sharing personal difficulties and triumphs, teachers frequently used the pronouns 'we', 'us' or 'our' to describe school life, for example:

> we work together, meditate together and share everything with the children…day by day we are updating ourselves, using many incidents from the daily life of our children in our teaching.
>
> (SV, India)

Curriculum directly championed certain values in each country. Rwanda's primary curriculum, for example, aims to teach values necessary to rebuild a country after the horrific genocide of 1994. Its 'Social and Religious Studies' curriculum for 9–11-year-olds covers: 'Environmental conservation, Financial education, Gender issues, HIV/AIDS, Nutrition, Peace education, Genocide and Inclusive… approaches.' (Rwanda Board of Education, 2015). Primary children should be:

> liberated from all kinds of discrimination, including gender based discrimination, exclusion and favouritism…to contribute to the promotion of a

culture of peace and emphasize Rwandan and universal values of justice, peace, tolerance, respect for human rights, gender equality, solidarity and democracy.

(Rwanda Board of Education, 2015, p. 8)

Tamil Nadu's primary curriculum lists values for a tolerant, religiously diverse country. 8-year-olds, for example, should know that 'our well-being is connected to the well-being of others'; 9- and 10-year-olds how 'different people in India are expected to live together and respect each other'; and 11-year-olds must study 'prejudice, discrimination, inequality and... [the benefits of] diversity' (Tamil Nadu, 2017).

Children themselves were often credited with affirming teachers' values, 'giving joy' through their enthusiasm. Several stressed how children 'grow quickly into the dominant values of the school' (MM, Japan).

Prayer was an unexpectedly regular theme in values-discussions. Most (13/16) directly raised its importance in sustaining sensitive, meaningful teaching. In India the day started with children's extemporary prayer addressing current needs (sick animals, poorly children, repairs, uniforms, school bags, transport) and gratitude for gifts (food donated, their rabbit's safe delivery of five young, house painting finished). Prayer was interfaith, fervent and emotional. Calling to mind such important details of daily life brought the whole day into one inter-related experience. Each day ended with the school community cross-legged in a white-painted, religious image–filled 'meditation room' considering the impact of their actions.

Religion was important in holding together each school context. 'Without religion how do we find our values?' asked one Japanese teacher. An Ethiopian teacher stressed the importance of religious inclusion: 'We do not name God. Giving God a name divides us, we just believe in a creator God that is good and preserves us – we pray to that God only'. A Buddhist teacher remarked:

> imparting knowledge is less important than understanding, we must try to impart wisdom. We should pray for the child's happiness, then you can bring forth wisdom, through prayer.

Living in the direction of values (McNiff and Whitehead, 2009) was central to each school's ethos. Values were frequently cited in casual conversation, referred to in posters, written into lesson introductions and assemblies and highlighted in public meetings. Teachers related many challenges and compromises too, but insisted that despite them school management helped every teacher maintain their fundamental beliefs. Teachers were appointed for their integrity as well as experience and retained if they continued to build on school values, while in Rwanda, for example, an academically able teacher was dismissed with the words, 'you failed to live the trust and love expected by the school'.

Teachers' values in the classroom

In lessons teachers often shared key stories relevant to the curriculum area being covered. These stories generated matching tales from children and education became personalised and meaningful:

- A Japanese teacher described organising a residential trip for 9-year-olds. Aware of a cultural reluctance to speak about emotions, she asked each parent to write a 'love letter' to their child which she would bring and distribute one evening of the trip. She described a memorable response from a usually violent, disaffected, depressed child:

  > he just became more cheerful after this letter and within a week nominated himself to be on the student council and shared that he'd written back to his mother three times that he was sorry to have caused so many problems…this reminds me of why I became a teacher.

- A Rwandan teacher told of a class visit to Rwanda's Parliament and other activities connected with inclusion and democracy. He was 'so deeply proud' of the 'wisdom and awareness of their questions'. Even greater satisfaction followed when they asked to hold mock elections in school and teach another class about democracy.
- In Ethiopia, nursery-aged children held a discussion on what to do if they found something that was not theirs. A child had found some glasses dropped by a 'Rough Guide' visitor to their village.

Values like love, democracy, selflessness and honesty did not appear to arise from fear or externally enforced discipline, but from children and teachers together *living* the values of community, responsibility and beauty that characterised their institution.

Learning from non-Western classrooms

Values *creation* made the schools in this study special. The 16 volunteer teachers were experienced, respected upholders of school values. The high profile of 'Utopian' ideals in their classrooms may seem exotic, but I believe they offer an agenda for education everywhere. Study findings suggested strong links between institutionally supported, altruistic values, high educational standards and school environments modelled on the possibility of the 'good society'. Teachers felt fulfilled in these places. Classrooms had not yet attained Utopian heights (each had its own inclusion and equality issues; socio-economic inequality impacted heavily upon learning, and sustainability and care for the natural world were rarely mentioned), but they aimed in that direction. For its teachers, each classroom *was* a 'laboratory for a more just society than the one we now live in' (Bigelow, 2004) and they had many attributes in common. These included:

1 High degrees of resilience. Teachers claimed this grew from *congruence between their own and their school's values*;

2 The use of *key-stories* founded upon personal experiences as school children. These stories were sources of stamina, vison and creativity and sustained the journey towards equal, kind and hopeful class communities;

3 Assurance that their *pedagogical and moral successes were recognised* and appreciated by management;

4 Awareness that such *acknowledgement* built capacity to risk further creativity and greater visions;

5 An appreciation of opportunities to *talk about values*;

6 A pedagogy with emphasis on security, meaning, positive relationships, faith, hope and community.

Claims of Utopian potential in these primary classrooms require more research and discussion, but many aspects of our conversations suggest promising starting points for debates in Western education. Questions arising from this study are particularly relevant to current concerns about teacher recruitment and retention:

1 How do teachers' values link to curriculum, teaching and learning?

2 What do we do about differences in values?

3 Are there universal values?

4 Can we build versions of Utopia in Western classrooms?

How do values link to curriculum, teaching and learning?

All interviewed teachers wanted to improve the quality of life and learning for children. Values were essential to this quest, but teachers agreed values must be well-tended and lived, not simply preferred[4] or iterated. The research gathered plentiful evidence that virtuous values influenced decisions and actions throughout the teaching day.

Observation and conversation analysis provided evidence that for the 16 teachers in this study, effective teaching involved frequent and acknowledged opportunities to:

- Develop personal *confidence*;
- Encourage *positive emotions*[5];
- Show *kindness* in a wide variety of contexts;
- Emphasise *common humanity* and human *interdependence*;
- Display *commitment*, *tenacity* and *selflessness*;
- Discover, exercise and develop *creativity*.

Through these values and attitudes, demonstrated throughout curriculum and pedagogy, teachers sought to construct and sustain democratic, just and inclusive communities. These features discussed below are arguably essential to building a more resilient, fulfilled and healthy teaching workforce in the West.

Confidence arises from the application of many values discussed. Children and teachers in the study schools exhibited unusual degrees of 'self-efficacy' (Bandura, 1994). Examples of the mutual equality, compassion, respect, trust and hope that sustain such confidence were common (see Halpin, 2003; Seligman, 2004).

Western perspectives see confidence as a desirable *personal* prerequisite for lasting, transferrable learning and successful social functioning (Bandura et al., 2003; Layard & Clark, 2017; Dweck, 2017). These non-Western schools, however, showed that *individualistic* confidence is not as highly prized (Cave, 2001), but should serve community, conformity, cooperation and culture. A binary choice between personal and collective confidence is unnecessary, however. In Japan teachers considered what to change in themselves when facing challenges offered by individual children. They regarded negative dispositions as open to positive change and expected personal confidence to grow towards collegiate responsibility. Teachers used terms like conviction, courage, power, energy, direction, diligence, growth and tenacity to describe the characteristics of confidence desired for their children. Such thoughts pose challenging curriculum questions for primary teachers in the West – for example:

- How can I show conviction in action in history projects?
- Where in the world are current geographical examples of courage?
- What moral or immoral uses of power could we discuss in PSHE or religious education?
- How can we understand energy using the contrasting languages and skills of PE, art, music or technology?

Positivity towards values and *as* a value frequently coloured discussions. 'Values of spirit'[6] (Booth, 2012) dominated teachers' key-stories. Their positive mind-sets did not result from a comfortable upbringing, however. Optimistic, constructive attitudes had arisen from wider environments where they experienced the virtuous values of others in action. Neither did positivity imply Pollyanna-like[7] disregard of the negative. Daily confrontations with the consequences of poverty, insecurity and sadness were standard for the teachers in Rwanda, Ethiopia and India. Japanese staff were equally conscious of the negative effects of affluence.

Positivity is a strongly embodied emotion in all cultures. Many classroom observations recorded the impact of mirror neurones (Rizzolatti & Craighero, 2004) as children reflected teachers' positive body language with similar physical stances. The somatic expression of feelings has become a major focus for educational neuroscience (see Damasio, 2018; Immordino-Yang & Faeth, 2011; Panksepp, 2004; LeDoux, 1996). Facial or body-language signals of positivity indicate mental states that enable more trusting and open relationships, readiness to interpret past experiences positively, creative and constructive ideation, greater muscular control and physical confidence (Fredrickson, 2009). Positive feelings like Booth's values of spirit are fundamental to mind-sets that can envision a better world (Dweck, 2017).

One value, *kindness,* was claimed by every teacher. Described as gentleness, love, caring, compassion or empathy, this benevolence was recorded abundantly in observations. Teacher kindness was, however, often coupled with equally strong beliefs in challenge, service and diligence. Pairings like these suggest questions about how we should interact in corridor, playground, staffroom and class:

- How can we encourage both kindness and challenge in a games lesson?
- How do we provide opportunities for both service and care in the dining hall?
- What can we do to make the social and physical environment more joyful?
- How do we balance empathy and challenge in our teaching?

Beliefs in *common and interrelated humanity* are central to the African concept of *Ubuntu*[8] (Battle, 2009; Sibanda, 2019) raised by Rwandan teachers. Similar exhortations to love our neighbour and reduce inequalities unite the major religions (ARC, 2016). Buddhist, Hindu, Christian and Muslim teachers separately recognised human interdependence and frailty (ARC, 2015) and honoured generosity, compassion and fairness – applying them across their curricula. What 'Big Ideas' in our secular Western contexts fulfil a similar motivating role? Can the UN's sustainability goals, humanitarianism, environmentalism, conceptions of social justice or politics be used to frame values-focussed:

- Foreign language lessons?
- Football matches?
- Musical composition?
- Science examples and experiments?
- Interdisciplinary approaches to 'Big Issues'?

Commitment characterised all teachers in this study. Beyond professional obligations, commitment showed in authentic involvement, giving 'more than required' and in managers' trust and gratitude. These teachers' hours were considerably longer than those of teachers in surrounding schools. Expectations were higher, yet each school had significantly lower rates of teacher sickness and early retirement. How can Western schools engender similar affirmative commitment from staff and children? Some have achieved commitment through:

- Sharing regular art or history sessions with a retirement home;
- Caring for bees, goats, chickens or buffalos (see West Rise website);
- Allowing a 'Green Team' to decide school policy;
- Working with architects to design a school extension;
- Building a school wild area.

Commitment becomes *creative* when imagination and novelty are involved in the process of teaching. Creative thinking transformed the experience of 4/16 teachers in this study. Parental 'love letters', democracy role play, opportunistic use of lost European glasses and interfaith prayer meetings and many more spontaneous, original ideas resulted from confidence in children's inherent creativity (see Sternberg, 1997; Robinson & Aronica, 2016), and a management that encouraged teachers to make personal decisions within agreed and upheld values. Access to creative inspiration is abundantly available to Western primary schools, but underexploited despite clear evidence (Barnes, 2018; Hall & Thomson, 2017; Roberts, 2006) of its well-being and job satisfaction benefits (see Room 13; Youth Music; Creativity Culture and Education; Creative Scotland; UNICEF).

What do we do about differences in values?

Every cultural context is unique. Cultures[9] arise from different histories, feelings and fortunes and generate wide variations in values. The communities served by the Tamil, Ethiopian and Rwandan schools *looked* and behaved differently from those in Japan. In diverse Western communities, values differ between social classes, families, regions and other subcultures. Though the cultural nature of values is recognised, this study revealed understandings of values that appear to lie beneath culture.

The value of *values themselves* was appreciated by all interviewees. Teachers' *key-stories* were quickly understood across cultures. Tales of pain or unhappiness, revelation, joy, compassion or courage touched on universal and emotional aspects of the human condition connecting people of vastly different histories (Gottschall, 2012). Several teachers now use key-stories from overseas in their lessons and report on their class's eagerness to hear them. The teachers uniformly valued the values-discussions – chances to express and consolidate their driving beliefs while sharing those of others. How might we ensure key-stories and values-discussions happen in Western primary schools?

- Plan regular values-discussions into staff, class, year group and parent meetings;
- Use story book stories to provoke class discussions or parallel stories from children's or teachers' lives;
- Use real stories to illustrate teaching points throughout the curriculum. Highlight the fundamental values illustrated;
- Use anecdotes and incidental illustrative personal stories to enliven every subject.

Are there universal values?

Aristotle, Thomas More and many others sought to identify universal values.[10] Values-universality is difficult to establish. In the super-diverse communities of the West, 'care', for example, means many things, from ultra-strict discipline, indoctrination and gender separation to total permissiveness. Teachers work with this diversity of interpretations every day. Common moral understandings like the 'Golden Rule' (treating others as you would wish to be treated) may persist (Hick, 1992), but few absolute agreements are likely. There are strong arguments, however, for prioritising dialogue about values. Discussion about values is good in itself, but aiming at common ground on them may be life-saving in the face of global risks like climate change, environmental degradation, species extinction, ultra-nationalism and economic instability.

Analysis of non-Western teacher conversations revealed close correlation across three out of four 'universal values' posited by Kinnier, Kernes, and Dautheribes (2000):

1   The recognition of something greater than self (e.g., faith, truth, justice);
2   Self-respect (attitudes of humility and responsibility);
3   Caring for others (recognising human connectedness, service, non-violence and kindness).

Kinnier's fourth value, *Caring for other living things and the environment*, however, was poorly represented in discussions, suggesting an urgent agenda item for education everywhere.

Areas of agreement between the study schools were encouraging, however. Teachers' key-stories evidenced the birth, growth and daily expression of values recognisable and appreciated across cultures. Though doubtless on their 'best behaviour', teachers were content to be judged by the values they articulated. The visits, observations and discussions revealed copious *lived* examples of beliefs in ultimate meaning, respect for self and care for others on personal and professional levels. Faith, care, kindness and respect in various forms appeared similar whether in Japan, Rwanda, Ethiopia or south India.

Can we build Utopia in Western classrooms?

Utopia is a feeling. Feeling in a 'good place' arises from the ways we interpret realities around us and how they compare to our core values. Scientists observing brain and body connections (Damasio, 2003; Panksepp, 2004; McGilchrist, 2019) are beginning to understand how subjective feelings affect physical realities. Positive feelings are known, for example, to impact positively upon physical functions like digestion, blood pressure, skin conductivity, muscle tone and the immune system (Fredrickson, 2009). The psychology of creativity, hope and trust is consistently linked with feelings of well-being and fulfilment.

Personal stories of virtuous values help shape and interpret realities around us too. This is significant for teachers wishing to create a positive classroom ethos and find long-term fulfilment in teaching. If classroom reality is one where *teacher and child* not only feel secure, but supported, fairly treated, listened to, trusted, empowered, hopeful, appreciated and appropriately stretched – the chances of existing for a while in the Utopias teachers once hoped for are high.

Summary

The researched schools represented an economic spectrum from destitution to wealth. They occupied rural, semi-rural, suburban, urban and metropolitan localities. Some classrooms were high-tech, others rudimentary. Whatever the context, after assuring safety, shelter and sustenance, teachers sought something greater than simply imparting knowledge. They wanted to make the world a better place and to start immediately by making their classrooms models of that healthier and sustainable world – little Utopias.

The evidence suggests that attracting and retaining teachers equipped to fulfil such hopes requires particular attention to their values. Statements of school aims and attention to 'British' values are not enough – values must be dynamic, promoting action, commitment and creativity. Values-discussions in five far from Western schools generated provocations to challenge any Western classroom, staff meeting and community.

Questions for reflection

How can the physical, social and emotional environment of classrooms be altered so that the chances of positive experiences are consistently higher than negative ones?

How can teachers use their and children's positive key-stories throughout the curriculum?

How can schools use values-discussions to identify, consolidate and share virtuous values?

Notes

1 Values: deeply held beliefs that strongly influence our real life choices, actions and aims.
2 Virtuous values: those that various cultures have seen as good, for example, those attributed to the work of Aristotle: courage, temperance, charity, joy, patience, respect, self-respect, equanimity, friendliness, honesty, humour and justice.
3 Utopia: an imagined place or state of things in which everything is perfect – literally Thomas More's combination of the Greek for a 'good place' (*Eu-topos)* and the word for 'no place' (*Ou-topos*).
4 For example: 'you shall know them by their fruits' (Matthew 7:16).
5 For example: peace, reflection, empathy, interest, joy, enthusiasm, fascination, curiosity, hope and friendliness.
6 These include: patience, hope, tenacity, selflessness, love, joy, beauty.
7 Pollyanna: an excessively cheerful person, the title and subject of a popular children's book by E.H Porter (1913).

8 Ubuntu: a traditional Central and East African philosophy expressed as 'I in you and you in me'.
9 Culture: the shared beliefs, actions and attitudes of a group of people.
10 Universal values: see Brown, 1991 for modern examples.

Further reading and resources

Freire, P. & Shor, I. (1987) *A Pedagogy for Liberation*, Basingstoke: Macmillan.
A philosophical book born of Paulo Freire's practical experience of education as a force for a better society.

Halpin, D. (2001) 'Utopianism and education: The legacy of Thomas More', *British Journal of Educational Studies*, 49, 3: 299–315. DOI: 10.1111/1467-8527. t01-1-00177.
A deeper examination of the concept of Utopia and its relevance for schooling.

Webb, D. (2009) 'Where's the vision? The concept of utopia in contemporary educational theory', *Oxford Review of Education*, 35, 6: 743–760. DOI: 10.1080/03054980903371179.
A reminder of the importance of keeping ideals and values at the forefront of educational planning and delivery.

References

ARC. (2015) *The Bristol Commitments*. Available at: http://www.arcworld.org/projects.asp?projectID=667.
ARC. (2016) *Faith in Finance*. Available at: http://www.arcworld.org/downloads/Faith-in-Finance.pdf.
Association of Teachers and Lecturers (ATL). (2015) *Why New Teachers Consider Leaving*. Available at: https://www.atl.org.uk/latest/new-teachers-already-demotivated-about-teaching-start-their-careers.
Bandura, A. (1994) 'Self-efficacy'. In: Ramachaudran, V. S. (ed.) *Encyclopedia of Human Behaviour*, San Diego, CA: Academic Press.
Bandura, A., Barbaranelli, C., Caprara, G. & Pastorelli, C. (2003) 'The Role of Affective Self-Regulatory Efficacy in Diverse Spheres of Psychological Functioning', *Child Development*, 74(3): 769–782.
Barnes, J. (2012) *What Sustains a Life in Education?* Unpublished PhD, Canterbury Christ Church University.
Barnes, J. (2018) *Applying Cross-Curricular Approaches Creatively*, London: Routledge.
Barnes, J. (2019) 'Teachers' Values: An International Study on What Sustains a Fulfilling Life in Education', *Journal of Education and Training Studies*, 7(5): 1–18.
Battle, M. (2009) *Ubuntu: I in You and You in Me*, London: Seabury.
Bigelow, B. (2004) *Rethinking Schools, Volume 2*. Available at: https://www.rethinkingschools.org/books/title/rethinking-our-classrooms-volume-2.
Booth, T. (2012) *Index for Inclusion*, Bristol: Centre for Studies in Inclusive Education.

Brown, D. (1991) *Human Universals*, New York: McGraw-Hill.

Cave, P. (2001) 'Educational Reform in Japan in the 1990s: 'Individuality' and Other Uncertainties', *Journal of Comparative Education*, 37(2): 173–191

Cooper, Gibson Research/DfE. (2018) *Factors Affecting Teacher Retention*. Available at: https://assets.publishing.service.gov.uk/government/uploads/system/upl oads/attachment_data/file/686947/Factors_affecting_teacher_retention_-_qual itative_investigation.pdf.

Creativity, Culture and Education Website. Available at: https://www.creativitycul tureeducation.org/programme/art-of-learning/.

Creative Scotland. Available at: https://www.creativescotland.com.

Damasio, A. (2003) *Looking for Spinoza: Joy, Sadness and the Feeling Brain*, Orlando FL: Harcourt.

Damasio, A. (2018) *The Strange Order of Things*, New York: Penguin Random House.

Department for Education. (2013) *Teachers' Standards*. Available at: https://assets. publishing.service.gov.uk/government/uploads/system/uploads/attachment _data/file/665520/Teachers__Standards.pdf.

Department for Education. (2018) *Statutory Guidance for Initial Teacher Training*. Available at: https://www.gov.uk/government/publications/initial-teacher-t raining-criteria/initial-teacher-training-itt-criteria-and-supporting-advice#c21 -programmes.

Dweck, C. (2017) *Mindset: Changing the Way You Think to Fulfil Your Potential*, New York: Little Brown Book Group.

Education Support Partnership. (2018) *Teacher Well-Being Index*. Available at: https ://www.educationsupportpartnership.org.uk/sites/default/files/resources/tea cher_wellbeing_index_2018.pdf.

Fredrickson, B. (2009) *Positivity*, New York: Crown.

Gottschall, J. (2012) *The Story Telling Animal*, New York: Houghton Mifflin Harcourt Miller, (2008). Available at: https://onlinelibrary.wiley.com/doi/abs/ 10.1111/j.1467-9752.2008.00646.x.

Guardian. (2018) 1st April 2018. Available at: https://www.theguardian.com/ed ucation/2018/apr/01/vast-majority-of-teachers-considered-quitting-in-past-y ear-poll.

Halpin (2003) *Hope and Education*, London: Routledge.

Hall, C. & Thomson, P. (2017) *Inspiring School Change: Transforming Schools through the Creative, Arts*, London: Routledge.

Hick, J. (1992) 'The Universality of the Golden Rule'. In: Runzo, J. (ed.) *Ethics, Religion and the Good Society, New Directions in a Pluralistic World*, Louisville KY: Westminster.

House of Commons (HC), Briefing Paper 7222. (2018) *Teacher Recruitment and Retention in England*. Available at: file:///Users/jbl142/Downloads/CBP-7222%20(5).pdf.

Immordino-Yang, M. H. & Faeth, M. (2011) 'The Role of Emotion and Skilled Intuition in Learning'. In: Souza, D. (ed.) *Mind Brain and Education: Neuroscience Implications for the Classroom*, Bloomington, IN: Solution Tree Press

Javid, S. (2019) *Statement at the Start of Serious Youth Violence Summit*, April 1st 2019. Available at: https://www.gov.uk/government/news/serious-youth-v iolence-summit-to-launch-public-health-duty-to-tackle-serious-violence.

Kell, E. (2018) *How to Survive in Teaching*, London: Bloomsbury.

Kinnier, R., Kernes, J. & Dautheribes (2000) 'A Shortlist of Universal Values', *Counselling and Values*, 45(1): 4–16.

Layard, R. & Clark, D. (2017) *Thrive: The Power of Evidence-Based Psychological Therapies*, London: Penguin.

LeDoux, J. (1996) *The Emotional Brain; the Mysterious Underpinnings of Emotional Life*, New York: Simon and Schuster.

McGilchrist, I. (2019) *The Master and His Emissary: The Divided Brain and the Making of the Western World*, New York: Yale University Press.

McNiff, J. & Whitehead, J. (2009) *Doing & Writing Action Research*, London: SAGE.

National Education Union (NEU). (2016) Available at: https://neu.org.uk/latest/how-bad-does-teacher-recruitment-crisis-have-be-dfe-calls-it-crisis.

National Education Union (NEU). (2019) Available at: https://neu.org.uk/press-releases/neu-survey-shows-widespread-funding-and-workload-pressures-school-support-staff.

National Union of Teachers (NUT). (2018) *Teacher Recruitment and Retention*, Available at https://www.teachers.org.uk/edufacts/teacher-recruitment-and-retention.

Panksepp, J. (2004) *Affective Neuroscience: The Origins of Animal & Human Emotions*, New York: Oxford University Press.

Rizzolatti, G. & Craighero, L. (2004) 'The Mirror-Neuron System', *Annual Review of Neuroscience*, 27(1): 169–192.

Roberts, P. (2006) *Nurturing Creativity in Young People: A Report to Government to Inform Future Policy*, London: DCMS.

Robinson, Sir K. & Aronica, L. (2016) *Creative Schools*, New York: Penguin Random House.

Room13 International. Available at: http://room13international.org/.

Rwanda Board of Education. (2015) *Education Statistical Yearbook*. Available at: http://mineduc.gov.rw/fileadmin/user_upload/pdf_files/2016_Education_Statistical_Yearbook.pdf.

Rwanda Board of Education. (2015) *Social and Religious Studies Syllabus for Upper Primary*, p.4–6. Kigali: Rwanda Education Board.

Seligman, M. (2004) *Authentic Happiness*, New York: Basic Books.

Sibanda, S. (2019) *In Search of Social Justice through Ubuntu*, Unpublished PhD thesis, Canterbury Christ Church University. Available at: https://repository.canterbury.ac.uk/item/89179/in-search-of-social-justice-through-ubuntu-a-critical-analysis-of-zimbabwe-s-post-colonial-education-for-all-efa-policy.

Sternberg, R. (1997b) *Successful Intelligence*, New York: Plume.

Tamil Nadu Board of Education. (2017) *Social Science Curriculum*. Available at: https://fullcircleeducation.in/wp-content/uploads/2017/11/Social-Science.pdf.

Telegraph. (2013) Available at: https://www.telegraph.co.uk/news/uknews/10442309/Michael-Gove-many-social-workers-not-up-to-the-job.html.

Times Educational Supplement (TES). (2016) Available at: https://www.tes.com/news/nearly-third-new-teachers-leave-profession-within-five-years-figures-show.

Times Educational Supplement (TES). (2017) 'Teachers Mental Health Problems'. Available at: https://www.tes.com/news/teaching-driving-too-many-teachers-mental-health-problems.

Time Magazine. (2018) Available at: http://time.com/magazine/us/5394910/september-24th-2018-vol-192-no-12-u-s/.

UNICEF Website. Available at: https://www.unicef.org/publications/files/Child_Friendly_Schools_Manual_EN_040809.pdf.

We Are Teachers (2018) *Why Teachers Quit*, Available at: https://www.weareteachers.com/why-teachers-quit-the-profession/.

Why Teach? (2015) Available at: http://whyteach.lkmco.org/wp-content/uploads/2015/10/Embargoed-until-Friday-23-October-2015-Why-Teach.pdf.

World Health Organisation (WHO). (2016) *Health Behaviour of School Aged Children, Report.* Available at: http://www.euro.who.int/en/health-topics/Life-stages/child-and-adolescent-health/health-behaviour-in-school-aged-children-hbsc.

Youth Music. Available at: https://www.youthmusic.org.uk/.

Chapter 3

Reconceptualising teacher identity

Paula Stone

Introduction

Should teachers be regarded as professionals? Technicians? Craft workers? Intellectuals? Scholars? Researchers? Practitioners, academics and policy makers cannot seem to agree. A recent global comparison of the teaching profession across a broad range of countries presents a picture of an array of ideologies; some of which celebrate and promote the professionalism of teachers (Finland and Singapore), and others where, driven by politics, neoliberal ideology and expediency, teaching is being de-professionalised (United States and England) (Darling-Hammond and Lieberman, 2012).

The conceptualisation of the teaching profession has been central to debate amongst policymakers, teachers and academics alike for decades. In the UK, the debate about teacher identity in England has become particularly polarised with the discourse of 'the competent craftsperson', the dominant and hegemonic definition maintained by the British Government, at one end of the continuum, and a model of the professional teacher, which I am calling 'the reflective professional', based on an amalgam of ideas from the academic community, at the other. I have decided to shine a spotlight on teaching in England because the popular perception of teaching as a craft is distinct from other countries in the United Kingdom.

I would like to suggest that the notion of what it is to 'be' a teacher (Dall'Alba and Barnacle, 2007) starts at the point of initial teacher education (ITE). The experiences and opportunities available to student teachers in this initial phase of teacher development play a crucial role in shaping teacher identity. It is interesting to note that even amongst the home nations there are stark differences in the way student teachers are educated. Since 2010, in England and Wales there has been a move away from universities toward a more school-based practice approach to teacher education, led by schools, academies and teaching school alliances. In Northern Ireland, however, universities still play a major role in teacher development; whilst in Scotland student teachers undertake a more academic route leading to a Master's qualification and the award of Chartered Teachers, which sits alongside other 'chartered' professionals (Biesta, 2012).

This chapter will aim to discuss a range of viewpoints relating to the conceptualisation of teachers' identity and the implications of these for teacher preparation and the teaching profession which, of course, are closely intertwined. It begins with a brief history of how teachers have been positioned over time, before examining what might be meant by teacher identity and the two dominant discourses around this – teacher as craftsperson and teacher as professional scholar. It then suggests that a reconceptualisation of the teaching profession is necessary, before summarising how this might look and be enacted.

Teachers' and student teachers' positioning – a brief history

It is widely recognised that the discourse surrounding the role of teachers, and indeed teacher preparation, is not just theoretical; it is also political. To locate and contextualise the debate I shall first offer a very brief historical overview of the 'identity' or status of teaching, which is often premised on teachers' experiences of initial teacher education.

Over the past two hundred years the pendulum has swung between the dominance of either a school-based apprenticeship model or a college- or university-based approach to teacher preparation. School-based apprenticeship models dominated in the nineteenth century, whilst college and university-based academic models were favoured for much of the twentieth century (Robinson, 2006).

From the 1960s onwards, teacher education became increasingly embedded within universities and colleges of teacher education, and teaching moved closer to becoming a graduate profession (Labaree, 1992). In England and Wales especially, teachers enjoyed unprecedented autonomy over curriculum development and decision-making. However, in 1976, James Callaghan made his now infamous 'Ruskin College' speech on education which raised questions about the monopoly of university-based teacher education and the link to unsatisfactory standards of school performance (Ball, 2017). Accordingly, the period that followed witnessed a significant shift in government policy and a reduction in teacher autonomy, which included the introduction of the National Curriculum and a set of standards for teachers.

The debate about whether student teachers should be trained in schools or educated within universities continues. In more recent times, New Labour (1997–2010), whilst introducing a new school-based model of teacher preparation enabling graduates to gain Qualified Teacher Status (Graduate Teaching Programme) without an academic qualification to teach, paradoxically attempted to raise the status of teaching through making it a Master's-level profession. Government funding for Master's study was, however, withdrawn by the Conservative–Liberal Democrat Coalition Government in 2011. Since then, Conservative Government reform has been predicated on a model which is highly centralised and controlled, through accountability, standardisation, curriculum prescription, and inspection – despite the rhetoric around free schools and academies. Within this ideology, teaching is now characterised as a skill that can be developed solely through professional practice. In consequence, there has been a focus on more practical and school-based models of teacher preparation.

Ball (2017) argues that it is the interrelationship between performativity and the state that is not just changing the way teachers work and how they are employed, but is also changing who they are, how they act, and importantly, how society defines what a good teacher is. What I want to debate here is how this ideology might affect teachers' identity, and more importantly, their ways of being (Dall'Alba and Barnacle, 2007).

Teachers' identity

While literature on teaching emphasises the importance of identity, understanding what is meant by teacher identity is a complex issue. Sachs (2005) presents a useful starting point which shows the centrality of the concept of identity for teaching but also indicates the dynamic nature of it:

> Teacher professional identity then stands at the core of the teaching profession. It provides a framework for teachers to construct their own ideas of 'how to be', 'how to act' and 'how to understand' their work and their place in society. Importantly, teacher identity is not something that is fixed nor is it imposed; rather it is negotiated through experience and the sense that is made of that experience.
>
> (Sachs, 2005, p.15)

This definition encompasses both the personal and professional aspects of identity (Beauchamp and Thomas, 2009) and involves an understanding of the self in relation to others (Mead, 1934). In this definition, teachers' identity is shaped in interaction with others in a professional context. The discourses in which policy-makers, academics and teachers themselves engage contribute to the shaping of their identities. Currently, there are two dominant yet binary discourses of the 'good teacher':

- *The competent craftsperson* (Moore, 2004), currently favoured by the British government in England. This conception of teaching emphasises situated professional knowledge (Moore, 2004; Winch, Oancea and Orchard, 2015);
- *The teacher as professional scholar* – this conception of teaching, based on an amalgam of ideas from a number of educational theorists (Moore, 2004; Biesta, 2012; Winch, Oancea and Orchard, 2015), combines situated understanding and tacit/intuitive knowledge, technical knowledge and critical reflection based on an understanding of educational research.

These discourses will be discussed in turn before a consideration of their impact in terms of how they contribute to the way teachers construct their identities.

Teacher as competent craftsperson

This, the current and most dominant ideology in England, is monopolising the discourse about teaching (Biesta, 2012). As articulated by the Secretary of State for Education in 2010, predicated largely on government critique of what was perceived as overly theoretical approaches to teaching based in universities, there has been a significant shift in government policy regarding the status of teaching:

> Teaching is a craft and it is best learnt as an apprentice observing a master craftsman or woman. Watching others, and being rigorously observed yourself as you develop, is the best route to acquiring mastery in the classroom.
>
> (Gove, 2010)

The aim was that 50% of student teachers would be trained through school-based routes (Gove, 2010), and in 2016–2017, 57% of postgraduate teachers *were* trained in this way.

The main concept emerging from this discourse is the notion of competence: 'the ability to perform the tasks and roles required to the expected standards' (Eraut, 2003, p.117), which suggests that the notion of competence is practical, and builds on knowledge, skills and action (Biesta, 2012). Such discourses tend to emphasise the technical aspects of teaching, based on the acquisition of a set of skills and competencies with which to meet the Teachers' Standards (2014). Underpinning this ideology of teaching as a craft is a belief that teachers need to have sufficient subject knowledge and pedagogical knowledge to teach their students effectively; which, as Biesta (2012) adroitly argues, is hardly contentious in itself.

In this model, teachers and student teachers predominantly learn from experienced practitioners, and through attention to their own development as resourceful, discerning and insightful professionals (Biesta, 2012). From this perspective, teaching can be delivered as a series of strategies to be learnt, applied and mastered; and advocates argue that school settings are well equipped and best placed to support this practical and technical knowledge. For example, Lemov (2015) in his book *Teach Like a Champion 2.0*, offers 'sixty-two techniques that put students on the path to college'. This popular book, endorsed by a highly regarded route into teaching, offers a set of teaching techniques to improve teachers' classroom practice. The techniques are practical and, according to Lemov, easy to implement.

Models like this, which Biesta (2012) argues are driven by fear, oversimplify the nature of teaching so that it is reduced to a set of outcomes and competencies that can be measured and compared. This, I would argue, reduces teachers to mere technicians who carry out instrumental tasks. In this model, pedagogy is reduced to the implementation of strategies, subordinating teachers' knowledge to a set of skills to be mastered (Aronowitz and Giroux, 2003).

Furthermore, the discourse of the teacher as craftsperson is now so dominant (Biesta, 2015), it is now the identity of the teacher that is expected and recognised socially, politically and professionally. Indeed, it is so much part of the professional norm, many teachers and school leaders think it is the only way to develop good practice. In this way, the discourse of teacher as competent craftsperson has been cultivated and embedded.

Winch, Oancea and Orchard (2015) argue that this popular conception of teaching, which relies purely on practical wisdom passed on from more experienced others, could limit theories of practice to a community consciousness in which theories of teaching and learning are localised and implemented without question. Brookfield (2017) supports this idea and contends there runs a risk of ideological homogeneity in schools, whereby there is a reinforcement of particular pedagogical approaches and a corresponding dismissal of alternative perspectives. In this way the discourse surrounding the competent craftsperson is obscuring the language of purpose, content and relation in education. This model of the teacher seems to rest on the assumption that practice is seen as more relevant than educational theory and, during initial teacher education, the more time a student teacher spends in school 'inevitably and unproblematically leads to better and "more relevant" learning' (Brown, Rowley and Smith, 2015, p.22).

The current education system in England is being eroded by forms of accountability and increasing managerialism alongside the intensification of workload that restricts the amount of time teachers have for critical reflection and intellectual development. The competent craftsperson discourse, with its emphasis on education based on educational qualifications, standards and accountability presents a threat to the status of teaching as a profession; reducing teachers to the status of high-level technicians. This has created a situation in which measurement and accountability have become ends in themselves rather than means to achieve a good education system in the fullest sense of the term (Biesta, 2015). This discourse of competence over technique focusses attention on what teachers *do* rather than what they *know* and limits teachers' ability to think (Biesta, 2015). Instead of posing questions about the principles underpinning different classroom methods, research techniques and theories of education, teachers are often preoccupied with mastering the best way to teach a given body of knowledge. All this, Giroux (n.d.) argues, is proletarianising the profession; reducing teachers to specialist technicians merely managing and implementing the curriculum.

As previously mentioned, in other countries in the United Kingdom, particularly Northern Ireland and Scotland, there is a strong emphasis on critical reflection and active engagement in research for teachers across each phase of their professional development. In England, however, the value of educational theory and research in initial teacher education has diminished over time as the shift away from university-led programmes continues. This model of teacher education in England is in opposition to other highly regarded international education systems, such as those of Singapore and Finland, where teachers rely heavily on rigorous research-based knowledge to inform their practice (BERA/RSA, 2014).

This idea of practitioner as researcher has not, however, gone unnoticed in English government circles, and in a recent and welcome development, Sir

Andrew Carter, in his review of initial teacher training [sic], recommended that trainees (and teachers) 'should understand how to interpret educational theory and research in a critical way, so they are able to deal with contested issues' (DfE, 2015, p.8) and that 'ITT should teach trainees why engaging with research is important and build an expectation and enthusiasm for teaching as an evidence-based profession' (DfE, 2015, p.8). This is the first occasion in recent government policy that acknowledges that teaching is, and should be, a scholarly, evidence-based activity in which research and research activity can enhance teachers' ability to make a difference to students' outcomes. Whilst this may seem a positive step towards enabling teachers to be critically reflective practitioners, Winch, Oancea and Orchard (2015) and Biesta (2012) point out that Carter's (DfE, 2015) definition of an evidence-based profession implies that research evidence can tell teachers what they should do and how they should do it, based on the assumption that particular forms of research, for example, the research found on the Education Endowment Foundation website (the research website favoured by the Government), 'can provide clear and unambiguous knowledge about "what works"' (Biesta, 2015, p.80). The issue for Biesta (2015) and Winch, Oancea and Orchard (2015) is that 'what works' always has to be set in relation to a particular purpose or set of purposes determined by policy makers, and teachers should be able to make their own professional judgments about the validity and reliability of the evidence; to do this they must be 'educationally wise' (Biesta, 2012, p.8). This leads on to an alternative model of teacher identity.

The teacher as professional scholar

In their model of teacher as professional, Orchard and Winch (2015) argue that while substantial teaching experience is required for the 'creation of good teachers' (2015, p.14), it is the teacher who is able to engage with the findings of educational research who is more able to judge the appropriate and effective action in school and classroom contexts.

Derived from their own empirical research, Oancea and Furlong (2007) conclude that there should be a complementary relationship between theory and practice. In a more recent paper, Winch, Oancea and Orchard (2015) offer a conception of the teacher – the teacher as professional – which encompasses a complementary and mutually enriching relationship between three different aspects of professional knowledge and practice: situated understanding, technical knowledge and critical reflection. They argue that professional practice makes the following demands of teachers: a practical understanding and knowledge of teaching and learning; a good conceptual understanding of education; and, importantly, the ability to understand, interpret and form critical judgements based on empirical research and its relevance to their particular situation. All of these depend on the disciplinary study of education and research, which plays a complementary role in relation to each of these dimensions. They argue that it is the appreciation of both theory and practice that has the most impact on being a reflective and reflexive practitioner.

Brookfield (2017) also argues that teachers should draw on a body of theory that has been mastered by teachers through years of study and reflection, so that they are able to question received wisdom about identified classroom practices. Brookfield (2017) asserts that engagement with theory helps teachers investigate their instincts and tacit knowledge that shapes practice and helps critical reflection. He argues that it can help teachers to break the circle of familiarity and can help prevent 'group think' or ideological homogeneity within the setting. Furthermore, he suggests that if teachers hope to encourage critical thought in their students, they must engage in it themselves. Cordingley et al. (2005) highlight how engagement in collaborative enquiry is crucial to create the conditions for enquiry-orientated teaching, which is associated with the greatest gains for pupils' learning and educational outcomes.

Biesta (2012), like Dall'Alba and Barnacle (2007), argues that educational wisdom starts with the formation and the transformation of the person, and it is only from there that knowledge, skills and dispositions develop. This means raising questions about the content, purpose and relationships in educational discourse (Biesta, 2015). He argues that the real work is to make teachers more thoughtful and wise. However, unlike Winch, Oancea and Orchard (2015) who argue that teachers should be engaged in educational research, Biesta (2007) argues that teaching and research are different, and the rhetoric of the practitioner researcher is undermining the identity of the teacher and the student, and may also be creating 'professional uncertainty'.

Winch, Oancea and Orchard (2015), however, argue that it is only through engagement with research that teachers are able to make decisions as to whether, and how, research-based considerations are relevant to how and what they teach. Boyd, Hymer and Lockney (2015) argue that engagement with, or in, research has the potential to inform and improve teachers' technical knowledge. They suggest that it is the interplay between practical wisdom (situated and technical knowledge) and public knowledge (theory, research, professional guidance and policy) that enables teachers to understand and evaluate the relevance of research findings to their own situation. In this way, theory, policy and research do not replace practical judgement in the classroom, but support or substantiate it.

The current focus on situated and technical knowledge often leaves teachers with the difficult task of integrating this knowledge into their practice without question. But teachers are human beings and knowing is situated within a personal, social, historical and cultural setting. I would contest that all teachers need to take an active responsibility for raising serious questions about what they teach, how they teach and the purpose of education. To do this, teachers need to challenge their assumptions about the world and their place within it as educators.

Reconceptualising 'the teacher'

Across the UK there has been increasing divergence in policy discourse surrounding teaching. However, in England the drive for school-based initial teacher education, with its focus on the acquisition of skills and competencies, seems to be inconsistent with the conception of teachers as reflective professionals. In particular, a focus on the acquisition of knowledge and competencies treats learning as unproblematic and renders irrelevant the necessity to educate student teachers to be able to make wise educational judgements (Biesta, 2012).

In contrast to this notion of the competent craftsperson, drawing on Orchard and Winch's (2015) concept of the professional teacher, I argue that teachers should be 'reflective professionals', which captures the notion of the professional and the scholar or intellectual (Giroux, n.d). This model emphasises not only the necessary discrete practical skills, techniques and areas of knowledge, but also skills needed to reflect constructively upon experience and theory as a way of improving the quality and effectiveness of a teacher's practice (Moore, 2004). In contrast to the competent craftsperson, the reflective professional is configured as someone who thinks and acts creatively, flexibly and thoughtfully based on their informed assessments of what is happening in their classroom (Moore, 2004). This educational wisdom (Biesta, 2015) enables teachers to articulate their position and provide justification for their decisions, based not only on doing, but also on reading and critical reflection which, he argues, goes beyond technical judgement (Biesta, 2012). I would also like to debate that teachers *should* engage in research, not in the way that Stenhouse (1983) espoused, i.e., as a public endeavour, but by utilising small-scale research as a means for teachers to examine their practice and challenge their assumptions.

Effective teaching demands engagement with a broad range of knowledge bases, which I would like to argue are much more powerful when they are research-informed. Of course teachers need to be competent, and their work needs to draw on evidence of 'what works', but most importantly teachers need to be able to make wise educational judgements (Biesta, 2012) to develop the capacity to be critical of policy, practice and research. Critically reflective teachers cease to rely only on methods and activities that have worked well in the past. Instead there is a recurrent checking of assumptions, a continual viewing of practice through different lenses and a persistent rethinking of what works and why. This can only be accomplished effectively if teachers are given opportunities to reflect on 'how to act', 'how to understand' and, importantly, 'how to be' (Sachs, 2005). Thus, it is important for teacher educators and school leaders to create space and opportunities for teachers to encounter the familiar in unfamiliar ways so that they can see teaching from an alternative perspective.

Summary

If teachers want to reject the notion of teacher as craftsperson, and instead reclaim teaching as a profession, we, as a profession, need to work beyond a set of shared standards (competencies) of practice. In contrast to this narrow conception of teaching, the reflective professional needs to develop educational wisdom (Biesta, 2015) whereby they can exercise their own judgement in the classroom and make decisions as to whether and how research-based considerations are relevant to how and what they teach (Winch, Oancea and Orchard, 2015). Whilst I am not suggesting that teaching can be learnt from theory alone, research processes and findings could contribute to the richness of reflection required in practical deliberation.

The conception of teaching as a reflective profession celebrates the fact that both systematic knowledge and educational research can have a valuable role to play in informing teachers 'how to act', 'how to understand' and, importantly, 'how to be'; but this is not enough. Instead, I suggest an embracing of what Biesta calls a 'virtue-based conception of teaching' (2012, p.18) in which there is a focus on the formation or transformation of the person as a professional.

Questions for reflection

What do you see as your professional identity? Think about your autobiography and how this has shaped who you are as a practitioner.

To what degree should teaching be an intellectual/academic endeavour? Should teacher preparation and ongoing professional development have an academic or theoretical underpinning?

If we, as a profession, advocate teaching as a craft, are we in danger of reducing its professional reputation?

Further reading and resources

Ball, S. (2017) *The Education Debate (Policy and politics in the twenty-first century)*, Bristol: Policy Press.

In this book, Ball captures key debates and themes in this fast-changing education field. He guides us through recent government initiatives and policies and looks at the politics of these policy interventions and how they have changed the face of education. This text does not simply describe education policy; Ball also considers the influence of neuroscience, the increased interest of business in education and the impact of austerity.

Brookfield, S. D. (2017) *Becoming a Critically Reflective Teacher*, San Francisco: John Wiley & Sons.

This text provides a practical guide to the essential practice of critical reflection. Brookfield describes what critical reflection is and why it is important, providing expert insight and practical tools to facilitate a journey of constructive self-critique. He shows how teachers can uncover and assess their assumptions about practice by viewing them through the four lenses; students' eyes, colleagues' perceptions, relevant theory and research and your own personal experience.

Day, C. (2017) *Teachers' Worlds and Work: Understanding Complexity, Building Quality*, Oxon, UK: Routledge.

Teachers' Worlds and Work provides a new, research-informed consideration of key elements which independently and together influence teachers' work and lives: policy and workplace conditions, teacher professionalism, identity, emotions, commitment and resilience, types of professional learning and development and the importance of the contribution to these made by high-quality leadership. In bringing these elements together, the book provides new, detailed and holistic understandings of their influence and suggests ways of building and sustaining teachers' abilities and willingness to teach to their best over their careers.

References

Aronowitz, S. & Giroux, H. A. (2003) *Education Under Siege: The Conservative, Liberal and Radical Debate Over Schooling*, Abingdon, UK: Routledge.

Ball, S. J. (2017) *The Education Debate*, Bristol: Policy Press.

Beauchamp, C. & Thomas, L. (2009) 'Understanding teacher identity: An overview of issues in the literature and implications for teacher education', *Cambridge Journal of Education*, 39(2): 175–189.

BERA-RS (2014) 'The role of research in teacher education – Reviewing the evidence. Interim report of the BERA-RSA Inquiry into the role of research in teacher education'. Available at www.bera.ac.uk/wp-content/uploads/2014/02/BERA-RSA-Interim-Report.pdf.

Biesta, G. (2007) 'Why "what works" won't work: Evidence-based practice and the democratic deficit of educational research', *Educational Theory*, 57(1): 1–22.

Biesta, G. (2012) 'The future of teacher education: Evidence, competence or wisdom?' *Research on Steiner Education (Rose)*, 3(1): 8–21.

Biesta, G. (2015) 'What is education for? On good education, teacher judgement, and educational professionalism', *European Journal of Education*, 50(1): 75–87.

Boyd, P., Hymer, B. & Lockney, K. (2015) *Learning Teaching: Becoming an Inspirational Teacher*, Northwich, UK: Critical Publishing.

Brookfield, S. D. (2017) *Becoming a Critically Reflective Teacher*, San Francisco: John Wiley & Sons.

Brown, T., Rowley, H. & Smith, K. (2015) *The Beginnings of School Led Teacher Training: New Challenges for University Teacher Education*, Manchester: Metropolitan University. Available at https://e-space.mmu.ac.uk/602385/2/School%20Direct%20Research%20Report.pdf. (Accessed 12.12.2018).

Cordingley, P., Bell, M., Evans, D. & Firth, A. (2005) 'The impact of collaborative CPD on classroom teaching and learning. Review: What does teacher impact data tell us about collaborative CPD?' In: *Research Evidence in Education Library*, London: Institute of Education: EPPI-Centre, Social Science Research Unit, Institute of Education, University of London.

Dall'Alba, G. & Barnacle, R. (2007) 'An ontological turn for higher education', *Studies in Higher Education*, 32(6): 679–691.

Darling-Hammond, L. & Lieberman, A. (eds.) (2012) *Teacher Education around the World: Changing Policies and Practices*, New York: Routledge.

Department for Education (DfE) (2015) *Carter Review of Initial Teacher Training*, London: Crown Copyright. Available at https://dera.ioe.ac.uk/21832/7/Carter_Review:16012015_Redacted.pdf (Accessed 12.01.2019).

Eraut, M. (2003) 'The many meanings of theory and practice', *Learning in Health and Social Care*, 2(2): 61–65.

Giroux, H. (n.d.) 'Teachers as transformatory intellectuals', *Symposium on Understanding Quality Education Conference on Re-envisioning Quality in*

Education. Available at http://www.itacec.org/afed/document/henry_giroux_2 _ok.pdf. (Accessed 12.12.2018).

Gove, M. (2010) 'Speech at national college annual conference, Birmingham'. Available at https://www.gov.uk/government/speeches/michael-gove-to-the-n ational-college-annual-conference-birmingham (Accessed 12.12.2018).

Labaree, D. (1992) 'Power, knowledge, and the rationalization of teaching: A genealogy of the movement to professionalize teaching', *Harvard Educational Review*, 62(2): 123–155.

Lemov, D. (2015) *Teach Like a Champion 2.0: 62 Techniques That Put Students on the Path to College*, San Francisco: Jossey-Bass.

Mead, G. H. (1934) *Mind, Self and Society*, Chicago: University of Chicago Press.

Moore, A. (2004) *The Good Teacher: Dominant Discourse in Teaching and Teacher Education*, London & New York: Routledge Falmer.

Oancea, A. & Furlong, J. (2007) 'Expressions of excellence and the assessment of applied and practice-based research', *Research Papers in Education*, 22(2): 119–137.

Robinson, W. (2006) 'Teacher training in England and Wales: Past, present and future perspectives', *Education Research and Perspectives*, 33(2): 19.

Sachs, J. (2005) 'Teacher education and the development of professional identity: Learning to be a teacher'. In: Denicolo, P. & Kompf, M. (eds.), *Connecting Policy and Practice: Challenges for Teaching and Learning in Schools and Universities*, 5–21. Oxford: Routledge.

Stenhouse, L. (1983) *Authority, Education, and Emancipation: A Collection of Papers*, Portsmouth, USA: Heinemann.

Winch, C., Oancea, A. & Orchard, J. (2015) 'The contribution of educational research to teachers' professional learning: Philosophical understandings', *Oxford Review of Education*, 41(2): 202–216.

Chapter 4

Fundamental British Values

Are they *fundamental?*

Imran Mogra

Introduction

Since its re-emergence as a political yardstick, by now, fundamental British values (FBV) would be expected to be securely embedded within the fabric of life in English schools. The two-pronged policy strategy from the Department of Education (DfE) may be considered as the main contributing factor for raising such expectations as the requirement to actively promote FBV became part of *being* a teacher (DfE, 2013), and later, post–the Trojan Horse Affair (THA), in making FBV the centrepiece of spiritual, moral, social and cultural development (SMSC). Thus, it becomes significant for us all to examine in-depth the issues related to teaching and learning.

This chapter will examine, as background, the historical development of nebulous FBV to demonstrate the origins being outside educational discourse; namely in counterterrorism. As part of this, a critical analysis of the Prevent agenda will be undertaken and the implications of both of these on the educational sector considered. A section of the chapter will present a descriptive analysis of the notions of FBV and deliberate their controversial nature to assist engagement with the social, cultural, ethical and pedagogical issues related to teaching the primary curriculum.

Introducing fundamental British values

FBV are defined as democracy, the rule of law, individual liberty and mutual respect and tolerance of those with different faiths and beliefs. From the perspective of the curriculum, the government advises schools to teach them as part of the spiritual, moral, social and cultural (SMSC) development of pupils and provides specific suggestions for their delivery (DfE, 2014). An immediate issue raised by Eaude (2018, p.72) is that a significant number of people would not subscribe to the four values highlighted as being fundamental to Britishness, either in the sense that those selected are fundamental or that others are omitted. Others argue that the values chosen create confusion, as those listed are considered part of universal human rights (Elton-Chalcraft et al., 2017; Struthers, 2017), and yet there is no reference made to human rights and a failure to acknowledge the United Kingdom's commitments to international human rights treaties (Struthers, 2017). Some have argued that these 'values' are actually not values but 'legal ethics' (Mansfield, 2019; Struthers, 2017) and that the root problem is that Britons often see themselves as Scottish, Welsh or (Northern) Irish and to a lesser extent English first, but not necessarily British (Mansfield, 2019, p.43).

A further concern, of course, is that if teachers do not move beyond a narrow and restricted conceptualisation and application of FBV to widen the scope of discussion in classrooms, the outcome might be to place Britain on a 'higher' pedestal in relation to other nations. This troublesome notion was further exacerbated by the then–Prime Minister, Theresa May, who declared the need to 'assert "the superiority" of British Values' (Travis, 2017, p.8).

Some years ago, the Ajegbo Report accentuated the complexity of understanding diversity and inclusion and recognised the different understandings of the term 'British' and that defining the term is problematic (Ajegbo, 2007). The Report also acknowledged that people construct identities in multiple ways and revealed that some respondents were concerned that the term 'Britishness' had the potential to be divisive. At that time, some academics had appealed for the vague term 'Britishness' to be replaced with citizenship and equal rights (Bhopal and Rhamie, 2014; Khan, 2007; Parekh, 2007). These concerns have persisted into the debate about the active promotion of FBV. Though the definition of British values accords with the findings in the above-mentioned report, even then, critical questions were voiced as to whether democracy, the rule of law, individual liberty, fairness/equality, respect and tolerance are actually values distinctive to Britain (Maylor, 2016, p.315). In fact, many other democracies have similar values and freedoms enshrined in their constitution (Beck, 2018; Eaude, 2018; Kymlicka, 2010).

Before going on to examine FBV and the issues surrounding them in more depth, the next section will discuss the Prevent Strategy and the Trojan Horse Affair, as these are often mentioned in connection with FBV and their influence needs to be understood.

Role of the Prevent Strategy and the Trojan Horse Affair

As part of a counterterrorism strategy, the *Prevent Strategy* was introduced in 2006 as a cross-governmental initiative to ensure that young people were not radicalised and did not engage in acts of violence. It involved the police, education and health professionals and local communities. It had four aims: to prepare for attacks, protect the public, pursue the attackers and prevent radicalisation in the first place (Miah, 2017).

The Strategy proved very controversial and, consequently, it was adapted. Despite this, it continues to be a source of considerable debate and anxiety. Although it was emphasised that Prevent was applicable to all communities and that in any area individuals may be open to radicalisation, the danger was generally thought to be greater in some geographical areas, notably in larger cities (Holmwood and O'Toole, 2018). Two main concerns apply in this respect. First, although possible radicalisation of young people by right-wing, ultra-nationalistic groups was recognised, the perception among Muslim communities and more widely was that the Prevent Strategy concentrated on and targeted mainly Muslims (Awan, 2018; Busher, Choudhury, Thomas and Harris, 2017; Miah, 2017). Secondly, schools and college staff (and other adults) were expected to report students perceived to be at risk of radicalisation, so that an assessment of appropriate support – and if need be, intervention – could be made. This has had an impact on the role of staff becoming part of a bigger 'surveillance' team across the country and goes against the idea that the primary role of teachers is to *educate* their pupils, not to view them automatically as suspects and potentially dangerous (Healy, 2018; Sant and Hanley, 2018). It is also noteworthy that the Prevent duty required publicly funded, registered early-years childcare providers to have due regard to the need to prevent pupils from being drawn into terrorism. This enforced a political agenda of securitisation onto such practitioners and those working directly with pupils (Lander, 2016). This role was made ever more untenable by evidence which suggested that radicalisation nearly always happens outside school or college, either through the internet or involvement in groups in young people's local communities (Eaude, 2018).

The five FBV are seen to be an attempt by government to define Britishness in opposition to a perceived extremist threat to wider society and to the next generation of citizens being educated in British schools (Mansfield, 2019). Research suggests, however, that the Prevent strategy in its policy directives on the teaching and learning of FBV has served to produce responses by schools that validate 'whiteness' as power, dominance, normativity and privilege (Moncrieffe and Moncrieffe, 2019, p.67). This will be discussed in more depth later in the chapter.

Something which propelled FBV to a new height in the public consciousness, especially in schools, was the so-called Trojan Horse Affair. Media reports unfolding in spring 2014 alleged that some academies in Birmingham were being targeted by hard-line 'Islamists' to be 'taken over' and that, allegedly, radicalisation and extremism were being promoted there. These allegations appeared in an anonymous letter, the authenticity of which was questioned (some deeming it to be a forgery) (Awan, 2018; Richardson, 2015). Despite the suspicious nature of the letter, several investigations into the matter took place and lifetime bans from teaching were imposed on a chairman of an education trust and more than 10 teachers.

Subsequently, a report by Birmingham City Council's Review Group found 'no evidence of a conspiracy to promote an anti-British agenda, violent extremism or radicalisation in schools' (Kershaw, 2014, p.4). Along similar lines, a study by Mogra (2016) of 21 Ofsted inspection reports of these non-religious schools revealed no evidence of a concerted and deliberate plot to promote radicalisation of Muslim children in these schools. It is worth emphasising that a House of Commons report had concurred with such findings (HM Government, 2015b).

Nevertheless, a few individuals were found to be trying to introduce an intolerant and aggressive ethos in a deliberate and sustained way. As a result of this, the THA raised many issues about the accountability of academies, school governance, leadership, school ethos and improvement, curriculum and equality, the relationship between religion and education and political ideology and systems of education. Later, the National College for Teaching and Leadership panel hearings found an abuse of justice by the Department for Education's legal team. They had withheld interview transcripts from key witnesses, which meant that the senior leadership team had their bans overturned and were free to return to the classroom (Adams, 2017; Awan, 2018).

Despite the outcome of this affair, the role of schools and teachers in the prevention of extremism and radicalisation was brought into sharper focus. At least three differences can be noted in relation to FBV:

- *All* schools were required to address FBV as the Government took unprecedented steps to further embed FBV in independent schools (HM Government, 2014);
- Initially these values were to be respected but now they were to be *actively* promoted;
- To ensure compliance, Ofsted's inspection framework was revised to check and ensure that schools were compliant, and also the criteria for unannounced inspections were broadened (HM Government, 2015b, p.16, S38).

Though the allegation to operationally and ideologically take control of these schools remained unproven, it gave government agencies impetus to intervene and pursue an assimilationist agenda conceptualised as national identity in the form of FBV (Poole, 2018).

Origins of FBV

The origins of FBV lie in the political landscape of the UK, where the concept of British values has been fluid and amorphous. To illustrate, when Tony Blair became prime minister in 1997 he announced that such values included fighting poverty, securing justice and opportunity and being a compassionate society. Later in 2000 his conception changed to fair play, creativity, tolerance and an outward-looking approach to the world, which led Struthers (2017) to note that successive governments have struggled with determining British values. The initiative to teach about 'traditional British values' in schools was initially mooted by Bill Rammell, the New Labour government minister in 2006, and Michael Gove eventually enacted it in 2014 in response to the THA (Vincent, 2019). The definition of FBV currently used has existed since at least 2011. Crucially, it was not a direct attempt at defining the values; rather, it was a reaction to the phrase embedded within the explication of extremism which stated that, 'Extremism is the vocal or active opposition to fundamental British values, including democracy, the rule of law, individual liberty and mutual respect and tolerance of different faiths and beliefs' (Richardson, 2015; Tomlinson, 2015). This explanation of extremism was set out in the government's Prevent counterterrorism strategy (HM Government, 2011, p.107; HM Government, 2015a) – in other words, the context was far from being educational; it was conceived rather from the viewpoint of national security and international policies of the Home Office. Thus, there is an evident link between anti-radicalisation, anti-extremism and the requirement to promote FBV in the education sector. Concurrently, it is also the justification for positioning FBV within what is considered to be 'safeguarding' of children (Vincent, 2019).

The introduction of FBV into education needs also to be examined within its broader socio-political and historical contexts. This includes a history of Britain that embraces colonial exploitation, imperialism, racial arrogance and oppression and militarism, potentially affecting how discussions of so-called British values are received by minority ethnic groups (Vincent, 2019; Beck, 2018). It is important to be mindful that the FBV tend to be presented as a 'new' curriculum policy. However, Winter and Mills (2020, p.47), employing a psycho-political approach and informed by anti-colonial work, highlight the often-silent workings of power within the FBV policy. They propose that the underlying rationale of FBV duties are symptoms of the much older colonial education–security relationship, and thus, of white British supremacist subjectivity deployed by government to defend white privilege. Therefore, ethically, for some British citizens, 'British' represents *un*-freedom, *in*tolerance, *denial* of democracy and *oppression* of indigenous religions. Though there are divergent views about the legacy of the empire, deeply held views coexist which are unlikely to be resolved (Beck, 2018). Unsurprisingly, some have argued that FBV have been selected to promote a particular ideology that opposes dissent from the current political norms and is grounded in a traditional view of Britain's political past: one that claims Britain as a bastion of perpetual progress and elevated civilisation (Mansfield, 2019, p.43).

A further issue which needs to be appreciated is that the foregrounding of the British values rhetoric is an element of a broader agenda seeking to address wider concerns about religious, cultural and ethnic diversity in the twenty-first century, with some arguing that these divisions are deepening seriously (Beck, 2018).

The policy: the problem

Criticism immediately emerged. To begin with, the policy itself was wanting in conceptual clarity as it represented a random selection of values. Richardson (2015) contended that the definition of extremism, wherefrom the FBV originated, lacked any explanation, illustration, rationale or discussion. It was conceptually unclear because its key terms – 'rule of law', 'liberty', 'democracy', 'tolerance' – are notoriously open to conflicting interpretations, and over the years have had different meanings at different times and in different contexts (Richardson, 2015, p.41). Secondly, the government was criticised for adopting a simplistic assumption that radicalisation results mainly from contact with and indoctrination into extremist ideology, whereas the reality is that the pathway to violent extremism involves several factors including psychological, socioeconomic, religio-political factors and a process of indoctrination into an ideology (Panjwani, 2016, p.331). Indeed, Arthur (2015) posits that there is difficulty in understanding extremism and radicalisation fully because both words lack an objective or universally accepted definition. Radicalisation can be viewed as a process by which someone adopts an extreme position, but it may not involve violent behaviour in support of the position adopted (Arthur, 2015, p.313). Significantly, the meaning of *undermining* is also left undefined. Unsurprisingly, school leaders in Revell and Bryan's (2016) study expressed uncertainty in its interpretation, and in the absence of a sophisticated discourse to discuss undermining FBV, an atmosphere of fear and uncertainty characterised their perspectives.

Another problem with the policy is its duality. On the one hand a separate guidance was issued and applied to independent schools, free schools and academies (DfE, 2013). Independent schools are regulated and inspected by bodies different from those which regulate and inspect publicly funded schools, and are privately funded whereas free schools and academies, while publicly funded, are not under local authority control, but are inspected under the Ofsted Framework. Eaude (2018) questioned why something 'fundamental' should be treated in different ways when the schools are otherwise similar. This anomaly, he suggested, without this being stated explicitly, meant that certain types of school, especially independent Muslim schools, were regarded as particularly likely to encourage radicalisation and so were in need of separate guidance (Eaude, 2018, 70).

Janmaat (2018) highlights another oddity in that the government concentrated on primary and lower secondary education and not on 16–19 colleges, although the latter were still obliged to engage with the Prevent duty. In the absence of any specific guidance from the DfE on how to deliver FBV for this group of education providers, they were advised 'to train staff to help them "exemplify British values" in their management and teaching, "challenge extremist ideas" and decide when to share information about individuals at risk of radicalising' (Janmaat, 2018, p.251–252).

The mandate to promote FBV can be conceived as a liberal (or civic) nationalistic approach to citizenship (Vincent, 2019), the key ingredients of which are the creation of a shared national identity. FBV has thus shifted from shared universal and common values (Lander, 2016). People are more likely to demonstrate widespread trust and solidarity when they identify with each other as compatriots, beyond the specifics of their gender, ethnic, cultural or religious identities (Miller and Ali, 2014). Hence it would seem that the phrase 'British values' has a nationalist flavour to it with the aim of arousing patriotism within the school population for nation-building, which might result in an intertwined net of simplistic stereotypes about race, ethnicity, multiculturalism and religion.

At a time of considerable uncertainty and upheaval, the imposition of FBV with limited diligence, consultation and debate is viewed by some as being part of a higher scheme in determining the relationship of the state and the public. Some Muslim teachers in the study of Panjwani (2016) did not find any conflict between FBV and Islam. Nevertheless, they were still critical of the FBV project and its implementation. Their criticisms ranged from claims of the moral deprivation of contemporary society to sophisticated observations such as the widespread perception among them that Western establishments displayed double standards in practising democracy and human rights. In addition to the arbitrary choice of values, some felt that they would be deprived of their role of creating critical minds through a fear of criminalisation. A respondent thought that the encouragement to follow rule of law was nothing more than an attempt to create a compliant citizenry when such laws were being made under the shadow of corporate and economic lobbies (Panjwani, 2016, p.337).

Reconsidering 'fundamental' and 'Britishness'

It is important to bear in mind that the values themselves are not being questioned per se; rather it is their portrayal as 'fundamental' and 'British' which is seen as unfitting and contentious (Janmaat, 2018). This, in turn, might lead to the alienation of some among minority communities, especially Muslims (Bolloten and Richardson, 2015; Tomlinson, 2015), and to the exclusion of a sizeable minority of pupils of minority backgrounds from the current historical narrative of Britain as delineated by the National Curriculum (2013) (Mansfield, 2019). It is crucial to minimise any sense of and perception of alienation experienced by pupils in school and in society. Social identity theory, in part, suggests that radicalisation develops as a result of individuals being confused about their identities and their search for the meaning of their role within society. Within the discussion of British values, in Awan's (2018, p.207) research, some children expressed feelings of lacking a sense of identity and belonging. 'Kamran stated that: "I must confess I have started to question what it means to be British. I honestly feel like I don't belong here anymore"'.

In addition, Smith (2016) advanced the view that the policy might instil fear among teachers of addressing sensitive themes in the classroom, pressuring them to avoid or close down open discussions of topical social and political issues. As a result, this could seriously undermine the dialogic and democratic processes of teaching and learning – the very ideas that the government purports to promote.

Significantly, there are philosophical problems in determining a fixed set of values in a diverse society. Eaude (2018, p.72) questions whether FBV can reasonably be described as being *fundamental* on the basis that there exist two sets of guidance for different types of schools. He goes on to highlight difficulties in relation to situations when any individual or group is not prepared to subscribe to one or more of the statements and how they are interpreted. Eaude (2018, p.72) contends that 'as soon as someone questions whether they espouse any fundamental value, this may bring into question their patriotism and commitment to the nation'. He submits that such a position may not be a source of great concern to someone like himself, 'who is British-born and white-skinned, about whom no serious questioning of [his] Britishness is likely'. However, those born outside Britain or perceived to be, and whose religion and culture may lead to their Britishness being open to question, may experience more scrutiny; a serious issue. Thus, he concludes that 'any statement of values can easily become exclusive, even when it claims, or seeks, to be inclusive; and those likely to be excluded are those whose membership of a group is already in question'.

As a reaction to the movement of people, integration of minorities, social cohesion, radicalisation and terrorism, the constitution of Britishness has become an increasingly visible part of the political discourse throughout this century (Beck 2018; Vincent, 2019). The attachment of the adjective 'British' to FBV has attracted the most controversy and debate in diverse ways and at various levels as it embraces the notion of insider/outsider Britishness. This is where the outsider is cast as the deficient, racialised 'Other' and who is 'not quite British enough', which is an attempt to centre whiteness. In other words, it could be conceptualised as an exercise to reinforce the privilege and status of whiteness. This concern was highlighted in the research by Elton-Chalcraft et al. (2017) who evidenced that some students, with strongly held values of their own, were able to evaluate FBV as being a government instrument created to 'control' a particular section of society and impose an assimilationist view of Britishness (ibid., 2017, p.41). Within an assimilationist agenda, there is concern that this might lead to an entrenched prejudiced outlook among teachers who may feel justified in their quest for the development of Britishness in pupils, and who may assume that some pupils are deficient for not embodying Britishness enough (Smith, 2013, p.443).

The assumption of associating Britishness with whiteness exposes a further dilemma. In their interviews with 30 trainee teachers in the UK, Bhopal and Rhamie (2014) found that when trainees discussed white identities, they talked about them in relation to being privileged, advantaged and in powerful positions, unlike those who were Black. Whiteness, they discovered, was considered the 'norm'. It was from this 'norm' that all other non-white identities were judged and it was considered to be the point of departure from where other identities were defined. Moreover, it was the single identity which was considered acceptable and the norm, not only for British society but globally. They concluded that whiteness carried a universal connotation of acceptance and privilege (ibid., 2014). Another investigation of white teacher trainees reported a dearth of reflexivity about white privilege and lack of assertiveness in dealing with race-related issues in school (Lander, 2011). This would suggest a lack of problematisation of notions related to British values and their role in promoting social cohesion. Furthermore, some RE and citizenship teachers in another study appeared to be disappointed, as the word 'British' places an ownership on these values when they were attempting to teach children about a global world (Vincent, 2019). Significantly, research over the years has shown that children's notions of who is and is not British are based on skin colour, with some holding the view that only white people born in Britain could be British (Barton and Schamroth, 2004; Elton-Chalcraft, 2009; Elton-Chalcraft et al., 2017, pp.41–43; Maylor, 2010; Roberts-Holmes, 2004).

Since the definitions of 'Britishness' are unclear and consist of multiple interpretations, Rhamie, Bhopal and Bhatti (2012), based on their study with secondary students, suggested that the normalisation of whiteness and its associations with 'Britishness' and power contributes to some students struggling with their identity and connectedness to 'Britishness' and schooling. Thus, the term 'Britishness' in FBV could potentially exclude as well as include (both white and minority ethnic) students. In their research, Bhopal and Rhamie (2014) reported the complexity of students' own experiences of diversity, 'race' and inclusion, which led them to suggest the need for further opportunities for trainees to address these issues in depth rather than relying on often superficial and simplistic approaches. A sophisticated understanding of 'Britishness' would minimise its potential of being both exclusionary and inclusive. In part, a complex conception can be created by challenging the assumption that minority ethnic students are all immigrants rather than some being British born, and by recognising the diversity which exists among the white majority and that the self-definition of people varies and may be in a flux. In other words, ignoring a sensitive and nuanced exploration of 'Britishness' in FBV has the potential for different groups feeling excluded rather than included (Maylor, 2016, p.325). Many teachers and others have expressed particular reservations regarding the perceived targeting of British Muslims within this policy and its divisive nature, as it is making some of them question their presence in England and is developing perspectives of 'us' and 'others' and of being seen as a 'suspect community' (Awan, 2018; Farrell and Lander, 2019; Poole, 2018; Vincent, 2019).

It is clear that from the outset, the concept of Britishness created debates about identity, race, colonisation, imperialism, integration and assimilation. Panjwani (2016, p.331), reflecting on subsequent discourses and debates, suggested that the focus on the adjective 'British' stole the limelight, leaving very little space to discuss more important issues around the utility and adequacy of the proposed values themselves. Richardson (2015, p.41) thought that considerable agitation could have been avoided if a general phrase such as 'the fundamental values and principles which underlie public life in the United Kingdom' had been adopted. Beck (2018) seems to concur, asserting that many people would consider these as noble principles and that they ought to be foundational in a liberal pluralistic society. However, it was suggested that they need closer specification and institutional embodiment to be effective, and to insist that these are *British* (sic), in his view, is likely to do more harm than good (Beck, 2018, p.232).

Schools and FBV

Prior to the introduction of FBV, values education has had a long history in British education, and has always been loaded with controversy (Deakin-Crick,

2002; Eaude, 2018; Halstead and Taylor, 1996). In relation to the curricula of schools, this controversy has been exacerbated by the positioning of the active promotion of FBV within the existing requirement for schools to promote the spiritual, moral, social and cultural (SMSC) development of pupils. Ministers described the inclusion of FBV in schools as a decisive shift away from moral relativism in the classroom (Adams, 2017). In other words, teachers would be expected to adopt a particular stance, the scope of which would be left to individual teachers to determine, even though contextually, it is only assumed that FBV builds pupils' resilience to radicalisation (Vincent, 2019), with doubts regarding the impact of 'regular encounters' with FBV in the school context and how this is able to ensure pupils develop a sense of belonging at a national level (ibid., p.28).

FBV curriculum policy is not a separate curriculum strand or a discrete subject in the school curriculum; rather the active promotion of FBV permeates the curriculum to form part of the requirement for pupils' SMSC development. In other words, all curricula in school have a contribution and role to play. Confusingly, however, the DfE requires head teachers, on the one hand, to help pupils 'distinguish' the difference between 'right' and 'wrong', while on the other hand, acknowledging that 'different people may hold different views about what is "right" and "wrong"' (DfE, 2014, p.4; Elton-Chalcraft et al., 2017, p.30). For successful FBV, schools must now demonstrate deliberativeness in their planning and engagement and 'challenge opinions or behaviours in school that are contrary to fundamental British values' (DfE, 2014, p.5) and to move from the minimal level of promotion (passive) to maximal (active) level (Healy, 2018).

Empirically, based on nine case study schools, both primary and secondary, Vincent (2019) found four hybrid ways rather than discrete approaches through which FBV were promoted.

The first was *Representing Britain* and consisted of two elements. One had posters and displays listing FBV, usually with Union Jack-themed decoration. The other focussed on teaching about symbols commonly associated with Britain, such as cups of tea, the Queen, Shakespeare, and so on rather than on values (vide Beck, 2018; Elton-Chalcraft et al., 2017). Vincent (2019, p.23) reported that this approach has been criticised by Ofsted's Chief Inspector of Schools, who argued that 'crafting a picture of the Queen out of sequins' was 'charming' but 'not teaching children about our common values'. However, despite such criticisms, such features persist and, in some cases, Darwin, Dawkins, famous British sport personalities and landmarks are added with bunting hanging around the display frame.

In the second approach, nearly all their case study schools had '*Repackaged*' their current activities to some extent. In other words, schools present their existing practices as evidence of their work. For instance, the long-established school councils were merged with FBV. For Vincent (2019), this showed the ability of these schools to absorb the FBV policy. It was also noted that some organisations who offer support to schools recommend auditing current practice and using a cross-curricular approach to FBV.

The third approach, '*Relocating FBV as school values*', describes schools which had particularly strong values frameworks. According to Vincent (2019), in this approach a school signals particular values on its website, and disseminates values such as respect and resilience throughout its practices, teaching those values explicitly (sometimes called character education). In such schools, the tendency is for FBV to be absorbed into their general values work.

The fourth approach, '*Engagement with FBV*', adopts a critical stance in terms of the values. Here, pupils critically examine the advantages and limitations of democracy. Although some components of this approach were sometimes implemented by some of the case study secondary schools, these were found not to be systematic, and none followed an explicit programme of engagement with FBV, instead tending towards absorption (ibid., p.24).

The research by McGhee and Zhang (2017) into the enactment of FBV policy analysed school websites. In response to the introduction of the securitising instrument in schools and a retreat from multiculturalism, they found some schools deploying 'local discretion'. The work of these schools and colleges was innovative and defused some of the securitising features by celebrating the UK as a multi-racial, multi-faith and multi-cultural society. These schools also ensured that their promotion of FBV was consistent with their own existing values and ethos, which included the SMSC development of their pupils.

Robson (2019) researched the way in which the new requirement to promote a predetermined set of FBV as a specific measure to counter terrorism has been mediated by the ECEC sector practitioners in their pedagogical practice in England. Some practitioners adopted a critical perspective regarding the selection of resources where there was an explicit strategy of avoiding symbols of nationalism. In examining displays of children's (aged two to four) work in ECEC, Robson found that they were part of a deliberate process of evidencing compliance, and although the practitioners were clear about the rationale for the displays – an explicit public commitment to FBV – they were nevertheless afforded lower status relative to other aspects of the visual environment. Values education was found by Robson to be embedded within their pedagogy. In all Robson's research settings, practitioners planned with parents and communities and the visual records of these meetings were displayed as a way of validating and celebrating children's contribution to planning. The practitioners felt these meetings gave opportunities for children to learn about the FBV of democracy.

The research by Moncrieffe and Moncrieffe (2019) examined the use of imagery on display boards in 27 primary schools across the country. They found that generally they projected dominant white British majoritarian perspectives and discourses of British identity. However, the data from their teachers shows them producing a mixture of shared and different responses in their interpretations of FBV that construct a sense of British identity. Teachers interpreted most of the dominant images of common icons and symbols of traditional British culture as not representing fundamental British values. Moreover, the display board chosen by all teachers as being least representative used images that were icons and symbols of an ethnocentric traditional and stereotypical white British culture (Moncrieffe and Moncrieffe, ibid., p.66). In other research, Mansfield (2019) reflected on the relationship between history in the National Curriculum and the active promotion of FBV within SMSC. He found that FBV were confusing, contradictory and exclusionary. He argued that pupils cannot be compelled to respect Britain's history or its democratic system of government if they are to learn how to be independent and generate 'self-knowledge'. In his experience, when applying the SMSC guidance and offering 'balance', the teacher is essentially policing free speech and thought. Mansfield (ibid., p.44) suggested that in the case of SMSC, FBV are presented as though they are correct and alternatives are erroneous and 'undesirable'. In such a situation, if schools are to promote 'self-knowledge' and independence, then pupils ought to be given a range of information and safe environments to discuss such views in order to decide for themselves (ibid.).

Summary

This chapter has highlighted key elements of the requirement to actively promote FBV in primary schools. Hopefully, it has facilitated deliberation of these controversial yet important values to assist an engagement with the social, cultural, ethical and pedagogical issues related to their inclusion in the ethos and life of schools. There is a long history of values in education in Britain and it is a contested phenomenon, with the origins of FBV lying outside educational discourse and in the securitisation agenda. The THA in Birmingham provided further impetus to strengthen FBV in the curriculum and to hold schools accountable for them through inspections. The policy has been problematised to expose the tensions that exist not only between policy and practice but also in terms of how teachers can become instruments of the state and affect their autonomy. As educators, we need to think about our own values and our role in shaping the worldview of pupils growing up in modern Britain. We need to challenge and debate our understandings and interpretations of the terms 'fundamental', 'British' and 'values' with a view to broadening our conception of Britishness and its political nature.

Questions for reflection

To what extent does the definition of FBV meet your expectations of FBV?
How would you defend the teaching of FBV on educational grounds?
How would you describe the relationship between SMSC and FBV?

Further reading and resources

Caroll, J., Howard, C. & Knight, B. (2018) *Understanding British Values in Primary Schools: Policy and Practice*, London: Learning Matters.

This text considers a whole school approach as being the best way to teach British Values. It offers a variety of ideas to assist teachers to take ownership and embrace the agenda. In addition to case studies, it also provides a useful audit of statements, evidence and impact.

Elton-Chalcraft, S., Revell, L. & Lander, V. (2018) 'Fundamental British values: Your responsibility, to promote or not to promote?' In: Cooper, H. & Elton-Chalcraft, S. (eds.) *Professional Studies in Primary Education*, (3rd ed.), London: SAGE.

This is an important chapter which invites critical reflection about the rationale to promote FBV and asks you to examine your own values. In fact, it questions whether student teachers should be promoting FBV. Based on their own research, the authors highlight the problematic nature of adhering to governmental instructions. A section offers some practical ideas for engaging with the requirement to promote and not to undermine FBV.

References

Adams, R. (2017) 'Five teachers Accused in Trojan horse affair free to return to classroom', *The Guardian*. Available at: https://www.theguardian.com/educati on/2017/may/30/trojan-horse-tribunal-fivebirmingham-teachers-islam.

Ajegbo, K. (2007) *Diversity and Citizenship Curriculum Review*, Nottingham: DfES.

Arthur, J. (2015) 'Extremism and neo-liberal education policy: A contextual critique of the Trojan horse affair in Birmingham schools', *British Journal of Educational Studies*, 63(3): 311–328.

Awan, I. (2018) "'I never did anything wrong' – Trojan Horse: A qualitative study uncovering the impact in Birmingham', *British Journal of Sociology of Education*, 39(2): 197–211.

Barton, P. & Schamroth, N. (2004) 'Understanding differences – Valuing diversity: Tackling racism through story, drama and video in mainly white primary schools', *Race Equality Teaching*, 23(1): 21–26.

Beck, J. (2018) 'School Britannia? Rhetorical and educational uses of "British values"', *London Review of Education*, 16(2): 228–238.

Bhopal, K. & Rhamie, J. (2014) 'Initial teacher training: Understanding 'race', diversity and inclusion', *Race, Ethnicity and Education*, 17(3): 304–325.

Bolloten, B. & Richardson, R. (2015) 'The great British values disaster – Education, security and vitriolic hate'. Available at: www.irr.org.uk/news/the-great-british-va lues-disaster-education-security-and-vitriolic-hate/ (accessed 01.05.2019).

Busher, J., Choudhury, T., Thomas, P. & Harris, G. (2017) *What the Prevent Duty Means for Schools and Colleges in England: An Analysis of Educationalists' Experiences*, London: Aziz Foundation.

Deakin-Crick, R. (2002) *Transforming Visions: Managing Values in Schools: A Case Study*, London: Middlesex University Press.

Department for Education (DfE) (2013) *Improving the Spiritual, Moral, Social and Cultural (SMSC) Development of Pupils: Departmental Advice for Independent Schools, Academies and Free Schools*. Available at: www.gov.uk/government/pub lications/improving-the-smsc-development-ofpupils- in-independent-schools.

Department for Education DfE (2014) *Promoting Fundamental British Values as Part of SMSC in Schools: Departmental Advice for Maintained Schools*, London: Department for Education.

Eaude, T. (2018) 'Fundamental British values? Possible implications for children's spirituality', *International Journal of Children's Spirituality*, 23(1): 67–80.

Elton-Chalcraft, S. (2009) *'It's Not Just About Black and White, Miss': Children's Awareness of Race*, Stoke-on-Trent: Trentham Books.

Elton-Chalcraft, S. Lander, Revell, V., Warner, D. & Whitworth, L. (2017) 'To promote, or not to promote fundamental British values? Teachers' standards, diversity and teacher education', *British Educational Research Journal*, 43(1): 29–48.

Farrell, F. & Lander, V. (2019) '"We're not British values teachers are we?": Muslim teachers' subjectivity and the governmentality of unease', *Educational Review*, 71(4): 466–482.

Halstead, J. M. & Taylor, M. J. (1996) *Values in Education and Education in Values*, Abingdon: RoutledgeFalmer.

Healy, M. (2018) 'Belonging, social cohesion and fundamental British values', *British Journal of Educational Studies*, 67(4): 1–16.

HM Government (2011) *Prevent Strategy*, London: HMSO. Cm8092.

HM Government (2014) *The Education (Independent School Standards) (England) (Amendment) Regulations 2014*. 2014 No. 2374, London: HMSO.

HM Government (2015a) *Revised prevent duty guidance: For England and Wales*, Crown Copyright. Available at: https://assets.publishing.service.gov.uk/gove rnment/uploads/system/uploads/attachment_data/file/445977/3799_Revised _Prevent_Duty_Guidance__England_Wales_V2-Interactive.pdf.

HM Government (2015b) *Extremism in Schools: The Trojan Horse Affair*, 17 March 2015.

Holmwood, J. & O'Toole, T. (2018) *Countering Extremism in British Schools?* Bristol: Policy Press.

Janmaat, J. G. (2018) 'Educational influences on young people's support for fundamental British values', *British Educational Research Journal*, 44(2): 251–273.

Kershaw, I. (2014) *Investigation Report – Trojan Horse Letter*, Birmingham: Birmingham City Council.

Khan, O. (2007) 'Policy, identity and community cohesion: How race equality fits'. In: Wetherell, M., Lafleche, M. & Berkeley, R. (eds) *Identity, Ethnic Diversity and Community Cohesion*, London: SAGE.

Kymlicka, W. (2010) 'The rise and fall of multiculturalism? New debates on inclusion and accommodation in diverse societies', *International Social Science Journal*, 61(199): 97–112.

Lander, V. (2011) 'Race, culture and all that: An exploration of the perspectives of white secondary student teachers about race equity issues in their initial teacher education', *Race, Ethnicity and Education*, 14(3): 351–364.

Lander, V. (2016) 'Introduction to fundamental British values', *Journal of Education for Teaching*, 42(3): 274–279.

Mansfield, A. (2019) 'Confusion, contradiction and exclusion: The promotion of British values in the teaching of history in schools', *The Curriculum Journal*, 30(1): 40–50.

Maylor, U. (2010) 'Notions of diversity, British identities and citizenship belonging', *Race, Ethnicity and Education*, 13(2): 233–252.

Maylor, U. (2016) 'I'd worry about how to teach it: British values in English classrooms', *Journal of Education for Teaching*, 42(3): 314–328.

McGhee, D. & Zhang, S. (2017) 'Nurturing resilient future citizens through value consistency vs. the retreat from multiculturalism and securitisation in the promotion of British values in schools in the UK', *Citizenship Studies*, 21(8): 937–950.

Miah, S. (2017) *Muslims, Schooling and Security: Trojan Horse, Prevent and Racial Politics*, Basingstoke: Palgrave Macmillan.

Miller, D. & Ali, S. (2014) 'Testing the national identity argument', *European Political Science Review*, 6(2): 237–259.

Mogra, I. (2016) 'The "Trojan Horse" affair and radicalisation: An analysis of Ofsted reports', *Educational Review*, 68(4): 444–465.

Moncrieffe, M. & Moncrieffe, A. (2019) 'An examination of imagery used to represent fundamental British values and British identity on primary school display boards', *London Review of Education*, 17(1): 52–69.

Panjwani, F. (2016) 'Towards an overlapping consensus: Muslim teachers' views on fundamental British values', *Journal of Education for Teaching*, 42(3): 329–340.

Parekh, B. (2007) 'The cultural particularity of liberal democracy', *Political Studies*, 40(1): 160–175.

Poole, E. (2018) 'Constructing "British values" within a radicalisation narrative', *Journalism Studies*, 19(3): 376–391.

Revell, L. & Bryan, H. (2016) 'Calibrating fundamental British values: How head teachers are approaching appraisal in the light of the Teachers' Standards 2012, Prevent and the Counter-Terrorism and Security Act, 2015', *Journal of Education for Teaching*, 42(3): 341–353.

Rhamie, J., Bhopal, K. & Bhatti, G. (2012) 'Stick to your own kind: pupils' experiences of identity and diversity in secondary schools', *British Journal of Educational Studies*, 60(2): 171–191.

Richardson, R. (2015) 'British values and British identity: Muddles, mixtures, and ways ahead', *London Review of Education*, 13(2): 37–48.

Roberts-Holmes, G. (2004) 'I am a little bit brown and a little bit white': A dual heritage boy's playful identity construction', *Race Equality Teaching*, 23(1): 15–20.

Robson, J. V. K. (2019) 'How do practitioners in early years provision promote Fundamental British Values?' *International Journal of Early Years Education*, 27(1): 95–110.

Sant, E. & Hanley, C. (2018) 'Political assumptions underlying pedagogies of national education: The case of student teachers teaching 'British values' in England', *British Educational Research Journal*, 44(2): 319–337.

Smith, H. (2013) 'A critique of the teaching standards in England (1984–2012): Discourses of equality and maintaining the status quo', *Journal of Education Policy*, 28(4): 427–448.

Smith, H. J. (2016) 'Britishness as racist nativism: A case of the unnamed 'other', *Journal of Education for Teaching*, 42(3): 298–313.

Struthers, A. (2017) 'Teaching British values in our schools: But why not human rights values?' *Social and Legal Studies*, 26(1): 89–110.

Tomlinson, S. (2015) 'The empire disintegrates', *Ethnic and Racial Studies*, 38(13): 2208–2215.

Travis, A. (2017) 'A tougher response than after Arena Attack', *The Guardian*, 05-06-17, p. 8.

Vincent, C. (2019) 'Cohesion, citizenship and coherence: Schools' responses to the British values policy', *British Journal of Sociology of Education*, 40(1): 17–32.

Winter, C. & Mills, C. (2020) 'The psy-security-curriculum ensemble: British values curriculum policy in English schools', *Journal of Education Policy*, 35(1): 46–67.

Chapter 5

What is effective pedagogy in the Reception Year?

Zoe Lewis

Introduction

In 2016 the Teaching Schools Council (TSC) set out to define the factors that contributed to pupil outcomes across the curriculum in Primary education. They concluded that there was confusion and inconsistency between practice in Reception and Year 1 classes and that a more structured approach to teaching in Early Years should replace what were considered to be 'aimless activities' (2016, p.3). The report called for a review of teaching in the Reception Year, the idea being to draw upon research and expertise from those with Reception teaching experience; what actually followed was the 2017 Ofsted report 'Bold beginnings: The Reception curriculum in a sample of good and outstanding primary schools', which echoed the calls for more formalised approaches and proposed an increased focus on reading, writing and mathematics.

This chapter will draw upon my own experiences as an Early Years teacher and lecturer to reflect critically on the current debate around the 'what works' approach to early education. It will question the reliance on developmental approaches, accountability measures and the notion of school readiness to argue that there is no 'one size fits all' solution to effective early years pedagogy. A more localised, democratic pedagogical approach with a focus on social development and play-based methods will be considered as a more inclusive alternative to develop the learning dispositions that will equip children to be successful both within and beyond their future schooling.

The central role of developmental psychology

The TSC report summarises how children learn, in a text box containing just five paragraphs. It claims that children are naturally curious and gain satisfaction from 'successful thinking'. However, it also states that 'thinking and reasoning are difficult' and that this deters children from continuing with their problem solving or exploration of new concepts (TSC, 2016, p.13). This produces a deficit model, emphasising what children cannot do and implies that effective pedagogy offers a range of strategies to rectify the perceived problem. The report's assertion is taken from cognitive developmental psychology and it cites Willingham (2009) as a source of more information. Willingham's research explores the biological and cognitive basis of learning and his book claims to offer scientifically-based approaches to classroom practice underpinned by a list of nine set principles that can be applied to children's thinking and learning regardless of any differences in circumstances or context, whether that is a laboratory or a Reception classroom.

Developmental psychologists such as Willingham seek to explain the processes involved in children's learning and development and offer biological explanations for individual differences. Their research produces developmental norms against which teachers can measure children's progress. Therefore, in this context children are often understood through their ages and stages of development, and effective pedagogy requires a repertoire of strategies that will enable children to move onto the next stage as quickly as possible. From this perspective, development is seen as linear, predictable and generalisable and research is seen as a scientific way of providing evidence about what works in education. Wood and Hedges (2016) claim that developmental psychology has created these normative discourses and an approach to effective pedagogy that implies a positivist ontology and methodology with what other researchers have described as a 'one size fits all' philosophy that does not take into account the diversity of children's backgrounds and experiences (Ang, 2014, p.195). Given the fundamental differences in children's cultures and social experiences, many of these norms are likely to be inappropriate, therefore reproducing social inequality when children fail to meet developmental expectations (Brooker, 2011) and teachers provide interventions that encourage them to conform (Farquhar and White, 2014). In this way, developmental psychology determines the ways in which children are understood and positioned (Dahlberg et al., 2013), which leads Brooker (2011) to question whether this developmental approach to pedagogy matches the principles of early education, including listening to children and following their interests – a question that will be explored in more detail later in this chapter. However, it is also developmental norms that underpin the learning goals in the Curriculum Guidance for the Early Years Foundation Stage (EYFS) (DfE, 2017) whereby teachers must ensure that children meet each goal in order to achieve a good level of development and be ready for school (Booker, 2011). Although Roberts-Holmes (2012) found that practitioners generally welcomed the EYFS because they felt that it validated their child-led pedagogy, he noted that there were tensions between this approach and the National Curriculum which was more focused on subject knowledge, possibly explaining some of the inconsistences that were identified in the TSC report (2016) and addressed in *Bold Beginnings* (Ofsted, 2017). Alternatively, Cox (2011, p.20) argues that as learning is situated in social and cultural contexts, the behaviourist approaches that underpin much of the practice in primary education are 'inadequate', and instead she claims that teachers should be seen as 'fellow participants' in children's learning rather than 'acting upon' them to bring about learning.

Interestingly, Pugh (2010) found that the policy focus on narrowing the gap between more and less disadvantaged children in Reception classes had, despite its positive intentions, created unintended pressures to limit what was designed as a broad and balanced curriculum to just literacy and numeracy, and this seems to be reflected in the 2017 Ofsted report. Clearly this approach significantly narrows the focus of early education and places time pressures on both children and adults to achieve these goals, leaving little opportunity to develop relationships, make meaningful connections or engage fully in child-initiated play (Carter and Curtis, 2017). It is particularly concerning, then, that House (2011) found policy-makers' desire for children to meet developmental norms as quickly as possible is not effective in the long term and conversely, it has the potential to damage their well-being, self-esteem and their ability to learn, with serious consequences for the rest of their lives.

While the implied certainty of developmental and psychological approaches to pedagogy is likely to appeal to policy-makers who seek accountability and generalised rules that can be applied nationally, young children learn and develop at different rates. The ages and stages of their development overlap and their learning is situated in different local and cultural contexts that all impact on how and what they learn (Farquhar and White, 2014). As Jones and Holmes (2014) argue, there are too many other variables involved in young children's learning for it to be fostered effectively within the current developmental and positivist approaches. Assuredly, there are limits to what can be generalised to all settings and there are significant dangers in this rather simplistic approach to teaching and learning. It is important, therefore, to explore alternative interpretations of what constitutes effective pedagogy, particularly the interpretations of Reception teachers and the children themselves, which appear to have been excluded from the TSC policy-makers' analysis.

Child-centred learning and free play as a meaningful context for learning

Traditional early years philosophy and the work of early education pioneers has suggested that young children learn best by being active, cooperating with others and playing together (Nutbrown, Clough and Atherton, 2014), and this has led some practitioners to believe that child-led, play-based learning may be the only effective pedagogy in the early years (Wood and Hedges, 2016). However, Farquhar and White (2014, p.822) argue that research provides two contrasting views of pedagogy; the first being a 'liberal' approach that values the autonomy of the child and the second being a 'conservative' view that is underpinned by the authority of the teacher. They claim that traditional Western early childhood discourse follows the first view and emphasises a child-centred approach that is based upon children's individual needs and interests rather than externally agreed developmental norms, and that play is a key way in which children learn through this liberal approach. Play itself is generally accepted as being an innate, natural and free activity that provides opportunities for children to learn by trying things out and acting upon the real world in ways that are meaningful and exciting to them (Pramling Samuelson and Asplund Carlsson, 2008). Moyles (2010) argues that play enables children to learn holistically through their own active engagement, at their own pace and at a time that is appropriate to them. Furthermore, this approach enables communication, play and learning to occur simultaneously in an environment that gives children a feeling of belonging (Pramling Samuelsson and Asplund Carlsson, 2008). Research has shown that play-based pedagogy develops children's content or subject knowledge across the curriculum as well as developing their social skills and positive attitudes towards learning. As one teacher explained:

> I used to think that I had to find the time for all the subjects and then play as well! Now I see that play teaches children lots about the curriculum – and in ways far more enjoyable than any of my adult planned activities would have been!
> (Year 1 teacher 1, project log cited in Fisher, 2011, p.39)

These views have been described by other researchers, however, as romanticised or idealised versions of play whereby it is always seen as positive and progressive (Dockett, 2011), whereas in fact play is not necessarily inclusive, democratic or educational. There is research to suggest that genuinely child-initiated play can be chaotic and may not be purposeful at all (Roberts-Holmes, 2012). Similarly, Wood (2010) argues that it is important to question current assumptions regarding play and goes on to analyse the ways in which play is not always fun; some children are unfamiliar with Western and middle-class forms of play; and others may use their freedom and power in free play contexts to behave in antisocial ways.

A BERA Early Years Special Interest Group (2003) found that it was not easy to produce a single agreed definition of play-based pedagogy and even more challenging to articulate the ways in which play might be used to support teaching, therefore the whole approach was deeply problematic in practice. Their review of research showed that there was particular concern regarding play in Reception classes and the experiences of four- and five-year-olds. Although Reception teachers spoke enthusiastically about the value of play and its role in children's learning, the reality was that they focussed mainly on literacy and numeracy while play was used to occupy children and fill time with low expectations of what might be achieved. A key challenge was that the outcomes of play were not easily linked to the curriculum goals or measured to demonstrate effectiveness.

Pramling Samuelsson and Asplund Carlsson (2008) found that young children do not separate play and learning when they engage in self-chosen activities, although the school culture often does so by giving specific times and spaces for each. They conclude that to adopt a play-based pedagogy in such a goal-orientated setting, teachers also need to view playing and learning together, so that children are able to make their own choices, be creative and take the initiative while still having the opportunity to meet curricula goals.

Effective pedagogy requires a balance between adult and child-led activities supported by interaction, joint problem solving and sustained shared thinking (Siraj-Blatchford et al., 2002), but again research has shown that while teachers understand and support this at one level, their practice is often variable. They struggle to apply these approaches when supporting children's learning and may be reluctant to give children choice and control over their activities (McInnes et al., 2011). Stephen (2010) suggests that children's choices in play activities are not always genuine and it was evident that, in some settings, they could only select from a limited range of options that had already been chosen by the teacher. Sometimes the free choice of play activities was only an option after children had finished their written work, meaning that there were limited opportunities for play in school settings (Carter and Curtis, 2017; Stephen, 2010). Rogers and Lapping (2012, p.258) describe these pedagogies of play 'as an attempt to tame the potentially incoherent, disordered and disruptive aspects of children's activity' and 'to give the illusion of coherence, order and control' while focusing mainly on the cognitive aspects of the process.

Cousins (1990) explains that much of the practice in Reception classes makes little sense to young children. She gives an example of a five-year-old traveller child named Sonnyboy who was a gifted storyteller and mathematician and yet struggled with many of his experiences of formal schooling. From his cultural background, he believed that questions were something people asked when they genuinely did not understand the answers; he could not see why children didn't just eat when they were hungry; why the school bell often interrupted his play activities when he was just getting to the interesting part; or how the words that he used every day took on different meanings in the school setting. Therefore, the classroom created a confusing social context which, for Sonnyboy, just did not make sense. As Fleer (2006) argues, these cultural constructions of early education do not sufficiently address the needs and understandings of the culturally and linguistically diverse populations that they serve, and therefore there is scope for further research and a rethinking of these practices if they are to become truly inclusive. After all, surely the celebration of diversity and the promotion of inclusive practices should be a priority for any pedagogy in the Reception Year.

Despite an apparent enthusiasm for play-based learning among some teachers, Martlew et al. (2011) found that they held differing views about its value and purpose when translated into a pedagogical approach. Many Reception teachers had not received any specific training for teaching this year group (Martlew et al., 2011) and few of them were able to write clear objectives for children's play (Stephen, 2010). Early years practitioners also tended to position themselves outside of the play, focusing on observation and assessment rather than engaging as partners in children's activities (Fleer, 2015). Martlew et al. (2011) and Bodrova (2008) all identify the performative culture and accountability measures in schools as a constant source of difficulty when using play as a means of achieving school readiness or meeting predetermined academic outcomes. Within the current system, children need to meet the curricular goals in order to achieve the 'good level of development' that is required for the next stage of their schooling, and teachers risk being judged badly against inspection criteria if they cannot demonstrate progress. This accountability culture has the potential to block further exploration of alternative views of play-based pedagogy. Cox (2011, p.53) found that teachers were frustrated by these competing values in school classrooms and they reported their disappointment at 'not being able to be the kind of teacher they hoped to be'. However, Wood (2004, p.361) found that despite these challenges there were 'processes of creative mediation, adaptation and resistance' whereby the teachers in her study continued to apply their professional knowledge and expertise within their own classrooms. Cox (2011) asserts that teachers are still able to exercise some local control over their pedagogical decisions, but this is dependent of course on confidence, subject and pedagogical knowledge and understanding and the support of senior leaders in the setting.

It would appear, then, that if play-based pedagogies are to be taken seriously and the confusion suggested in the TSC report (2016) is to be avoided, teachers need to be able to articulate their values and make their pedagogical principles explicit. They need access to research evidence and appropriate training to give them the confidence to defend their professional status and avoid being seen as ineffective when they are juggling the competing demands of teaching in Reception classes (Rogers and Lapping, 2012; Stephen, 2010). It could be concluded, therefore, that much is taken for granted when the philosophical interpretations of play are applied to the pragmatic concerns of pedagogy, and there are differences between the rhetoric of child-led learning and the reality of outcomes-led practice. It seems that the performative culture in schools has created conflict between the interests of children, teachers and policy-makers and as a result it tends to be the adults' needs that are privileged.

Learning dispositions

Positive learning dispositions are highly influential in the ways that children respond to their learning experiences as well as the wider world around them. These dispositions include resilience, perseverance, playfulness, creativity, problem solving and a willingness to explore, ask questions and contribute their own ideas (Daniels, 2013). Some researchers argue that children are born with a natural curiosity and disposition to learn (Nutbrown, 2011), but it is generally agreed that positive dispositions can be fostered in an educational culture that enables children to be confident and successful in their learning (Daniels, 2013). This suggests that effective pedagogy needs to provide a learning environment where teachers recognise children's achievements and, as a result, the children come to see themselves as successful learners.

When considering the development of these important learning dispositions, it is important to recognise key differences between early years and primary education (Pramling Samuelson and Asplund Carlsson, 2008). Many children in Reception are just four years old and among the youngest in Europe to be in schools (Sharp, 2002), making it essential that the goals that are set for them are appropriate to their individual levels of development. If these differences are ignored and pedagogical decisions lead to inappropriate learning goals, children are unlikely to see themselves as successful learners, with serious consequences for their future educational success. Failure, fear and anxiety are likely to impact upon their persistence, confidence and engagement with future tasks (Stephen, 2010), and as Ailwood (2010) notes, children are rarely in a position to challenge these dominant and inappropriate practices.

Cox (2011, p.20) draws on sociocultural perspectives and the work of Lave and Wenger (1991) to consider an alternative, more supportive role for the teacher as a fellow participant in the 'socially situated activities' that constitute learning rather than 'acting upon' children to bring about learning. From this perspective, effective pedagogy incorporates the many different ways in which teachers help children to learn and to develop positive dispositions. Carter and Curtis (2017) note that this involves interaction, communication, explaining, modelling, thinking aloud, questioning, observation, documentation, offering encouragement and providing challenge so that the curriculum is co-created by children and adults through a process of shared meaning-making. They argue that the learning environment is fundamentally important in supporting these interactions and creating an appropriate, nurturing classroom culture, which in turn requires ongoing reflection about the values and understandings of young children that underpin it. Carter and Curtis conclude that the emotional environment and the process of teaching and learning itself also contribute to the content of what children learn, therefore alongside delivery of the curriculum, children are 'deeply affected by the quality of the teaching environment in which it takes place' (Carter and Curtis, ibid., p.6). Again, this would suggest that relationships between children and adults and a culture that respects children as competent, confident and capable learners are crucial in determining the holistic, dispositional outcomes of children's learning.

Hedges and Cooper (2014) claim that widening the focus of effective pedagogy to include these more holistic outcomes would develop children's identities as competent learners and may prove to be crucial in their long-term social and academic success. Conversely, while the didactic teaching and adult-directed transfer of knowledge seen in more formal models of pedagogy are based on a belief that they will prepare children for later schooling, they may actually be harmful to these very dispositions that children will need to be successful in education. Similarly, Moss (2014) argues that instrumental approaches to pedagogy deny children the opportunity to be creative, imaginative, curious and original, when the aim of early education should be to support them so that they see themselves as capable learners (Jordan, 2009) and are able to reach their full potential (Moss, 2014). As Katz so clearly argues, 'Any educational approach that undermines that disposition is miseducation' (1993, p.1). Therefore, the literature suggests pedagogy in the Reception Year should focus on these important learning dispositions as well as more subject-based curriculum content if it is to be truly effective in supporting children's learning. Perhaps, then, an important next step is to explore the question of what it means to be effective in the context of the Reception class.

Discourses of quality and effectiveness

Wood and Hedges (2016) reflect on the current political interest in the potential of early years to address socioeconomic issues and inequality and they note that this has resulted in significant expenditure on provision. In turn, policy-makers require evidence of a return on their investment, leading to some researchers arguing for a return to more formal whole-class teaching so that schools can compete in international comparisons of more measurable subjects such as maths and science (O'Hear, 2000). These perspectives have led to particular definitions of quality, and therefore effectiveness, that have been built on a political desire to increase human capital, labour market participation and global economic competition. This, in turn, has led to a particular view of what constitutes a good education, and the term 'quality' has come to represent all that is desirable in effective practice. However, it has also been argued that the term 'quality' has been taken for granted in current educational debate (Dahlberg et al., 2013). It is seen as being an obvious requirement and has become the 'dominant discourse' and a 'regime of truth' (Foucault, 1980 cited in Dahlberg et al., 2013, p.31), so that other possibilities or ways of knowing are excluded. Consequently, this regime of truth limits what it is possible to think, privileging some voices while silencing others (Moss, 2014), marginalising teachers' professional knowledge and taking away their power to make pedagogical decisions (Carter and Curtis, 2017).

Many arguments about traditional early years pedagogy, including child-centred learning and the role of play, are dismissed as being 'laissez-faire', with little evidence of their effectiveness when compared to the more 'scientific' approaches of developmental psychology (Wood and Hedges, 2016, p.388). It is argued that they represent a rejection of the high standards that are associated with the term 'quality', and as a result, alternative views of effective pedagogy have received relatively little attention in national policy (Moss, 2014). However, a pedagogical approach that is based on such narrow learning outcomes is questionable when it attempts to simplify what is such a complex process of pedagogical interaction. Furthermore, postmodernist researchers argue that quality itself is not an objective or neutral term, and it is infused with the political values outlined above. It is, therefore, open to critique and perhaps there is an option to reject the term altogether and work with a different set of values to evaluate pedagogy (Dahlberg et al., 2013).

Fisher (2011) found that the current performative culture presents further challenges to teachers' autonomy in the form of other people's expectations, especially those of head teachers and senior management. Often these are expectations around planning and assessment, perhaps with a requirement for written evidence of children's learning, despite the fact that young children cannot always express their knowledge, skills and understanding in words at this age. Aubrey (2002, p.67) traced this concern with 'basic literacy and numeracy' back to the 1980s and 1990s when children and teachers felt the impact of the National Curriculum and a constant pressure to teach academic skills at an increasingly early age. Although children clearly need these skills to be successful in later life, it is important for them to develop more concrete understandings of maths and to explore literacy in multi-modal, culturally relevant ways if these academic skills are to be meaningful and useful to them (Bodrova, 2008). However, children's deeper understandings and more child-centred pedagogical approaches appear to take second place when compared to the key measure of quality and effectiveness, which appears from the Ofsted report (2017) to be school readiness.

School readiness

The purposes and aims of effective early years pedagogy have become centred around a clear goal of school readiness, implying that the Reception Year might be seen as simply preparation for what is yet to come (Ang, 2014). Similarly, this philosophy is demonstrated in the recommendations of the TSC report, which calls for an '*evidence-based*' review of practice in this year group 'to ensure that children enter Year 1 fully equipped' (2016, p.44).

However, the term 'school readiness' is not clear, and it is also open to multiple interpretations. Brown (2010) argues for more clarity, claiming that from a sociocultural perspective, children can be seen as being ready for school in one context but not ready in another. This has the potential for conflict between home and school cultures, a lack of respect for children's understandings and therefore a sad repetitive cycle of failure (Moss, 2008). Wood (2014) suggests an alternative, more positive view of school readiness which might be seen as children developing learning dispositions, asking questions and thinking for themselves rather than conforming to the requirements of more formal pedagogical approaches. Or perhaps children do not need to be developed or readied at all, as often it is the pedagogy that is unsuitable and difficult for them to understand rather than children themselves being in deficit. In this context, the 'school ready' child might be seen as a 'tamed child' (Wood and Hedges, 2016, p.392) and pedagogy used as a 'form of inscription' (Luke, 1992, p.109).

Moss (2008, pp.229–230) offers a solution to this 'stand-off' regarding school readiness in his 'vision of a meeting place' whereby the different phases of education work together to share their understandings, values and meanings in a more democratic approach. This requires mutual respect and ongoing collaboration in what would be a 'strong and equal partnership', but it seems to offer a more constructive approach to the challenges of producing a definition of effective pedagogy that is meaningful and appropriate across all phases of primary education.

The political nature of pedagogy

Learning, teaching, society and politics are all interrelated and therefore any analysis of effective pedagogy is political in nature. It is important, then, to consider the wider political questions that define education in order to address the complexity and differing contexts in which pedagogical interactions are situated (Moss, 2014). Brooker (2011, p.137) argues that 'in general researchers have been looking for "answers" to the wrong questions' because effective pedagogy can be interpreted from a variety of perspectives and value positions. Perhaps then the critical questions are: what works with respect to what? What is the broader aim of early education and what are the purposes of the current measures of effectiveness (Cox, 2011, p.46)? Is the goal of education to produce compliant workers for economic functions or is its purpose to help children grow and develop to their full potential so that they become engaged citizens who are equipped to make a contribution to society? Furthermore, what and whose knowledge is important in determining these aims and whose benefit is it likely to serve? Surely pedagogy should be about children's needs and be for their benefit as well as their families and communities. It should offer the enriched childhood experiences that give children the best chance of a better future, rather than focusing on that future alone.

Alexander (2010) explored these wider purposes of education and noted the dominance of the word 'standards' in educational politics. Rather than basing his views on what is easily observed, measurable and controlled, he argues for a 'pedagogy based on evidence and principle, not prescription' (p.3). Building on this desire for a principled approach to pedagogy, Farquhar and White (2014) call for a more philosophically informed perspective that challenges the existing dominant psychological and empirical approaches. Therefore, whereas Willingham (2009, p.213) claims that 'Education is the passing on of accumulated wisdom of generations to children...', these researchers see 'pedagogy as a relationship rather than a response or intervention' (p.822). Similarly, Stephen (2010) defines pedagogy as a moral practice that needs to combine technique with an ethical and caring dimension which would require teachers to think for themselves and reflect and engage with the wider philosophical aspects of pedagogy (Cox, 2011). This is a more respectful approach where children learn to learn in a democracy; rather than just acquiring knowledge, they become active participants in society. As Hedges and Cooper argue, these more

> Holistic outcomes require pedagogies that value relationships, emotional engagement, reflection and responsibility, attention to content and process, uncertainty and challenge and, above all, making learning visible to all with a vested interest in early childhood curricula, pedagogy and outcomes.
>
> (Hedges and Cooper, 2014, p.406).

By making learning visible, for example through pedagogical documentation, the values, principles and holistic outcomes of early years pedagogy can be made more explicit (Dahlberg et al., 2013). They can then be shared and debated with other stakeholders, including parents, teachers and policy-makers to create a more inclusive and democratic understanding of effective pedagogy. However, one group that is still likely to be excluded from the debate are the children themselves.

Who decides what is effective pedagogy?

Biesta (2007) claims that educational policy generally ignores children's agency, their potential and their ability to exceed the limits of curricular goals, while childhood is often seen as a transitional phase which simply leads towards maturity. From this perspective, children are constructed as being dependent on adults, deficient and often having few rights of their own. Alternatively, traditional child-centred early years pedagogy views the child as a competent co-constructor of knowledge in partnership with adults. Alderson (2008) analyses these differing ways in which children are conceptualised and highlights the ways in which this impacts upon services such as education. She questions the developmental ages and stages that schools currently use to conceptualise children and challenges them to reconsider adult-child relationships so that children's rights as human beings are upheld and schools work together with children to improve educational practice. This leads Brooker (2011) to ask what children would choose for themselves in the Reception Year and which experiences or goals they would prioritise if they shared power with adults. A potential way forward would be for research to develop new ways of working and reflecting together with young children and Reception teachers to explore alternative understandings of effective pedagogy.

Although this is probably not the answer that the TSC (2016) were looking for when they questioned the teaching practices in Reception classes, and it would certainly require a significant paradigm shift for policy-makers, this shared and dialogic approach does offer a means of creating multiple and shared understandings of what might constitute effective pedagogy in schools as genuine learning communities – with people, rather than performance, at their heart.

Summary

This chapter began with a TSC report (2016) that questioned effective pedagogy in the Reception Year on the basis of developmental psychology, quality and accountability measures, curricular goals and some apparent misunderstanding regarding play-based, child-centred learning. It has shown that developmental goals and normative discourses have created a 'one size fits all' approach to effective pedagogy that cannot fully address the complexity and diversity of children's learning experiences. This approach carries a risk of creating a repetitive cycle of social exclusion rather than challenging the inequalities that early childhood education is intended to address. It has been suggested that pedagogical approaches that aim to accelerate the rate at which children achieve these rather narrow curricular goals place additional pressures on both teachers and children and reduce the time available for meaningful, deeper-level understanding, building strong relationships and developing positive dispositions to learning – the very aspects that are most likely to equip children to be successful in and beyond their future schooling.

Some teachers may struggle to articulate their understandings, play-based practice can be variable, and the linking of children's freely chosen play activities to the expected outcomes for the Reception Year is particularly problematic. It might be concluded therefore that Reception teachers need access to training and ongoing professional development that enables them to translate their values and beliefs into an effective pedagogical approach. This would enable those teachers with Reception experience to enter into dialogue with colleagues from other phases of primary education with the aim of producing more inclusive understandings of effective pedagogy that are meaningful across primary education as a whole.

Perhaps the most important message from this chapter is the need to recognise and value the knowledge of children, Reception teachers and researchers who have questioned the reductionist and instrumental thinking of policy-makers and the current 'what works' approach to pedagogy. However, this requires transformational change that goes beyond a review of the Reception Year. Teachers and researchers would need to challenge policy-makers' desire to measure quality and performance against developmental norms, as well as the goal of school readiness, in order to address young children's different ways of knowing, the complexity of their learning and the values of democracy with their multiple interpretations of what might be considered to be effective pedagogy.

Questions for reflection

How would you define school readiness?

How can teachers achieve an appropriate balance between child-initiated play and teacher-led activities in Reception classes?

To what extent are the problems outlined in this chapter likely to require universal solutions, rather than more localised, contextually specific approaches to pedagogy?

Further reading and resources

TACTYC (2017) *Bald beginnings: A response to Ofsted's (2017) report, Bold beginnings: The Reception curriculum in a sample of good and outstanding primary schools.* Available at: http://tactyc.org.uk/wp-content/uploads/2017/12/Bold-Beginni ngs-TACTYC-response-FINAL-09.12.17.pdf.

This response from TACTYC, the association for professional development in Early Years, offers further debate concerning the formalisation of the curriculum and pedagogy in the Reception Year.

Bradbury A. & Roberts-Holmes, G. (2018) *The datafication of primary and early education: Playing with numbers*, Abingdon: Routledge.
This book gives a comprehensive analysis of the impact of accountability measures and the desire for performance data on teachers and the pedagogy in schools and early years settings.

Ephgrave, A. (2013) *The Reception Year in action: A month-by-month guide to success in the classroom (revised and updated edition)*, Abingdon: Routledge.
This book offers a practical child-centred approach to play-based pedagogy in the Reception Year.

References

Ailwood, J. (2010) 'Playing with some tensions: Poststructuralism, Foucault and early childhood education'. In: Brooker, L. & Edwards, S. (eds.) *Engaging Play*, Maidenhead: Open University Press, pp. 210–222.

Alderson, P. (2008) *Young Children's Rights: Exploring Beliefs, Principles and Practice* (2nd ed.), London: Jessica Kingsley Publishers.

Alexander, R. J. (2010) 'Cambridge primary review: Children, their world, their education. Final report'. Available at: http://www.robinalexander.org.uk/wp-content/uploads/2012/05/CPR-final-report-briefing.pdf.

Ang, L. (2014) 'Preschool or prep school? Rethinking the role of early years education', *Contemporary Issues in Early Childhood*, 15(2): 185–199.

Aubrey, C. (2002) 'Implementing the foundation stage in Reception classes', *British Educational Research Journal*, 30(5): 633–656.

Biesta, G. (2007) 'Why "what works" won't work: Evidence-based practice and the democratic deficit in educational research', *Educational Theory*, 57, 1: 1–22.

Bodrova, E. (2008) 'Make-believe paly versus academic skills: A Vygotskian approach to today's dilemma of early childhood education', *European Early Childhood Education Research Journal*, 16(3): 357–369.

Bradbury, A. & Roberts-Holmes, G. (2018) *The Datafication of Primary and Early Years Education: Playing with Numbers*, Abingdon: Routledge.

British Educational Research Association (BERA) Special Interest Group (2003) 'Early years research: Pedagogy, curriculum and adult roles, training and professionalism'. Available at: https://www.bera.ac.uk/wp-content/uploads/2015/09/beraearlyyearsreview31may03.pdf.

Brooker, L. (2011) 'Taking children seriously: An alternative approach for research?' *Journal of Early Childhood Research*, 9(2): 1–13.

Brown, C. P. (2010) 'Balancing the readiness equation in early childhood education reform', *Journal of Early Childhood Research*, 8(2): 133–160.

Carter, M. & Curtis, D. (2017) *Learning Together with Young Children*, St Paul, MN: Readleaf Press.

Cousins, J. (1990) 'Are your little Humpty Dumpties floating or sinking? What sense do children of four make of the reception class at school? Different conceptions at that time of transition', *Early Years*, 10(2): 28–38.

Cox, S. (2011) *New Perspectives in Primary Education: Meaning and Purpose in Learning and Teaching*, Maidenhead: Open University Press.

Dahlberg, G., Moss, P. & Pence, A. (2013) *Beyond Quality in Early Childhood Education and Care: Postmodern Perspectives* (3rd ed.), London: Falmer Press.

Daniels, K. (2013) 'Supporting the development of positive dispositions and learner identities: An action research study into the impact and potential of developing photographic learning stories in Early Years', *Education 3-13*, 41(3): 300–315.

Department for Education (DfE) (2017) 'Statutory framework for the early years foundation stage: Setting the standards for learning and development and care for children from birth to five'. Available at: http://www.foundationyears.org.uk/f iles/2017/03/EYFS_STATUTORY_FRAMEWORK_2017.pdf.

Dockett, S. (2011) 'The challenge of play for early childhood educators'. In: Rogers, S. (ed.) *Rethinking Play and Pedagogy in Early Childhood Education: Concepts, Contexts and Cultures*, London: Routledge, pp. 32–47.

Ephgrave, A. (2013) *The Reception Year in Action: A Month-By-Month Guide to Success in the Classroom (Revised and Updated Edition)*, Abingdon: Routledge.

Farquhar, S. & White, E. J. (2014) 'Philosophy and pedagogy of early childhood', *Educational Philosophy and Theory*, 46(8): 821–832.

Fisher, J. (2011) 'Building on the Early Years Foundation Stage: Developing good practice for transition into Key Stage 1', *Early Years*, 31(1): 31–42.

Fleer, M. (2006) 'The cultural construction of child development: Creating institutional and cultural intersubjectivity', *International Journal of Early Years Education*, 14(2): 127–140.

Fleer, M. (2015) 'Pedagogical positioning in play – teachers being inside and outside of children's imaginary play', *Early Child Development and Care*, 185(11–12): 1801–1814.

Hedges, H. & Cooper, M. (2014) 'Engaging with holistic curriculum outcomes: Deconstructing "working theories"', *International Journal of Early Years Education*, 22(4): 395–408.

House, R. (2011) *Too Much Too Soon? Early Learning and the Erosion of Childhood*, Stroud: Hawthorne Press.

Jones, L. & Holmes, R. (2014) 'Studying play through new research practices'. In: Brooker, E., Blaise, M. & Edwards, S. (eds.) *SAGE Handbook of Play and Learning in Early Childhood*, London: SAGE, pp. 128–139.

Jordan, B. (2009) 'Scaffolding learning and co-constructing understandings'. In: Anning, A., Cullen, J. & Fleer, M. (eds.) *Early Childhood Education: Society and Culture* (2nd ed.), London: SAGE, pp. 39–53.

Katz, L. (1993) 'Dispositions as educational goals', *Eric Digests*. Available at: http://ericae.net/edo/ED363454.htm.

Lave, J. & Wenger, E. (1991) *Situated Learning: Legitimate Peripheral Participation*, Cambridge: Cambridge University Press.

Luke, A. (1992) 'The body literate: Discourse and inscription in early literacy learning', *Linguistics and Education*, 4(1): 107–129.

Martlew, J., Stephen, C. & Ellis, J. (2011) 'Play in the primary classroom? The experience of teachers supporting children's learning through a new pedagogy', *Early Years: an International Journal of Research and Development*, 31(1): 71–83.

McInnes, K. Howard, Miles, J., G. & Crowley, K. (2011) 'Differences in practitioners' understanding of play and how this influences pedagogy and children's perceptions of play', *Early Years*, 31(2): 121–133.

Moss, P. (2008) 'What future for the relationship between early childhood education and compulsory schooling?' *Research in Comparative Education*, 3(3): 224–234.

Moss, P. (2014) *Transformational Change and Real Utopias in Early Childhood Education: A Story of Democracy, Experimentation and Potentiality*, Abingdon: Routledge.

Moyles, J. (2010) *The Excellence of Play*, Maidenhead: Open University Press.

Nutbrown, C. (2011) *Threads of Thinking* (4th ed.), London: SAGE.

Nutbrown, C., Clough, P. & Atherton, F. (2014) *Early Childhood Education: History, Philosophy and Experience*, London: SAGE.

OFSTED (2017) *Bold beginnings: The Reception curriculum in a sample of good and outstanding primary schools*. Available at: https://assets.publishing.service.gov.uk /government/uploads/system/uploads/attachment_data/file/663560/28933 _Ofsted_-_Early_Years_Curriculum_Report_-_Accessible.pdf.

O'Hear, A. (2000) 'Philosophy and educational policy', *Royal Institute of Philosophy Supplements*, 45: 135–156.

Pramling Samuelsson, I. & Asplund Carlsson, M. (2008) 'The playing learning child: Towards a pedagogy of early childhood', *Scandinavian Journal of Educational Research*, 52(6): 623–641.

Pugh, G. (2010) 'Improving outcomes for young children: Can we narrow the gap?' *Early Years*, 30(1): 5–14.

Roberts-Holmes, G. (2012) '"It's the bread and butter of our practice": Experiencing the early years foundation stage', *International Journal of Early Years Education*, 20(1): 30–42.

Rogers, S. & Lapping, C. (2012) 'Recontextualising "play" in early years pedagogy: Competence performance and excess in policy and practice', *British Journal of Educational Studies*, 60(3): 243–260.

Sharp, C. (2002) 'Starting school age: European Policy and recent research', *Paper Presented at the LGA Seminar 'WHEN SHOULD OUR Children Start School?* London, 1 November. NFER. Available at: https://www.nfer.ac.uk/media/1 318/44414.pdf.

Siraj-Blatchford, I., Sylva, K., Muttock, S., Gidden, R. & Bell, D. (2002) 'Researching effective pedagogy in the early years'. Available at: http://www.327matters.org/ Docs/RR356.pdf.

Stephen, C. (2010) 'Pedagogy: The silent partner in early years learning', *Early Years*, 30(1): 15–28.

TACTYC (2017) *Bald beginnings: A response to Ofsted's (2017) report, Bold beginnings: The Reception curriculum in a sample of good and outstanding primary schools*. Available at: http://tactyc.org.uk/wp-content/uploads/2017/12/Bold-Beginni ngs-TACTYC-response-FINAL-09.12.17.pdf.

Teaching Schools Council (TSC) (2016) 'Effective primary teaching practice'. Available at: http://www.tscouncil.org.uk/wp-content/uploads/2016/12/ Effective-primary-teaching-practice-2016-report-web.pdf.

Willingham, D. T. (2009) *Why Don't Students Like School? A Cognitive Scientist Answers Questions About How the Mind Works and What It Means for the Classroom*, San Francisco, CA: Jossey-Bass.

Wood, E. (2004) 'A new paradigm war? The impact of national curriculum policies on early childhood teachers thinking and classroom practice', *Teaching and Teacher Education*, 20(4): 361–374.

Wood, E. (2010) 'Reconceptualising the play-pedagogy relationship: From control to complexity'. In: Brooker, L. & Edwards, S. (eds.) *Engaging Play*, Maidenhead: Open University Press, pp. 11–25.

Wood, E. (2014) 'The play-pedagogy interface in contemporary debates'. In: Brooker, L., Blaise, M. & Edwards, S. (eds.) *The Sage Handbook of Play and Learning in Early Childhood*, London: SAGE, pp. 145–156.

Wood, E. & Hedges, H. (2016) 'Curriculum in early childhood education: Critical questions about content, coherence and control', *The Curriculum Journal*, 27(3): 387–405.

Chapter 6

Exploring how early years settings might promote high-quality communication and language opportunities through community-based projects

Vanessa Sawyer and Megan Stephenson

Introduction

Communication and language skills are often referred to as providing the foundation for children's learning, playing a key role in developing life chances (I CAN, 2019; Lee, 2013). Statistics show, however, that in some parts of the United Kingdom (UK), particularly where there are areas of social disadvantage, over 50% of children begin school without these essential communication and language skills (I CAN, 2019). According to the children's communication charity I CAN, by the time a child reaches the age of five, their vocabulary is considered to be a strong indicator in predicting future educational success and outcomes, emphasising the importance of the development of children's communication and language skills in the early years. This is not, however, reflected within recent Ofsted reports such as *Bold Beginnings* or the Department for Education (DfE) wherein they are restarting their attempts to develop a reception baseline; both of which have caused waves of anger from those in or connected with the early years sector, as this has the potential to have a detrimental effect on communication and language opportunities in early years settings.

This chapter aims to explore how particular early years settings have prioritised high-quality communication and language opportunities amongst children and practitioners through looking closely at case study examples (names anonymised) and exploring the lasting impact this could have on children's development. Debates are focused around the challenges which face school leaders and practitioners with regards to the curriculum, whilst opening up questions and reflections around whether particular approaches are sustainable and how we might raise the awareness and the status of exemplary practice happening currently in our school settings. There is no doubt that this is a significant time for early years educators as online social media platforms evidence an ever-growing number within the sector making a stand against developmentally inappropriate government-driven initiatives and demanding education be put back into the hands of teachers and schools (More Than a Score, 2019).

The community approach – developing an imaginary community as a resource

Role play can be viewed as an effective pedagogical strategy used to enhance communication and language development as it provides a play frame, nurturing social collaboration whereby children can take on and negotiate roles and responsibilities (Lillard et al., 2013). Jane, Assistant Headteacher at School N in North Leeds, places great emphasis on developing relationships through role play, where children and staff build their own community within their classroom, representing themselves as various characters within this imaginary setting. Through adopting this community approach, staff effectively weave the statutory requirements of the curriculum into their practice; maintaining children's intrinsic motivation by ensuring that they can relate to the subject matter through making it more meaningful.

Each child invents a character who will live in the community and it is the children's ideas and interests which ultimately shape the developments moving forward. Over time the communities develop and evolve as more and more is discovered about the characters and the place in which they live. Much of the learning develops through role play and drama and includes building up scenarios and debates based on the curriculum. Children are expected and are eager to write and communicate their ideas in specific community books. Using problem solving such as presenting the children with a situation which affects their community, requires deeper-level thinking, collaborative practices and ultimately high-quality narrative. This particular primary school has fully invested in this approach to teaching and learning, as have the children, with the strength lying in the school's 'natural propensity to enable and facilitate creativity and critical thinking' (School N, 2019). Jane emphasises that such an approach should not be viewed as merely a storytelling tool and that all staff need to be wholly committed to the approach, fully understanding the pedagogy and principles driving it, for this to be sustainable and have maximum impact.

The community approach provides a platform for creative and critical thinking as children's imaginations are encouraged to develop. Furthermore, as the community is seen as a 'microcosm of the real world' (School N, 2019), current issues occurring at that moment in the world can be explored, meaning that children are being prepared to deal with dilemmas, issues and problems whilst being given the opportunities to explore ethical considerations. As a result, the children develop a raft of problem-solving and debating skills whilst at the same time fully embedding the characteristics of effective learning (Early Education, 2013).

A further strength of this approach is exploring different opinions and looking at alternative viewpoints, emphasising active citizenship and social responsibility, with children learning how to work together as a group as they make decisions and deal with conflicts and problems in a fair and ethical manner. They learn the skills of debating, and divergent thinking is promoted as they are encouraged to communicate their ideas and thoughts based on their feelings for their character and the situation presented. They become exposed to other people's perspectives and views and the many possibilities and solutions that arise from such debates, teaching them that there is often more than one solution, that the one we present may not always be the 'right' one and that it is acceptable to be wrong or have different opinions.

Inspired by the Reggio Emilia philosophy, whereby relationships are at the very heart of the approach, the adult plays a vital role in creatively weaving the curriculum into the community. This is achieved through introducing a dilemma or a problem, questioning, scaffolding teaching and learning where appropriate and intentionally engaging 'children in meaningful work and conversation' (Biermeier, 2014, p.1; Palmer, 2014). Mirroring the Reggio Emilia philosophy, the environment is viewed as the third teacher and the setting is designed to be functional whilst reflective of children's learning (Wharton and Kinney, 2015; Wood, 2013). Children in this setting are confident in using the environment freely and teachers are flexible in their approach, allowing space for the learners' ideas.

There is no doubt that such an approach has the potential to significantly impact on children's communication and language abilities across the curriculum through providing rich, meaningful and context-embedded opportunities that will intrinsically motivate children as learning becomes real and children and their communities become interwoven into the curriculum. Simultaneously, the methods adopted support children's social and emotional development and ability to self-regulate, which Lee (2013) argues leads to better social outcomes in later life. This school have invested in this approach, led by Jane herself, who has visited the schools in Reggio Emilia and as a result has dedicated allocated time through timetabling sessions towards the end of the Reception year leading into Key Stage 1 to prepare children for this phase.

Pause for thought

Ofsted report that children at School N are always at the heart of the curriculum and that the school prioritise providing the 'best education possible' (School N Ofsted Report, 2017). It is unlikely that this approach would have a significant impact on children's progress if staff were not fully committed or did not completely understand or agree with the ethos behind it. This suggests that it is not an easy model to transfer to another setting as it relies on time to build and embed a whole-school vision in order to achieve maximum impact. There is also context to consider, as the nature of both the intake and local contextual factors impact on school processes and decisions regarding curriculum and pedagogy. This echoes the current Ofsted framework, which encourages schools to look closely at their whole-school curriculum and how the institutional context impacts and informs this (Gov.uk, 2019). Nonetheless, the approach is fascinating, and the school do see impact and progress in all areas of development with Ofsted observations stating that children at the school are happy. 'They love their school and enjoy the varied and enriched curriculum' (School N Ofsted Report, 2017).

You might at this point want to consider your local context and the impact that this might have on curriculum decisions and approaches adopted.

Outdoor excursions – using the local community as a resource

One of the challenges highlighted above is the practitioner's ability to weave curriculum content into innovative and creative approaches to teaching and learning whilst simultaneously developing soft skills, also referred to as learning dispositions, such as communication and language (Claxton, Costa and Kallick, 2016). The importance of developing soft skills amongst our youngest children is a much-debated area, with advocates stating that teaching children learning dispositions will ultimately have a positive impact on the economy when children become adults, as they have been well equipped with the skills to empower them to become lifelong learners and to manage and adapt their own learning in a rapidly changing world. Such arguments, from a human capital approach to education, strengthen the 'relevance of incorporating soft skills in early childhood education' (Laureta, 2018, p.29).

This next example demonstrates how this could be achieved by challenging the pupils to plan an event, in this case an outdoor excursion. Elena is an experienced Early Years practitioner and Senior Leader of the Early Years Foundation Stage (EYFS) and Key Stage 1 (KS1) phases. She has been commended for her approach to Early Years Teaching and Learning and for the skill with which she embeds the EYFS curriculum through a carefully structured programme of high-quality provision and discrete sessions in Prime and Specific Areas. Ofsted noted her use of 'Outdoor Excursions' and promoted them as an excellent example of developing pupils' independence and communication skills whilst covering the mainstay of the EYFS.

Each year in the summer term the pupils are presented with a 'challenge'. Due to a keen interest in the local village and the surrounding school environment, Elena and her team concluded that some exploration of this area would be a good way to develop the children's knowledge of the world. Careful planning, preparation and guidance of such a trip would facilitate learning in all the areas of the EYFS framework and would promote rich communication and language opportunities. Consequently, it was decided that the plan would be for the staff and children to walk into the local village near their primary school to buy something from the local bakery – the challenge being that the children were to be given ownership of this excursion and the responsibility of working out how to organise themselves for the day.

The children in the first instance were presented with a 'hook' to promote their curiosity and interaction. In this case, the stimulus was in the form of a letter from the Headteacher stating that the class had permission to take a day out of school to visit the local village. Great excitement ensued, and discussion followed around what the purpose of an outdoor excursion could be. The children took ownership in organising their visit and the practitioners facilitated the planning and preparing of resources, highlighting the importance of providing children with the opportunity to collaborate. The role of the practitioner in this situation is to provide the conditions whereby children can develop skills such as the ability to communicate needs and 'negotiate, plan, create and challenge one another' (Bottrill, 2018, p.40). However, as Bottrill (ibid.) argues, such skills lie outside the requirements for 'measurability in educational outcomes' and are therefore not always viewed as important or even necessary when planning teaching and learning opportunities. The children in Elena's setting were accustomed to having talk partners (Clarke, 2019) and were well practised in discussing ideas and listening to one another, emphasising the need to embed strategies that provide children with the opportunity to think, discuss and express themselves orally into a daily routine.

Similarly, children were given responsibility in small groups to discuss how certain activities would take place. For example, groups investigated how much money they would need, the time it would take to walk there and back, and the type of clothing and footwear required for an outdoor excursion. Solving practical problems challenges children's thinking skills and their ability to find solutions, which 'develops logical and creative thinking' (De Boo, 1999, p.155). Such practice not only develops children's confidence in problem solving but develops skills which are transferable to other activities or situations. The practitioner's role here is not merely to provide children with the solution but to support pupils in tackling the problems. After the excursion a review took place in the form of a presentation delivered to the whole school where pupils discussed their outing and presented their solutions to the original challenges. Enabling pupils to succeed in finding their own solutions is vital for the development of their self-esteem and problem-solving skills (De Boo, 1999).

Pause for thought

In the same way as the community approach, planning for outdoor excursions or any form of problem-solving challenge relies on the practitioner's ability to plan for a language-rich environment which promotes interactions between children and between adults and children. Such an approach requires dedicated staff with an excellent knowledge of the Early Years and KS1 curricula and a strong pedagogical stance in relation to the importance of developing communication and language skills. Such practice is most successful when delivered as a whole-school approach or at least with approval and even involvement from those in Senior Leadership positions. This is evidenced in Elena's setting, as the head-teacher's letter was used as the hook to stimulate enquiry and encourage children to ask questions. Similar to the community approach, outdoor excursions involve using a community as a resource to develop children's experiences; in this case the community being the local village in which the children lived. Such planned approaches enable pupils to broaden and deepen their knowledge within a familiar and relevant context, aligning with the new Ofsted framework (Gov.uk, 2019) which places emphasis on a knowledge-rich curriculum.

You might at this point wish to consider how you can create further problem-solving opportunities using the local community as a curriculum resource.

Resident artists – using the wider community as a resource

Louise is the acting executive Head Teacher at M Nursery in Bradford, which was graded outstanding by Ofsted in 2012 and again in 2016. In May 2013, the setting was 'designated as a National Support School' and Louise as a 'National Leader of Education' (M Nursery, School Website, 2019). With Children's Centre services on their site and a highly experienced staff team across the organisation, the Nursery prides itself on successfully meeting the needs of the whole family and is described as 'a special place that is deeply valued by families in our local community' (M Nursery, School Website, 2019).

Louise has a keen interest in the arts and is passionate about working with professionals in the wider community to provide children with real experiences and learning opportunities which develop a multitude of attitudes, dispositions and physical skills whilst at the same time promoting high-quality communication and language between all adults and children. This is captured in their Ofsted report (M Nursery, Ofsted Report, 2012) where the inspector emphasises the 'very strong focus on developing children's communication skills'. Most children in the school come from minority ethnic backgrounds and have English as an additional language, and these children 'achieve extremely well'. To promote this strong focus on developing both physical development and language, Louise employs resident artist Erica Jones once a week to work across the nursery schools in the collaboration. Erica works closely with the children and documents the communication she has with the staff and pupils in the form of a blog so that parents, carers and visitors to the school can engage with her work. Below are extracts from Erica's blog as she works in the provision with the adults and children, highlighting how she develops children's communication and language skills though the power of media.

Blog extract by Erica Jones, Resident Artist

> Daffodils and tulips look lovely in the room – Jo had set it up previously and it felt joyous with lots to have a go at. There had been interest with the magnifying glasses too. When I am drawing, and modelling, children are watching 'how' I'm describing the flowers – as I've said before – isn't that how we also learn to draw – by watching others do it too? It's another language to learn, not replicating reality but creating a way of describing something.

> S: *It's a tulip* (then she added some lines) *It's got arms* (her concentration hadn't gone but the drawing of the shape led her drawing to take on a life of its own).
>
> J is spending a lot of time drawing – he draws his tulip and then a character he created with the same shape on his head which he said was a 'crown' [*sic*].

Erica outlines the importance of children observing adults and of the adult modelling and vocalising their actions as they do so, which the children imitate as they begin to draw their pictures, accompanying this with language. Earlyarts (2019), an internationally acclaimed training and research consultancy company based in the UK, state that Early Years arts and cultural activities help children to make sense not only of their linguistic development but also their cognitive, physical, emotional, spiritual and moral development, emphasising the holistic nature of such practice. Interestingly, from a global perspective, The Compass School (2017) situated in Cincinnati, Ohio, use the word 'Art' to refer to a 'lively process of engagement that is reflective, creative and deliberate and that deepens and extends the children's learning'. Like School N, M Nursery are inspired by the Reggio Emilia philosophy embracing the 'hundred languages' of expression and representation (Smidt, 2013).

The Nursery setting boldly states that art activities offered in schools need to be reconsidered, as there needs to be a move away from so-called 'copycat' art activities in favour of more open-ended opportunities offering a range of media. Furthermore, they argue that the emphasis needs to be on the creative process rather than on the end product, to enable art to be used as a tool for developing thinking, communication and language. If we want to provide children with authentic and differentiated methods of learning, then we need to provide more open-ended activities that focus on the processes. Allowing children the opportunity to engage flexibly in a range of activities through selecting, representing and explaining their thoughts and actions (Marie and McLennan, 2010) leads to the development of communication and language skills necessary for future success.

At M Nursery, Erica introduces the children to various media, providing and modelling support regarding techniques in order to develop the children's skills. The underpinning idea behind this is that by providing children with repeated opportunities to explore a medium, they become 'more fluent in the language of art' (M Nursery, 2019; The Compass School, 2019).

> R and I talked about his shadow, although a bit later I said to him it may be a reflection rather than a shadow.
>
> R: *Look, I am waving, and my shadow is waving back!*

At The Compass School in Cincinnati, Ohio, along with the municipal schools in Reggio Emilia, there is a space which is known as the 'atelier'. The atelier is full of art equipment and houses a variety of materials for the children to explore. Alongside this, there is an 'Atelierista', similar to the role Erica plays in M Nursery, whose role it is to support the children in exploring the hundred languages through art projects. Erica's expertise enables her to examine the role of art in children's lives, and the extract below demonstrates how Erica uses art opportunities to invite children to look more closely at detail, encouraging questions, new perspectives, emotions, communication and listening.

Blog extract by Erica Jones, Resident Artist

I took some of the small clipboards out with the possible intention of drawing the growing daffodils. Two boys were interested – D, and Y – and I tried to encourage a look at the shapes and colours and had brought the "appropriate" (I clear my throat with irony here) colours. The two boys made lots of marks that didn't appear to me to be about looking at what I was talking about, but then they were drawing weren't they and chatting and so I diversified and changed my direction of seeing upwards (the sky was looking particularly dramatic with blue skies and scudding clouds and vapour trails criss-crossing)

Me: Look a plane
Y: The plane I saw at my house
Me: Look at the clouds moving
Y: The clouds are going home. I'm drawing the clouds now, I made it.
D: No, the sky is their home... they are going that way (and we looked at the direction the clouds were moving in)
Me: Where are they going? (I was completely in the dark as to how I would answer that)
Y: They are going to bed now cos they taking so long 'coz they so tired they going slowly (which of course they were except to us with experience of looking at clouds know they were actually moving relatively fast)
D: They going past the Baker's house (we were looking towards the horizon across the rooftops)
Me: What are they going to see?
D: The old man and the old woman making gingerbread man.
Y: They making cupcakes
Y: Who is blowing the wind? It's the cloud
D: No, it's the blue sky
D: Look I can see a dinosaur, a dinosaur cloud
Y: I can see a lion
D: That looks like a digger, it's turned into a giraffe.

This is one of those conversations that was particularly special to have been part of and there was loads more to it – like what happens to the clouds at night. D and Y had last half term played loads with rockets, space and the moon, weather, seasons, dragons, kites, flying, birds, space....The sky is a fantastic resource and I loved the way the children took it into fantasy without any encouragement or comments from me [*sic*].

In this instance, the development of process-focused art rather than product-focused is evident as Erica supports the children and provides opportunities for them to take the initiative, to be engaged and creative in their thinking. Like The Compass School, M Nursery have invested in this approach which they believe supports the learning and development of the whole child across all areas of the curriculum. This is reflected in their social and emotional development as well as their communication and language. Louise, like Jane, is drawing on the Reggio Emilia philosophy to enhance not only children's linguistic development but the development of the whole child, with the help of her resident artist. In the extract above, there is also evidence of cognitive development as children compare the clouds, predict what they might be, and develop their own enquiries about what happens to clouds at night. Similarly, art in the Reggio Emilia environment is seen as an expression of children's current interests and fascinations, making it a tool for making meaning and a way of constructing new forms of communication and language.

Pause for thought

As with both the community approach and outdoor excursions, this approach relies on a whole-school philosophy; in this case one inspired by Reggio Emilia where children are viewed as unique and capable. The role of the adult here is to co-navigate the learning journey, which is clear from the extracts as Erica provokes ideas, encourages dialogue and shares educational experiences alongside the children. However, it is important to note that simply employing a resident artist does not mean that this approach would be successful elsewhere and such expense could be considered a high-risk factor in a school with limited resources and a lack of research behind the implementation of this concept. As with the other two approaches, using a resident artist involves working with the community as a resource to develop children's experiences, in this case the focus being on the use of the wider community of professionals. Employing an Artist in Residence enables schools to work flexibly with an artist, and the aim and purpose needs to be clear and transparent to all staff. In this case the artist is utilised to enrich the curriculum, focusing on developing necessary communication and language skills as well as physical development whilst embedding a culture of creativity within the school. Such a focus is deemed of high importance by the Headteacher, who has invested in this practice taking into consideration the context of the school and the needs of the local community.

You might, at this point, want to consider why employing a resident artist may not be successful elsewhere. What are your thoughts on the quality of discussion taking place? Do you think the setting is all the richer for having a resident artist, or could this experience be achieved using the staff in the setting?

Summary

There is no doubt that developing high-quality communication and language opportunities should be a priority in education, however, the reality is that it continues to have a low profile in education policy (Lee, 2013) and there remains an ever-widening gap between the communication skills of disadvantaged children and their peers when they begin school (DfE and Hinds, 2018). It could be argued that developing communication and language skills should be central to policy and practice and that money should be invested into approaches such as community-based projects to show evidence of closing the communication and language attainment gap. Would this not be a better investment of the Department for Education's ten million pounds rather than the proposed second attempt at a Reception baseline which is causing such controversy amongst the Early Years community (More Than a Score, 2019)? Fortunately, despite the backdrop of ill-considered policy, it is clear that there are settings who are passionate about developing the whole child and preparing well rounded individuals. Such settings place considerable emphasis on communication and language and providing teaching and learning opportunities that leave space in the curriculum for children to be the experts. Dissemination of this exemplary practice is essential, within Initial Teacher Training providers and beyond.

Rather than coming up with a new proposed scheme run by an independent charity or local authority (what is left of them) or a one-size-fits-all Academy Trust model might we hand the responsibility to teachers and schools who, as the examples show, have developed rich communication and language experiences within their settings, utilising their diverse communities and showcasing their creativity in establishing approaches grounded in theory? Surely such approaches show impact because the settings have invested in quality research identifying what is right for their setting and their communities, not simply through transferring a model of 'best practice' or delivering a one-size-fits-all solution. This would, of course, mean the government putting their trust firmly in the early years experts, building on teachers' and school leaders' expertise and enlisting them in the design of curricula, policies and practices which would mean a radical change in our 'highly standardised industrial work organisation' (Schleicher, 2018, p.1). Recognition and recommendation are needed of the creative and innovative work that many settings are involved with, and this, then, could be the driving force behind education policy initiatives, ensuring that children, from an early age, are embraced within a culture that provides the building blocks for leading flourishing lives in the twenty-first century.

Despite the daily challenges, demands and pressures that face school leaders and teaching practitioners, the case studies drawn upon in this chapter evidence the way in which schools are building their own communities of practice (Wenger, 1998). Such practice holds communication and language in high regard, with an emphasis on developing social contexts for learning through building interaction with others – equipping children for life, not for the purpose of passing a test or a short-term target. In all three cases the approaches used are varied and personalised to each setting and the community they serve, highlighting that there is no one way to plan for children's communication and language experiences. With the National Literacy Trust (2019) welcoming government policy initiatives that focus on improving children's early language and literacy skills, rather than 'delivering a structured, targeted and explicit approach to teaching language' (National Literacy Trust, 2019, p.23), might we call upon such communities of practice in utilising their expertise in developing the skills of the early years and schools' workforce and initial teacher training programmes? Evoking the expertise of exemplary school leaders and practitioners in policy-making and securing long-term funding and grants to address the challenges of low literacy and delayed language would lead to lasting changes, significantly raise the status and awareness of exemplary practices grounded in research and theory, and ultimately may just lead to attracting and retaining the best teaching practitioners.

Questions for reflection

How do you envisage the planning and implementation of the practices discussed if they are to have maximum impact?

Consider your own timetable and the constraints that lie within this. How much of your time is spent on structured adult-led activity compared to adult–child or child–child interaction?

How much emphasis is placed on communication and language in a social context in your own setting?

Acknowledgements

With special thanks to:

Those on whom the examples are based. You are not named but you know who you are!

Further reading and resources

Earlyarts (2019). Available at: https://earlyarts.co.uk/.

The Earlyarts is an award-winning training, research and consultancy company providing online research studies and resources with a particular focus on the arts and creativity. The Earlyarts philosophy is that arts and creativity play an important role in early education and in cultural leadership, impacting positively on young children and their families.

Ofsted framework (2019). Available at: https://www.gov.uk/government/consultations/education-inspection-framework-2019-inspecting-the-substance-of-education/education-inspection-framework-2019-inspecting-the-substance-of-education.

The draft education inspection framework for 2019 outlines how Ofsted proposes to inspect schools and registered early years settings. There is acknowledgement of academic evidence around curriculum quality and a focus on restoring a broad and balanced curriculum.

The Compass School. Available at: https://www.thecompassschool.com/blog/the
-language-of-art-in-reggio-inspired-classrooms/.
The Compass School of Cincinnati, Ohio opened in 2000 as one of the first preschool
settings in southwest Ohio to offer a Reggio Emilia–inspired curriculum philosophy.
In 2011, the school achieved National Association for the Education of Young
Children (NAEYC) accreditation, recognised as the highest benchmark of quality for
a preschool program in the United States.

References

Biermeier, M. A. (2014) 'Teaching young children', *Teaching Young Children/
Preschool*, 7(4): 27–29.
Bottrill, G. (2018) *Can I Go and Play Now? Rethinking the Early Years*, London:
SAGE.
Clarke, S. (2019) *The On-Your-Feet Guide to Partner Talk*, London: SAGE.
Claxton, G., Costa, A. & Kallick, B. (2016) 'Hard thinking about soft skills',
Educational Leadership, 73(6): 60–64.
De Boo, M. (1999) *Enquiring Children, Challenging Teaching*, Buckingham: Open
University Press.
Department for Education & Hinds, D. (2018) *Multi-Million Fund to Boost
Children's Early Language Skills*. Available at: https://www.gov.uk/government/
news/multi-million-fund-to-boost-childrens-early-language-skills   (Accessed
21.03.2019).
Early Education (2013) *Development Matters Guidance*, The British Association for
Early Childhood Education. Available at: https://www.early-education.org.uk/
(Accessed 28.03.2019).
Gov.uk (2019) *Education Inspection Framework*. Available at https://www.gov.uk/g
overnment/collections/education-inspection-framework (Accessed 21.03.2019).
I CAN (2019) *How We Support Children. Getting the Support, You Need*. Available
at: https://www.ican.org.uk/how-we-support-children/ (Accessed 21.03.2019).
Laureta, B. (2018) 'Soft skills and early childhood education: Strange bedfellows or
an ideal match?' 5, 3 New Zealand Tertiary College. Available at: https://www
.hekupu.ac.nz/sites/default/files/2018-05/05%20Laureta.pdf.
Lee, W. (2013) 'A generation adrift', *The Communication Trust Every Child
Understood*: 5–27. Available at: https://www.thecommunicationtrust.org.uk/
media/31961/tct_genadrift.pdf (Accessed 28.03.2019).
Lillard, A. S., Lerner, M. D., Hopkins, E. J., Dore, R. A., Smith E. D. & Palmquist,
C. M. (2013) 'The impact of pretend play on children's development: A review of
the evidence', *Psychological Bulletin*, 139(1): 1–34.
Marie, D. & McLennan, P. (2010) 'Process or product? The argument for aesthetic
exploration in the early years', *Early Childhood Education Journal*, 38(2): 81–85.
More Than a Score (2019) *Stop Testing Four Year Olds*. Available at: https://www
.morethanascore.org.uk/what-we-do/ (Accessed 01.03.2019).
National Literacy Trust (2019) *Language Unlocks Reading: Supporting Early
Language and Reading for Every Child*. Available at: https://literacytrust.org.uk/
(Accessed 01.03.2019).
Palmer, J. (2014) 'Role play areas for early years foundation stage, key stage 1 and
beyond'. In: Bower, V. (Ed.) *Developing Early Literacy 0–8: From Theory to
Practice*, London: SAGE.

Schleicher, A. (2018) *Want to Improve Education? Give Teachers Professional Freedom TES.* Available at: https://www.tes.com/news/want-improve-education-give-teachers-professional-freedom (Accessed 01.03.2019).

Smidt, S. (2013) *Introducing Malaguzzi: Exploring the Life and Work of Reggio Emilia's Founding Father,* London & New York: Routledge.

Wenger, E. (1998) *Communities of Practice: Learning, Meaning, and Identity,* Cambridge: Cambridge University Press.

Wharton, P. & Kinney, L. (2015) *Reggio Emilia Encounters: Children and Adults in Collaboration,* London: Routledge.

Wood, E. (2013) *Play, Learning and the Early Childhood Curriculum* (3rd ed.), London: SAGE.

Chapter 7

Teaching early reading
The phonics debate

Rebecca Austin

It is obvious to all considered persons that one great reason why so much time is taken to learn children [to read], and the work at last done by halves, is the late beginning with them, when their heads are filled with variety of plays and tricks of idleness. Therefore my first advice to parents is, to begin with their children betimes, even as soon as they can speak, though more imperfectly; and whoever followeth it in any moderate degree, spending an hour or two in a day...shall find that most children will be able to read by four years of age...Even nature itself in all learning teaches us to begin with the letter and go on to the greater things.

Is. C. (*sic*) (c.1725) *The London New Method and Art of Teaching Children to Spell and Read Distinctly and Perfectly*, London: ECCO

The thing that hath been, it is that which shall be; and that which is done is that which shall be done: and there is no new thing under the sun.

Ecclesiastes 1:9

Introduction

This chapter takes as its focus the debates surrounding the role of phonics in the learning, teaching and assessment of reading. Phonics refers to the teaching of sound–symbol correspondences in words. The two main approaches are 'synthetic' and 'analytic' – current policy preferring the synthetic approach. Synthetic phonics teaches all the sound–symbol relationships as individual grapheme (written)-phoneme (sound) correspondences, for example 'l/igh/t'. In analytic phonics, children are taught to recognise longer phonically regular 'rimes' such as 'ight' or 'and'. There are concurrent debates about the way in which phonics relates to writing – specifically spelling – but that discussion requires another chapter on another day. The 'reading wars' (Pearson, 2004; Nicholson, 1992; Goodman, 1998) are the context for the 'great debate' (Chall, 1967) or the 'never-ending debate' (Smith, 1992) that I examine here.

Learning to read

We all want children to learn to read. We understand how reading can enrich lives and support children in developing into full and rounded members of society.

Reading enables children to find out about and engage with the world, to find out about themselves and others like and not like them, to explore worlds beyond themselves and imagine and take hold of possible worlds for their future. That our children learn to read is important for individuals, it is important for societies and it is important for the world.

There is great investment, therefore, in getting children reading – and a great number of investors: educators, researchers, politicians, parents and publishing companies all have something to say about how children learn to read and how children should be taught. It matters to all of them; it matters to us all. With so many interested and knowledgeable and/or powerful parties involved, all of whom are motivated (with varying degrees of altruism) to the same cause, one might think that getting children reading would be something that engenders consensus and harmony. After all, we all want the same thing. But maybe it is precisely because of its perceived importance that the debates about how children should be taught to read have been so fierce: it matters to everyone; and it matters a lot.

The act of reading is not straightforward. But even how reading is defined – what we decide counts as reading and whether reading is a single, objective, definable act – is problematic. We talk of reading people, situations, maps and films – there must be something, therefore, in how we approach these multimodal tasks that mirrors what we do when we engage with printed texts. But even when considering printed texts, we might ask whether reading a set of instructions is the same as reading a poem. One is about reading to find out in order to do – the other about reading in order to engage in an intangible, emotional response (see Rosenblatt, 1938) – these are quite different, nevertheless most would see both of these responses as essential aspects of reading.

We might find consensus around the idea of the 'simple view of reading' (Gough and Tumner, 1986) – that reading is a combination of decoding and comprehension – we crack the code and make the meaning from it. We decode faces, contexts, lines and symbols and the *mise-en-scène*. And we decode print in order to work out what it has to say to us. This decoding aspect might be clear, but how we come to the meaning of what we read is hugely complex. Neisser called reading 'externally guided thinking' (1967, p.136) and brain studies (Wolf and Stoodley 2008) show that the whole brain is engaged when we read – we are bringing our whole selves to bear (O'Neill, 1970) on the words (and other semiotic representations) we read in the process of making it make sense to us – comprehending. Just as we do when we engage in the world on a day to day basis. Reading is as complex as life.

Furthermore, Tennent (2014) suggests there are many different kinds of comprehension related to print-based reading – from understanding the meaning of individual words to understanding how they work together to make meaning in sentences right through to the kind of inferential comprehension required to make sense of something like a poem or character development in a novel. And what you understand from your reading will depend in part on what you already know (Freire, 1985) – what you bring to the piece (Rosenblatt, 1938;

Chambers, 1993). No two people can ever comprehend the same text in identical ways because we have to allow for the role of the reader and all of their life and language experience in the sense-making process of reading.

Yet we might also see reading print as a set of skills that require us to work from the 'bottom up' – recognising letters, associating them with sounds, blending those sounds to make words and building sentences from the words we read, and so moving on to reading whole texts. If we know about the relationship between letters and sounds – phonics – we can access the words and their meanings and so make sense of what we read. This is, broadly, the psychological model of learning to read (reading is a learned set of skills which have to be taught) whereas the more complex exploration of reading and meaning-making describes a messier sociocultural model of learning to read.

These models represent perceptual, conceptual, ideological, ontological and epistemological differences in thinking about what reading is and how it is described, enacted and learned, what it is for – and therefore how it should be taught. And the subsequent debates about the role of phonics in teaching reading ('the reading wars' of 1967) are rooted in these different perspectives on reading – on the world. These differences lead to distinct ways of assessing reading, understanding progress in reading and specific approaches to the teaching of reading – particularly for those children who do not find learning to read easy (Smith, 1992).

In addition, governments have a vested interest in getting children reading – high levels of literacy are seen to relate to a successful society and a flourishing economy (Pearson, 2004). Politicians need, therefore, to be seen to get this right. When measured against other countries we need to prove our worth and our potential – what better way than to see how well our children read when compared with those from elsewhere? Mechanisms such as the Progress in International Reading Literacy Study (PIRLS) amplify this intercountry competitiveness and can lead to state interventions to address the perceived issues.

Governments across the world can take a more or less active role in education – in England governments intervene in significant ways to influence practice through policies which are enforced through the school inspection system. The school inspection system also extends to higher education where teachers must be trained in ways laid down by government policy. Government intervention in England in relation to the expectations for phonics teaching in primary schools and the training that primary school teachers received is unprecedented. The increase in weight of political support for the teaching of phonics has fuelled the debate and the passionate responses of those who feel that the emphasis on phonics for beginner readers is not appropriate for all children.

A potted history 1988–present

Phonics – both synthetic and analytic (Goswami, 1999) – has a long history in the teaching of reading in schools – particularly in relation to learning to read in

English-speaking countries. It has rarely been completely absent, though, from the learning and teaching repertoire. Other approaches such as 'look and say' where whole words are learned to be read on sight, or the searchlights model promoted by the National Literacy Strategy (NLS) (1998) which suggests that children should make informed guesses by drawing on a range of 'cues' (Clay and Cazden, 1990; Goodman, 1967), come more or less into favour or are more or less vilified within policies and practice. Policies and practices then influence the resources used to teach reading – including the kinds of texts children are given access to. This also has an impact on the way in which reading is included in the school day and the constraints and freedoms of time and instruction. When and what do children read for themselves? When, what and why do they read for others? Beliefs about the teaching of reading and the role that phonics plays have a significant impact on what happens in schools.

The Education Reform act in 1988 paved the way for the first National Curriculum in England. *English for ages 5 to 16* (1988) – otherwise known as the Cox Report – provided the basis for the English section of the National Curriculum (1989) and came from the work of an advisory working group appointed by the government. The Cox Report was broadly welcomed by educationalists and seen as an attempt to bring together different perspectives about English and how it was taught – although more conservative elements bemoaned the liberal approach to knowledge about language – particularly in relation to the teaching of grammar and Standard English.

In relation to reading, the Cox Report – echoing the Bullock Report (DES, 1975) findings from more than a decade earlier – states:

> 16.9 A prime objective of the teaching of reading must be the development of the pupil's independence as a reader. But 'there is no one method, medium, approach, device, or philosophy that holds the key to the process of learning to read ... Simple endorsements of one or another nostrum are of no service to the teaching of reading' (Bullock, 1975). In their quest for meaning, children need to be helped to become confident and resourceful in the use of a variety of reading cues. They need to be able to recognise on sight a large proportion of the words they encounter and to be able to predict meaning on the basis of phonic, idiomatic and grammatical regularities and of what makes sense in context; children should be encouraged to make informed guesses. Teachers should recognise that reading is a complex but unitary process and not a set of discrete skills which can be taught separately in turn and, ultimately, bolted together.
>
> (DES, 1989)

Twenty years later this statement will be completely turned on its head within government policy documents.

The National Curriculum (DfEE, 1988) did not achieve the results that had been hoped for. Standard Assessment Tasks (SATs) scores in English were not what they should be and children did not appear to be making progress. By 1996, an Ofsted report (Ofsted, 1996) which focused on low literacy levels in a number of inner-London primary schools fuelled calls for reform in the teaching of English in primary schools (Mortimore and Goldstein, 1996). This led to the introduction in 1998 of the NLS framework for teaching – with a highly structured literacy hour which was divided into timed sections which focused on different aspects of teaching and learning, drawing on a large number of discrete learning objectives at word, sentence and text level which had to be addressed in each year group. Reading at word level – decoding – was taught through shared and guided reading approaches led by the teacher. This included explicit phonics teaching related to the texts which were being studied. The role of phonics in the teaching of reading was emphasised:

> Most teachers…have often been over-cautious about the teaching of phonics – sound and spelling. It is vital that pupils are taught to use these word level strategies effectively. Research evidence shows that pupils do not learn to distinguish between the different sounds of words simply by being exposed to books. They need to be taught to do this…At Key Stage 1 there should be a strong and systematic emphasis on the teaching of phonics and other word level skills.
>
> (DfEE, 1998, p.4).

However, when the NLS failed to deliver the required improvements in performance in the Standard Assessment Tasks (Goodwyn and Fuller, 2012), further reforms were required. The introduction of *Progression in Phonics* (DfEE, 1999), after the first couple of years of the implementation of the NLS – a government-funded and -produced scheme for explicit teaching of phonics – was a means of countering criticisms of the searchlights model (Stuart, Stainthorp and Snowling, 2008) for not being sufficiently focused on phonics as the most important cueing system for beginner readers. This scheme drew on a range of activities in relation to phonics teaching and used both analytic and synthetic phonics approaches as tools for decoding:

> Most focused phonics teaching should therefore be done through play, games and activities and then applied alongside other reading cues to meaningful reading of appropriately matched, good quality texts in other parts of the Literacy Hour, particularly in shared and guided sessions with the teacher. Although much of this teaching will necessarily be taught away from the text, it should relate to texts in three important ways:
>
> - by using particular words from texts as starting points for instruction and investigation;
> - by using patterned texts which exemplify particular phonemic structures e.g. rhyming, alliterative, assonant, onomatopoeic patterns;

- most importantly, through the application of phonic strategies to texts in shared and guided reading.

(DES, 1999, p.7)

There was an emphasis, therefore, on the application of the learning from discrete lessons in phonics to the wider literacy instruction within the literacy hour. Phonics was seen as important enough to have its own discrete teaching, but it was still positioned alongside other cueing systems such as meaning and syntax. High-quality texts were seen as starting points for selections of words to be investigated and to represent a range of linguistic features that support the identification of letter–sound relationships.

For some, this did not go anywhere near far enough, and influential individuals and pressure groups continued to lobby for a review of the 'multi-strategy' searchlights model for the teaching of reading as advocated by the NLS (Lewis and Ellis, 2006 p.113). This culminated in the instigation of the *Independent review of the teaching of early reading* which was undertaken by Sir Jim Rose in 2006. Central to this review was research undertaken in Clackmannanshire in relation to the role of synthetic and analytic phonics in the teaching of reading (Johnston and Watson, 2004; 2005). The research divided opinion – some criticised the approach taken and others questioned the fact that the gains in word reading (decoding), which were impressive, were not matched by a consequent gain in comprehension. Others, however, felt that research into the significant impact of phonics teaching on children's phonic knowledge was at last being taken seriously – and that synthetic phonics in particular was being given an appropriate platform. Rose concluded:

Despite uncertainties in research findings, the practice seen by the review shows that the systematic approach, which is generally understood as 'synthetic' phonics offers the vast majority of young children the best and most direct route to becoming skilled readers and writers.

(Rose, 2006, p.4)

This stood in stark contrast to the earlier findings from the Bullock Report which were advocated by the Cox Report: that no one way of teaching reading should be prioritised over any other. The recommendations of the Rose Review included the introduction of discrete, daily, systematic synthetic phonics lessons for all children from Reception to Year 2. The searchlights model was seen to be one which was more appropriate for understanding what skilled readers do (Stuart, Stainthorp and Snowling, 2008) and the argument for phonics as a requirement for beginner readers as the prime approach to decoding, taught 'first and fast', was propounded. The government-produced SSP programme *Letters and Sounds* explained this:

In the early stages...children will encounter many words that are visually unfamiliar, and in reading these words their attention should be focused on decoding rather than on the use of unreliable strategies such as looking at the illustrations, rereading the sentence, saying the first sound and guessing what might fit. Although these strategies might result in intelligent guesses, none of them is sufficiently reliable and they can hinder the acquisition and application of phonic knowledge and skills, prolonging the word recognition process and lessening children's overall understanding. Children who routinely adopt alternative cues for reading unknown words, instead of learning to decode them, find themselves stranded when texts become more demanding and meanings less predictable. The best route for children to become fluent and independent readers lies in securing phonics as the prime approach to decoding unfamiliar words.

(DfEE, 2007, p.12)

Letters and Sounds was freely available for all schools and all those training to teach, but schools could also buy into schemes which met government-produced criteria. Matched funding was provided for such schemes and other resources for the teaching of reading. The revised core criteria advised that in a 'good' SSP scheme:

7. It is important that texts are of the appropriate level for children to apply and practise the phonic knowledge and skills that they have learnt. Children should not be expected to use strategies such as whole-word recognition and/or cues from context, grammar, or pictures.

(DES, 2010)

This was a move away from the text-led contextualised phonics teaching advocated by the NLS in *Progression in Phonics.* The requirement for children to access texts which relate to their phonic ability was taken up again and further emphasised in the revised primary curriculum in 2013, which advises that:

Pupils need to develop the skill of blending the sounds into words for reading and establish the habit of applying this skill whenever they encounter new words. This will be supported by practice in reading books consistent with their developing phonic knowledge and skill and their knowledge of common exception words. At the same time, they will need to hear, share and discuss a wide range of high-quality books to develop a love of reading and broaden their vocabulary.

(DfE, 2013, p.19)

Since the Rose Report, schools and initial teacher education programmes have been subject to close scrutiny in the requirement that children are taught phonics daily and discretely from a scheme which meets government approved criteria. Children's progress (and by implication teachers' efficacy) has been assessed through a phonics screening check at the end of Year 1, introduced in 2012.

The results of these checks at school level are made public and used to identify schools and authorities where teaching of phonics is deemed to be poorer. In 2019, 'English Hubs' were introduced – schools with excellent records of results in the phonics screening check who would be invited to support other schools in developing similarly successful practice supported by phonics roadshows led by Ruth Miskin Training. An overall budget of £26.3 million has been allocated to this (Hinds, 2018). The teaching of phonics in primary schools at the point of writing this chapter remains high stakes and big business.

What works?

In education there is a peculiar imperative to find out 'what works' in terms of teaching and learning – as if there is always, somewhere, the elusive 'one way' that will work for all children and contexts. Research evidence is gathered, considered and cited by advocates of different approaches. Success in different countries is scrutinised for what could be borrowed and used here in England. The evidence which appears to be most compelling to those in positions of power is that which is used to influence policy and practice in schools, ultimately impacting on the experiences of all children.

There is an assumption that what works in one context with one group of children will be generally applicable across all contexts and all children, when there is no reason to think that this will be so. And 'those in positions of power' will have ideological and possibly personal agendas in which they are invested affecting the process of weighing up the evidence they have been shown. Biesta, in his article 'Why 'what works' doesn't work', says research is not about finding answers, but about giving teachers (not politicians) ways of thinking about how to approach the 'problem' of teaching – how do we meet the needs of our pupils?:

> Research can only tell us what has worked in a particular situation, not what will work in any future situation. The role of the educational professional in this process is not to translate general rules into particular lines of action. It is rather to use research findings to make one's problem solving more intelligent.
>
> (Biesta, 2007, p.20–21)

The ultimate failure of the National Literacy Strategy and the Literacy Hour was, in part, because no matter the level of prescription, of 'sameness' in terms of what is taught and how it is delivered, every school, every teacher and every single child who is taught is different (Stannard and Huxford, 2007). What works doesn't *always* work. In an ideal world, teachers would use evidence from research findings to develop their professional thinking and teaching approaches – in the real world they are influenced by the policies dictated by government on the basis of their interpretation of research, the vigour and rigour with which the policies are implemented and, ultimately, how their success or otherwise is measured.

How do we measure reading?

Interpreting data about using phonics to teach reading is tricky. The huge mass of research stretching back over decades comes from an extraordinary range of different perspectives related to the ontological and epistemological assumptions made about reading. The reader must first ask:

- 'Why was this research undertaken? Who has undertaken it?' (the political and ideological context);
- 'What do the researchers understand about what reading is?' (their ontological position);
- 'What data do they believe will tell them what children know and can do in reading?' (their epistemological position).

Then the data, findings and conclusions can be interpreted accordingly – and the inconsistencies can be explored and considered. And the reader can engage in their own critical reflection and analysis of the data to come to their own position and reading of the findings. Similarly, data garnered from assessments of individual children in school; schools' performance in SATs (and phonics checks); and countries' performance in PIRLS should all be subjected to the same critical interrogation. Where and how has this data come about? What is it measuring?

Assessing reading comes in many forms. The 1971 Schonell Reading Test was a list of words which children read out loud – the test is stopped when children have read 10 consecutive words incorrectly and the reading age calculated from how far along the list they got. The Holborn Reading Scale (first produced in 1948) required children to read a list of increasingly challenging sentences – the sentence in which they made their fourth error indicated their reading age. These two approaches represent different ways of measuring decoding – the context cues of the sentences in the Holborn approach might help children make a more accurate guess at a word (Smith, 1980) although 21st-century children may not get much contextual help from 'Quench your thirst with a bottle of our sparkling ginger ale'. The Schonell test is clearly simply about decoding isolated words.

These reading ages were used as the standard means of assessing progress, grouping children according to ability and determining the 'level' of reading book the child should be given. Many schools still use tests like these – it is interesting to consider why their perceived usefulness has endured. Sometimes it is about the simplicity of such tests as blunt instruments to provide a handy simplification that can be easily administered, interpreted and 'used'.

In contrast, reading comprehension is much more difficult to assess – especially if we allow for a range of 'right' readings of any text. The 2011 Reading Comprehension SATs test required children to read and answer questions on a text called *Caves and Caving in Davely Dale* (2012). Michael Rosen (2011) produced a critique of this as a text explaining how it was easier for some children than others because of the requirement to know things from experience of the world, not just what has been learned in the classroom. Children who do not know what a 'dale' is and have never been caving will inevitably understand the text less well. Comprehension cannot ever be tested from a level playing field – what we understand when we read is based, in part, on what we already know. Part of what was being assessed in this particular SATs year (and arguably every year, as each text will have a context) was children's experience of life outside school. Information such as this, though, was (and is) used to measure children's attainment and progress and to compare and rank teacher and school performance.

What do we know about the phonics check data?

The phonics check looks at children's ability to decode 40 words, 20 of which are 'names of imaginary creatures' or 'nonsense' words – that is, they are words which can be decoded phonically but do not have a meaning in English. Since its introduction there have been year on year improvements in the number of children achieving the expected level. Nick Gibb, Schools Minister, in his September 2018 press release about the improved scores in the phonics screening test stated:

> Phonics provides pupils with the building blocks they need to read fluently and confidently, as well as aiding future learning and giving them the tools they need to express themselves.

This is quite a lot to attribute to teaching children sound–symbol correspondences and then checking which they can remember and apply to isolated words in a test.

There are detailed instructions provided for those administering the check:

> Alternative pronunciations must be considered when deciding whether a response is correct. For real words, inappropriate grapheme-phoneme correspondences must be marked as incorrect (for example, reading 'blow' to rhyme with 'cow' would be incorrect).
>
> (Phonics Screening Check Administrative
> Guidance, 2019, p.15)

So, if the word is 'real', alternative pronunciations of graphemes are not allowed, but the nonsense word 'clow' would be accepted if pronounced to rhyme with either 'grow' or 'prow'. What is being assessed here? Phonics knowledge or vocabulary? If a child does not know a word – if it is not part of their vocabulary – to them, it is a nonsense word. In addition, a child's normal accent and/or pronunciation can be taken into account – so pronouncing 'think' as 'fink' is acceptable if that is how the child usually says the word. There are also rules about the extent to which children elongate sounds or the length of gap between sounding out each phoneme. It is not straightforward to assess. And what is it that is being assessed? Is it reading? There could be an argument that phonics might be best assessed through *only* 'nonsense' words. For those words, the only way to read them is by applying a sound–symbol rule – might that be harder to use as evidence for improved reading rather than simply improved decoding?

Nick Gibb, in the same press release, also links the improvement in phonics scores to the PIRLS success, which looks at reading comprehension across a range of countries.

> The focus on phonics – where children learn to read by sounding out and blending letters – has played a significant part in the improvement in primary school standards. England has risen from 19th place in 2006 to joint 8th in the world reading league table (PIRLS).

Krashen (2018, p.57), however, presents evidence from across a range of studies which suggests that there is no link between intensive phonics instruction and reading comprehension. Rather:

> High performance on tests of reading comprehension, such as PIRLS, are the result of doing lots of pleasure reading, which requires access to books.

Within the period that the phonics screening check has been implemented, there has been a contemporaneous push towards developing children's reading for pleasure – it might be that this has had an impact on the PIRLS score too.

The data from the phonics check tells us that children have got better at phonics. There is also a compelling argument that the data from the phonics test is used to assess school and teacher performance in the teaching of phonics as much as the performance of individual children (Clark, 2018).

Summary

A traditionalist view of literacy and reading sees an unproblematic hierarchy – language as either right or wrong with consistent, unchanging usage and standards – language as a sum of its parts, wherein studying the parts enables you to learn the whole. Changes in the way language is used are always seen as regressive. Language is seen as neutral – not affected by history, social context or culture. This view supports a straightforward assessment regime. It looks for a direct correlation between learning the 'code' and learning to read. If we look at how well children have learned their phonics, we will be able to ascertain how much better their reading is. Teaching phonics can be done discretely and systematically. We can test comprehension through one-size-fits-all standardised testing, too, and we can interpret that as the impact of decoding on comprehension.

A progressive, liberal approach argues for language as a socio-cultural practice embedded in ways of doing and being and intricately tied up within power structures. It sees language as necessarily fluid and changeable, and that change is inevitable and good. But this would take the view that all texts are encultured, all readers are individual and there is no one right way to comprehend a text. This is tricky to assess. Phonics as part of a repertoire of reading skills would be seen to be best used and taught and assessed in the context of reading – where it is much more difficult to isolate the role it plays. Those taking this kind of perspective might consider that knowing sound–symbol correspondences in isolation is not at all the same thing as 'reading'.

Others would argue, too, that schools are necessarily positioned in ways that make access to learning unequal:

> Education and the teaching of reading is a cultural act and therefore will privilege some and deny others.
>
> (Lambirth, 2007, p.119)

There are differences of opinion, however, as to whether systematic synthetic phonics is the problem or the cure when we look at evidence of underachievement for certain groups of children from particular socioeconomic or cultural backgrounds. The evidence about phonics and reading is an enormous mixed bag – for every view citing evidence to support it, there is another waiting in the wings to refute it.

The Reading Reform Foundation is an organisation which has lobbied consistently for systematic synthetic phonics to be the prime approach to teaching reading. The front page of their website states:

> For too long now the teaching of reading has been affected by the idea that children should learn by discovery and "incidental" phonics teaching, leading to the rejection of systematic, explicit phonics instruction. This idea is deeply ingrained in education and still has a powerful influence on how reading is taught, despite having no scientific validity.
>
> (RRF, no date)

Many of the articles on their site offer an interrogation of the criticisms of synthetic phonics approaches and provide detailed data and analyses – for example, Rhona Johnston's examination of two significant meta analyses that found that synthetic phonics was no better at getting children reading than analytic phonics. Johnston concludes that these studies got it wrong:

> A close examination of the C. Torgerson et al. (2006) meta-analysis shows evidence of multiple errors in the selection of the studies to be included and in the selection of the data entered into the analysis. The number of studies included was also too small to allow for a meaningful meta-analysis.
>
> (Johnston, 2018, no page)

Jeff McQuillan's (2018, p.27) analysis of Machin et al.'s (2016) data from nearly 500,000 children in the UK concludes that his evidence is sound:

The evidence Machin et al presented is consistent with experimental studies that have found intensive phonics instruction makes a modest initial impact but has very small effects on reading achievement later.

These are scholars and researchers engaging with the evidence in ever-decreasing circles – meta analyses; critiques of each other's work; inspection of evidence from a different perspective – through a different lens. Agreement about any element of the reading process where phonics is concerned would seem to be unlikely – even when looking at the same evidence, we hear different interpretations of what it means.

So does phonics work? 'Yes!' exclaim one group of people with great passion; 'It's more complicated than that!' roar another with equal fervour. 'Maybe,' say some more cautiously, 'Sometimes?' say others even more cautiously. 'It depends,' say the canny group in the middle quite decisively. 'I just don't know,' say the confused.

I started this chapter with a quote from a 'phonics' scheme in use in 1725 – if we are still caught up in the debates about phonics nearly 300 years later, I suspect that Frank Smith (1992) is right and the debate is 'never-ending'. If that is the case, then evidence will continue to be produced, debated, deified, debunked and derided. The imperative for all practitioners must be, then, that they position themselves within the debate, not outside it. We need teachers who know the big picture about the detail of what they do in the classroom – where policies come from and how they influence practice. We need professionals who look for answers and engage first-hand in the myriad evidence available to them. Leanne Chall (1967, p.7), writing about 'the Great Debate', was struck by the fact that she found 'emotion where reason should prevail'. But perhaps emotion is both inevitable and good in the world of teaching reading. We need teachers who care about the teaching of reading and how they teach it.

After all, it matters to all of us. And it matters a lot.

Questions for reflection

Where has the government policy emphasis on teaching early reading through phonics come from?

What is the difference between being able to decode text and being able to comprehend it?

What do you know, understand and believe about the role of phonics in learning to read? How have you come to that position?

Further reading and resources

Hall, K. (2005) *Listening to Stephen Read: Multiple Perspectives on Literacy*, Milton Keynes: OUP.

This book provides the opportunity for a number of educationalists to give their perspectives on the reading process. A good way to challenge yourself to think about what your beliefs are about learning to read.

Rose, J. (2006) *Independent Review of the Teaching of Early Reading*, Nottingham: DfES Publications.
This is the report which triggered significant changes in the primary reading curriculum in England. It is important that you engage with this first-hand so that you understand the key aspects that were (and were not!) identified as reasons to adopt the systematic synthetic phonics approach.

United Kingdom Literacy Association 'Fact Sheet' about the teaching of reading, available at: https://ukla.org/downloads/Fact_Sheet.pdf.
This is a helpful resource which identifies reading 'facts' and then points you in the direction of further reading to support each point or explore it further.

References

Biesta, G. (2007) Why "what works" won't work: Evidence-based practice and the democratic deficit in educational research. *Educational Theory*, 57(1): 1–22.

Bullock, A. (1975) *A Language for Life: Report of the Committee of Inquiry Appointed by the Secretary of State for Education and Science under the Chairmanship of Sir Alan Bullock*. London: Her Majesty's Stationery Office.

Caves and Caving in Davely Dale (2012) KS2 SATs Paper. Available at http://www.satstestsonline.co.uk/past_papers/2011_english_reading_answer_booklet.pdf.

Chall, J. (1967) *Learning to Read: The Great Debate*, New York: McGraw-Hill Book Company.

Chambers, A. (1993) *Tell Me: Children, Reading & Talk*, Primary English Teaching Association. Stroud: Thimble Press.

Clark, M. M. (ed.) (2018) *Teaching initial literacy: Policies, Evidence and Ideology*, Birmingham: Glendale Education.

Clay, M. M. & Cazden, C. B. (1990) A Vygotskian interpretation of reading recovery. In: Moll, L. (ed.) *Vygotsky and Education*, New York: Cambridge University Press.

Cox Committee (1988) *English for Ages 5–11*, National Curriculum, HMSP. London: Her Majesty's Stationery Office.

DES (1975) *A Language for Life* (The Bullock Report), HMSO. London: Her Majesty's Stationery Office.

DES (1989) *English for Ages 5 to 16* (The Cox Report), London: HMSO.

DfE (2010) *Phonics Teaching Materials: Core Criteria and the Self-Assessment Process*, London: HMSO.

DfE (2013) *The National Curriculum in England: Key stages 1 and 2 Framework Document*, London: HMSO.

DfEE (1998) *National Literacy Strategy: A Framework for Teaching*, London: HMSO.

DfEE (1999) *Progression in Phonics*, London: HMSO.

DfEE (1999) *The National Curriculum: Handbook for Primary Teachers in England*, London: HMSO.

DfEE (2007) *Letters and Sounds Principles and Practice of High Quality Phonics*, London: HMSO.

Freire, P. (1985) Reading the world and reading the word: An interview with Paulo Freire. *Language Arts*, 62(1): 15–21.

Gibb, N. (2018) Press release. Available at https://www.gov.uk/government/news/more-children-on-track-to-be-fluent-readers-in-primary-school.

Goodman, K. S. (1967) Reading: A psycholinguistic guessing game. *Literacy Research and Instruction*, 6(4): 126–135.

Goodman, K. S. (Ed.) (1998) *In Defense of Good Teaching: What Teachers Need to Know about the "Reading Wars"*, Teachers Publishing Group Incorporated. York, ME: Stenhouse.

Goodwyn, A. & Fuller, C. (Eds.) (2012) *The Great Literacy Debate: A Critical Response to the Literacy Strategy and the Framework for English*, London: Routledge.

Goswami, U. (1999) Causal connections in beginning reading: The importance of rhyme. *Journal of Research in Reading*, 22(3): 217–240.

Gough, P. B. & Tunmer, W. (1986) Decoding, reading, and reading disability. *Remedial and Special Education*, 7(1): 6–10.

Hinds, D. (2018) Press release. Available at https://www.gov.uk/government/news/new-education-and-skills-measures-announced--2.

Johnston, R. S. & Watson, J. E. (2004) Accelerating the development of reading, spelling and phonemic awareness skills in initial readers. *Reading and Writing*, 17(4): 327–357.

Johnston, R. & Watson, J. (2005) The effects of synthetic phonics teaching on reading and spelling attainment: A seven year longitudinal study. Available at https://dera.ioe.ac.uk/14793/1/0023582.pdf.

Johnston, R. (2018) Examining the evidence on the effectiveness of synthetic phonics teaching: The Ehri et al (2001) and Torgerson et al. (2006) meta-analyses. Available at https://rrf.org.uk/2018/06/17/examining-the-evidence-on-the-effectiveness-of-synthetic-phonics-teaching-the-ehri-et-al-2001-and-c-torgerson-et-al-2006-meta-analyses-by-rhona-johnston-emeritus-professor-of-psychology-univers/.

Krashen, S. (2018) Does Phonics deserve the credit for the improvement in PIRLS? In: Clark, M. M. (Ed.) *Teaching Initial Literacy: Policies, Evidence and Ideology*, Birmingham: Glendale Education.

Lambirth, A. (2007) in Goouch, K. & Lambirth, A. (2011) *Teaching Early Reading and Phonics: Creative Approaches to Early Literacy*, London: SAGE.

Lewis, M. & Ellis, S. (Eds.) (2006) *Phonics Practice Research and Policy*, London: UKLA/Paul Chapman Publishing.

Machin, S. J., McNally, S. & Viarengo, M. (2016) 'Teaching to Teach' literacy. IZA Discussion Paper, 9955.

McQuillan, J. (2018) Is synthetic phonics working in England? A comment on the 'teaching to teach literacy' report. In: Clark, M. M. (ed.) *Teaching Initial Literacy Policies, Evidence and Ideology*, Birmingham: Glendale Education.

Mortimore, P. & Goldstein, H. (1996) *The Teaching of Reading in 45 Inner London Primary Schools: A Critical Examination of Ofsted Research*, London: Institute of Education, University of London.

Neisser, U. (1967) *Cognitive Psychology*, New York: Appleton-Century-Crofts.

Nicholson, T. (1992) Reading wars: A brief history and an update. *International Journal of Disability, Development and Education*, 39(3): 173–184.

Office for Standards in Education (1996) *The Teaching of Reading in 45 Inner London Primary Schools*. London: Publications office, Institute of Education.

O'Neil, W. (1970) Properly literate. *Harvard Educational Review*, 40(2): 2.

Pearson, P. D. (2004) The reading wars. *Educational Policy*, 18(1): 216–252.

Phonics Screening Check Administration Guidance (2019) Available at https://assets.publishing.service.gov.uk/government/uploads/system/uploads/attachment_data/file/798235/2019_phonics_screening_check_administration_guidance.pdf.

Reading Reform Foundation. Available at: www.rrf.org.uk.

Rose, J. (2006) *Independent Review of the Teaching of Early Reading*, Nottingham: DfES Publications.

Rosen, M. (2011) Available at https://www.facebook.com/notes/michael-rosen/heres-the-lecture-i-gave-yesterday-at-nottingham-trent-uni-it-includes-an-analys/10150196276022225/.

Rosenblatt, L. M. (1938) *Literature as Exploration*, New York: Modern.

Smith, F. (1980) *Understanding Reading: A Psycholinguistic Analysis of Reading and Learning to Read*, London: Routledge.

Smith, F. (1992) Learning to read: The never-ending debate. *The Phi Delta Kappan*, 73(6): 432–441.

Stannard, J. & Huxford, L. (2007) *The Literacy Game: The Story of the National Literacy Strategy*, London: Routledge.

Stuart, M., Stainthorp, R. & Snowling, M. (2008) Literacy as a complex activity: Deconstructing the simple view of reading. *Literacy*, 42(2): 59–66.

Tennent, W. (2014) *Understanding Reading Comprehension: Processes and Practices*, London: SAGE.

The Holborn Reading Scale. Available at http://staff.anzacterrace.wa.edu.au/wp-content/uploads/2015/03/Holborn-Reading-Scale.pdf.

The Schonell Reading Test. Available at http://www.readingtest.co.uk/schonell-reading-test/.

Torgerson, C., Brooks, G. & Hall, J. (2006) *A Systematic Review of the Research Literature on the Use of Phonics in the Teaching of Reading and Spelling*, Nottingham: DfES Publications.

Wolf, M. & Stoodley, C. J.. (2008) *Proust and the Squid: The Story and Science of the Reading Brain*, New York: Harper Perennial.

Chapter 8

The arts as handmaiden

Hermione Ruck Keene

Introduction

At a moment in history when schools face unprecedented financial and account-ability pressures within a fragmented society, arguments to protect the teaching of the arts gain urgency. Their proven contributions to 'human flourishing' (Matarasso, 2019, p.20) in terms of creativity, wellbeing, social cohesion and cognitive and academic development make a persuasive case for their inclusion in school curricula. The question debated here is whether the arts – music, dance, drama, media and visual arts – should be protected in the curriculum by virtue of these instrumental benefits, or their intrinsic value as unique and highly skilled forms of human communication and expression.

The debate surrounding teaching the arts 'for art's sake' or as a 'handmaiden' is a long-running one, to which I bring my perspective as a music educator in primary school and university contexts. Whilst teaching music within a generalist primary teacher education programme, I find myself arguing for the inclusion of the arts in primary curricula in the context of low trainee confidence levels, little university teaching time to develop subject and pedagogical knowledge and teaching placements with very varied arts provision. By making these arguments, I hope that trainees will reach their own understandings of why the arts should be protected, so that they become advocates for high-quality arts education as teachers or leaders. Choosing to ground these understandings in the instrumental or intrinsic qualities of the arts is a personal decision, as is the conclusion reached by readers of this chapter.

Drawing on my own expertise in music education throughout, I begin by contextualising the debate and outlining the arts education landscape in England; I then explore some claims made for the benefits to children of arts education, using El Sistema as an example, before discussing the arts as unique subjects and in a transdisciplinary context.

The debate in practice

I open with a vignette from my own experience as a music teacher in a London school. I was given space and time to run a small music-based intervention with children from Nursery to Year 2, all of whom had specific educational needs related to communication and language processing. I had observed that they participated confidently and happily in class music lessons, despite in some cases having profound learning challenges and limited speech. Working with the school's Speech and Language Therapist, I devised a programme to improve their language, communication and interpersonal engagement. At the time I was engaged in study for an MA in Music Education, and had recently discovered the literature discussing the innate connections between music and language from the pre-natal to the end of life (Chen-Hafteck and Mang, 2018) and the attendant capacity of music to aid linguistic and cognitive development (Hallam, 2017; Knight and Rabon, 2017; Pitts, 2016). This group allowed me to put my burgeoning academic knowledge into practice.

Each week, seated around a large gathering drum with their Learning Support Assistants, children played the rhythms of their names and other words, used the drum to express their emotions, explored the different timbres, textures and dynamics of the instrument, took turns to be leaders and enjoyed sitting in the upturned drum as we moved it to the pulse and sang together. Their engagement and improved communication and social skills were notable, as was their immediate and embodied connection with the drum and with each other, and ability to express themselves musically. At the same time, they built on the musical skills they were acquiring during weekly lessons with their respective classes. This learning was, though, incidental to the goal of the sessions, which was to use music for the purposes stated above. Due to the diverse ages of the children, I was only able to make limited connections to their learning in their weekly class music lessons and did not include objectives linked to musical skill development in my planning for these sessions.

This brief vignette encapsulates many of the issues surrounding this debate and can be 'read' from both sides of the argument. The instrumental value of music in developing these children's language and communication skills was incontrovertible, reflecting the findings of research in this area (Hallam, 2017; Pitts, 2016; Sharda et al., 2018). Yet as an example of high-quality music teaching it could be perceived as lacking in many ways, particularly in terms of progression and range of music skills and activities. Nevertheless, it embodied the many benefits that making music can bring to a group of children whose school experience often included a feeling of isolation, challenges in accessing learning or inability to make their voices heard. Each week, the children, other adults and I formed a joyful community of music-makers, sharing in a moment of meaningful creativity and communication outside the constraints of classroom teaching and learning; I recognise now what a golden opportunity this was, and how lucky I was to be able to share in those dialogues and be present to witness the children conversing and developing through music.

There is no 'correct' way to interpret this vignette in terms of the instrumental or intrinsic value of the music-making, just as there is no right answer to the question under debate here, as I hope to illustrate. I begin my discussion by contextualising it within the wider arts education landscape in the UK, with a focus on the English context; although many of the issues discussed are highly relevant in the rest of the UK and indeed internationally.

The arts education landscape: teaching and accessing the arts

The *National Plan for Music* (Henley, 2011) set out a vision for music education based on a belief in the historical quality of music education in the UK and the potential contribution made by musicians to the economy, a sentiment echoed in the 2015 Warwick Commission report, *Enriching Britain: Culture, Creativity and Growth*. The 2013 OECD report *Art for Art's Sake* (Winner, Goldstein and Vincent-Lancrin, 2013), a meta-analysis of research into arts education, promotes the view that the role of education is to foster the skills fuelling economic and social innovations, such as creativity, imagination, communication and teamwork, and that arts education is particularly effective in this regard. The Durham Commission on Creativity and Education Report explores the benefits of a creative education in the context of: economic growth, skills and social mobility; community identity and social engagement; and personal fulfilment and wellbeing (Durham University, 2019). These aspects of a creative education sit behind the debate explored in this chapter, representing an instrumental, futures-orientated view of creative education first set out in the 1999 NACCCE report *All our futures* (National Advisory Committee on Creative and Cultural Education).

Whilst valuing creativity as an essential skill in post-industrial societies has had significant benefits in terms of increased recognition of the contribution of the arts to education and society more broadly, the focus on the potential of arts education to contribute in seemingly every other area than the arts themselves can be problematic. As Payne and Hall (2018, p.170) observe, to view the arts in terms only of their economic potential perpetuates a globally pervasive neo-liberalist agenda 'positioned centre-stage politically, and engendering market-driven forces within institutions previously founded on egalitarian practices'. The authors also highlight the fundamental disconnect present in the promotion of the economic value of the arts without promoting the intrinsic educational value of art forms and associated skill development.

The arts education landscape in England sits within a broader global culture of accountability, testing, and curriculum reform which has been well documented and informs many of the debates under question in this volume. Devolution within the English system through the academisation and free schools agenda has impacted on the provision for arts education (Cultural Learning Alliance, 2017a), in particular through the removal of the requirement for all schools to follow the National Curriculum, which, although patchy in its provision for the arts and subject to much critique (e.g. Payne and Hall's 2018 analysis of the Art and Design curriculum), does embed the arts as a statutory requirement from ages 5–14. A further significant factor has been the introduction in 2010 of the EBacc accountability measure for secondary schools, which excludes arts subjects from the set of subjects used to measure school achievement at GCSE level. The subsequent appearance in 2016 of the Progress 8 and Attainment 8 headline measures, which also excluded arts subjects, dealt a further blow to arts education.

Numbers of pupils entering GCSE and A level in the arts have been consistently falling since the introduction of the EBacc and Progress 8 (Johnes, 2017; Parameshwaran and Thomson, 2015). Although not targeted at primary schools, the impact on arts education of these measures cannot be overlooked, if only in terms of the long-term supply of teachers sufficiently educated in the arts to teach them at primary level. The exclusion of the arts from accountability measures reinforces their role as 'not a proper subject' or, in Payne and Hall's (2018) words, a 'bimbo', a perspective exemplified by the then–Secretary of State for Education Nicky Morgan's infamous remarks that students who chose to study arts and humanities rather than STEM (Science, Technology, Engineering and Maths) subjects were being 'held back' in their future careers (Paton, 2014). This perception is at odds with the view of arts education as a valued contributor to the development of skills required in the post-industrial world presented in the policy documents and reports discussed above. This illustrates one of the risks of viewing the arts in a predominantly instrumental role: that the level of skill and expertise required for individual art forms is undermined by a desire to extrapolate transferable skills from participating in artistic endeavour.

A further worrying development is the increasing socio-economic divide in terms of access to the arts; Youth Music (2019) noted a significant increase in young people taking a 'DIY' or informal approach to learning a musical instrument, particularly those from lower socio-economic backgrounds. This supports earlier findings that access to music education, particularly instrumental and vocal tuition, is becoming increasingly the preserve of those whose parents can afford it (Associated Board of the Royal Schools of Music, 2014). Inequality of access is not confined to music; as Payne and Hall (2018, p.167), citing research from Arts Council England, state:

> Far from the cultural wealth apparent on the surface of British society, growing inequality is evident in creative sector employment, cultural participation and educational opportunities in the visual arts.

In the primary education context, the 2014 revised National Curriculum's shift towards higher knowledge-based expectations, particularly in English and Maths, combined with the increasingly demanding requirements of SATs testing, has led to a progressive and inevitable 'squeezing out' of arts subjects in terms of curriculum time and resources allocated to them (Brill, Grayson, Kuhn, O'Donnell, and National Foundation for Educational Research, 2018; Hennessy, 2018; NSEAD, 2016; Savage and Barnard, 2019). The Fabian Society's recent report on the state of arts education in England (Cooper, Bailey, Media, Manager, and Khan, 2018) found that 68% of 350 primary teachers surveyed reported a reduction in quantity of arts teaching in England, with 49% also reporting a drop in the quality of provision. The same report found that the impact of budget cuts in education had impacted significantly upon the arts, which, apart from dance as part of PE, do not benefit from ring-fenced or protected funding. Arts education organisations have repeatedly called for Ofsted to take account of provision for the arts in their inspection frameworks (Savage and Barnard, 2019). Recently, Ofsted have recognised the detrimental impact of the narrowing of the curriculum (Ofsted, 2018) and their proposed revised inspection framework promises to take into consideration both breadth of subject provision and a curriculum which 'extends beyond the academic, technical or vocational and provides for learners' broader development, enabling them to develop and discover their interests and talents' (Ofsted, 2019).

A final significant feature of the arts education context in England is the shifting landscape of Initial Teacher Education (ITE). A push towards school-based models of training, combined with reduced teaching time on university PGCE courses, has contributed to very varied levels of professional development in the Arts for trainee teachers. There are few remaining BA Education or PGCE courses which offer a specialist pathway in the Arts; this, combined with the picture of often limited Arts teaching in school contexts described above, means that NQTs, regardless of how they have trained, may enter the profession with little or no experience of teaching the Arts. Hennessy (2018) finds further that:

> Initial teaching training programs have limited capacity to change the attitudes and values students bring with them. Factors that contribute to changing these involve well-supported school-based practice with sustained opportunities to engage practically with and to teach music; observing good examples of practice; and lots of time for reflection.
>
> (Hennessy, 2018, p.268)

Within an Arts education and teacher development landscape where the Arts are sadly often absent, the argument for their instrumental role seems to gain credence; the picture seems to be that the Arts are simply not valued for their own sake in many contexts, so increased evidence from other sources is needed to advocate for them.

Specialist or generalist teachers?

Related to the central debate of this chapter is the question of whether the Arts should be taught by specialist or generalist teachers, another thorny issue with convincing arguments on either side. There is a wealth of literature in the music education field, for example, exploring the confidence levels of generalist teachers and trainee teachers in teaching music; Hennessy (2018) found that between 1999 and 2015, 50% of the articles in a major music education journal related to music education at Primary level were concerned with this very issue. With research consistently finding confidence levels to be low, the solution does appear to be to employ specialist teachers whose subject and pedagogical knowledge allows them to deliver high-quality arts education, as advocated by Cooper et al. (2018), for example. However, arguments that the arts should be taught by generalist class teachers are equally persuasive; these teachers' knowledge of their pupils, ability to adapt pedagogy to the specific learning culture and needs of their classroom context and flexibility to integrate the arts within other areas of the curriculum give them strengths which in many cases may balance those of the specialist teacher. Hennessy (2018) offers an insightful summary based on many years of working in ITE; although she refers here to music specifically, this perspective applies equally to other art forms:

> What is needed is both: generalists who can confidently engage in the music learning of their classes, understand how to combine musical experiences and learning with other subjects, lead and facilitate music-making with imagination and enthusiasm, with the support of specialist colleagues; and enough specialists to provide adequate support to generalists and develop high-quality music learning opportunities for all children. Such specialists might be school-based or not, qualified teachers or musicians. Whoever they are, they need good education and training in music education and in the range of different roles they might fill as specialists.
>
> (Hennessy, 2018, p.269)

Hennessy's view to some extent reflects the debate under question in this chapter; the generalist teacher might be perceived here as the 'handmaiden', whilst the specialist supporting them represents the Arts for their own sake. However, to describe these roles in this way is somewhat reductive and undermines the potential of the generalist teacher, with the right support and training, to integrate the Arts into their teaching with confidence and enthusiasm.

Instrumental value of the arts

The Cultural Learning Alliance's 2017 research summary *Key research findings: the case for cultural learning*[1] (2017b) was designed to provide research evidence for those advocating for the arts. Drawing together the results of empirical studies with large cohort sizes or with control groups, the report concluded that the 'CLA can state emphatically that there are key skills delivered by cultural learning' (ibid., p.2). Headline findings included that participation in structured arts activities increases cognitive abilities; learning through arts and culture increases attainment in Maths and English; and that arts and culture education develop skills and behaviours that enable children to do better in school, impact on university attendance for children from lower socio-economic backgrounds, increase the likelihood of voting, boost employability and reduce the risk of offending. This report is the latest in a series of such research and policy documents arguing for the instrumental value of the arts and their capacity to develop transferable skills and impact on lifelong outcomes for young people.[2] This is not an isolated piece of research, focusing on the positive impacts of arts education and participation for young people; there is a wealth of similar empirical studies of the benefits of the arts to people reaching the ends of their lives, and throughout adulthood.[3] It does not lie within the scope of this chapter to explore each of these fully, so I propose to use the example of El Sistema to illustrate the arguments set forth in this debate.

Founded in Venezuela in 1975 by musician and political activist José Antonio Abreu, El Sistema was established to promote social change by bringing orchestral music-making to young people living in poverty. Its programme of intensive teaching and playing has spawned offshoots around the world, including In Harmony in the UK. The core values and pedagogy of these programmes, underpinned by a conception of the symphony orchestra as 'a society in miniature' (Bergman, Lindgren and Sæther, 2016), are based on social development, partnership, 'ensemble based instruction to cultivate socio-behavioural benefits', immersion, peer mentorship and a common goal to strive for 'musical excellence' (Osborne, McPherson, Faulkner, Davidson and Barrett, 2016). El Sistema is not without its critics, notably Baker, whose 2014 critique raised thought-provoking questions about the programme, in particular the neo-colonialist overtones of choosing exclusively Western classical music, hierarchical power structures and claims to bring about social justice (Baker, 2014). The performance, product-based orientation of the programme also raises questions about the potential for creativity for young people participating in the programmes. Bergman, Lindgren and Sæther's (2016) study interrogates the very notion of the symphony orchestra as a site for democracy. The authors explored socially constructed ideas of segregation within an El Sistema–inspired programme established in Sweden in 2010, through the twin lenses of universalist or separatist discourses on enabling integration, exploring how repertoire choices in particular might reinforce a universalist – 'we are all fundamentally the same and music brings us together' – or separatist – 'we are all individuals and our cultural musical heritage emphasises our individuality' – discourse.

Osborne, McPherson, Faulkner, Davidson and Barrett (2016) evaluated the impact of an El Sistema–inspired programme in two Australian schools whose socio-economic makeup represented high levels of generational poverty and refugee or immigrant populations. Assessments of the non-verbal reasoning, verbal and mathematical ability and psychosocial well-being of 92 students in Y3–6 were conducted after a 12-month programme. Although the results across the two schools were inconsistent, School 1 pupils demonstrated increased non-verbal reasoning and problem-solving abilities, and significantly higher levels of well-being in terms of personal happiness, self-esteem, sense of belonging and positive relationships with school. The inconsistent findings of this research, however, are an apt illustration of the challenges arising in proving the instrumental benefits of participating in the arts.

The El Sistema programme as a whole invites us to question whose arts are being offered, and with what aim; is performance or product the goal, or equipping young people with the tools to become participating, creative artists in whichever is their chosen art form? An experimental evaluation of El Sistema in Venezuela using RCTs in 16 music centres by Aleman et al., (2017, p.873) found that 'exposure to El Sistema might serve an important role as a preventive strategy to promote positive outcomes among disadvantaged children', but it is also necessary to wonder what the *musical* benefits might be, how many El Sistema participants carry on making music into adult life, and how the programme prepares or equips them for independent self-regulated music-making? The group approach to pedagogy favoured by the El Sistema model presents considerable challenges in terms of ensuring individual progression and engagement, and the focus on orchestral repertoire inevitably means that the participants' repertoire of music that they can play independently of others is more limited.

This programme gives just one example of how the arts may serve purposes beyond the artistic; it illustrates the challenges of this approach to arts education, and further raises the question, pertinent to an instrumental role for the arts in general, of how the 'extra-artistic' benefits of arts activities can be planned for. Planning for progression and skill development in a specific art form should be no different to any other discipline or subject area; predicting the impacts on learner well-being, for example, is much more complex.

Perspectives on the arts 'for their own sake'

> It is [the arts'] sensuous mode of operation which makes them stubbornly specific and differentiates them from other forms of enquiry into human existence. Arts make visible the cognitive life of the senses and the imagination.
>
> (Abbs, 2003, p.56)

Philosophical, sociological and psychological perspectives on the value and status of the arts abound, addressing variously their relationship to the individual, to society and to 'aesthetics'. These perspectives raise questions of process and product, creator and audience and aesthetic value, all of which impact on the pedagogical approaches and choices of arts educators, as well as upon arguments to justify their inclusion within formal education. Abbs' words above offer one possible view; others might argue for other 'stubbornly specific' qualities within the arts, and furthermore might suggest that visibility of the 'cognitive life of the senses and the imagination' is not restricted to the arts. A further challenge in discussing the arts 'for their own sake' is that many of the insights offered into their uniqueness relate to their capacity to facilitate communication, self-expression and the essence of what it is to exist in the world.

Eisner (2002) argued that it is the ways of thinking developed through learning in and about the arts which gives them their value and centrality to our environment and education. These 'distinctive forms of thinking' (p.8), such as 'learning to pay attention to the way in which form is configured' (p.9), the 'pursuit of surprise' (p.11) and the insight that 'not everything knowable can be articulated in propositional form' (p.12) are:

> relevant not only to what students do, they are relevant to virtually all aspects of what we do, from the design of curricula, to the practice of teaching, to the features of the environment in which students and teachers live.
>
> (Eisner, 2002, p.8)

These 'forms of thinking' may translate in practical terms into pedagogical approaches to planning, teaching and assessing the arts; educators' perceptions of the creative process become, therefore, key to their methods. Writing in 1934, Dewey described the relationship between art products, their creators and their audiences thus:

> When an art product once attains classic status, it somehow becomes isolated from the human conditions under which it was brought into being and from the human consequences it engenders in actual life-experience.
>
> (Dewey, 1934, p.1)

This perspective neatly encapsulates many of the issues surrounding arts education debated in this chapter and elsewhere. A view of creativity which privileges only the completely novel product – and, by extension, its potential economic value – and discounts the 'everyday' or 'little-c' creativity (Craft, 2001) risks undervaluing the developing creative skills of young children in favour of a product-orientated model of artistic creation such as that which El Sistema may promote. The 2014 English National Curriculum suggests that children must learn about – and perhaps aspire to be – 'the best in the musical canon', the 'great composers and musicians' and 'great artists, craft makers and designers' (DfE, 2013), a perspective which undermines a 'democratic' vision of children's everyday creativity (Banaji, Burn and Buckingham, 2010) where novelty may only be apparent to the creator (Beghetto and Kaufman, 2007; Craft, 2013). Isolation from the 'human conditions under which [the art product] was brought into being' (see Dewey above) devalues the role of the skills and capabilities associated with individual art forms and their creators, and separation from 'actual-life experience' suggests that the arts exist in a vacuum, away from the rest of life.

The experiential quality of the arts described by Dewey grants them a unique capacity to facilitate communication, collaboration, empathy and self-expression, as discussed above.

As Abbs (2003) describes, this capacity inspired in the past a somewhat unstructured approach to pedagogy in the arts, driven by psychology and sociology as opposed to aesthetics, and where:

the teacher was essentially the releaser of the child's innate creativity through acts of self-expression and self-discovery [...] all the collective resources were seen to reside in the natural self, not in the collective culture and not in the specific art form the teacher was claiming to teach. One released; one did not initiate or transmit.

(Abbs, 2003, pp.49–51)

Abbs adds to Dewey's conception the necessity of considering the specificity of different art forms and their associated resources, or skills. He later describes a short-lived 'new paradigm' of arts education, coinciding with wide-spread educational reform during the 1970s, crushed by the accountability and assessment culture, and during which:

the arts were not seen primarily as acts of self-expression and psychological adaptation, but as the fine vehicles of human understanding. At their best and most typical they are cognitive to the very core. In their double aspects, of making and of receiving, the arts are in pursuit of meaning.

(Abbs, 2003, p.56)

Van Boeckel (2015) builds on this conception of the arts as pursuing, or making, meaning for their producers and receivers, stating the need to shift the focus from product to process:

every human being can participate meaningfully in some form of artistic activity – if we sever the notion from the nouns 'artist' and 'artwork' and instead shift our attention to the act of creating and releasing something new and meaningful into the world. Rather than referring to art-making as exclusively coming forth from talent, skill or mastery, I want to bring to the fore its basic meaning as a human activity that consists of deliberately arranging items in a way that influences and affects one or more of the senses, emotions and intellect.

(van Boeckel, 2015, p.115)

This call to shift the focus from 'talent' is important; as argued above, valuing the everyday creativity of children is not a question of seeking out talent, an agenda which often comes to the fore in the English government's approach to funding arts education. Funding places for children to attend specialist arts schools through the Music and Dance Scheme[4] whilst the economic picture for arts education in England is so bleak, as discussed above, is a system that is not only open to abuse (Lightfoot, 2018) but suggests that the promotion of 'talent' is more important than the benefits of participation in the arts for all.

Haseman and Osterlind (2014), in their review of the 2013 OECD report *Art for Art's Sake*, provide a perspective which to some extent undermines the premise of this chapter, arguing that the question of whether the arts should be taught for their own sake or instrumentally is a 'false dichotomy':

> The primary 'justification' for the arts in schools is as subjects in their own right, for their 'intrinsic importance'. Of course. But have the authors constructed a false dichotomy here? Surely the power of aesthetic learning flows from the capacity of the arts to engage the experiential domain of affect while at the same time expand bodies of knowledge and improve cognitive, technical and creative skills. In rich arts education experiences, as with art, there is always more than one thing going on.
>
> (Haseman and Osterlind, 2014, p.412)

I agree with this point of view, but might add to it that the same could be said of any learning, or indeed living, experience; to break it down into discrete subjects or labelled experiences is often a reductive and ultimately impossible task.

Transdisciplinary approaches to arts education

Variously referred to as arts integration, arts infusion or cross-curricular approaches to the arts, combining the arts with one or more other curriculum subject is an approach which could be debated as fully as the central question of this chapter. Barnes (Barnes, 2012, 2015, 2018; Cremin and Barnes, 2014) has written and researched extensively in this area and provides thoughtful insights into curriculum design, planning and the contribution made by teachers' own interests and areas of expertise to cross-curricular teaching and learning. Again, there is not scope in this context for a full discussion of the issue, so I have chosen to focus on the emergent question of transdisciplinarity, drawing on evidence from a recent research project.

The term 'transdisciplinary' has become increasingly widespread, replacing 'interdisciplinary' and describing a true sense of dialogue between disciplines. As Tobias-Green (2017, p.338) states:

> transdisciplinary arts education differs from cross- and inter-disciplinary approaches. It is not about knowing or tolerating the representation of more than one branch of knowledge. Instead, rather than make boundaries permeable, malleable or consanguineous, it renders them both void and productive. By showing how knowledge systems are socially constructed they are laid open to inquiry, deconstruction and reconstruction [...] Art can be a site of challenge, discourse, expression, protest and compassion.

This perspective offers valuable insight on the example of El Sistema above; unpicking the social construction of knowledge systems, in the form of the symphony orchestra and its associated core repertoire, can enable discussion of the fundamental principles underlying the programme, opening up the possibility of modifying them to encompass a more musically and socially inclusive vision. According to Tobias-Green, an 'exploratory, interventionist and questioning pedagogy helps to promote a sense of transdisciplinarity' (ibid., p.343), a perspective echoed by Chappell et al. (2019, p.300):

> We see transdisciplinarity as rooted in asking questions beyond disciplines and (particularly in educational contexts) fuelled by students' and teachers' curiosity. It is in response to curious questions in education that transdisciplinarity emerges.

This pedagogy of 'curious questioning' lies at the root of a transdisciplinary approach. The project giving rise to the above statement involved action research with arts and science teachers to develop new ways of working in the context of an EU-funded Horizon 2020 project, the overarching goals of which are fundamentally economic: to produce 'world class science' within Europe.[5] This project illustrates how instrumental goals for the arts – to use pedagogies derived from the arts to increase student engagement in the sciences as part of a wider STE(A)M[6] agenda – might give rise to genuinely transdisciplinary teaching and learning, where aesthetic quality is not compromised. The final pieces made by lower secondary pupils as part of a project exploring the sea represented the end product of a genuine fusing of pedagogical approaches from the arts and the sciences, where teachers were able to consider both content and skill development from the perspective of dialogue between pedagogies.

Writing about this project through the lens of a post-human perspective on research and pedagogy, Chappell et al. (2019, p.315) conclude that:

> Rather than education being about the emergence through dialogue of unique human subjects, creative arts-science education is about the emergence of unique assemblages in which embodied teachers, students, ideas, and objects emerge.

The concept of the 'assemblage', derived from Barad (2007), proposes that the 'human' and the 'material' (or non-human) are equally significant in their relationship to one another; a post-human view of pedagogy suggests therefore that ideas and objects are equally as important as teachers and students in a dialogic exchange, giving rise to new pedagogical spaces moving beyond the conception of 'education-as-transmission' (Chappell et al., 2019, p.315).

To conclude, I return to my opening vignette, asking myself whether I could reframe this teaching and learning as transdisciplinary, whether its value as an instrumental opportunity to improve children's communication was sufficient, or whether it should have been reconceptualised as a purely musical activity, with the other learning becoming incidental. Again, I have no answer to this question, but in the spirit of reflective practice describe by Barnes (2018), I will continue to interrogate how my positionality as educator and academic might affect my perspectives on the debate I have discussed and on the future of arts education in this country and beyond. In terms of the long-term sustainability of arts education, perhaps choosing to protect the arts because of their instrumental benefits is a 'safer bet'. Recent funding and policy initiatives seem to suggest growing support for and understanding of their role, such as the decision to allocate funding for 'social prescribing' of the arts to address mental and physical health issues (Whitelaw et al., 2017). Arguments drawn from the economic potential of arts education seem often to omit to note, as Payne and Hall (2018) observe, that without high-quality arts education based on progressive skill development, the UK may not continue to produce the same number of successful artists, dancers, actors, filmmakers and other contributors to the cultural sector. As has been seen throughout this chapter, the two sides of the debate are inextricably bound together and their influence of the future of arts education is somewhat interdependent. What cannot be questioned though is that educators and policy makers must continue to fight to protect the arts in a local, national and international context; to some extent, the evidence they choose to draw on to aid that battle is up to them.

Summary

The debate addressed in this chapter – whether the arts should be protected within primary curricula due to their instrumental or intrinsic benefits – does not, as I have outlined, have a simple solution. Situated within the current educational landscape of accountability, budget constraints and rapidly reducing provision for the arts at secondary level, the role of primary teachers and leaders in protecting and promoting the arts becomes even more fundamental. Arguments from both sides of the debate can provide evidence and ammunition for the fight to advocate for the arts. The proven contribution of the arts to children's emotional, cognitive and social development, as well as the necessity, in a post-industrial, post-humanist society, for the skills of creativity, collaboration, empathy and communication fostered by the arts, provide powerful justifications for why they should be taught – whether by specialist or generalist teachers. Their unique and almost intangible status as channels of communication, representations of the cognitive in sensuous form, and in many ways the essence of what it is to be alive, is an equally valid justification for why they should be given equivalent curriculum status to other subjects and disciplines. Transdisciplinary approaches provide a further lens through which to view this debate; integrating pedagogical approaches, skills and content from multiple disciplines in dialogue with one another allow both the intrinsic and instrumental qualities of the arts to flourish. Ultimately, for the arts to have a viable future within primary schooling systems, individual educators and leaders of education must form their own perspectives on why they matter; the fundamental issue is to realise that they do.

Questions for reflection

How might planning from an 'instrumental' or 'intrinsic' perspective look different?

What might transdisciplinarity look like in your own practice?

What might be the implications for your future professional development of your positionality within this debate?

Notes

1 The CLA defines 'cultural learning' as 'an active engagement with the creation of our arts and heritage'. https://culturallearningalliance.org.uk/about-us/cultural-learning-key-terms-and-definitions/.

2 Examples include Cooper et al. (2018) for a summary of the benefits of the arts; Hallam (2017) for a research synthesis of the impact of making music on aural perception and language skills; Hallam (2015) for a research synthesis of the impact of making music on the intellectual, social and personal development of children and young people; Maury and Rickard (2016) on the possible contribution of group singing to wellbeing from an evolutionary perspective.

3 Examples include Creech, Hallam, Varvarigou and McQueen (2013) and Hallam, Creech and Varvarigou (2017) on the value of music in the lives of older adults; Pitts (2017) on fostering lifelong engagement in music; and Veblen (2012) on formal and informal learning in adult education contexts.

4 https://www.gov.uk/music-dance-scheme.

5 https://ec.europa.eu/programmes/horizon2020/en/what-horizon-2020.

6 Science, Technology, (Arts), Engineering and Maths.

Further reading and resources

Chappell, K. A., Pender, T. Swinford, E. & Ford, K. (2016) 'Making and being made: Wise humanising creativity in interdisciplinary early years arts education', *International Journal of Early Years Education*, 24(3): 254–278.

Drawing on extensive practitioner and researcher work in early years settings, this paper uses the lens of Wise Humanising Creativity to explore arts and interdisciplinary practice, with implications for both early years settings and primary education more broadly.

Colucci-Gray, L., Burnard, P., Davies, R. & Stuart Gray, D. (2017) *Reviewing the potential and challenges of developing STEAM education through creative pedagogies for 21ˢᵗ century learning: How can school curricula be broadened towards a more responsive, dynamic and inclusive form of education*. British Association for Research in Education (BERA)

This recent and comprehensive review of issues arising from the move from STEM to STEAM raises some interesting questions for school curriculum designers, at both primary and secondary level.

www.nsead.org.

The National Society for Education in Art and Design (NSEAD)'s website holds a wealth of research and resources related to the teaching of Art and Design in formal and non-formal education settings, including a searchable database of publications.

References

Abbs, P. (2003) *Against the Flow: Education, the Arts and Postmodern Culture*, Abingdon and New York: Routledge.

Aleman, X., Duryea, S., Guerra, N. G., McEwan, P. J., Munoz, R., Stampini, M. & Williamson, A. A. (2017) 'The effects of musical training on child development: A randomized trial of el Sistema in Venezuela', *Prevention Science : the Official Journal of the Society for Prevention Research*, 18(7): 865–878.

Associated Board of the Royal Schools of Music (2014), *Making Music: Teaching, Learning and Playing in the UK*. London: ABRSM

Baker, G. (2014) *El Sistema: Orchestrating Venezuela's Youth*, Oxford: Oxford University Press.

Banaji, S., Burn, A. & Buckingham, D. (2010) *The Rhetorics of Creativity* (2nd ed.), London: Arts Council England.

Barad, K. (2007) *Meeting the Universe Halfway: Quantum Physics and the Entanglement of Matter and Meaning*, Durham and London: Duke University Press.

Barnes, J. (2012) 'Creativity and autonomy for music in a creative and cross-curriculum'. In: Philpott, C. & Spruce, G. (Eds.), *Debates in Music Teaching*, London: Routledge.

Barnes, J. (2015), *Cross-Curricular Learning 3–14*, London: SAGE.

Barnes, J. (2018) *Applying Cross-Curricular Approaches Creatively*, London: Routledge.

Beghetto, R. A. & Kaufman, J. C. (2007) 'Toward a broader conception of creativity: A case for "mini-c" creativity', *Psychology of Aesthetics, Creativity, and the Arts*, 1(2): 73–79.

Bergman, Å., Lindgren, M. & Sæther, E. (2016) 'Struggling for integration: Universalist and separatist discourses within el Sistema Sweden', *Music Education Research*, 18(4): 364–375.

Brill, F., Grayson, H., Kuhn, L., O'Donnell, S. & National Foundation for Educational Research (2018) *What Impact Does Accountability Have on Curriculum, Standards and Engagement in Education? A Literature Review*, National Foundation for Educational Research, Slough: National Foundation for Educational Research.

Chappell, K., Hetherington, L., Keene, Ruck, Wren, H., Alexopoulos, H., Ben-Horin, A. O. & Bogner, F. X. (2019) 'Dialogue and materiality/embodiment in science|arts creative pedagogy: Their role and manifestation', *Thinking Skills and Creativity*, 31: 296–322.

Chappell, K. A., Pender, T., Swinford, E. & Ford, K. (2016) 'Making and being made: Wise humanising creativity in interdisciplinary early years arts education', *International Journal of Early Years Education*, 24(3): 254–278.

Chen-Hafteck, L. & Mang, E. (2018) 'Music and language in early childhood development and learning'. In: McPherson, G. E. & Welch, G. F. (Eds.), *Music Learning and Teaching in Infancy, Early Childhood and Adolescence: An Oxford Handbook of Music Education*, New York: Oxford University Press.

Cooper, B., Bailey, O., Media, K. M., Manager, C. & Khan, R. (2018) *Primary Colours: The Decline of Arts Education in Primary Schools and How It Can Be Reversed*. London: Fabian Society.

Craft, A. (2001) 'Little c creativity'. In: Craft, A., Jeffrey, B. & Leibling, M. (Eds.), *Creativity in Education*, London and New York: Continuum.

Craft, A. (2013) 'Childhood, possibility thinking and wise, humanising educational futures', *International Journal of Educational Research*, 61: 126–134.

Creech, A., Hallam, S., Varvarigou, M. & McQueen, H. (2013) 'The power of music in the lives of older adults', *Research Studies in Music Education*, 35(1): 87–102.

Cremin, T. & Barnes, J. (2014) 'Creativity and creative teaching and learning'. In: Arthur, J. & Cremin, T. (Eds.), *Learning to Teach in the Primary School*, Abingdon and New York: Routledge.

Cultural Learning Alliance (2017a) *Imagine Nation: The Value of Cultural Education.* London: Cultural Learning Alliance.

Cultural Learning Alliance (2017b) *Key Research Findings: The Case for Cultural Learning.* Available at: https://www.culturallearningalliance.org.uk/images/uploads/CLA_key_findings_2017.pdf.

Dewey, J. (1934) *Art as Experience*, New York: Penguin.

Department for Education (2013) Music Programme of Study: Key Stages One and Two. Available at: https://assets.publishing.service.gov.uk/government/upl oads/system/uploads/attachment_data/file/239037/PRIMARY_national_curri culum_-_Music.pdf

Durham University (2019) Available at: https://www.dur.ac.uk/creativitycommission/.

Eisner, E. W. (2002) 'What can education learn from the arts about the practice of education?' *Journal of Curriculum and Supervision*, 18(1): 4–16.

Hallam, S. (2015) *The Power of Music: A Research Synthesis of the Impact of Actively Making Music on the Intellectual, Social and Personal Development of Children and Young People.* London: iMerc.

Hallam, S. (2017) 'The impact of making music on aural perception and language skills: A research synthesis', *London Review of Education*, 15(3), 388–406.

Hallam, S., Creech, A. & Varvarigou, M. (2017) 'Well-being and music leisure activities through the lifespan'. In: Mantie, R. & Smith, G. D. (Eds.), *The Oxford Handbook of Music Making and Leisure* (Vol. 1), Oxford: Oxford University Press.

Haseman, B. & Osterlind, E. (2014) 'A lost opportunity: A review of art for art's sake? The impact of arts education', *Research in Drama Education: the Journal of Applied Theatre and Performance*, 19(4): 409–413.

Henley, D. (2011) *The Importance of Music: A National Plan for Music Education*, London: Department for Education.

Hennessy, S. (2018) 'Improving Primary teaching: Minding the gap'. In: McPherson, G. E. & Welch, G. F. (Eds.), *Music and Music Education in People's Lives*, New York: Oxford University Press.

Johnes, R. (2017) *Entries to Arts Subjects at Key Stage 4.* London: Education Policy Institute.

Knight, A. & Rabon, P. (2017) 'Music for Speech and Language development in early childhood populations', *Music Therapy Perspectives*, 35(2): 124–130.

Lightfoot, L. (2018) *Music School Grants for Poor Students Going to 'Comfortable Middle Class'.* Available at: https://www.theguardian.com/education/2018 /oct/02/music-school   grants-poor-middle-class-yehudi-menuhin-chethams (Accessed on 12.04.2019).

Matarasso, F. (2019) *A Restless Art*, London: Calouste Gulbenkian Foundation.

Maury, S. & Rickard, N. (2016) 'Wellbeing in the classroom: How an evolutionary perspective on human musicality can inform music education,', *Australian Journal of Music Education*, 3(1): 3–15.

National Advisory Committee on Creative and Cultural Education (NACCCE) (1999) *All Our Futures*. London: DfEE.

NSEAD (2016) *The National Society for Education in Art and Design Survey Report 2015 16*. Available at: www.gov.uk/government/upl oads/syste m/upl oads/attac hment_data /file /415874/Go vernm ent Response_to_the_Workload_Challenge.

Ofsted (2018) *Chief Inspector Sets Out Vision for New Education Inspection Framework*. Available at: https://www.gov.uk/government/news/chief-inspector-sets-out-v ision-for-new education-inspection-framework (Accessed on 08.04.2019).

Ofsted (2019) *Education Inspection Framework: Draft for Consultation*. Available at: https://www.gov.uk/government/publications/education-inspection-framew ork-draft-for consultation (Accessed on 08.04.2019).

Osborne, M. S., McPherson, G. E., Faulkner, R., Davidson, J. W. & Barrett, M. S. (2016) 'Exploring the academic and psychosocial impact of el Sistema-inspired music programs within two low socio-economic schools', *Music Education Research*, 18(2): 156–175.

Parameshwaran, M. & Thomson, D. (2015) 'The impact of accountability reforms on the Key Stage 4 curriculum: How have changes to school and college Performance Tables affected pupil access to qualifications and subjects in secondary schools in England?', *London Review of Education*, 13(2): 157–173.

Paton, G. (2014) 'Nicky Morgan: Pupils "held back" by overemphasis on arts', *The Telegraph*. Available at: https://www.telegraph.co.uk/education/educationnew s/11221081/Nicky   Morgan-pupils-held-back-by-overemphasis-on-arts.html (Accessed on 25.04.2019).

Payne, R., & Hall, E. (2018). The NSEAD survey report 2015–16: political reflections from two art and design educators. International Journal of Art & Design Education, 37(2), 167–176.

Pitts, S. E. (2016) 'Music, language and learning: Investigating the impact of a music workshop project in four English early years settings', *International Journal of Education and the Arts*, 17: 20.

Pitts, S. E. (2017) 'What is music education for? Understanding and fostering routes into lifelong musical engagement', *Music Education Research*, 19(2): 160–168.

Savage, J. & Barnard, D. (2019) *The State of Play: A review of Music Education in England 2019*. Available at: https://www.musiciansunion.org.uk/StateOfPlay.

Sharda, M., Tuerk, C., Chowdhury, R. Jamey, Foster, K., Custo-Blanch, N., Hyde, M. (2018) 'Music improves social communication and auditory–motor connectivity in children with autism', *Translational Psychiatry*, 8(1): 231.

The National Curriculum in England Framework Document (2013) Available at: https://assets.publishing.service.gov.uk/government/uploads/system/upload s/attachment_dat /file/210969/NC_framework_document_-_FINAL.pdf.

The National Society for Education in Art and Design (2019) Available at: www .nsead.org.

The Sound of the Next Generation: A Comprehensive Review of Children and Young People's Relationship with Music (2019) Available at: https://www.youthmusic.or g.uk/sites/default/files/PDFs/The, Sound of the Next Generation.pdf.

Tobias-Green, K. (2017) 'Challenging the cult of normalcy: Arts education and transdicplinary practices', *Visual Inquiry: Learning and Teaching Art*, 6(3): 335–346.

van Boeckel, J. (2015) 'Angels talking back and new organs of perception: Art-making and intentionality in nature experience', *Visual Inquiry*, 4(2): 111–122.

Veblen, K. K. (2012) 'Adult musical learning in formal, nonformal, and informal contexts'. In: Mcpherson, G. E. & Welch, G. F. (Eds.), *Oxford Handbook of Music Education*, New York: Oxford University Press.

Warwick Commission (2015) 'Enriching Britain: Culture, creativity and growth'. Available at: http://www2.warwick.ac.uk/research/warwickcommission/futureculture/finalreport/warwick commission_report_2015.pdf (Accessed on 27.11.2015).

Whitelaw, S., Thirlwall, C., Morrison, A., Osborne, J., Tattum, L. & Walker, S. (2017) 'Developing and implementing a social prescribing initiative in primary care: Insights into the possibility of normalisation and sustainability from a UK case study', *Primary Health Care Research and Development*, 18(2): 112–121.

Winner, E., Goldstein, T. R. & Vincent-Lancrin, S. (2013) *Art for Art's Sake?: The Impact of Arts, Education, Educational Research and Innovation, Books Abroad* (Vol. 10). Paris: OECD Publishing.

Youth Music & Ipsos MORI (2019) The Sounds of the Next Generation: A Comprehensive review of children and young people's relationship with music. Available at: https://www.youthmusic.org.uk/sound-of-the-next-generation

Chapter 9

The place of foreign languages in the primary school

Louise Pagden

> Those who know nothing of foreign languages know nothing of their own.
> Johann Wolfgang von Goethe

Introduction

The notion of foreign languages in the primary classroom has been long debated, but it is only in the last five years that it has finally become part of the statutory curriculum. However, whilst for many people this has been considered a forward step, new questions arise as the effective implementation of foreign languages is tackled. This chapter will briefly outline the historical and cultural context in which foreign languages resides, as well as considering the challenges in this area. The chapter will go on to consider key questions in this field, including whether younger is really better; if all schools should teach the same language and, if so, who is best placed to teach the language; and if a language awareness programme would provide a more secure foundation for language learning.

The historical and cultural context of foreign languages in the primary school

Whilst languages are a recent addition to the primary National Curriculum (DfE, 2013), the importance of the subject for early learners has long been under discussion. Ever since the Languages Project in the 1960s (funded by the Nuffield Foundation and Schools Council), people have attempted to introduce the subject to primary schools. In this initiative, children between the ages of 8 and 11 were taught French. The impact on their progress (and attitudes towards language learning) at secondary school were then evaluated. However, despite significant investment, there was little or no evidence of progress beyond that made by children who had had no prior language instruction. The Nuffield Foundation (online) state that,

> The British government's French pilot scheme was troubled by over-rapid expansion. It turned out that for the majority of schools there were other

priorities for their limited resources, and the lack of continuity between primary and secondary schools meant that pupils were not able to build on what they had already achieved in French.

Unfortunately, 50 years later, the country seems to be in a similar position.

Whilst the languages project of the 1960s and 1970s may not have had the impact hoped for, many people kept the flame burning for the place of languages in the primary curriculum. By 2000, the Nuffield Foundation again commissioned a review of languages in the UK. In the introduction, Trevor MacDonald and John Boyd (the chairmen of the review) stated,

> Capability in other languages – a much broader range than hitherto and in greater depth – is crucially important for a flourishing UK... Educational provision is fragmented, achievement poorly measured, continuity not very evident. In the language of our time, there is a lack of joined-up thinking.
>
> (The Nuffield Foundation, 2000, p.5)

Again, the country appeared to be haunted by the same issues as 30 years earlier, ones which continue to persist today. One of the many recommendations from the report was that the government appoint a languages 'supremo' and that they 'Drive forward a national strategy. The government should establish a national strategy for developing capability in languages in the UK and a system capable of supporting such a strategy.' The following year a National Languages steering group was set up and the 'Languages for All: Languages for Life' national languages strategy was published (DfES, 2002).

Whilst the remit of the languages strategy was to enable a coherent and 'joined up' approach to life-long language learning, one of the key aims of the vision was,

> To improve teaching and learning of languages, including delivering an entitlement to language learning for pupils at Key Stage 2, making the most of e-learning and ensuring that opportunity to learn languages has a key place in the transformed secondary school of the future.
>
> (DfES, 2002, p.5)

The strategy endeavoured to provide all children in Key Stage 2 with an *entitlement* to learn languages, although it did not ever go so far as to make this a statutory part of the curriculum. Nonetheless, in 2005, the Key Stage 2 framework for languages was developed and this enabled a clear progression in literacy, oracy and intercultural understanding skills, as well as pupils developing their knowledge and understanding of knowledge about language and language learning skills. Across the country, there was significant investment in the training of pre-service and qualified teachers, as well as investment in the resourcing of this 'new' subject. Whilst the initiative continued to be led by a small but very committed group of individuals, teaching in a range of languages developed across the country.

For a period of time, it appeared that languages would form part of the new National Curriculum emanating from the Rose review. In this version of the curriculum, languages were included as an integral part of one of the six areas of learning: 'Understanding English, communication and languages'. Rose (DCSF, 2009) hoped that this would enable teachers and pupils to exploit the links between English and the chosen language(s). Sadly, in 2010, in the 'wash-up' prior to the general election, the Rose curriculum was scrapped, along with the hopes that languages might finally form part of children's daily diet of learning.

Following a period of curriculum review, a new curriculum was finally published by the coalition government in 2013. In this new, knowledge-based curriculum, Michael Gove promised to rid the curriculum of 'vapid happy talk' and ensure pupils had a structured 'stock of knowledge' (Coughlan, 2013). Whilst there was criticism of the narrowness of the new curriculum, it did, for the first time ever, contain a statutory programme of study for languages at Key Stage 2. Programmes of study in subjects other than the core subjects were to be much shorter to allow for the maximum level of innovation at school level for the development of content in these areas. Teachers were to be given freedom to develop more innovative and effective approaches to teaching (Holmes and Myles, 2019, p.5). However, for some teachers, the reduced content (when compared to the Key Stage 2 framework for languages) was disabling – especially people who were expected to teach this subject without a strong subject knowledge themselves.

Whilst the programme of study for foreign languages was succinct, the curriculum was also very ambitious: 'The teaching should enable pupils to express their ideas and thoughts in another language and to understand and respond to its speakers, both in speech and in writing'. The purpose goes on to state, 'It should also provide opportunities for them to communicate for practical purposes, learn new ways of thinking and read great literature in the original language.' Whilst these were exciting times for the passionate and committed linguists, the content of the curriculum intimidated many teachers who did not have a background in languages. In addition to learning a language in its own right, a further aim of the National Curriculum was to 'establish the foundations of learning how to learn a language and enable pupils to develop an appreciation of how language works in addition to making substantial progress in one language' (DFE, 2013, p.193).

In September 2018, the first cohort of pupils who had studied a foreign language at primary school reached secondary school; this has provided a yard stick to begin to understand the impact that these four years of language learning may have.

Current context

According to Holmes and Myles (2019) and *Language Trends* (Tinsley and Doležal, 2018; Tinsley, 2018), the majority of primary schools are responding to statutory requirements to introduce a language at Key Stage 2. However, they recognise that progress towards full implementation is uneven across the country:

Around 80% of schools allocate on average between 30 minutes and up to one hour per week for language learning, although comments indicate that this is often irregular or eroded by other priorities.

(Tinsley and Doležal, 2018, p.12)

It is worth noting, also, that these figures are well below the several hours per week offered in many countries (European Commission, 2012; OECD, 2014a).

Whilst *Language Trends* is often regarded as *the* authority on the current situation of language learning, it should be noted that only 776 primary schools out of 24,281 actually completed the survey in 2019; approximately 3% of England's primary schools (this was the highest number of schools to complete the survey in recent years). It is possible to assume that those who completed this survey are more engaged with the teaching of foreign languages than those who did not respond. The 80% quoted in *Language Trends* actually represents 620 schools or 2.6% of English primary schools. Nonetheless, whilst the picture in England may not be as rosy as they would like to suggest, Holmes and Myles (2019, p.6) recognise that it is 'improbable that policy requirements will be fully met without further central guidance and support in a number of key areas'.

Times are changing?

Until recently, the assessment regime in primary schools has been the tail which wags the curriculum dog. Given the significance which has been placed on examined results, this has been to the detriment of the broader curriculum (Pells, 2017). However, the new Ofsted Framework (2018) attempts to redress the balance and puts the wider curriculum at the heart of the inspection process (Holmes and Myles, 2019). Amanda Spielman (Ofsted Chief Inspector), in the review of the inspection process, noted that the team 'saw curriculum narrowing, especially in upper Key Stage 2, with lessons disproportionately focused on English and mathematics' (Spielman, 2018a). In an effort to counteract the narrowed curriculum and education, Spielman stated in a speech to the National Association of Headteachers:

Our central aim is to encourage a focus on the substance of education... One aspect of this is to restore Ofsted's former focus on curriculum, in its proper place at the centre of education... We want to look at what children are being taught; how well it is being taught; and how effectively it is setting them up to succeed at the next stage of their lives.

(Spielman, 2019, online)

The renewed inspection focus on the broad curriculum should, therefore, mean a higher status for subjects other than English and mathematics, including foreign languages (Holmes and Myles, 2019). Nonetheless, foreign languages have rarely featured in the inspection process nor in inspection reports since the introduction of the statutory requirement for children in Key Stage 2 to learn a language. Holmes and Myles, in their White Paper for primary languages, state that,

> If the subject is to be taken seriously, primary languages must feature more prominently in the Ofsted inspection process from September 2019. This ... should incentivise schools to develop more detailed planning of the primary languages curriculum to ensure depth and breadth of learning and clear progression.
>
> (2019, p.10)

This view echoes the recommendation which Rose (DCSF, 2009) made ten years earlier.

The earlier, the better?

Early language learning policy has often been premised on the assumption that the earlier children embark on language learning, the better their progress will be. Tony Blair (the then–Prime Minister) communicated this view in 1999: 'Everyone knows that with languages, the earlier you start, the easier they are'. This was the initial thesis on which the 1960s–70s Languages Project rested. Likewise, the Languages Strategy (DfES, 2002, p.10) was also premised upon the benefits of early language learning: 'If a child's talent and natural interest in languages is to flourish, early language learning opportunities need to be provided, and their aptitude needs to be tapped into at the earliest opportunity when they are most receptive'.

The perceived benefits of early language learning have their theoretical foundations in the 'Critical Period Hypothesis'. This hypothesis suggests that children are born with an innate language faculty which deteriorates with age. Therefore, it is important to tap into these innate mechanisms before the critical age when they disappear (Myles, 2017). Whilst this view is debated, evidence shows that children's neural plasticity reduces over childhood, thus critical periods for learning specific skills can come and go during this time. For example, Mundkar (2005) suggests that the critical period for *natural* language learning is up until the age of 6 (Mundkar, 2005, p.855). However, it is also suggested that the period in middle childhood (between approximately 6 and 12 years of age) plays an equally important period of time for language learning where implicit language learning through immersion is supported by carefully planned opportunities for the application of these new skills and knowledge (Muñoz, 2006; Lindgren and Muñoz, 2013). Hence the importance of pedagogical approaches (and policy) being effectively underpinned by the research in this area.

However, research has shown that young classroom learners do not have an advantage over older learners in terms of linguistic development, unless input is plentiful (Holmes and Myles, 2019). Nonetheless, when taught in a consistent, systematic and engaging way, young classroom learners can and do make linguistic progress commensurate with the amount of input (Holmes and Myles, 2019; Muñoz, 2006).

Other, more emotional factors also come into play in later years, such as our willingness to speak out in front of a group and to make mistakes and take risks, which often reduces with age (Guz and Tetiurka, 2016; Muñoz, 2006). Learners become more self-aware and less likely to have the confidence to put the language into practice, speak new vocabulary aloud and try out new learning in grammar construction (Hawkins, 2005). Nonetheless, while children are still primarily driven by emotional engagement and intrinsic motivation, they are increasingly capable of concentration and sustained attention and begin to be motivated by more goal-orientated activities (Holmes and Myles, 2019, p.10); these can become increasingly cognitively and linguistically challenging (Muñoz, 2006).

What is questionable is whether early language learning will support successful language learning and foster a life-long love of languages. In a systematic literature review of early language learning, Singleton concluded (1989, p.137), 'The available evidence does not consistently support the hypothesis that younger second language learners are globally more efficient and successful than older learners'. Often the arguments in support of early language learning largely focus on oral communication. Whilst spoken language is a key skill, the ability to read, write and listen effectively are all skills which are best supported by having first developed in our mother tongue. Underpinning these skills are a sound knowledge of the concept of 'grammar' (and a base understanding of grammar in our first language), which the Key Stage 2 framework described as part of 'knowledge about language', as well as language learning strategies. As Myles (2017) notes, older children are able to use their more developed cognitive capabilities and literacy skills to support their learning; something which younger children are not yet able to do.

Another question surrounding early language learning is whether early investment translates into long-term progression or commitment to language learning. In Gamble and Smalley's (1975) article which critiqued the NFER evaluation of the Language Project in the 1960s–70s, they noted that the project evaluation had been conducted on a very small group of pupils. They highlighted the high drop-out of those pupils participating in school language learning. Hawkins' (2005) article also considers whether the early investment in languages at primary school in the NFER project of the 1960s and 1970s impacted on the longevity of their relationship with languages. He, too, draws attention to the high attrition rate and concludes that, 'It certainly does not suggest that early starting by itself will avert early dropout' (Hawkins, 2005, p.16). Significantly, Blondin et al. (1998) highlight that research findings into the lack of long-term benefits of an early start can, at least in part, be attributed to a lack of continuity in teaching across phases. However, Courtney (2014) and Graham et al. (2014) (contrary to previous transition studies) both demonstrated that learners made progress across transition from Key Stage 2 to 3.

Many scholars (Cable et al., 2010; Martin, 2012; Holmes and Myles, 2019) believe that the place of foreign languages in the statutory National Curriculum can only be a good thing. The next question, therefore, is who is best placed to teach this subject?

Who is best placed to teach foreign languages?

Language Trends and Doležal (2018) suggested that, of those surveyed, 62% of language teaching is taught by the class teacher. However, the level of language proficiency of these teachers is varied and this could be attributed to recent government policy. Since the implementation of the Languages Strategy, language learning is only compulsory until Key Stage 3. Despite government aims for over 90% of young people to study a language to age 16, 'over the past five years, there has been a 19% reduction in entries for GCSE languages' (Tinsley and Doležal, 2018, p.3; drawing on Department for Education, GCSE and equivalent results in England 2017–18 [revised]). In 2018 only 46% of pupils took a language to Key Stage 4 (Jeffreys, 2019), with an all-time low of 40% of pupils taking a language at GCSE in 2011. Consequently, anyone who was at secondary school between 2005 and 2014 would have only had three years of *compulsory* language learning. It is highly likely, therefore, that a primary teacher may have stopped learning a language at 14 and only have a rudimentary grasp of core language skills. In Tinsley's (2019) survey, 16% of participants had a language level below GCSE.

Unsurprisingly, Tinsley (2019, p.6) goes on to note,

> Schools with higher attainment levels (percentage of pupils reaching the expected standard in reading, writing and maths), are statistically more likely to employ higher qualified staff to teach languages, i.e. with an A level or above in the language they are teaching.

This poses an important challenge for the continuing professional development, in both pedagogy and subject knowledge, of those who teach this subject.

The majority of people entering the teaching profession will embark on a one-year postgraduate course, with a minority undertaking a three- or four-year undergraduate course. In the Carter review of initial teacher education (Carter, 2015), it was noted that one-year Initial Teacher Training programmes are too short to fully address subject knowledge. He recommended that schools, therefore, should include subject knowledge as an essential element of professional development, particularly in the NQT year and for early career practitioners. Carter made further recommendations about Continuing Professional Development, proposing that the DfE should make funded in-service subject knowledge enhancement courses available for primary teachers to access as professional development – particularly in subjects such as foreign languages. At present, there are few funded opportunities for professional development in foreign languages. Tinsley (2019) notes that participation in professional development for languages is low. Only one in five schools where classroom teachers are responsible for language teaching have provided these teachers with language-specific CPD in the past year.

However, despite issues surrounding subject knowledge for many primary teachers, these professionals are experts in the age-phase they teach and the associated pedagogy. Primary teachers know their class well and are able to make connections between other areas of the curriculum and learning which the children may be undertaking. This 'specialist' knowledge should not be underestimated, nor overlooked. Nonetheless, teachers with less developed subject knowledge are more likely to make mistakes, stick to nouns and adjectives (without teaching children key elements of grammatical knowledge, which is vital for independent language construction) and may even communicate a fear or dislike of languages to children. At worst, languages may not occur in the primary classroom at all. In McLachan's (2009) research, she explored staff views on the teaching of primary foreign languages. Her findings suggested that not everyone perceives the teaching of modern foreign languages as important. This sentiment is echoed in Legg's (2013) research: 40% of the participants in her study explained that they felt languages as a subject was less important than other areas of the curriculum. They suggested that many pupils struggle to master their first language and that these pupils would need to gain a better understanding of English before learning a new language.

Many schools and organisations favour specialist teachers of languages, for whom this is their key area of focus. In Tinsley's (2019, p.5) *Language Trends* survey,

> 46% of schools employ language specialists, whether as peripatetic teachers or staff members... One third of schools rely entirely on specialists to provide language teaching, while in a further 13% of schools, specialist language teachers work in conjunction with class teachers.

Whilst these teachers have been referred to as the 'Spanish and Vanish' teacher or 'Russian and rush out', teachers with a good grasp of subject knowledge have a lot to offer. Specialist teachers of language are able to pre-empt and understand where misconceptions arise (Muij et al., 2005; Driscoll et al., 2013) and their planning for learning will demonstrate a deep subject knowledge which will enable children to make connections in their language learning (Driscoll, 2014).

Language teachers will know why a sentence is constructed in a certain way and will be able to support children to apply this in other contexts; they will be able to use their excellent subject knowledge to support children's progression. Not only that, their love for the subject may engender this in their pupils. Perhaps unsurprisingly in Cable et al.'s (2010) study, in schools where there was a specialist teacher, there was evidence of increased gains in pupil attainment; conversely, children in the schools with the lowest performance were taught by those with the least developed subject knowledge, pedagogical knowledge and experience. In summary, specialist teachers offer, as Driscoll (2014, p.263) notes, 'a rich source of learning which cannot be replaced by a commercially produced resource'.

Nonetheless, specialist teachers are not without their own set of challenges. Occasionally, specialist teachers are not familiar with the pedagogical practices of the primary classroom and consequently this can reduce children's engagement and progression (Driscoll, 2014). There is also an issue with long-term sustainability, as any expertise stays with the teacher should the teacher leave. It might be argued that, in the best-case scenarios, specialist teachers work alongside class teachers to develop their confidence and subject knowledge (this is the case in 13% of schools surveyed in *Language Trends*, 2019); however in Cable et al.'s (2010) study, most of these class teachers leave the room as soon as the specialist is present. This clearly, as both Cable et al. and Wade et al. (2009) note, reduces the possibility of both modelling and coaching.

It is clear that the continued development of teachers' knowledge and skills is vital if foreign languages are to be a subject where children make progress. Whilst the ideal candidates for teaching languages in the primary school are rare, a teacher who knows the child, knows how to teach the child, knows the subject and knows how to teach it will arguably provide the best conditions for success.

Should all schools teach the same language?

The current situation of languages taught in English primary schools is varied: French is taught in 75% of primary schools, and Spanish in 29% (the total does not reach 100% as some schools teach more than one language). Very few schools teach other languages, with German taught in 5% of schools, Chinese in 3%, Latin in 2% and other languages in 1% or fewer schools in each case. Whilst the percentages for most languages have stayed relatively static, Spanish has increased from 16% in 2012 (Tinsley, 2019) making it one of the fastest-growing foreign languages in England. The reasons for these choices are largely due to staff expertise and availability of suitable resources, or due to the primary school being led by the actions of the local secondary school (Cable et al., 2010).

Whilst the initial trials in foreign languages all involved the teaching of French (for example, the Pilot Scheme for the Teaching of French in primary schools – see Nuffield [online] and Burstall [1977] for further information), the programme of study in the National Curriculum allows schools to teach whichever language they feel is most appropriate: 'Teaching may be of any modern or ancient foreign language and should focus on enabling pupils to make substantial progress in one language' (DfE, 2013, p.194). The Languages Strategy also did not stipulate which language(s) should be taught at primary level; indeed, Lord Dearing, in the 2007 Languages Review (DfES, 2007a, p.9) stressed the importance of widening the range of languages that can be offered in primary school beyond French (Barton, Bragg and Serratrice, 2009, p.145).

The Nuffield Foundation (2000, p.6) suggested that,

> The UK needs competence in many languages – not just French – but the education system is not geared to achieve this. Schools and colleges do not provide an adequate range of languages and levels of competence for the future. Curricular, financial and staffing pressures mean that we teach a narrowing range of languages, at a time when we should be doing the opposite.

They found that there was a firm belief in society that English is no longer enough in today's global community; but paradoxically, while languages were perceived as important, schools were failing to offer a range of languages (Nuffield Foundation, 2000) and there was a great need for more language teachers.

However, set amongst the backdrop of support for language diversity, transition from Key Stage 2 to 3 has become highly problematic. Within feeder schools to a secondary school there is often a diversity of languages represented, and when these pupils arrive in their new school they will be placed with children from a variety of schools, representing a variety of languages and experiences (Courtney, 2017). It is almost impossible, therefore, for the language teacher to accommodate all of these different levels of expertise in the language, from no exposure to the foreign language to four years of structured language learning. Sadly, teachers faced with this variety may start from the beginning again (Driscoll, Jones and Macrory, 2004).

In their White Paper, Holmes and Myles (2019) suggest that to raise standards in language proficiency in line with other major jurisdictions, certain strategic decisions need to be addressed to facilitate improved cross-phase learning and teaching and a smooth transition between Key Stage 2 and 3. These strategic decisions include: determining a time allocation to language teaching; an agreement of core content; planning for progression; and determining age-related expectations for each Key Stage. Significantly for this discussion, they also stress the importance of a strategic decision surrounding the choice of language to be taught, albeit at a local level.

Whilst on one level, legislating the language choice for primary schools may result in a reduction of language diversity, there are several advantages for this model. Investment in subject knowledge enhancement at pre-service and in-service training could be targeted. By teaching just one language, training could be clearly focussed; entry requirements could include a qualification in the language; and schools would ensure that children transferring from another primary school could have a similar experience. Finally, as children transition to secondary school, their prior learning could be built upon, rather than children starting language learning again, thus risking demotivating the pupils. Diversification of languages should not be jettisoned outright, however; instead, perhaps this could be for the remit of secondary schools where teachers are more likely to have the expertise to approach this effectively.

Whilst it may appear sensible to advocate just one foreign language to enhance both the training and expertise of teachers, support the progression of learners and avoid transition issues, there may be an alternative approach to language teaching that could be considered.

Could a language awareness programme provide a more secure foundation for language learning?

It has long been debated whether the primary years should actually provide a foundation for understanding the workings of language, as opposed to progression in just one language. In the Key Stage 2 Framework for Languages (DCFS, 2005), alongside oracy, literacy and intercultural understanding, two key strands provided children with key workings of language: knowledge about language (understanding basic grammatical structures and concepts which are common to other languages) and language learning strategies (which can apply to the learning of any language). No matter what languages a child went on to learn, these two 'cross cutting' strands provided a grounding in fundamental skills and knowledge related to foreign language learning per se. Given the issues surrounding both the choice of language and the depth of subject knowledge of some primary teachers, a clearly structured language awareness programme may go some way to addressing this.

Ultimately the question of whether children should learn one language or embark on a language awareness programme comes down to the aims and purpose of language learning. Hawkins (2005) reminds us of the two different purposes (or ends) which Stanley Leathes laid out in his report to the Prime Minister in 1918: the first was 'instrumental' where the given or chosen language is used for a real or instructional reason. The second, 'educational' purpose provides learners with an understanding of how languages work and strategies for learning a language, or inspires the pupil to learn other languages. Hawkins (ibid.) suggests that it is impossible to predict the future language needs of an English-speaking 7-year-old and therefore suggesting an instructional purpose for language learning at this age is a fallacy. He goes on to say that whilst there is a time and a place for instrumental instruction, 'language choices can only be made later by the individual learner' (Hawkins, 2005, p.4).

Interestingly, an *educational* purpose which is concerned with laying the foundations for language learning, rather than an individual's progression in a given language, chimes a chord with a range of research in this area. Studies by Driscoll (2000); Wade et al. (2009); Cable et al. (2010) all suggest that teachers value languages for promoting intercultural understanding, and that they wish to motivate their pupils in language skills and encourage positive attitudes. An educational purpose for language learning would, therefore, promote a language awareness programme. These programmes expose children to a range of languages, foster an interest and love of languages, explore basic knowledge about language, make connections with English and develop a range of language-learning strategies (Hawkins, 2005; Barton, Bragg and Serratrice, 2009).

A key aspect of language awareness programmes enhances children's understanding of their own language. Developing children's metalinguistic awareness (broad understanding of how language works and its cultural associations) is seen to have clear benefits in children's learning (Murphy, 2018). A strong understanding of grammar (and phonological awareness) in children's mother tongue will support explicit grammar instruction in the foreign language. An understanding of the interrelationship between the mother tongue and the foreign language has also, on the whole, been seen to have benefits for the development of both languages (Sparks, 2012). In Muñoz's (2014) study exploring children's understanding of language and language learning, she found that young children can have a good awareness of both language and their self-efficacy. Pupils' answers showed an early awareness of foreign language learning and learning conditions as well as the influence of the learning environment and experience on the changes that reshaped their views through primary education. These findings are significant, as if teachers are to effectively support children's language awareness and development, it is important that they understand the learner's perspective (Andrews, 2007, p.29).

There have been several studies which have explored the benefits and limitations of language awareness programmes. Barton et al. (2009) conducted a study into the success of a language awareness programme in seven schools. They found that the teachers were apprehensive about teaching languages, as they felt they did not know the language well enough. They also learnt that there were concerns about where a traditional approach to language teaching would fit into the already crowded curriculum. However, teachers and headteachers felt that, unlike a single–foreign language model, there were distinct advantages for a language awareness programme, as it did not require specialist language knowledge (or teachers) to deliver it (Barton et al., 2009, p.145). The initiative also appeared to boost pupils' motivation, and pupils appreciated that learning a variety of languages could be more interesting than learning just one.

Nonetheless, when we refer back to the earlier discussion on the benefits of early language learning, it is clear that children in the middle years have the capacity to effectively learn a foreign language (Wade et al., 2009). Progress in a single language and the opportunity to use it for meaningful purposes is a key motivator in itself. Research by Courtney (2014; 2017) and Graham et al. (2014; 2016; 2017) has shown that when children are making good progress in a given language, they become more motivated to learn. This is especially important in the period of transition between Key Stage 2 and 3 where motivation can diminish if prior learning is not recognised nor progress made (Chambers, 2016). Consequently, it would be interesting to see whether a language awareness programme (which lacks progression in one language) would provide the best foundation for language learning.

Summary

This chapter may have raised more questions than answers, but it highlights the controversy and debates which surround this minority subject. Whilst there are still significant issues to address, languages, as a subject in the primary school, has come a long way in its chequered history. Issues of teacher proficiency and training, language choice and a limited programme of study have meant that children's progress in a foreign language may have been impaired. Further challenges have arisen in the transition from primary to secondary school where issues persist in the diversity of experiences with which children arrive. However, agreeing the language choice (at the very least on a local level) and targeting the training of teachers may go some way to addressing this. Alternatively, a language awareness model may be more appropriate if we engage with the *educational* purposes of language learning.

Most importantly, at a time of political turmoil and national division, the appealing and attractive purpose in the National Curriculum should be embraced: 'Learning a foreign language is a liberation from insularity and provides an opening to other cultures' (DfE, 2013, p.193). Whichever language is taught, through whatever approach and by whomever, it is important that this subject retains its place in the National Curriculum and that sufficient investment and training enables all teachers to make good progress in this vital subject.

Questions for reflection

Foreign languages currently have a low priority in the primary school. Do you feel that a change to a language awareness approach would help or hinder this? Why?

What do you consider the benefits and limitations of moving to a single foreign language in all primary schools?

Should only those teachers with a certain proficiency in a foreign language be able to teach this subject?

Further reading and resources

Association of Language Learning https://www.all-languages.org.uk/.
ALL is one of the main subject associations for those involved in teaching modern foreign languages at all levels. The association exists to represent and support language teachers and is committed to their ongoing professional development.

Holmes, B. & Myles, F. (2019) *White Paper: Primary Languages Policy in England – The Way Forward, RiPL.* Available at: www.ripl.uk/policy/.
As foreign languages in the primary school becomes more embedded, this timely report outlines responses to the current challenges for both policy makers and practitioners. The paper poses a number of pertinent questions and draws on a range of important literature.

Driscoll, P., Earl, J. & Cable, C. (2013) 'The Role and Nature of the cultural dimension in primary foreign languages', *Languages Culture and Curriculum*, 26(2): 146–160.
This article highlights the significance of the cultural element of languages which is often overlooked. Whilst this aspect is implicit within the National Curriculum, there are no learning outcomes relating to this aspect, so despite good intentions, planning relating to the cultural dimension can be sadly lacking.

References

Andrews, S. (2007) *Teacher Language Awareness*, Cambridge: Cambridge University Press.

Association of Language Learning. Available at: https://www.all-languages.org.uk/.

Barton, A., Bragg, J. & Serratrice, L. (2009) '"Discovering language" in primary school: An evaluation of a language awareness programme', *Language Learning Journal*, 37(2): 145–164.

Blondin, C., Candelier, M., Edelenbos, P. Johnstone, R., Kubanek-German, A., & Taeschner, T. (1998). Foreign Languages in Primary and Pre-School Education: Context and Outcomes. A review of Recent Research within the European Union. London: CILT.

Burstall, C. (1977) 'Primary French in the balance', *Foreign Language Annals*, 10(3): 3.

Cable, C., Driscoll, P., Mitchell, R., Sing, S., Cremin, T., Earl, J., Eyres, I., Holmes, B., Martin, C. & Heins, B. (2010) *Languages Learning at Key stage 2, A Longitudinal Study: Final Report*. Research Report. London: DCSF.

Carter, A. (2015) *Review of Initial Teacher Training*,Sir Andrew Carter OBE, January 2015. Available at: https://assets.publishing.service.gov.uk/government/uploads/system/uploads/attachment_data/file/399957/Carter_Review.Pdf (accessed 02.07.2019).

Chambers, G. (2016) 'Pupils' perceptions of Key stage 2 to Key stage 3 transition in modern foreign languages', *The Language Learning Journal*, 47(1): 1–15.

Coughlan, S. (2013) 'Gove sets out "core knowledge" curriculum plans', *BBC News*, Available at: https://www.bbc.co.uk/news/education-21346812 (accessed 12.07.2019).

Courtney, L. (2014) *Moving from Primary to Secondary Education: An Investigation into the Effect of Primary to Secondary Transition on Motivation for Language Learning and Foreign Language Proficiency*, (PhD), Southampton: University of Southampton.

Courtney, L. (2017) 'Transition in modern foreign languages: A longitudinal study of motivation for language learning and second language proficiency', *Oxford Review of Education*, 43(4): 462–481.

DCSF (2005) *Key Stage 2 Framework for Languages*, London: DCSF_RR198: Department for Children Schools and Families.

Department for Children Schools and Families (DCSF) (2009) Independent review of the primary curriculum. Final report.

Department for Education (2013) The national curriculum in England: key stages 1 and 2 framework document. Available at: https://www.gov.uk/government/publications/national-curriculum-in-england-primary-curriculum [Accessed: 22.06.20]

DfES (2002) 'Languages for all: Languages for life: A strategy for England'. Available at: https://www.languagescompany.com/wp-content/uploads/the-national-languages-strategy-for-england-1.pdf (accessed 02.07.19).

DfES. (2007) *Languages Review*. Online at: https://www.languagescompany.com/wp-content/uploads/the-languages-review.pdf [accessed 22.06.20]

Driscoll, P. (2000). Reconstructing primary modern foreign languages: an inclusive process towards the development of competence. Early Language Learning Bulletin 5.

Driscoll, P. (2014) 'A New Era for primary languages'. In: Driscoll, P., Macaro, E. & Swarbrick, A. (eds.), *Debates in Modern Language Education*, London: Routledge.

Driscoll, P., Earl, J. & Cable, C. (2013) 'The Role and Nature of the cultural dimension in primary foreign languages', *Languages Culture and Curriculum*, 26(2): 146–160.

Driscoll, P., Jones, J. & Macrory, G. (2004) *The Provision of Foreign Language Learning for Pupils at Key Stage 2*, Research Report No. 572, Canterbury, UK: Canterbury Christ Church University College.

European Commission (2012) *First European Survey on Language Competences: Final Report*. Brussels: European Commission.

Gamble, C. J. & Smalley, A. (1975) 'Primary French in the balance – "Were the scales accurate?"' *Journal of Modern Languages*, 35(2): 94–97.

Graham, S., Courtney, L., Marinis, T. & Tonkyn, A. (2017) 'Early language learning: The impact of teaching and teacher factors', *Language Learning*, 67(4): 922–958.

Graham, S., Courtney, L., Tonkyn, A. & Marinis, T. (2016) 'Motivational trajectories for early language learning across the primary-secondary school transition', *British Educational Research Journal*, 42(4): 682–702.

Graham, S., Marinis, T., Tonkyn, A. & Courtney, L. (2014) *Primary Modern Languages: The Impact of Teaching Approaches on Attainment and Preparedness for Secondary School Language Learning*, Final Report to the Nuffield Foundation. Available at: http://www.nuffieldfoundation.org/primary-modern-languagesim pact-teaching-approaches. (accessed 01.08.2019).

Guz, E. & Tetiurka, M. (2016) 'Positive emotions and learner engagement: Insights from an early FL classroom'. In: Gabryś-Barker, D. & Gałajda, D. (eds.), *Positive Psychology Perspectives on Foreign Language Learning and Teaching*, pp. 133–153, Cham: Springer.

Hawkins, E. (2005) 'Out of this nettle, drop-out, we pluck this flower, opportunity: Rethinking the school foreign language apprenticeship', *The Language Learning Journal*, 32(1): 4–17.

Holmes, B. & Myles, F. (2019) *White Paper: Primary Languages Policy in England – The Way Forward. RiPL*. Available at: http://www.ripl.uk/policy/ .

Jeffreys, B. (2019) Languages Learning: German and French drop by half in UK schools. BBC News. Online at: https://www.bbc.co.uk/news/education-473 34374 [accessed 22.06.20]

Legg, K. (2013) 'An investigation into teachers' attitudes towards the teaching of modern foreign languages in the primary school', *Education 3-13*, 41(1): 55–62.

Lindgren, E. & Muñoz, C. (2013) 'The influence of exposure, parents and linguistic distance on young European learners' foreign language comprehension', *International Journal of Multilingualism*, 10(1): 105–129.

Martin, C. (2012) 'Pupils' perceptions of foreign language learning in the primary school – findings from the Key Stage 2 Language Learning Pathfinder evaluation', *Education 3-13 International Journal of Primary, Elementary and Early Years Education*, 40(4): 343–362.

McLachan, A. (2009) 'Modern languages in the primary curriculum: Are we creating conditions for success?' *Language Learning Journal*, 2: 183–203.

Mundkar, N. (2005) 'Neuroplasticity in children', *Symposium on Behavioural and Developmental Disorders*, 1(10), 855–857.

Muñoz, C. (2006) 'The effects of age on foreign language learning: The BAF project'. In: Muñoz, C. (ed.), *Age and the Rate of Foreign Language Learning*, pp. 1–40, Clevedon: Multilingual Matters.

Muñoz, C. (2014) 'Exploring young learners' foreign language learning awareness', *Language Awareness*, 23(1–2): 24–40.

Muijs, D., Barnes, A., Hunt, M., Powell, B., Arweck, E., Lindsay, G. & Martin, C. (2005) *Evaluation of the Key Stage 2 Language Learning Pathfinders*, London: DfES.

Murphy, V. A. (2018) 'Literacy development in linguistically diverse pupils'. In: Miller, D., Bayram, F., Rothman, J. & Serratrice, L. (eds.), *Bilingual Cognition and Language: The State of the Science Across Its Subfields, Studies in Bilingualism*, p. 54, Amsterdam: John Benjamins.

Myles, F. (2017) *Learning Foreign Languages in Primary Schools: Is Younger Better?* Available at: http://www.meits.org/policy-papers/paper/learning-foreign-la nguages-in-primary-schools-is-younger-better (accessed 01.08.2019).

Nuffield Foundation (online) *Nuffield Primary French*. Available at: https://www .nuffieldfoundation.org/nuffield-primary-french-1963.

The Nuffield Languages Inquiry/ Foundation (2000) *Languages: The Next Generation*, London: The Nuffield Foundation.

OECD (2014a) *Education Indicators in Focus: How Much Time Do Primary and Lower Secondary Students Spend in the Classroom?* Paris: OECD Publishing.

Ofsted (2018) *Chief Inspector Sets Out Vision for New Education Inspection Framework*, Press release. Available at: https://www.gov.uk/government/news/chief-insp ector-sets-out-vision-for-new-education-inspection-framework.

Pells, R. (2017) 'SATs having "damaging consequences" for both children and schools, teachers warn', *The Independent*. Available at: https://www.ind ependent.co.uk/news/education/education-news/sats-having-damaging -consequences-children-schools-teachers-nut-survey-a7806571.html (accessed 17.07.2019).

Singleton, D. (1989) *Language Acquisition. The Age Factor*, Clevedon: Multilingual Matters Ltd.

Sparks, R. L. (2012) 'Individual differences in L2 learning and long-term L1–L2 relationships', *Language Learning*, 62: 5–27.

Spielman, A. (2018) *HMCI Commentary: Curriculum and the New Inspection Framework*. Available at: https://www.gov.uk/government/speeches/hmci-c ommentary-curriculum-and-the-new-education-inspection-framework.

Spielman, A. (2019) *Amanda Spielman's Speech to the NAHT Conference*. Available at: https://www.gov.uk/government/speeches/amanda-spielmans-speech-to -the-naht-conference.

Tinsley, T. & Doleżal, N. (2018) *Language Trends 2018: Language Teaching in Primary and Secondary Schools in England*, Survey Report, British Council. Available at: https://www.britishcouncil.org/sites/default/files/language_trends_2018_report.pdf.

Tinsley, T. (2019) Language Trends 2019: Language Teaching in Primary and Secondary schools in England Survey report. British Council. Available at: https://www.britishcouncil.org/sites/default/files/language-trends-2019.pdf [accessed 22.06.20]

Wade, P., Marshall, H. & with O'Donnell, S. (2009) *Primary Modern Foreign Languages Longitudinal Survey of Implementation of National Entitlement to Language Learning at Key Stage 2, Research Report No RR127*, London: DCSF.

Chapter 10

Promoting a bilingual approach in the primary classroom

Virginia Bower

Introduction

This chapter argues that a bilingual approach in *all* primary classrooms would benefit *all* pupils. From the outset I would like to clarify that by 'bilingual approach' I am not referring to practice whereby the curriculum is delivered in more than one language. There are, indeed, highly successful schools who adopt this method, but this is not practical for most educational settings in the United Kingdom. Instead, a 'bilingual approach' within the confines of this chapter implies an overt celebration of languages beyond English, and the deliberate and ongoing promotion of languages every day and across the whole curriculum. This approach does not require practitioners to be bilingual themselves; instead, it assumes that what is needed is an open attitude to the use of different languages in the classroom and an understanding of the benefits of promoting language learning.

Pupils in educational settings in the UK are, for the most part, exposed to a monolingual, monocultural curriculum and assessment system designed by a sector of society far removed from the realities of the diversity of classroom life. At a time of unprecedented uncertainty, with the potential for uninformed opinion, dogmatic perspectives and devotion to a small island mentality to prevail, it is worth considering this quote from the National Centre for Languages:

> There is no evidence to support the view that speaking languages other than English in the home is socially divisive or that it is incompatible with a British identity. Rather, the evidence would suggest that bilingualism promotes a respect for diversity and an ability to navigate different cultural realities.
>
> (CiLT, 2006, p.4)

The history of research into bilingualism demonstrates how the knowledge and understanding relating to being bilingual has changed over decades, and the benefits of being bilingual are firmly rooted in the areas of educational and scientific research. Despite this evidence, however, there remain disturbing messages from educational settings, and more general societal settings, that it would be better for children to focus on one main language – in this case English – in order to be successful. What is useful to remember here is that approaches to education 'need to be understood as potential tools for social control rather than automatically as a means to social emancipation' (Pennycook, 1998, p.82), and that a debate needs to be had at every opportunity to challenge any attempt to marginalise learners' voices.

The chapter begins with an overview of the history of attitudes towards, and knowledge and understanding of, bilingualism and bilingual learning and the debates therein. In order to contextualise the current position, it is useful to have an understanding of the research, policy and practice which have led us to this point. In exploring the landscape, past and present, the debates surrounding this topic will become apparent and the next section will examine how these debates manifest themselves in educational settings and the challenges perceived by practitioners. The final section, before the summary, will examine what I regard as the dangers of the continuance of a monolingual education system within a 'super diverse' (Vertovec, 2007) society, heightening the debate to one of urgency if we are to counter the damaging effects of curricula and assessment designed with just one language in mind. It is not the intention of this chapter to suggest 'how' a bilingual approach might be promoted (there are several publications which provide practical suggestions [Bower, 2017; Conteh, 2012]), but to explore 'why' and to examine the debates that might challenge this approach.

Note: The terms 'bilingual learners' and 'children with EAL' will be used interchangeably in this chapter.

History of the debates around bilingualism

Since the mid-twentieth century, much has changed in terms of how bilingualism is perceived (Baker, 1988). Until the 1960s, traditional research findings indicated that there was no advantage to learning a second language; in fact it was suggested to be potentially damaging to the brain. Behaviourist approaches and a focus on individual cognition (Cross, 2010) were prevalent, whereby learning was perceived to emanate solely from the mind of the individual and that this learning was influenced by their personality, attitude, beliefs and innate abilities.

Significant changes occurred from the 1960s, when emergent research indicated that bilingual learners were able to think in more flexible and abstract ways, 'resulting in superiority in concept formation' (Baker, 1988, p.17). It was found that these learners could adapt more readily to different contexts and environments and were able to use the knowledge and understanding of one language when learning another. Around this time, the government was recognising the status of immigrants from 'new Commonwealth nations' (Safford and Drury, 2013, p.71) and schools received specific funding for resources. There was active promotion of children's first languages in schools, supported by that most influential publication – the Bullock Report – which stated that 'no child should be expected to cast off the language and culture of the home as he crosses the school threshold and the curriculum should reflect those aspects of his life' (DES, 1975, para20.5).

More research was being undertaken into contrastive analysis (where learners use their knowledge of language 1 (L1) to support their growing understanding of language 2 (L2), and there was a movement towards a more sociocultural approach by some, acknowledging the existence of high and low status languages, additive and subtractive bilingualism, integration and acculturation (Bialystok, 1991). At the same time, the idea that bilingual learners might have particular characteristics which enabled them to be more successful at learning *further* languages was being explored.

In 1985, the next significant government report was published – the Swann Report (DES, 1985). The recommendations in this report had what Rampton, Harris and Leung (2002, no page) view as a long-lasting and damaging precedent for a monolingual approach in schools. Although there was support for respecting cultural diversity and integration of bilingual children into mainstream classrooms, the key focus was on learning English and a perception of children with English as an additional language being at a disadvantage because they did not have English as their first language. There was no support for the active promotion of minority language and:

> Rather than cultivating any specialised cultural or linguistic resources that ethnic minorities might have, the Swann Report sought in effect to nationalise them.
>
> (Rampton, Harris and Leung, 2002, no page)

Despite this, the debate about how languages are learnt continued, and a significant influence was that of Canale and Swain's (1980) ideas on 'communicative competence' – grammatical competence, sociolinguistic competence, discourse competence and strategic competence – acknowledging that learners of another language need to develop skills in each of these. These ideas had a long-lasting effect on how approaches are taken towards bilingual learners and are still influential today (Leung, 2005).

The 1980s saw the centralisation of education, which manifested itself in the introduction of a National Curriculum (NC); power and budgets moving from Local Authorities to schools; the advent of statutory testing; league tables; and parental choice over which schools their children attended. All of this was detrimental to perceptions of children with EAL and the support and funding available specifically for this group. It was 'no longer in a school's interest to welcome refugee children and other newcomers to England' (Rampton, Harris and Leung, 2002, no page), because accountability and reported league tables put extreme pressures on schools to achieve results and children for whom English was not their first language were viewed as having the potential to lower those results. Schools became businesses, vying for pupils, some of whom were more desirable than others (Kenway and Bullen, 2001), depending on what they were perceived to offer the setting, or whether they might add 'negative value' (Kenway and Bullen, 2001, p.139). The NC brought with it a focus on Standard English, reducing the status of minority languages; something further exacerbated by the introduction of the National Literacy Strategy (DfEE, 1998) and the Literacy Hour, which largely excluded reference to the 'heteroglossia and multilingualism of the global city' (Rampton, Harris and Leung, 2002, no page). Conteh (2003, p.13) notes that, 'Through centrally developed and imposed curricula, national governments establish the knowledge that counts' and that the NC originally 'aimed to promote a model of uniformity and cultural cohesion' (Conteh, 2003, p.14). Around this time, specialist language support systems were disbanded.

In the research world, focus has shifted evermore towards a Vygotskian view of language learning, seen as 'intricately related to the construction of social roles, cultural affiliations, beliefs, values, and behavioural practices among participants in a community' (Lam, 2004, p.46). There has been a move towards the view that bilingual learners need to be seen in the different contexts of their lives, and appreciated for how they adapt, adjust, and are influenced by the myriad environments they encounter. Linking with this, Garcia (2009) introduced the term 'translanguaging' in relation to how learners use languages in different ways to suit the circumstance, context and their individual needs. She writes about 'translanguagings' which she defines as 'multiple discursive practices in which bilinguals engage in order to make sense of their bilingual worlds' (Garcia, 2009, p.45).

Scientific research in the last few decades has also had a significant impact on our understanding of bilingual brains, finding that bilingual children have a 'more highly developed linguistic and social awareness as well as a cognitive and intellectual flexibility' (Gregory and Williams, 2000, p.6) exceeding that of monolingual peers. Bilingualism specifically impacts on executive functions – including memory, problem solving, flexibility around completing tasks and reasoning – leading to higher levels of functioning (Bialystok, 2011). The very nature of learning L2 (as opposed to L1), with its tendency towards the conscious and deliberate, promotes more effective use of metacognitive and metalinguistic strategies, and EAL learners may have greater recognition that language can be arbitrary (Jimenez, Garcia and Pearson, 1996).

Despite these positive findings, however, there is still a tendency to view children with EAL as 'lacking' (Rodriguez, 2013), because they are not necessarily fully literate in English. Because of this, the approaches are more towards transitional bilingualism (Conteh, 2012), where L1 is seen as a 'bridge' to L2 and can then be discarded. Cummins (2005) notes the irony of an education system that gradually robs a child of their bilingual status whilst endeavouring to teach foreign languages to English monolingual children; and this in a world where the majority of the population are bilingual or multilingual (Marian and Shook, 2012). A lack of knowledge and understanding in the field of education – whether it be the government, teachers or parents – of the benefits of bilingualism and a bilingual approach means that children are denied the opportunity to recognise and capitalise on 'their own power, and the potential for learning that bilingualism gives them' (Conteh, 2012, p.38).

So, this then is the current context. We have 'education policy which encourages teachers and schools to celebrate children's linguistic diversity but which does not require or promote mainstream teachers' linguistic knowledge and training' (Safford and Drury, 2013, p.73), and we have increasing numbers of bilingual learners in many areas of the UK. This situation has led, inevitably, to debate around how children might best be supported in different contexts, and the next section will look at some of the questions and debates that often arise in relation to planning for, teaching and assessing bilingual learners.

The debates in schools

Knowing the historical background allows us to understand some of the questions and debates which arise in educational settings. This section will identify and challenge some of these debates, continuing to defend the position that a bilingual approach would ensure a higher level of teaching and learning for all practitioners and pupils. The questions chosen for debate arise from my conversations and interactions with students and teachers over the last two decades:

- Does it confuse children to use and learn in more than one language and will it inhibit their progress?
- Will 'normal' planning, teaching and assessment support the needs of bilingual learners?
- Would it not be better if children just learnt English, so that they can do well in England in terms of exam results and jobs?

Does it confuse children to use and learn in more than one language and will it inhibit their progress?

The concept of using L1 as a tool for learning is neither straightforward nor universally accepted. This is predictably reflected in the approaches to pedagogies and practices adopted in English primary classrooms. Park (2013) describes traditional classrooms as being places where the target language and the child's first language are divided, and if a child switches to their home language it is seen as a sign that they are not strong in the target language and therefore it is discouraged. In reality, children might switch for any number of reasons: for more challenging activities where they need more vocabulary than they have in the target language; to maintain their identities; because they feel that their grasp of English does not enable them to put across their ideas as well as they would wish; or of course because it is more sociable to talk with their peers in a common language.

There is increasing evidence to suggest that the maintenance of L1 does not in any way impede the progress of L2 (Cummins, 2001; Garcia, 2009; Hyltenstam and Abrahamsson, 2012; Marian and Shook, 2012), although there will inevitably be some temporary confusion when children are not only learning more than one language, but are *learning to learn* in a bilingual way. Not only does a bilingual approach *not* inhibit learning, but research indicates that there are significant benefits and that bilingual learners 'enjoy cognitive and social advantages over monolinguals' (Garcia, 2009, p.11–12). Although there may be initial barriers to learning for those at the early stages of learning English, fluent bilingual learners outperform monolingual learners in tests at the end of Key Stage 2 and GCSE level (Demie, 2013).

There is also evidence to support taking a bilingual approach as early as possible, as very young bilinguals have been found to understand the 'symbolic function of letters' (CiLT, 2006, p.4) more quickly than monolingual pre-school children, and with the opportunity to hear and explore stories in more than one language, will be at an advantage when learning to read. If children's L1 is promoted in school and learners are encouraged to draw on their knowledge and understanding of language generally, the languages will nurture each other (Cummins, 2001), leading to improved academic performance. If, however, children are discouraged from using L1, their development of this language will stagnate and 'their personal and conceptual foundation for learning is undermined' (ibid., no page).

Kenner's (2007) research with second- or third-generation British Bangladeshi children (who were usually more fluent in English than in their mother tongue) found that all those questioned would prefer to learn in both languages and they recognised the advantages of retaining their first language:

> slowly, slowly we forget Bengali and then we will be like the English people only speaking one language.
>
> (Kenner, 2007, p.20)

Even though they were more fluent in English, the children considered Bangla to be their mother tongue and were disappointed that this was not acknowledged. As the project continued, and the use of Bangla was more overtly encouraged, the teachers felt that they got to know the pupils better and had a better understanding of their identity. Some children became more motivated to learn; some understood concepts more readily when they were presented in both languages; they were often more confident; and they were able to apply their knowledge to different contexts.

Unfortunately, the benefits of a bilingual approach can take many years to manifest themselves and this is not what the current education system supports. Quick fix results are what is required and Conteh (2003) identifies this as one of the reasons why bilingualism is not capitalised upon in English classrooms.

Will 'normal' planning, teaching and assessment support the needs of bilingual learners?

I believe the short answer to this is no, this will not suffice. However, the reassuring aspect, I would argue, is that planning, teaching and assessment to support bilingual learners will support and benefit *all* learners. Language issues are central to *all* learners, not just bilingual learners, and all teachers must 'consciously teach language' (Elorza and Munoa, 2008, p.94). The classroom environment 'needs to be planned in terms of language enhancement so as to make the most of the great opportunities it can offer to strengthen and develop linguistic production' (ibid.). As suggested in the introduction, this chapter does not set out to discuss *how* this might be successfully achieved – the aim is merely to debate *why* a bilingual approach is so powerful. However, I shall briefly examine some ideas from researchers who have explored different approaches and whose ideas suggest how planning, teaching and assessment might be enhanced to raise the profile of language.

Leung (2005, p.249) writes that bilingual learners in the early stages of second language development benefit from 'context-embedded communication', and this might involve children being supported with tangible objects, a range of visuals and being involved in active learning where communication and collaboration are key aspects of the learning. Planning for this might involve a greater attention to resourcing, timings, grouping and so forth, but these are all everyday considerations for teachers and might simply need more of a language focus. These types of activities often enable the teacher to take a less prominent role and this in turn allows more opportunities for ongoing assessment. This approach can also lead to more of a focus on language, as children work together to problem solve, play, create and discover. Kotler, Wegerif and Levoi (2001, p.404) believe that there are not enough opportunities for children to use and explore language in the classroom and that this a grave concern when it might be the 'only opportunity that a bilingual pupil has to learn the language she or he needs for educational success.' Giving attention to how pedagogies and practices, resources and materials might provide these opportunities is potentially a way of creating a classroom culture which promotes the promotion and use of a range of languages (Conteh, 2003).

Gutierrez, Bien, Selland and Pierce (2011, p.240) found that the practices promoted in their study, where children were encouraged to use multiple languages, were 'meaningful to their identities as learners and meaning-makers'. They found that using different languages both mediated children's learning whilst countering 'the hegemonic, English-only discourses of current educational arrangements' (ibid.). The researchers examined an after-school club which used a mythical cyber wizard as the main character with whom children communicated using different languages. The club was based on humour, play and communication in different languages using multimodal forms. The wizard was always there to prompt and invite the children to explore the languages, whilst not putting any pressure on or having one language as dominant. In this way they were able to play with language in a non-threatening environment. The wizard was deliberately used to promote the value of multilingualism 'while respecting children's language practices and choices' (ibid., p.250). Findings indicated that children often defaulted to English because they thought that was what was expected, but because the wizard valued multilingualism, it gave them the freedom to use the language best suited for a particular situation, thus promoting bilingualism as valuable. The wizard was the prime mediator and 'knew' all about the children and their interests, referring to these in its communications as well as referring to popular culture with which they were familiar. The researchers believed that the way this club was set up and organised promoted 'hybrid literacy practices that extend children's repertoires of practice, while leveraging their expertise' (ibid., p.259).

In her study of writing systems, Kenner (2002, p.8) encouraged the children to teach each other their writing systems. This was to ascertain what their ideas were about different ways that writing is produced, and was a powerful way to engage children with language. The children began discussing differences, pointing out useful aspects, e.g., directionality, thereby bringing about language awareness and promoting meta-cognition and meta-linguistic awareness. Velasco and Garcia (2014, p.8) recognise the 'interconnections of language practices' even if languages do not share the same writing systems and argue that being literate in one language will support the development of literacy in another language, as learners develop an 'integrated reasoning' (ibid., p.9). Activities such as those described by Kenner promote this biliteracy and raise the profile of all languages in the classroom.

Teachers have the power and position to effect change by challenging dominant ideologies which constrain and prescribe, and developing spaces 'where students' hybrid language practices are incorporated, privileged, and leveraged to promote learning' (Palmer and Martinez, 2013, p.289). If sometimes this seems a lot to ask of us as teachers – to be thinking of how to support bilingual learners on a day-to-day basis – it is worth facing up to what might be an uncomfortable truth, as described by Palmer and Martinez (ibid, p.273): that 'teachers' monolingualism is not generally problematized, only students' bilingualism'.

Would it not be better if children just learnt English, so that they can do well in England in terms of exam results and jobs?

There are three key points to debate here:

- What do bilingual learners gain from developing both L1 and L2?
- What do bilingual learners lose from shedding L1 in favour of L2?
- What does it say about us as teachers if we choose to ignore the knowledge about language bilingual learners already possess?

I shall address each of these in turn. Earlier in the chapter, brief mention was made of the gains in terms of the benefits of bilingualism in cognitive terms: improved executive functions and more effective use of metacognitive and meta-linguistic strategies. Evidence suggests that 'Bilingual children as young as seven months can better adjust to environmental changes, while bilingual seniors can experience less cognitive decline' (Marian and Shook, 2012, p.1). Bilingual learners have both languages 'simmering' at the same time, and one of their key challenges is to choose which language is best suited to the context. Research indicates that this constant decision-making and switching between languages goes towards explaining the high levels of academic performance demonstrated by many bilingual children: 'the plasticity of cognitive systems in response to experience' (Bialystok, 2011, p.233).

The social advantages are just as great, if not more so. In order to achieve social competence within a particular community, a person needs to become aware of the practices and routines in order to be able to function confidently. Language is the medium through which this is mediated. Becoming literate in a new language is not simply about responding to instruction; it is related to 'a set of practices, that is, discourses, that enact the cultural norms of a particular social group' (Lam, 2004, p.46). Having access to more than one language has been found to promote better social communication skills, as bilingual learners – particularly if exposed to diverse linguistic environments – develop a 'a profound understanding of differences between people's perspectives, naturally enhancing their communicative abilities' (Fan, Liberman, Keysar and Kinzler, 2015, p.1091).

The loss from gradually replacing L1 with L2 can be significant. Kumaravadivelu (2008) describes a U-shaped cultural phenomenon where children up to their teenage years are comfortable with their home cultural beliefs and the fact that the language spoken is different than the one in school, and are happy to celebrate with their families; then in their teens they may be under pressure from their peers, the media and the community around them and they rebel against their inherited culture and language, not wanting to be any different from those from the dominant culture. As they reach early adulthood, however, they often realise how useful it is to have more than one language and experience of diverse cultures and they blame their parents for not promoting the inherited culture and language. This can lead to disaffection and a real problem in terms of identity and a feeling of not belonging anywhere.

Most teachers would agree that one of the key elements of a lesson is discovering children's prior knowledge about a subject and building on this in future learning. With bilingual learners there is an existing language to build on, as well as the potential for utilising children's prior experiences, knowledge and understanding; their culture and their diverse backgrounds. To replace an existing language, rather than building on what is already there, can thus be viewed as a failure in terms of our duties as teachers. The privileging of a single language means that the potential for building upon the richness and wealth of linguistic experience that bilingual children bring to the classroom is threatened (Parke et al., 2002, p.200), and they are marginalised before they even set foot in the classroom (Le Roux, 2001). Toohey (2003, p.91) writes that children with EAL are 'defined as something like "benignly deviant", in Foucault's terms, in that their language departs from accepted standards and that as a group they constitute a rank "requiring normalisation"'. It is axiomatic that teachers want the best for their pupils and this marginalisation and normalisation would not be their intention. However, working in settings where English is the dominant language in terms of the curriculum and assessment system, it takes a determined mind-set to fight the system. The next section examines the dangers, however, of not putting up that fight.

The dangers of a monolingual approach

Language is very much tied up with self and other, us and them. To 'belong' you need to speak the majority language; the dominant group and the dominant language wield the power, particularly within institutions such as schools (Heller, 1995). Throughout history, language has been influenced by 'the phenomena of prestige and reverse prestige, the strongly supported pull towards a normative language created by education and the national media' (Dentith, 1995, p.36). Despite the cultural and linguistic diversity within England, it is still one of the few countries where being monolingual is the norm (Lyon, 1996; Bunch, 2013). This may be due to the problematic label attached to linguistic diversity and the way this 'problem' is continually broached by raising the status of English and privileging it above all others (Safford and Drury, 2013). A monolingual nation state with a multicultural, multilingual society suggests that there will be power struggles and conflict and a narrow, prescribed approach to education.

The education system is geared to blame the children and their families, or the teachers, if children do not conform to age-related expectations. The pressure thus exerted means that we might fail to see what bilingual learners bring to the classroom and only see the narrow perspective of test results. In her interviews with teachers, Conteh (2003, p.103) encouraged them to talk about the cognitive and linguistic advantages of children speaking more than one language, but they were more concerned with the 'affective' implications, in that they felt it empowered the children. When pushed to discuss the academic element, the teachers began to talk about the children as if they were at fault, because their bilingualism was perceived as a language 'problem' which was not allowing them to achieve the appropriate levels.

Even at pre-school level, children recognise the status accorded to different languages (Day, 2002). Recognising the low status of their first language, children may begin to turn away from it and thus begins the gradual loss of L1 (Cummins, 2005). Full assimilation into a culture implies a rejection of L1 or at the very least ensuring that English is the dominant language used. Although there may not be overt and active dissuasion, the dominance of a curriculum and assessment system in English ensures that effective use of the English language is what is valued:

> Children understand very quickly that the school is an English-only zone and they often internalise ambivalence and even shame in relation to their linguistic and cultural heritage.
>
> (Cummins, 2005, p.590)

Any use of L1 in the classroom tends to be regarded – often by children, teachers and parents – as temporary and transitional (Conteh and Brock, 2011), used as a bridge towards acquiring English and to be discarded once English is established. This, despite the overwhelming evidence in support of the benefits of bilingualism.

Summary

Many classroom pedagogies and practices, school routines and structures normalise monolingualism and it is this ideology that needs the strongest of challenges before bilingual learners can be successfully engaged and bilingualism can achieve the celebrated status it deserves (Palmer and Martinez, 2013). Safford and Drury (2013, p.70) observe that 'linguistic diversity has always been problematic to Westerners, who continually try to "solve" this problem by privileging or imposing a single language or variety'. If we are genuinely to adopt an inclusive attitude to language, an imperative is to address deep-rooted beliefs in the superiority of one language over another. We need to change the whole discourse around bilingualism – acknowledging that our roles are not so much supporting bilingual learners' access to English but rather enabling them to capitalise on the benefits of having at least two languages.

A central contention is that there is also a job to do on our own knowledge and understanding of bilingualism and a need to dispel popular myths. In her research into teachers' beliefs about language – in Italy, Austria and Great Britain – De Angelis (2011, p.229) found that teachers showed little awareness of the interaction of languages in learners' minds and there was a belief that 'language interactions give rise to confusion and delays when learning the host language'. Her findings revealed that teachers lacked understanding of the importance of L1 promotion at home, within the family, and that teachers were sometimes actively discouraging this. De Angelis advocates a more proactive approach to teacher development in terms of developing pedagogies and practices for multilingual classes.

Garcia (2009, p.53) argues that the 21st century requires language practices which are 'multiple and ever adjusting to the multilingual multimodal terrain of the communicative act', and that the monolingual, traditional approaches and resources in schools neither recognise nor promote these. If, instead, an approach can be taken which reflects the myriad ways children use language each day, in different contexts and situations and for different audiences, there is the chance that the untapped potential of a bilingual approach might be accessed. Keeping up the debate around this subject is essential and a final thought to finish the chapter might enable you to take up the debate, whatever setting you are in:

> What is surely needed is not somehow to mould all children to fit the static model of 'Englishness' that is perceived to be required for success in the

education system, but to develop and broaden the model itself of what it means to be English.

(Conteh, 2003, p.115)

Questions for reflection

In what ways might you take up this debate in your own setting?

What professional development might be useful to you in order to promote a bilingual approach?

Why is it important to consider both the social language required by bilingual learners and the academic, curriculum language?

Further reading and resources

Garcia, O. (2009) *Bilingual Education in the 21st Century: A Global Perspective*, London: Wiley-Blackwell.

Look no further if you want a text to inspire you to take a bilingual approach in your classroom. Garcia writes with authority and feeling, leaving you keen to seek ways to promote bilingualism in as many ways as possible.

Conteh, J. (ed.) (2006) *Promoting Learning for Bilingual Pupils 3–11: Opening Doors for Success*, London: SAGE.

Jean Conteh has published widely in this field and there is much to be learned from her experiences, taken directly from her work with children with English as an additional language. Conteh provides practical strategies, firmly rooted in research and theory around this much debated topic.

NALDIC – this is the National Association for Language Development in the Curriculum and can be found here: https://naldic.org.uk/.

NALDIC is an excellent association, promoting effective teaching and learning of EAL and bilingual pupils across the UK.

References

Baker, C. (1988) *Key Issues in Bilingualism and Bilingual Education*, Clevedon: Multilingual Matters.

Bialystok, E. (ed) (1991*) Language Processing in Bilingual Children*, Cambridge: Cambridge University Press.

Bower, V. (2017) Supporting Pupils with EAL in the Primary Classroom, Berkshire: OU Press.

Bunch, G. C. (2013) 'Pedagogical Language Knowledge: Preparing Mainstream Teachers for English Learners in the New Standards Era', *Review of Research in Education*, 37: 298–341.

Canale, M. & Swain, M. (1980) 'Theoretical Bases of Communicative Approaches to Second Language Teaching and Testing', *Applied Linguistics*, 1(1): 1–47.

CiLT (The National Centre for Languages) (2006) *Positively Plurilingual*, London: CiLT.

Conteh, J. (2003) *Succeeding in Diversity*, Stoke on Trent: Trentham Books.

Conteh, J. (2012) Teaching bilingual and EAL learners in primary schools, London: Sage.

Conteh, J & Brock, A. (2011) "Safe spaces'? Sites of bilingualism for young learners in home, school and community', *International Journal of Bilingual Education and Bilingualism*, 14(3): 347–360.

Cross, R. (2010) 'Language Teaching as Sociocultural Activity: Rethinking Language Teacher Practice', *The Modern Language Journal*, 94(3): 434–452.

Cummins, J. (2001) *Bilingual Children's Mother Tongue: Why Is It Important for Education?* Available at: https://inside.isb.ac.th/nativelanguage/files/2015/11/Bilingual-Childrens-Mother-Tongue.pdf (Accessed 09.05.19).

Cummins, J. (2005) 'A Proposal for Action: Strategies for Recognising Heritage Language Competence as a Learning Resource with the Mainstream Classroom', *The Modern Language Journal*, 898(4): 585–592.

Day, E. M. (2002) *Identity and the Young English Language Learner*, Clevedon: Multilingual Matters.

De Angelis (2011) 'Teachers' Beliefs about the Role of Prior Language Knowledge in Learning and How These Influence Teaching Practices', *International Journal of Multilingualism*, 8(3): 216–234.

Demie, F. (2013) 'English as an Additional Language Pupils: How Long Does It Take to Acquire English Fluency?' *Language and Education*, 27(1): 59–69.

Dentith, S. (1995) *Bakhtinian Thought: An Introductory Reader*. London: Routledge.

Department for Education and Employment (DfEE) (1998) *The National Literacy Strategy: Framework for teaching*. London: DfEE.

Department of Education and Science (DES) (1975) *The Bullock Report A Language for Life*, London: Her Majesty's Stationery Office.

Department of Education and Science (DES) (1985) *Education for All: Report of the Committee of Inquiry into the Education of Children from Ethnic Minority Groups*, Cmnd. 9453, London: HMSO (Swann Report).

Elorza, I. & Munoa, I. (2008) 'Promoting the Minority Language Through Integrated Plurilingual Language Planning: The Case of the Ikastolas Language', *Culture and Curriculum*, 21(1): 85–101.

Fan, S. P., Liberman, Z., Keysar, B. & Kinzler, K. D. (2015) 'The Exposure Advantage: Early Exposure to a Multilingual Environment Promotes Effective Communication', *Psychological Science*, 26(7): 1090–1097.

Garcia, O. (2009) *Bilingual Education in the 21st Century: A Global Perspective*, London: Wiley-Blackwell.

Gregory, A. & Williams, A. (2000) *City Literacies Learning to Read Across Generations and Cultures*, London: Routledge.

Gutierrez, K. D., Bien, A. C., Selland, M. K. & Pierce, D. M. (2011) 'Polylingual and Polycultural Learning Ecologies: Mediating Emergent Academic Literacies for Dual Language Learners', *Journal of Early Childhood Literacy*, 11(2): 232–261.

Heller, M. (1995) 'Language Choice, Social Institutions and Symbolic Domination', *Language in Society*, 24(3): 373–405.

Jimenez, R. T. Garcia, G. E. & Pearson, P. D. (1996) 'The reading strategies of bilingual Latina/o students who are successful English readers: Opportunities and Obstacles', *Reading Research Quarterly*, 31(1): 90–112.

Kenner, C. (2002) 'Early Biliteracy: Signs of Difference', *NALDIC News*, 27: 6–8 NALDIC.

Kenner, C. (2007) *Developing bilingual learning strategies in mainstream and community contexts*, Full Research Report ESRC End of Award Report, RES-000-22-1528, Swindon: ESRC.

Kenneth Hyltenstam, K. & Abrahamsson, N. (2012) 'High-Level L2 Acquisition, Learning and Use', *Studies in Second Language Acquisition*, 34: 177–186.

Kenway, J. & Bullen, E. (2001) *Consuming Children*, Buckingham: Open University Press.

Kotler, A., Wegerif, R. & Levoi, M. (2001) 'Oracy and the Educational Achievement of Pupils with English as an Additional Language: The Impact of Bringing "Talking Partners" into Bradford Schools', *International Journal of Bilingual Education and Bilingualism*, 4(6): 403–419.

Kumaravadivelu, B. (2008) *Cultural Globalization and Language Education*, New Haven and London: Yale University Press.

Lam, W. S. E. (2004) 'Second Language Socialisation in a Bilingual Chat Room: Global and Local Considerations', *Language Learning and Technology*, 8(3): 44–65.

Le Roux, J. (2001) 'Social dynamics of the multicultural classroom', *Intercultural Education*, 12(3): 273–288.

Leung, C. (2005) 'Convivial Communication: Recontextualising Communicative Competence', *International Journal of Applied Linguistics*, 15(2): 119–144.

Leung, C. (2005) 'Language and Content in Bilingual Education', *Linguistics and Education*, 16(2): 238–252.

Lyon, J. (1996) *Becoming Bilingual*. Clevedon: Multilingual Matters.

Marian, V. & Shook, A. (2012) 'The Cognitive Benefits of Being Bilingual'. Available at: http://dana.org/news/cerebrum/detail.aspx?id=39638 (Accessed 20.04.19).

Palmer, D. & Martinez, R. A. (2013) 'Teacher Agency in Bilingual Spaces: A Fresh Look at Preparing Teachers to Educate Latina/o Bilingual Children', *Review of Research in Education*, 37(1): 269–297.

Park, M. S. (2013) 'Code-Switching and Translanguaging: Potential Functions in Multilingual Classrooms', *TESOL & Applied Linguistics*, 13(2): 50–52.

Parke, T. Drury, R. Kenner, C. & Helavaara Robertson, L. (2002) 'Revealing Invisible Worlds: Connecting the Mainstream with Bilingual Children's Home and Community Learning', *Journal of Early Childhood Literacy*, 2(2): 195–220.

Pennycook, A. (1998) 'The Right to Language: Towards a Situated Ethics of Language Possibilities', *Language Sciences*, 20(1): 73–87.

Rampton, B., Harris, R. & Leung, C. (2002) 'Education in England and Speakers of Languages Other Than English', *Working Papers in Urban Language and Literacies*, London: King's College London.

Rodriguez, G. M. (2013) 'Power and Agency in Education: Exploring the Pedagogical Dimensions of Funds of Knowledge', *Review of Research in Education*, 37(1): 87–120.

Safford, K. & Drury, R. (2013) 'The 'problem' of Bilingual Children in Educational Settings: Policy and Research in England', *Language and Education*, 27(1): 70–81.

Toohey, K. (2003) *Learning English at School Identity, Social Relations and Classroom Practice*. Clevedon: Multilingual Matters.

Velasco, P. & Garcia, O. (2014) Translanguaging and the Writing of Bilingual Learners, *Bilingual Research Journal*, 37(1): 6–23.

Vertovec, S. (2007) 'Super-Diversity and Its Implications', *Ethnic and Racial Studies*, 30(6): 1024–1054.

Chapter 11

Debates in primary science education

Leigh Hoath

Introduction

Ask people about science and you will hear a variety of responses ... science is difficult, science is facts, science is all around us. There seems to be little doubt that for the adult population science falls into one of two camps – those who do and those who don't – with very little in between. I think it is reasonable at this point to set out my position. I was a teacher of secondary science and drifted into primary science education. I was a scientist – the sort who looked for a truth, who believed in objectivity. I am still a scientist but now have much softer views on what science is. For me it is *a* truth, not *the* truth; it is a way of seeing the world and exploring everything around us. It is the future and it holds many answers to questions as yet unasked.

I do not believe that science is taught sufficiently well in many schools – and I broad sweep that judgement across primary and secondary schools. There are pockets of excellence and of that there is no doubt. But ... there are issues over the content-focused approaches in secondary schools. Too often the teachers are teaching *subjects* rather than *learners*, and the key aspects of working scientifically and enquiry are lost in the learning of content of the National Curriculum. In primary schools the sterling effort of teaching a child science is often lost in the haze of grinding through the Maths and English content, or a lack of confidence with science and its wider applications. Or, in the worst case scenario, both of these. There is a middle ground here, where both the learner and science are brought together in a more holistic way, but for that to happen there are a number of challenges which need to be embraced and it is these that form the basis of this chapter.

The abolition of the SATS science KS2 tests in 2009 was expected to yield great things in primary science ... has it? Science is identified within the Curriculum as a 'Core Subject' ... but is this translated into a reality in the classroom? Science capital is something which has become prominent within the science education world ... again, what does this mean for the primary classroom and the teachers? Science is something that forms part of the STEM subject group where there is an alleged gap in skills and workforce – to what extent is this being addressed if it does really exist? So, with science 'up against it' in so many ways, where do we go from here? This chapter aims to answer these big questions and outline the key debates within the science education sector and beyond.

The 'coreness' of science

As a lecturer in science education I have often been shocked (but not surprised) to hear how little science is going on within some of the schools in which the trainees undertake their school experience. I wish I had a pound for every time I hear one of them say, "But it's not a core subject anyway, is it ...?" The debate around 'coreness' is an interesting one. Within the world of education, we all know that what should have happened with the abolition of Key Stage 2 SATS for Science (announced in May 2009) was the opening up of a world of science exploration, enquiry and engagement. Many science bodies (SCORE, ASE, Society of Biology, Royal Society, Royal Society of Chemistry) supported the move away from such testing. Views included the Vice-President of the Royal Society, Sir Martin Taylor, stating that he was 'delighted that SATS in science for 10- and 11-year-olds are to be abandoned' (SCORE report, 2009) and the move was warmly welcomed by others. There was great hope from the RSC that removal of teaching to the test would free up valuable time for inspirational science lessons. However, each of these science bodies, in one way or another, issued a caveat to their enthusiastic support for the divorce of this testing and the learners ... the RSC, for example, warned of science being seen as the poor relation to the still formally tested subjects.

So rather than our much-anticipated primary science utopia, we find ourselves in a position where Ofsted are reporting on findings that support the worst-case scenarios outlined over 10 years ago, and primary science finds itself in a sorry state. Ofsted (2019a, p.4) reported their observations as:

> Little consideration was given to understanding scientific concepts and skills nor how they could be sequenced to aid pupils' understanding. We understand the incentives that have led some schools to deprioritise science. However, there is clearly enough room within the timetable to ensure that young people can master the essentials of English and mathematics at the same time as building their knowledge in science.

Now, to defend this damning position a little, I *know* that there are many pockets of excellence with primary science. I work with some schools undertaking their Primary Science Quality Mark and, with increasing numbers each year across the country completing the awards, we know that this is one positive impact on the quality of science in the primary age phase. The situation remains, however, that science is rarely given the teaching time it should have; opportunities for science-related professional development are not prioritised (despite Ofsted recognising that a 'wealth of high-quality resources exists to support primary science leaders' [Ofsted, 2019a, p.5]); and it has indeed become that predicted poor relation.

Should science be a core subject? If that means it is given status and recognition within schools, then yes. Whilst Ofsted recognised that these concerns were shared in other subject areas, they stated that 'because science is a core subject within the national curriculum, this is a particular worry' (2019a, p.4).

Currently, the term 'core' is meaningless and carries little weight, it seems. Being core has not done much for the status of primary science since SATS were abandoned in this subject – and the consequence appears to be that science finds itself in what might be described as a no man's land between a disrespected core subject and not having the credibility of being a foundation one. I appreciate the arguments about the time given to foundation subjects but at least they have a label that is accepted and gives them some context and meaning.

One of the greater issues amongst this is finding a solution. It feels as though we are left with the need to reintroduce testing to raise the profile of science again. Currently random sampling takes place every two years – four in 1500 children will be tested in science at the end of KS2. The DfE (2017) report summarises the outcomes from this testing but it indicates that less than 25% of the children were at the standard expected by the end of the KS2 in science. There are arguments about why this is, one such being that the introduction of the new curriculum compared with the previous cohort sampled meant that the content to be taught was not as embedded as it had been previously. This aside, the 2014 sample shows 28% of pupils achieved the expected standard in science … which I would argue is still not enough. By reintroducing formal testing, science would at least have to be given the time and recognition it (arguably) deserves.

However, this sits rather uncomfortably with me. Whilst this may solve one problem, it creates others. It does not improve the *quality* of science teaching and *support* for teachers having to teach this subject. We may, indeed, recreate the situation where science is 'taught to the test'. The exploration and enquiry element of science has not been exploited sufficiently with the abolition of the formal testing – so if it is reintroduced there is the danger of exacerbating this. The 'good stuff' is not happening enough to be constrained by this testing!

Moreover, should we be testing children in this way, particularly at this age? Two of the other key debates that will be addressed in this chapter are 'science capital' and the 'STEM gap'. My greatest fear of the reintroduction of testing is that it will curtail the growth of these areas even further. Unfortunately, what I do not have is an answer to this conundrum. I just have to hold on with some optimism and hope that at least now Ofsted are recognising that the core status of science is not being upheld. They, along with the professional bodies who once supported the abolishing of SATS and aimed to work closely with the government to provide a safety net for science provision, have the potential to turn this ocean vessel in the right direction.

In May 2019, Ofsted outlined their methodology for approaching curriculum inspections (Ofsted, 2019a) and introduced the notion of a 'deep dive', which:

involves gathering evidence on the curriculum intent, implementation and impact over a sample of subjects, topics or aspects. This is done in collaboration with leaders, teachers and pupils. The intent of the deep dive is to seek to interrogate and establish a coherent evidence base on quality of education.

(Ofsted, 2019b, p.4)

Since the inspection framework was implemented in September 2019, science-based and primary school–focussed social media and support networks have been seen to engage with a great deal of discussion about such 'deep dives'. Many teachers are making reference to science being one of the subjects that Ofsted are including within the inspections, although no individual subject is specifically mentioned within this document, which suggests there is a translation of Ofsted's findings from their earlier report on science into an action. Clearly, the longer-term impact of such focus will not be known for some time and it is held in the balance if this shift will support science teaching and learning in a positive way or not.

Science capital

The Institute of Education, University College London, is the centre which is undertaking a wealth of research into and around science capital. The current work is seated in the context of previous ASPIRES projects which were undertaken through King's College London. UCL (2019) describe capital as:

a concept that can help us to understand why some young people participate in post-16 science and others do not. In particular, it helps shed light on why particular social groups remain underrepresented and why many young people do not see science careers as being 'for me'.

The concept of science capital can be imagined like a 'holdall', or bag, containing all the science-related knowledge, attitudes, experiences and resources that you acquire through life. It includes what science you know, how you think about science (your attitudes and dispositions), who you know (e.g. if your parents are very interested in science) and what sort of everyday engagement you have with science.

Science capital is a very interesting concept. Professor Louise Archer and team at UCL have identified eight dimensions of science capital from research analyses that together comprise what you know, how you think, who you know, and what you do:

Science capital dimensions

1. Scientific literacy
2. Science-related attitudes, values and dispositions

3. Knowledge about the transferability of science
4. Science media consumption
5. Participation in out-of-school science learning contexts
6. Families science skills, knowledge and qualifications
7. Knowing people in science-related roles
8. Talking about science in everyday life

(KCL, 2019)

The ASPIRES2 project is the second phase of a 10-year study. The key finding relevant from here is that if children do not see science as being 'for me' by the time they are 11, then the chances are they will not change their minds. If it is known that 11 years of age is the 'cut off' for engagement with science in the longer term, then the primary age phase is where efforts need to be targeted in order to change this state of play. To date, the majority of the research has been located in the secondary age phase, although this is extending with further research into developing a 'science capital teaching approach' within the primary age phase through collaboration between the Ogden Trust, Primary Science Teaching Trust (PSTT) and the IoE at UCL.

The danger with this is the misinterpretation of what constitutes a science capital teaching approach and how it is utilised. It is far more than simply setting learning in the context of science, or a visit to a science-based industrial site or having a visiting speaker. The Science Capital Teaching Approach for secondary schools was produced as a support pack in 2017 and is described as working:

within any science curriculum. It is not a new set of materials and it does not mean a dilution of science ideas and concepts. Instead, it is a reflective framework that involves making small tweaks to existing practice so as to re-orientate science lessons in ways that can better connect with the reality of students' lives and experiences.

(Godec, King and Archer, 2017, p.5)

This approach suggests a shift in pedagogy for teachers. The advantage for secondary school teachers doing this is the access they have to secure science subject knowledge. They are steeped within the science contexts to draw upon on a day to day basis. This is not necessarily so for primary teachers who often lack confidence (and knowledge) with teaching science. The challenges with this are embedded in how primary teachers are supported with making such a shift, with the already identified lack of professional development opportunities. And again, as Ofsted (2019) suggest, if there is insufficient science already taking place, how will improving the quality of the teaching and provision through such a teaching approach ever materialise?

However, the development of the teaching approach can only go towards supporting the engagement of teachers and learners in schools with primary science and start to build foundations for the future. If more children see that science is or could be for them, this has the potential to give the subject more intrinsic value than a subject that is formally examined. The challenge lies around the Senior Leadership Team (SLT) within the school to perceive this value and take the step towards supporting science fully. I am currently working with one school who are refreshingly redesigning their curriculum so *all* subjects are taught through science as a context – but not all schools are so fortunate to have such SLT support. In the Ofsted (2019b) publication one of the statements that was perhaps most alarming was 'a few headteachers were shocked to find during the research fieldwork just how limited their science curriculum really was' (Ofsted, 2019b). I fully appreciate that headteachers, and their team, are extremely busy individuals and issuing blanket criticism is unfair … but to be 'shocked' at the quality of provision indicates that there is little engagement with it, which subsequently proffers a position in terms of how valued science is within their setting. And whilst all of this unfolds within the education system, the learners are being given a very clear message about the importance of science – it is no real wonder that they do not see it as being 'for me' if they are not really seeing it at all.

The notion of science capital is a very familiar one – it feels right and whether it is a formal label for something that has already been happening in some places or not is irrelevant in this context. It is a tangible measure of the value and relevance of science to the lives of young learners, and if this can try to fill some of the gaps created by the supposed positive move of SATS abolition then much is to be celebrated.

STEM gaps

The STEM (Science, Technology, Engineering and Maths) employment shortage is something that is met with interesting conversation of late. I started as a secondary science teacher over 20 years ago. There was talk then about the need to support girls in particular in science and the general lack of science graduates to take up jobs within industry and the wider scientific community. I am not sure when those particular debates started but what I do know is that they are ongoing. It feels that over the years there has been an increasing awareness of the STEM gap in terms of post-16 uptake of the sciences and suitably qualified science graduates for jobs, and within teaching itself we see the issues around recruitment and retention of science (and other) teachers. In February 2019 the BBC reported that 'teacher training providers have accused the government of "lowering the bar" on teacher recruitment to address teacher shortages within the classroom' (BBC, 2019) despite bursaries of up to £26,000 for some secondary subjects, including the sciences.

At the same time a parallel debate is emerging. Studies from the University of Warwick and University of Leicester suggest that the issue is not around the uptake of sciences at post-16 and degree level, but rather that graduates are choosing not to go into jobs related to science and their degree, stating:

There is no evidence of a shortage of STEM graduates per se. Only a minority of STEM graduates ever work in HS STEM occupations, and an even smaller proportion are employed in key 'shortage' areas. Any mismatch between the supply and demand for STEM workers cannot, therefore, be attributed to the number of students graduating with STEM degrees. Problems with the 'supply' of STEM workers are more likely to be explained by the willingness of graduates to pursue careers in STEM fields and the recruitment practices of employers.

(Smith and White, 2018, p.7)

This would suggest that although there is a 'gap' somewhere in the system, there is some uncertainty as to where the supply chain of scientists and other STEM professionals breaks down.

The recruitment practices of employers are not something up for debate here, but the aspirations of the students offer an interesting discussion. If students' expectations of what science-related degrees and jobs involve are not being met, there is an argument that they are not being sufficiently prepared, and schools could be doing them a disservice by not aligning the curriculum with what is needed out in the employment market. Perhaps the gap is in connections between 'real-life' science jobs and the demands of degrees and A-level sciences.

Solutions are neither simple nor straightforward, but it is evident that interventions and initiatives up to this point are not having a significant effect. The conclusion from the Ofsted report (2019a, p.5) declares that:

Science has clearly been downgraded in some primary schools … this is likely to have a serious impact on the depth and breadth of science understanding and knowledge that pupils take with them into secondary school, which may in turn stifle pupils' later curiosity and interest in the sciences.

If there is a solution to making science more attractive to learners, it does not lie within the secondary age phase – this Ofsted report and the ASPIRES2 work demonstrates that. If learners are to be the scientists of the future then this needs to start in primary school, and it will be another 15 years before the rewards are seen. If an approach like that being developed by IoE UCL can encourage children to see science as 'for me', and their expectations of what science-related employment and post-18 study look like are realised, there is a chance that the STEM gap (whether through more pupils taking the subjects in and beyond GCSE or more following the route through to employment within the sector) may be filled.

Science and lifelong learning

What appears to be in little debate is the need for science education throughout school to create a more consistent path for learners towards their futures. In terms of having a scientifically literate society, Abrahams et al. (2019, p.7) state that:

> The reality of the complex society in which we live is such that we depend on experts and professionals. Most of us are not scientists or designers of technology and yet irrespective of our academic achievements are all able to use mobile phones, send e-mails and fly around the world without needing to know, or in many cases having any desire to know, anything about the underlying science that enables such technology to function.

As science and technology progress we seem to accept more without question, and there is a danger in that through doing so children simply acknowledge advances, and the inquisitive future generations of scientists are not encouraged. I wonder what it will take to really 'wow' the children in schools now as there is so much technology at their fingertips. Abrahams et al. (ibid.) offer five arguments as to why people should continue to develop their knowledge of science, which fall under the headings of Economic, Democratic, Utility, Social and Cultural. The economic argument has already been touched upon within this chapter, and the cultural debate is too large to engage with here; however, their other arguments make interesting points about the changing society we live in and the challenging nature of engaging with lifelong learning in science. Their democratic argument suggests

> that science knowledge enables individuals living in a scientific society to engage in debate and decision-making in contexts that involve scientific information ... However, this argument fails to consider the level of scientific conceptual understanding that is required to make scientifically rational informed decisions.
>
> (Abrahams et al., 2019 p.2)

Their stance on the Utility argument suggests that:

> science knowledge is of value to individuals living in a society dependent on science ... it is important to teach science in order for students to develop the knowledge they will subsequently utilise in decision making about science related issues at an individual level (for example, nutrition, health and safety) thereby enabling them to make rational, scientifically, informed choices as consumers.

In the wider social context, they argue that:

> the increasing specialisation and remoteness of much scientific knowledge has created a gap between society at large and science, which threatens both. It can be argued that a scientifically educated individual – it is unclear what

level of science education is required – would feel less alienated from science and scientific research, and perhaps better sympathise with the aims of science.

All of these points make it clear that to really make sense of science and to be informed about decisions that influence generations of people in a progressive society is a considerably complex task. We want for the public to understand and think like scientists, without being scientists. And can the younger generations lead the way with this if they are not fully exploring these approaches themselves and having them modelled within their education? This goes beyond having a qualification in science; it asks for people to potentially have conceptual understanding and a way of thinking that to this point they may not have experienced. This does not mean, however, that there should not be a push to recognise the importance of lifelong learning – and arguably, particularly with science – as it holds many of the answers to the questions of a future society that have not yet been asked.

Summary

Perhaps being at the heart of science education in the roles I currently work in is why, despite all the challenges that science, particularly in the primary age phase, faces, I am optimistic that there is a positive change afoot. It feels as though recognition through inspection of science as a 'core' subject is on balance a good thing. The focus of projects on developing such areas as science capital, again, can only be a good thing for the subject. Proactive engagement of learners early in their school career with science has the potential to fill some of the gaps that are seen further down the line in terms of recruitment to science roles and the development of a truly scientifically literate society. The paradox comes with the progressive nature of the subject and whether education and society will always be chasing the tail of the development of science and what it can do and is doing. This is not, however, a reason to avoid engaging with science throughout our lives, and rather should spur us on to learn more and be able to make more informed decisions about issues that have both personal and global impact, such as sustainability and climate change.

The status of science in education will most probably remain a political one for some time. Its demise over the last 10 years in school was caused by a change in assessment policy ... but as suggested, a revisit to such testing will not necessarily result in the science we *need* to be taught *being* taught.

Questions for reflection

To what extent is science recognised as a core subject within your school and how can its profile be raised without creating burdensome workload for teachers?

How can science capital of both teachers and pupils within the school be developed to improve the engagement with science as a long-term goal?

How can schools try to maintain pace with the progress of science within the constraints of the curriculum?

Further reading and resources

The Science Capital Teaching Approach: engaging students with science, promoting social justice. Available (free of charge) at: https://www.ucl.ac.uk/ioe/depa rtments-and-centres/departments/education-practice-and-society/science-capi tal-research/science-capital-teaching-approach.

This resource identifies opportunities to integrate approaches which will develop science capital into everyday teaching. It is accessible and offers case studies which contextualise the strategies. Although initially intended for use within the secondary age phase, there are many principles which can be drawn on to support the learning of children in the primary school.

Association for Science Education: https://www.ase.org.uk/.

There is a significant volume of supportive material which is available to non-members (although membership provides access to all resources). The Association works alongside all of the key science education bodies to distil changes in guidance into teacher talk and action within the classroom. They are working to inform policy and best practice within science education across the primary (and secondary) age phases.

Primary Science Teaching Trust: https://pstt.org.uk/.

The PSTT have a vision which aims to 'see excellent teaching of science in every primary classroom in the UK'. As well as having established networks of Fellows, Academic Collaborators and Clusters of schools, they offer a range of resources which are aimed at developing effective primary science teaching.

National STEM Learning Centre: Future Learn: https://www.futurelearn.com/pa rtners/stem-learning.

This website offers a range of online courses for teachers to access free CPD based on their own needs and the school's areas for development. As well as practical support there are many courses which also engage with developing understanding of theory and pedagogy.

References

Abrahams, I., Potterton, B., Fotou, N. & Constantinou, M. (2019) 'Scientific literacy: Who needs it in a "Black Box" Technological Society?' In *New Perspectives in Science Education*, 21–22 March 2019, Florence, Italy.

ASPIRES2 Available at: https://www.kcl.ac.uk/sspp/departments/education/r esearch/ASPIRES/Index.aspx.

BBC (2019) *Ministers Accused of Pressure Over Teacher Recruits*. Available at: https://www.bbc.co.uk/news/education-47132288.

DfE (2017) *Key Stage 2 Science Sampling 2016 Methodology Note and Outcomes.* Available at: https://assets.publishing.service.gov.uk/government/uploads/

system/uploads/attachment_data/file/630681/2016ScienceSamplingMethodol ogyOutcomesPaper.pdf.

Godec, S., King, H. & Archer, L. (2017) *The Science Capital Teaching Approach: Engaging Students with Science, Promoting Social Justice*, University College London: London.

King's College London (2019) *Science Capital*. Available at: https://www.kcl.ac.uk /ecs/research/research-centres/cppr/research/currentpro/enterprising-science /01science-capital.

Ofsted (2019a) *Intention and Substance Findings of Primary School Science*. Available at: https://assets.publishing.service.gov.uk/government/uploads/system/upl oads/attachment_data/file/777992/Intention_and_substance_findings_paper _on_primary_school_science_110219.pdf.

Ofsted (2019b) *Inspecting the Curriculum: Revising Inspection Methodology to Support the Education Inspection Framework*. Available at: https://assets.publishing.serv ice.gov.uk/government/uploads/system/uploads/attachment_data/file/8146 85/Inspecting_the_curriculum.pdf.

SCORE (2009) Available at: http://www.score-education.org/news/press-releases -and-media-coverage/abolishment-of-ks2-sats.

Smith, E. & White, P. (2018) *The Employment Trajectories of Science Technology Engineering and Mathematics Graduates*, University of Leicester: Leicester.

Chapter 12

Religious Education – what is it trying to do?

Rhiannon Love and Alasdair Richardson

Introduction

Primary teachers know that it can be difficult enough trying to teach a subject when you have a National Curriculum document and scheme of work to plan from. Religious Education (RE) occupies a unique place in Primary education in the United Kingdom (UK) in that it is statutory (it must be taught), but the content is locally agreed. As such, the content, intentions and pedagogical approaches taken in RE lessons can differ widely from school to school. This chapter hopes to give Primary practitioners an overview of what RE is (and is not) and what it might (or could) be, and challenges the reader to think about the way forward for RE. Our key question is: what is RE trying to do? As teachers with a broad experience teaching RE from the Early Years to Advanced Level (and to undergraduate and postgraduate trainee teachers), the authors will take a pragmatic disciplinary approach. By this we mean that we will not align ourselves to a particular local syllabus, philosophical school of thought, or pedagogical approach. Rather, we will offer the history of RE in the UK, its current position and recent developments to challenge the reader to think about what this might mean for them in their practice.

What is the purpose of RE?

An interesting exercise to complete with RE professionals, student teachers or even pupils is to ask them what they think the purpose of RE is. Opinions are invariably divided, with some opting for statements around academic rigour and knowledge-based content; some argue intentions around preparing for the modern, diverse world (understanding and tolerance of all in society, for example); whilst others argue about finding meaning and answering 'big questions' (such as those around life and death); with still others promoting various government initiatives such as Fundamental British Values (FBVs), countering extremism and Spiritual, Moral, Social and Cultural Development (SMSC), to name but a few. It can be confusing for subject practitioners of other disciplines to understand how there is such a diversity of views and opinions around something so fundamental as the 'purpose' of a school subject.

Even government-issued guidance on good practice in RE does not make the purpose any clearer. The aims and purposes of the 2010 non-statutory guidance for RE (DCSF, 2010) are varied and broad:

- developing pupils' knowledge and understanding of principal religions;
- understanding and respecting beliefs and traditions;
- considering questions of meaning and purpose in life;
- considering ethical teaching to make reasoned judgements;
- developing identity and belonging;
- building resilience to anti-democratic or extremist narratives;
- building community cohesion.

Similarly, Conroy et al.'s research found that the purposes of RE reported by stakeholders were multiple, complex and often contradictory or competing (see Table 12.1).

How is it possible that one subject can be expected to address these contrasting, and some might argue, conflicting areas? In their attempt to define what RE is, the Inter Faith Network (IFN) suggest that:

> for many children and young people religious education (RE) lessons will be the first place they learn about people different from themselves and often the first context in which they will meet a person who belongs to a religious belief tradition different from their own. Pupils are encouraged to learn about and develop their own beliefs and learn about the beliefs and practices of others, whilst learning to respect those who hold beliefs different to their own.
>
> (IFN, 2019)

Table 12.1 Competing imperatives on Religious Education (Conroy et al., 2012, p.312)

a. Religious literacy (knowledge and understanding of religious ideas and language and their social and cultural impact)
b. Dealing with truth claims and pluralism
c. Philosophical understanding
d. Understanding heritage
e. Citizenship education
f. Multicultural sensitivity and awareness
g. Spiritual and social cohesion – contributing to school ethos
h. Nurturing pupils in particular communities (including catechesis)
i. Moral development
j. Spiritual life and religious observance
k. Enhancing local demographic considerations
l. Very particular 'Socratic dispositions'
m. Sex and relationships education

For the IFN, RE appears to be a place where children can encounter others who have different beliefs from them, and to learn about those beliefs in an atmosphere of mutual respect. The IFN was established in 1987 with the explicit aim of building cohesion and understanding between different faith traditions, and is one of several committees, bodies or organisations who represent the views of those involved in RE. These organisations include (but are not limited to) the RE Council for England and Wales (REC), the National Association for Teachers of RE (NATRE), the National Association of Standing Advisory Councils on RE (NASACRE), and the Association for Religious Education Inspectors, Advisers and Consultants (AREIAC). All of these organisations produce teaching guidance or resources for teachers and educators, but the diversity of opinions and organisations reflects the disparate nature and evolution of RE policy and practice in UK schools over the last century – and all contribute to the feeling that we lack coherence in our sense of purpose for our subject. Since there is no National Curriculum for RE in UK Schools, the content of a RE lesson will vary for children of the same age, depending upon which UK country they live in, which area they live in within the country, and the type of school they attend. In this respect, RE is unlike any other discrete curriculum subject. It is a subject that finds itself in a unique (and arguably precarious) position. The reasons behind this are connected to the long and complex history of the subject in schools. To try to explore our key question further, we need to consider this historical background in order better to understand the intentions behind its evolution.

Religious Education in the UK – a brief history

The history of Religious Education in British schools can be traced back to before the 1902 Education Act, in which the government formalised the status of the Anglican and Catholic churches in running schools. The centrality of the churches in the delivery of education (and curriculum design) remained evident in the 1944 Education Act. At a time of war, the Government of National Unity chose to work with (rather than against) the churches to enshrine its vision of a post-war, peaceful education system. There was undoubtedly 'a shifting social climate' at that time that facilitated collaboration between church and state (Barber, 1994, p.3). Such cooperation meant both sides had to compromise. Following the 1944 Education Act, all schools were required to teach RE (or 'Religious Instruction' as it was first known – because the intention was to 'instruct' children in their Christian faith), and to provide a daily act of collective worship. Since the 1902 Education Act each local authority (usually a county council, or in some cases a larger city council) has been required to have a committee known as the Local Education Authority (or 'LEA', now often referred to simply as the Local Authority or 'LA') (Byrne, 1986). Since the 1944 Act, each LEA has been required to have an Agreed Syllabus Conference (ASC) to oversee the creation and revision of the Locally Agreed Syllabus, and to have a Standing Advisory Council on Religious Education (SACRE) to advise them on matters relating to RE and collective worship. The different committees are expected to have representatives from different interested groups – such as teachers, members of faith communities and elected local politicians (and additional members can be co-opted to better inform their work). Following the 1988 Education Reform Act, the law stated that RE 'shall reflect the fact that the religious traditions in Great Britain are in the main Christian whilst taking account of the teaching and practices of the other principal religions represented in Great Britain', while the daily act of collective worship (which is separate from RE, but legislatively linked) 'shall be wholly or mainly of a broadly Christian character' (HMSS, 1944, sections 8.3 and 7.1, respectively).

RE and devolution in the UK

Since the late 1990s, the UK has seen greater devolution of control over education policy to its constituent countries (England, Wales, Scotland and Northern Ireland). Consequently, there are important variances between RE provision in the different countries which need to be understood when approaching our discussion.

England and Wales

Maintained schools in England and Wales are expected to follow the National Curriculum (https://www.gov.uk/government/collections/national-curriculum). Since its inception in 1989, the National Curriculum has set out expectations of curriculum coverage and attainment in the full range of school subjects across the compulsory school age range (5–18 years of age). Although independent schools (sometimes called 'private' schools in the UK) are not required to follow this curriculum, they are free to do so. The most recent revision to the National Curriculum was published in 2013 and retained the legal status of RE as a part of the 'statutory' curriculum. As such (along with Sex and Relationships Education, or 'SRE'), RE is a compulsory subject but does not have a prescribed curriculum document (unlike Geography or Music, for example). All of the National Curriculum subjects are studied from 5–14 years of age, whilst SRE is obligatory from age 11. RE is compulsory from the ages of 5–18 for all children in all state-funded schools. To complicate things further the National Curriculum documentation states that, 'Schools have to teach RE but parents can withdraw their children for all or part of the lessons, and pupils can choose to withdraw themselves once they're 18' (https://www.gov.uk/national-curriculum/other-compulsory-subjects). This means that while the subject is compulsory, parents have the right to withdraw their children for all or part of the curriculum (for which they do not have to provide a reason, and for which the school is not expected to offer an alternative educational provision beyond supervision of the child).

In an attempt to clarify the statutory (legal) requirements for schools, NATRE reiterate that in keeping with the National Curriculum documentation, 'Every maintained school in England must provide... RE for all registered pupils at the school' (DCSF, 2010, p.10). Given the diversity of types of school that now exist in the UK (such as Free Schools or Academies – which are state-funded, but technically independent schools), NATRE also set out the legal requirements for the different schools: 'All maintained schools [including] Academies and free schools are contractually required through the terms of their funding agreement to make provision for the teaching of RE' (NATRE, 2019). Broadly speaking, the legislation makes it clear that every pupil in a state-funded school from 5–18 must receive some form of Religious Education. Usually this will follow the Locally Agreed Syllabus as set down by the local SACRE, although schools with a religious character can follow an alternative syllabus in line with their foundation (such as a scheme of work specifically written for Catholic schools).

Scotland

In Scotland, the Education (Scotland) Act 1980 established provision for RE, and in school these lessons are delivered through Religious and Moral Education (RME). Education Scotland (https://education.gov.scot) define this as being 'two distinct areas' which 'involves exploring Beliefs, Values and Issues and Practices and Traditions through the context of Christianity, World Religions... and belief groups independent of religion' (Education Scotland, 2011). In the country's Catholic schools there is a separate programme of Religious Education – Religious Education in Roman Catholic schools (RERC). RME must be provided for all pupils in Primary and Secondary schools (from 5–18 years of age) and is one of the eight core curriculum areas within *Curriculum for Excellence* (the national curriculum for schools) (Scottish Government, 2011, sections 5 and 6, respectively). In Scotland RME is clearly a 'values based framework for learning and teaching', which supports 'the values of compassion, wisdom, justice and integrity that underpin Curriculum for Excellence' (Education Scotland, 2014, sections 3 and 6, respectively). As such the explicit outcomes of RME appear to be more broadly impactful on pupils' moral development than in England and Wales.

Let us consider the question of aligning religious with moral education for a moment. Which other subject would presume to both engage in moral teaching whilst still aiming to be considered an academic subject with specific subject knowledge to impart (Barnes, 2011; Conroy et al., 2012; White, 2004)? Teachers should consider if it is desirable or acceptable that RE should be used as 'a vehicle of moral education' (Barnes, 2011; White, 2004, p.156). This goes beyond engaging with ethical questions, which the pupils might encounter in other subjects (such as discussing climate change in Geography, for example). White cautions that such connections 'may engender or reinforce in some children the notion that morality is impossible without religion' (White, 2004, p.158). He does not suggest that engaging with moral and ethical questions is unimportant, rather he proposes that the logical place for such discussions might sit more comfortably in Personal, Social and Health Education (PSHE) or Citizenship lessons, or even in collective worship. This, White suggests, would enable pupils to view RE as a purely academic subject, rather than being confused by its purpose.

Collective worship is called 'Religious Observance' (RO) in Scotland, and is less focused on Christianity, being required to reflect instead on 'a variety of faiths and belief perspectives' that echo the diversity of Scottish school populations (Scottish Government, 2017, section 13). The expectation is that RO happens 'several times in a school year' rather than daily, as it must in England and Wales.

Northern Ireland

In Northern Ireland the RE curriculum is defined by the Department of Education, together with the four largest Christian denominations in the country (Roman Catholic, Presbyterian, Anglican and Methodist) through the Council for the Curriculum, Examinations and Assessment (CEA) (http://ccea.org.uk/curric ulum/key_stage_3/areas_learning/religious_education). The prescribed curriculum is almost exclusively Christian in content. In each Key Stage the first three Learning Objectives (LOs) focus on: the revelation of God (LO 1), the Christian Church (LO 2) and morality (LO 3). Only in Key Stage 3 (for 11–14 year olds) is there a fourth LO focusing on world religions, with the expectation that pupils learn about two world religions other than Christianity. Consequently, children of primary age are not expected to study beliefs other than Christianity at school. As with the curriculum in Scotland, the Northern Irish documentation appears to have a wider focus on spiritual and moral development (albeit from a predominantly Christian perspective) than in England and Wales. However, like England and Wales the requirement for a daily act of (Christian) collective worship is more robustly required, enshrined within the Education and Libraries (Northern Ireland) Order (Northern Ireland Orders in Council, 1986, section 21).

RE pedagogy

In considering what we are trying to do in RE (and having established what the law requires us to be providing in RE above), it is important to think about how pedagogy in RE has developed, and how this has been viewed and interpreted by policy makers. Given its long history as a school subject, RE has been the focus of considerable research and evaluation by educationalists and different faith groups. In response to the introduction of the National Curriculum, Michael Grimmitt's *Pedagogies of Religious Education* drew together the major schools of thought from the previous 40 years (Grimmitt, 2000). Grimmitt saw the National Curriculum as being increasingly underpinned by an 'outcome, objective-led, competencies or standards driven educational ideology' (2000, p.9), whereby teachers were under pressure to commodify subjects. Although RE was not a National Curriculum subject, he felt it had been drawn into this process of commodification by default. His book was intended to 'liberate' RE teachers from this by ensuring 'that the subject's very rich repository of pedagogical research and development' was made available to them (2000, p.5). Gearon has since suggested that the developments in RE pedagogy over the years could be summarised in six paradigms (Gearon, 2013). These move from a Christian confessional model of Religious Instruction (RI) to more contemporary non-confessional, socio-cultural and historical-political models of Religious Education (RE) and Religious Studies (RS). Broadly speaking, he believes that RE has become less about what we collectively believe and more about a sociological study of what we, as a community, *variously* believe (or, indeed, do not believe).

Thinking around pedagogy has led to the publication of several key reports, briefings and position papers in the last decade. In 2010 the Department for Children, Schools and Families (DCSF, now the Department for Education) issued non-statutory guidance on the provision and teaching of RE for schools (DCSF, 2010). This guidance was intended to clarify schools' responsibilities amid the legal confusion and to provide case studies of good practice in a rapidly changing educational and social landscape (which was becoming increasingly multi-faith). In 2013, the Office for Standards in Education, Children's Services and Skills (Ofsted) published a review of RE provision from nearly 200 school inspections in the previous four years (Ofsted, 2013). Their findings presented a fairly dismal overview of an ailing subject – poorly resourced, with weak teaching and inadequate leadership, all culminating in restricted examination attainment by pupils later on in Secondary schools. A key finding of this report was that 'confusion about the purpose and aims of RE had a negative impact on the quality of teaching, curriculum planning and the effectiveness of assessment' (Ofsted, 2013, p.14). Specifically, they found that in primary schools, teachers were struggling to separate RE from spiritual, moral, social and cultural development (SMSC), whilst they also found too great a focus on pupils' own reflections or experience, to the detriment of rigorous in-depth study and evaluation of religion and belief. In summary, the inspectors reported that the rationale for RE lacked coherence and was too complex; resulting in what they saw as a confusion between academic content and personal development.

Consequently, the report lamented that 'the subject's potential is still not being realised fully' (Ofsted, 2013, p.4). More recently, Charles Clarke (a former Secretary of State for Education in England and Wales) and Professor Linda Woodhead published their vision of *A New Settlement Revised: Religion and Belief in Schools* in 2018 (an update to their similarly titled 2015 paper), principally advocating a National Curriculum for RE (Clarke and Woodhead, 2018). In 2018 the Commission on Religious Education (CoRE) published their final report *Religion and Worldviews: The Way Forward*. It is perhaps this report which (more than any other) sets out what RE is (or should be) trying to do, and which we will look at in greater detail now to explore our key question further.

Commission on RE – the way forward?

One of the most significant events for RE in 2018 was the long-awaited publication of the CoRE report (Commission on Religious Education, 2018). Launched in July 2016, the Commission was established to review the current legal, education and policy frameworks for RE, with the aim of improving the quality and rigour of RE. Published in September 2018, the report is the culmination of two years of work by the Commission, drawing on over 700 responses to their interim report *Religious Education for All* from across a wide range of stakeholders in RE. The authors of the final report challenge the Government to accept 11 key recommendations which, they claim, would not only transform the current RE curriculum, but also more truly reflect the diversity of modern society:

> Despite its central importance, RE in too many schools is not good enough to prepare pupils adequately for the religious and belief diversity they will encounter, nor to support them to engage deeply with the questions raised by the study of worldviews.
>
> (Commission on Religious Education, 2018, p.3)

Of these 11 recommendations, two warrant closer scrutiny for the purpose of our key question; Recommendation 1 – a proposed name change, and Recommendation 2 – regarding a proposal for a national entitlement.

Recommendation 1: The name of the subject should be changed to 'Religion and Worldviews'

The recommendation to change the name from 'Religious Education' to 'Religion and Worldviews' has caused much discussion amongst RE professionals. Many have welcomed the move, seeing it as embracing a wider, more inclusive outlook than 'religion' (Kuusisto et al., 2019), in particular to encompass non-religious worldviews (Erricker and Erricker, 2000). Authors such as Valk (2009) have long asserted that the term 'religion' is problematic, and can hinder discussions and restrict understanding of the diversity and variety of beliefs and values on offer, suggesting that:

> use of the term worldview, rather than exclusively religion, might enhance dialogue, broaden the discussion and expand the parameters to create a more level playing field, and to examine other perspectives which contrast or compete with religion in the public square.
>
> (Valk, 2009, p.1)

It could be suggested that the concept of worldview is more useful in our current era, where diversity is apparent in all walks of life, including the question of religious and non-religious beliefs (Valk, 2009). Valk suggests that this new focus can help us to move beyond a fixation on traditional religions to embrace other perspectives, leading to a 'greater understanding of ourselves and the world, and the fact that those thoughts and ideas hold great sway today in the public realm' (Valk, 2009, p.5). He argues that this will necessitate a rethink how not only religious, but also non-religious beliefs and values can impact on individuals' and societies' thoughts and actions. However, critics have raised concerns that this new name signals a dilution or a side-lining of the religious content (Cooling, 2019), as well as the possibility that the new focus might lead to a more individualistic approach at the expense of the communal, cultural and societal dimensions of religions (Kuusisto et al., 2019).

A further challenge is raised over the perceived lack of clarity around the definition of worldviews (Cooling, 2019). The Commission did try to address the latter point, including their own, detailed definition of Worldviews (see Table 12.2).

Recommendation 2: The National Entitlement to the study of Religion and Worldviews should become statutory for all publicly funded schools

The Commission found that, despite being a compulsory part of the curriculum, too many schools were failing to ensure that all pupils received their entitlement to Religious Education. Whilst some groups in the RE world had hoped that the Commission would advocate RE joining the National Curriculum, the reality was not quite as bold. Recommendation 2 suggested that the current statutory requirement for RE should be replaced with a National Entitlement which, they state, would 'reflect our vision for the subject, which is widely shared among teachers and subject experts, while retaining the flexibility for schools of all types to interpret it in accordance with their own needs, ethos and values'(Commission on Religious Education, 2018, p.1). This National Entitlement consists of nine statutory requirements that schools would need to meet and would be inspected against, including areas such as Point 9 – 'the different ways in which religion and worldviews can be understood, interpreted and studied, including through a wide range of academic disciplines and through direct encounter and discussion with individuals and communities who hold these worldviews' (Commission on Religious Education, 2018, p.11).

Table 12.2 CoRE definition of worldview (Commission on Religious Education, 2018, p.2)

The English word 'worldview' is a translation of the German *Weltanschauung*, which literally means a view of the world. A worldview is a person's way of understanding, experiencing and responding to the world. It can be described as a philosophy of life or an approach to life. This includes how a person understands the nature of reality and their own place in the world. A person's worldview is likely to influence and be influenced by their beliefs, values, behaviours, experiences, identities and commitments.

We use the term 'institutional worldview' to describe organised worldviews shared among particular groups and sometimes embedded in institutions. These include what we describe as religions as well as non-religious worldviews such as Humanism, Secularism or Atheism. We use the term 'personal worldview' for an individual's own way of understanding and living in the world, which may or may not draw from one, or many, institutional worldviews.

The question of a National Entitlement is a sensitive issue and one that is likely to split RE professionals. Its instigation would require a rethinking of the current role of SACREs and Locally Agreed Syllabi (see Recommendations 4 and 8 of the CoRE report), as it would replace the requirement in the Education Act 1996 (Section 375) for community, foundation and voluntary controlled schools to follow their Locally Agreed Syllabus.

Both of these recommendations would have significant implications on the structure of RE provision and monitoring locally, and redefine what RE is trying to do from a national perspective.

Summary

As we draw this chapter to a close we are presented with a problem – arguably we are no closer to answering our question 'what is RE trying to do?' than we were when we started! But this demonstrates the very problems that we have been discussing here, and the unique situation of RE in the curriculum... and RE is perhaps on the verge of further, radical evolution in the near future following the CoRE report. The subject remains bound up in a complex legal history, which has been the result of decades of negotiation between the Churches and the State. The result is that there is a lack of cohesion between the curriculum demands of each nation state of the UK, or even between neighbouring counties or authorities. We said at the outset of the chapter that we would take a 'pragmatic disciplinary approach'. We have tried to present balanced (if sometimes provocative) accounts of the possible purposes of the subject, its history, the legal requirements, the pedagogical approaches and more recent developments in opinion.

RE is about the 'big questions' in life, and claims of a 'search for meaning' are often at the forefront of discussions about the purpose of RE (Conroy et al., 2012, p.309). In examining Ofsted's subject report for RE (Ofsted, 2010) they found that while 'meaning' was explicitly mentioned 11 times as a central feature of RE, the same report proposed that success at Key Stage 4 (14–16 years) in RE was seen purely in terms of accredited qualification numbers (Conroy et al., 2012). This presents a potential tension for the subject between performative expectations around examination and curricular frameworks and 'nurturing certain perceived forms of human (personal) development and flourishing' (Conroy et al., 2012, p.316).

A further concern is the propensity for RE to be 'hijacked' by transitory government initiatives; for example Community Cohesion (DCSF, 2010), SMSC (Ofsted, 2015), Fundamental British Values (DFE, 2014) and the Prevent Agenda (HM Government, 2015), to name but a few in recent years. This can often be a challenging issue for RE teachers. It is undeniable that there are genuine connections with RE that can be made with many of these areas, however, when the suggestion or implication (from the government or senior leaders in school) is that these issues 'belong' to RE, this can cause issues. SMSC is a good example of this. Ofsted's (2013) report raised explicit concerns that primary teachers, including subject leaders, were often unable to separate RE from SMSC. Peterson et al. stress that whilst all staff need to share responsibility for SMSC, and indeed include SMSC 'teachable moments' where appropriate in lessons, there should not be an expectation that this needs to be in every lesson (Peterson et al., 2014, p.26). They do, however, concede that the methods of discussion that enable SMSC development are possibly more aligned with pedagogies of teachers of RE, Citizenship or Humanities.

Perhaps the greatest concern for RE teachers is the Prevent Agenda and related issues around preventing extremism. A key ingredient of a successful RE classroom is the ability of the teacher to create a 'safe space' for all pupils, where issues can be critically engaged within a supportive atmosphere. Farrell is openly critical of the government's attempts to incorporate extremism prevention in the RE curriculum, asserting that 'the aims of open pluralistic, critical RE are incompatible with the disciplinary incitements of the war on terror discourse as enacted in DfE education policy' (Farrell, 2016, p.283). His concern is regarding the invasion on the purpose of RE: 'RE is at risk of being territorialised as a strategic site for the government's domestic war on terror' (p.285), but also the challenges that it poses for RE teachers due to its depiction of Muslims in Islamophobic terms, and the need for RE teachers to be able to resist this narrative in their practice.

While it is important to consider all of the elements, contradictions and tensions we have discussed (above) and more, for many RE teachers they all play their part in the richness of RE debate. As Orchard states, 'contentious moral and ethical issues, beliefs about ultimate meaning and purpose that matter to children and young people and which have the potential to create divisions within communities are grist to the mill of the child-focused RE teacher' and we celebrate them (Orchard, 2015, p.49). What is important is that teachers have a clear understanding of what they are trying to achieve in *their* school and *their* classroom with *their* pupils, and that this can be articulated openly to the pupils, parents, wider community and external agencies (such as Ofsted), and equally what they are *not* trying to do. We believe that a National Curriculum for RE would go some considerable way to helping teachers with this – although we appreciate that such a document would be highly contentious in its design and implementation and will probably not be a reality for some time, if ever.

Questions for reflection

What should the subject be called? A name is important – should it include the words 'religion', 'belief' or 'worldview', for example?

What should the scope of RE be? Should RE include moral education, for example? Does collective worship have a place in RE (and if so, what should it be)? Should RE be predominantly focused on Christianity and would that reflect the national context? Should non-religious worldviews be included?

Should there be a National Curriculum for RE? Would a national entitlement help teachers in their planning and teaching? Could agreement about content ever be reached?

Further reading and resources

Commission on Religious Education (CoRE) https://www.commissiononre.org.uk/wpcontent/uploads/2018/09/Final-Report-of-the-Commission-on-RE.pdf. The CoRE Report is arguably the most significant appraisal of the state of RE in recent years. In its recommendations the Commission raise a number of issues which (whilst being potentially controversial and sensitive) can realistically not be avoided for much longer. For anyone with an interest in RE, this report is likely to have a significant influence on developments over the coming years.

Grimmitt, M. (2000) *Pedagogies of Religious Education: Case Studies in the Research and Development of Good Pedagogic Practice in RE*, Great Wakering: McCrimmons. This is an essential piece of work for anyone with an interest in RE pedagogy. Grimmitt's important work draws together thinkers from across several decades. In the absence of a national entitlement, teachers might use this volume to consider what their own pedagogy for RE might be.

The National Association for Teachers of RE (NATRE) https://www.natre.org.uk. The NATRE website provides access to information and resources for RE teachers. NATRE support RE teachers in various ways, including the organisation of conferences, as well as being a voice for RE nationally.

References

Barber, M. (1994) *The Making of the 1944 Education Act*, London: Cassell.
Barnes, L. P. (2011) *Debates in Religious Education*, London: Routledge.
Byrne, T. (1986) *Local Government in Britain: Everyone's Guide to How It All Works*, London: Penguin Books.
Clarke, C. & Woodhead, L. (2018) *A New Settlement Revised: Religion and Belief in Schools*. Available at: http://faithdebates.org.uk/wp-content/uploads/2018/07/Clarke-Woodhead NewSettlement-Revised.pdf (Accessed 30.07.2019).
Commission on Religious Education (2018) *Religion and Worldviews: The Way Forward: A National Plan for RE*, London: Religious Education Council of England & Wales. Available at: https://www.commissiononre.org.uk/wpcontent/uploads/2018/09/Final-Report-of-the Commission-on-RE.pdf.
Conroy, J. C., Lundie, D. & Baumfield, V. (2012) Failures of meaning in religious education. *Journal of Beliefs & Values*, 33(3): 309–323.
Cooling, T. (2019) The return to worldview: Reflections from the UK. *International Journal of Christianity & Education*, 23(1): 3–9.
DCSF (2010) *Promoting Community Cohesion: The Role of Extended Services*, Manchester: Training and Development Agency for Schools.
DCSF (2010) *Religious Education in English Schools: Non-Statutory Guidance 2010*. Available at: https://assets.publishing.service.gov.uk/government/uploads/syste

m/uploads/attachment_data/file/1　0260/DCSF-00114-2010.pdf (Accessed 30.07.2019.

DFE (2014) *Promoting Fundamental British Values as Part of SMSC in Schools.* Available at: https://assets.publishing.service.gov.uk/government/uploads/syste m/uploads/attachment_dat　/file/380595/SMSC_Guidance_Maintained_Sch ools.pdf.

Education Scotland (2011) *Curriculum for Excellence: Religious and Moral Education.* Available at: https://www.gov.scot/publications/curriculum-for-excellence-relig ious-and-moral-education/.

Education Scotland (2011) *Religious and Moral Education.* Available at: https:// education.gov.scot/scottish-education-system/policy-for-scottish-education/po licy-drivers/cfe-(building-from-the-statement-appendix-incl-btc1-5)/curriculu mareas/Religious%20and%20moral%20education (Accessed 30.07.2019).

Education Scotland (2014) *Religious and Moral Education 3–18.* Available at: https ://education.gov.scot/improvement/documents/rme30curriculumimpactrevie wrme.pdf.

Erricker, C. & Erricker, J. (2000) The children and worldviews project: A narrative pedagogy of religious education. In: Grimmitt, M. (ed.), *Pedagogies of Religious Education: Case Studies in the Research and Development of Good Pedagogic Practice in RE*, pp. 188–206, Essex: McCrimmons.

Farrell, F. (2016) 'Why all of a sudden do we need to teach fundamental British values?' A critical investigation of religious education student teacher positioning within a policy discourse of discipline and control. *Journal of Education for Teaching*, 42(3): 280–297.

Gearon, L. (2013) *MasterClass in Religious Education: Transforming Teaching and Learning*, London: A&C Black.

Grimmitt, M. (2000) *Pedagogies of Religious Education: Case Studies in the Research and Development of Good Pedagogic Practice In RE*, Great Wakering: McCrimmons.

HM Government (2015) *Revised Prevent Duty Guidance: For England and Wales*, London: HM Government.

HMSS (1944) *Education Act 1944.* Available at: http://www.legislation.gov.uk/ ukpga/Geo6/7-8/31/contents/enacted.

ITF (The Inter Faith Network for the United Kingdom) (2019) *Religious Education Across the UK.* Available at: https://www.interfaith.org.uk/activity/religious-e ducation (Accessed 30.07.2019).

Kuusisto, E., Hirsto, L. & Ubani, M. (2019) Introduction to religions and world views creating purpose and meaning for learning. *Journal of Beliefs & Values*, 40(1): 1–6.

NATRE (National Association of Teachers of Religious Education) (2019) *Legal Requirements.* Available at: https://www.natre.org.uk/about-re/legal-requi rements/ (Accessed 30.07.2019).

Northern Ireland Orders in Council (1986) *The Education and Libraries (Northern Ireland) Order 1986.* Available at: https://www.legislation.gov.uk/nisi/1986 /594/article/21(Accessed 30.07.2019).

Ofsted (2010) *Transforming Religious Education: Religious Education in schools 2006–09*, Manchester: Office for Standards in Education.

Ofsted (2013) *Religious Education: Realising the Potential*, Manchester: Ofsted Accessed at: https://www.gov.uk/government/uploads/system/uploads/at tachment_data/file/413157/Religo us_education_-_realising_the_potential.pdf.

Ofsted (2015) *School Inspection Handbook from September 2015*, Manchester: OfSTED. Available at: https://www.gov.uk/government/publications/school-inspection-handbookfrom september-2015 (Accessed 29.05.2016).

Orchard, J. (2015) Does religious education promote good community relations? *Journal of Beliefs & Values*, 36(1): 40–53.

Peterson, A., Lexmond, J., Hallgarten, J. & Kerr, D. (2014) *Schools with Soul: A New Approach to Spiritual, Moral, Social and Cultural Education*, London: RSA: Action and Research Centre.

Scottish Government (2017) *Curriculum for Excellence: Religious Observance*. Available at: https://www.gov.scot/publications/curriculum-for-excellence-relig ious-observance/ (Accessed 30.07.2019).

Valk, J. (2009) Religion or worldview: Enhancing dialogue in the public square. *Marburg Journal of Religion*, 14(1): 1–16.

White, J. (2004) Should religious education be a compulsory school subject? *British Journal of Religious Education*, 26(2): 151–164.

Chapter 13

Geography and history – a sense of time and place

Wendy Garner and Tony Pickford

Introduction

This chapter will explore geographical and historical education within the primary phase of compulsory education. Since the advent of the National Curriculum in 1988, there has been ongoing debate about the nature of history and geography, the focus of the curriculum in terms of the 'facts versus skills' debate and the value of these subjects within the context of the wider curriculum. These critical areas and issues will be explored from a range of perspectives which comprise historical, political, psychological and pedagogical.

Firstly, and importantly, the reasons why each subject evolved will be identified and discussed. Secondly, and also worthy of consideration, is an exploration of how over time, each subject has developed and changed. Aligned with this, there is also a need to reflect on how the changing nature of these subject areas impacts on young learners and their futures.

For over 20 years, relevant subject associations and subject-specific, pedagogical literature have advocated enquiry-based learning as an effective model of teaching and learning, as opposed to teacher-led instruction. Consideration of humanities pedagogy in this way is arguably an oversimplification of what represents a much more complex phenomenon and one which should be viewed through a variety of lenses. The humanities subjects are intrinsically valuable within the context of educating young people. Both subjects provide a rich context for the development of core subjects such as English and Maths, for example, in addition to the opportunities afforded by significant and ongoing developments in technology. Taking a cross-curricular approach and the value in doing so may be contested and adds another important layer to the discussion. These are some of the areas to be debated within this chapter.

Facts, skills and history

The so-called 'facts versus skills' debate in primary education has a long history. Put simply, the dispute revolves around two distinct ways in which the curriculum in primary schools might be organised – a teacher-led, traditionalist approach centring on the delivery of factual knowledge, or a more learner-centred approach where children are facilitated to develop subject-based and cross-curricular skills through discovery, questioning and enquiry. Although evident in other subjects across the curriculum, the development of teaching approaches in the humanities, and specifically primary history, illustrates the key elements of the debate particularly well. Although its roots may be much earlier, in sources such as the Hadow Report in 1931 with its recommendation that primary education should be thought of 'in terms of activity and experience, rather than of knowledge to be acquired and facts to be stored', the dispute became more explicit in the 1960s with differing responses to the Plowden Report and its emphasis on a Piagetian analysis of children's development and learning. Put simply, Piaget's view that most children of primary age learn best through activity based on concrete objects and events (the so-called stage of 'concrete operations') can be construed as having two key, mutually exclusive implications:

- As abstract thought and problem solving is beyond the capabilities of most children, then learning must be based on a simple transmission model – give children the facts of a subject at primary school age, so that they may be able to engage in more higher-order thinking and activities at some vague point later in their development.
- Or, base subject learning on Piagetian principles – make it as practical as possible through learner-centred, hands-on activities and engagement with concrete, real-world materials and sources.

The former approach was, perhaps, best reflected in the primary history textbooks of R. J. Unstead. His texts on British history, published in the 1950s and 1960s, presented the subject as an uncontested narrative of (mainly) great men and their contributions to the development and improvement of our island nation. Although the books were copiously illustrated with images and sources, children were given no scope for questioning or analysis, but presented with a single, chronological, highly Anglo-centric account with often idiosyncratic views about some historical characters. Whole-class teaching centred on Unstead's stories, with lessons being little more than shared reading exercises. The author can remember dreading these history lessons as a junior-age child in the mid-1960s and a less than fluent reader – the daunting prospect of being chosen to read a passage containing challenging words, such as 'medieval' or 'Elizabethan', hardly led to the development of a love for the subject.

The latter approach, embodying Plowden's child-centred philosophy, became increasingly more prevalent in teaching strategies in the 1970s and 1980s. In history, set whole-class textbooks, such as Unstead's, were disparaged and replaced by materials and sources, which became the focus of more learner-centred, question-led, often group-based activities. The author can remember, as a new teacher in the late 1970s, being informed by the deputy head in his first primary school that there were no longer any class sets of textbooks in the school and all lessons were now based on practical activities and group work. The surplus textbooks had apparently ended up in a skip!

By the mid-1980s, primary history began to reflect approaches pioneered in secondary schools and labelled 'new history' by advocates. The narrative of history still had its place but was accompanied by relevant primary source material and prompts/questions to encourage enquiry and interpretation. Materials produced by the Schools Council and source-based packs, such as the 'Jackdaw' series, supplemented teacher-produced materials, created using newly acquired photocopiers. Learning of history began to focus on understandings of key concepts, such as change and continuity, alongside conventional narratives. Not everyone was happy with these more learner-centred approaches and critical voices questioned the capabilities of young children when faced with original material and, sometimes, conflicting evidence. By the time of the 1988 Education Reform Act and the introduction of the National Curriculum in England and Wales, the proponents of traditional, knowledge-based approaches and others who supported 'new history' techniques were engaged in sometimes fierce debate.

The working party assembled to formulate the first National Curriculum programmes of study for history were faced with a considerable challenge. Content became the subject of newspaper articles and parliamentary debates – then–Prime Minister Margaret Thatcher even contributed, asking 'Why cannot we go back to the good old days when we learnt by heart the names of the kings and queens of England, the names of our warriors and battles and the glorious deeds of our past?' The author well remembers a prime-time BBC2 documentary from the period where the sides of the argument were represented by Sheila Lawlor (then–Deputy Director of the Centre for Policy Studies, a firm believer in the importance of 'facts') and Dominic Powesland, a landscape archaeologist and proponent of skills-focused learning. Ms Lawlor's arguments became increasingly vehement as the programme progressed, focusing on the bafflement of learners when asked to interpret sources and startling displays of ignorance she had witnessed in secondary school history classrooms, with one child claiming that Winston Churchill was an 'African'. Powseland's views were no less extreme in their claims, with one passage suggesting that children can have 'free form' when making interpretations about sources, with their views being as valid as those of academic historians. The programme concluded with a contribution from Carol White, a member of the history working party, who explained how their Programmes of Study (PoS) addressed these conflicting views.

The first National Curriculum for History, published in 1989, was a masterpiece of compromise. The report of the working group stated:

> to have integrity the study of history must be grounded in a solid knowledge of the past: must employ vigorous historical method – the way in which historians carry out their task – and must involve a range of interpretations and

explanations...together, these elements make an organic whole: if any one of them is missing the outcome is not history.

(Department of Education and Science, 1990)

The programme of study was divided equally between 'Key Elements' and 'Areas of Study'. The former were the skills of historical enquiry, reflecting the teaching approaches of 'new history' and the development of conceptual understandings. The latter were the areas of historical content to be covered in each key stage and the knowledge to be acquired. The fundamental idea underpinning the subject was that neither section of the PoS should be taught in isolation – content knowledge should be acquired through engagement with and interpretation of source materials; skills should be developed in the context of required areas of factual knowledge. The curriculum was, to an extent, a settlement that pleased everyone and no one, in that neither side of the 'facts versus skills' debate could claim ascendancy in relation to the PoS. It is significant, however, that criticism focused mainly, like other subjects in the first iteration of the National Curriculum, on the quantity of its requirements, rather than the structure of its content. Then–Secretary of State, Kenneth Baker, had succeeded in his aim of creating a broad (but not necessarily balanced) curriculum, rather than the expected narrow outline of core knowledge – the result being the infamous stack of subject ring binders delivered to every teacher.

The Dearing Review of 1993 squarely addressed concerns about quantity of content leading to a slimming down of all foundation subjects. The dual approach of the History PoS was retained, however, with the balanced knowledge and skills structure being adopted by other subjects. Further modifications in the National Curriculum followed in 2000, with more reduction of foundation subject requirements. The final months of the Labour government in 2009–2010 saw the publication of two significant reviews of the primary curriculum – the Cambridge Primary Review, chaired by Robin Alexander, and the government-sponsored, so-called 'Rose Review', chaired by Sir Jim Rose. Both reviews argued for a more holistic curriculum, incorporating more flexible and cross-curricular approaches to teaching and learning. Significantly, Rose's plans challenged the subject-based structure of the curriculum established in 1988 – 14 subjects were reduced down to six areas of learning. History would be subsumed into a humanities area of learning labelled 'Historical, geographical and social understanding'. The knowledge and skills elements were retained, however, with 'Essential Knowledge' and 'Key Skills' being identified under separate headings, alongside a detailed 'Breadth of Learning' section which contained concepts, skills and factual knowledge to be acquired during early, middle and later phases of primary schooling. A separate outline of 'Cross-curricular Learning' signalled clearly the new approach to more holistic planning that underpinned the 'Rose' curriculum.

Although many schools had started planning for delivery of this curriculum, one of the first acts of the coalition government, which came to power in May 2010, was to abandon Rose's ideas and commence a new review of the National

Curriculum. The incoming Secretary of State for Education, Michael Gove, was very clear in setting parameters for this review. In an interview on the Radio 4 *Today* programme in January 2011, he stated 'I just think there should be facts... One of the problems that we have at the moment is that in the history curriculum we only have two names [of historical figures]'. Ofsted's 2010 subject report, *History for All*, in some ways gave support to this view, with its criticism of primary children's chronological knowledge and their inability to construct a connected narrative. The history curriculum that emerged from the review was as radically different to the original National Curriculum as Rose's holistic, cross-curricular structure. The settlement that gave equal weighting to skills and facts through 'Key Elements' and 'Areas of Study' was no more. Instead, requirements focused only on factual knowledge to be taught, with only brief references to historical skills in the aims of the subject.

The first draft of the new history curriculum, published in February 2013, was controversial, to say the least. This was not just a curriculum based on factual knowledge, but one which provided immense detail and required children at Key Stage 2 to learn British history from the Stone Age to the 'Glorious Revolution of 1688'. Voices, ranging from teachers to academic historians, not only criticised the amount of content specified by the new requirements, but also the unrealistic nature of its demands. Speaking at the Hay Festival in May 2013, Simon Schama is reported as saying:

> 'This is a document written by people who have never...taught...in a class-room. None of you should sign up to it until we trap Michael Gove in a classroom and tell him to get on with it. You want to say to him, "Let's go into a class of nine-year-olds and do the kingdom of Mercia with them". I would love to see how you would do that!'
>
> (Furness, 2013)

Although there was a reduction in the amount of content in the final version of the curriculum that became statutory in September 2014 (1066 became the end-date for the detailed study of British history in Key Stage 2), the structure was unchanged from the draft and a fundamental remodelling of the history curriculum had been achieved. To a large extent this change was also reflected in other subjects, such as geography. The debate that had begun in the 1960s as a response to Plowden's learner-centred, active curriculum appeared to have reached a conclusion, at last, with traditionalist ideas, values and attitudes in the ascendancy. The 'facts versus skills' debate has not ended, however, with anecdotal evidence suggesting that many primary teachers are continuing to give equal weight to skills-based learning alongside the development of factual knowledge. Former BBC education correspondent Mike Baker has summed up the current shape of the debate well when he states, 'The history curriculum should teach both facts and skills. The real question is where to put the balance'.

The nature of geography

So, what is geography? Certainly Eliot Hurst's prediction in 1985 that 'geography has neither existence nor future' (as cited in Johnston, 1985) has been proven wrong. Five years later in 1989, geography secured a place within the National Curriculum for England and within all future iterations (Department for Education and Science [DES], 1991; Department for Education [DfE], 1995; Department for Education and Employment [DfEE/QCA], 1999; DfE, 2013). When considering the 'facts versus skills' debate within the context of geography, it is worth reflecting first on the evolution of geography as a subject, which some would argue is inextricably linked to the development of society; a subject designed to serve the political agenda and to perform related socio-economic functions. For example, it has been argued that school geography helped to promote acceptance of territorial acquisition and the concept of imperialism (Eliot Hurst, 1995). The purpose and nature of geography as a school subject is, therefore, an important consideration when exploring how it might be most effectively taught in school.

Definitions of geography as a school subject can vary significantly and this has often been viewed as problematic in terms of making appropriate pedagogical decisions. As early as 1914, it was noted that 'the difficulty of teaching geography, [is due] to the vagueness of the concept of the subject' (March, p.297). Even earlier in 1901, it was described as 'dull and uninteresting...a dreary recitation of names and statistics...of little use except, perhaps, in the sorting office of the post office' (Rooper, p.4). Over a hundred years later, it is described more optimistically by Professor Alistair Bonnett as 'the world discipline...an unwieldy yet utterly necessary and very human project to seek order and meaning in the diversity and complexity of the world. Uniquely among academic subjects, geography has a roughly equal emphasis on science and social science' (Geographical Association [GA], 2019). Indeed, within the context of primary geography, it is seen as bridging the gap between arts and sciences, 'from science and history to art and design' (Catling and Wiley, 2018). It can thus be seen as an overarching term representing an association of various sciences and disciplines, which, when studied together, will contribute to a deeper understanding of a particular set of facts about the world in which we live.

Evolving pedagogies

As early as 1918, Carpenter discusses the nature of geography teaching in primary schools and states boldly that 'the third form child is frankly not interested in the lives of others' (p.233). Instead, it is the 'world-wide sweep and its encyclopaedic collection of place-names, race-names, facts and formulas' which interests the young mind (p.234). Carpenter emphasises here the importance of the knowledge base of geography; in particular, names and facts traditionally learnt by rote.

A short time after this, and with a degree of contrast, Ballyntyne (1922) describes a scheme of work in an Elementary School as being essentially place-based, but with the integration of theory through 'special lessons on physical laws' (p.214). This notion bears a resemblance to the use of 'models' advocated by specialists sometime later (Crisp, 1969; Walford, 1969; Cole and Benyon, 1970). References to questioning and research are limited here (Ballyntyne, 1922), but there is some movement away from a purely facts-based curriculum.

The problems associated with teaching geography are acknowledged from an early stage, and the paramount importance of subject knowledge is questioned in terms of primary school teaching:

> I must not give the impression that training in geography is all that is required. The geography teacher should be a teacher first, a geographer second...I would say that pedagogy is fully as important as geography.
>
> (Unstead, 1928, p.319)

Since the early 1970s, there has been a marked shift of pedagogical thinking towards 'enquiry-based' methods, with the concept of enquiry being generally perceived as the process of focused questioning and research and with a view to reaching a reasoned conclusion. The implication of this within the context of this debate is that enquiry as a pedagogical approach emphasises both content and process; acknowledging the significance of both facts and skills to geographical education. With this in mind, it is useful to reflect on how school geography has been planned and taught over time, and to discuss the extent to which enquiry methods are really a modern phenomenon or whether such methods have always been a part of geography curricula since as early as the start of the 20th century. For example, the idea that children need to be in control of their personal learning is not new; 'no boy likes to be taught, every boy likes to learn' (Fairgrieve, 1936, p.1), and the related concept of meta-cognition is certainly of relevance to the facts versus skills debate.

In reflections of 'what the primary school geography teacher should know and be', it is suggested that the teacher should 'encourage children to talk, and (dangerous as it may seem [!]) to ask questions about the subject' (Unstead, 1928, p.315). An early experiment in a Junior School found that pupils were encouraged to undertake independent enquiries. They had to identify a focus for research and were required to use a number of sources to actually present a lesson on their chosen topic to the rest of the class. This was with a view to '[encouraging] the children to take a sufficiently *active* part' in the lesson (Cullis, 1919, p.27). The project also reported a number of benefits, not least in terms of the enthusiasm of those involved. A later study had similar outcomes, finding that when the 'class literally teaches itself' (Haddon, 1948, p.190), the benefits might include increased motivation, proficiency in the use of sources and an increase in pupil questioning about geographical topics (Haddon, 1948). Small-scale experimentation in elementary schools also revealed that teaching seemed to be most effective when pupils' work was framed by the teacher but was self-directed in terms of choice of resources and methods of approach (Jones, 1925). The approach detailed in this case study is very similar to the model of a 'framed enquiry' which has been presented more recently (Roberts, 1987; Roberts, 2003).

The shifting sands with respect to the nature of geography and how it should be taught began to be felt by the early 1960s. For example, in 1963, the Geographical Association (GA) reported on a one-day conference for primary geography teachers, advocating a topic-based curriculum and stating that, through a cross-curricular approach, 'far more real geography is likely to be learnt and fully understood than was ever achieved in the traditional "chalk and talk" lesson' (GA, 1963, p.421). The move away from the traditional 'chalk and talk' – a facts-orientated and highly didactic curriculum for primary-aged children – continued, and within a report commissioned by the GA in 1964 (based on the structure of the Hadow Report of 1931), it advised that the 'curriculum...be thought of in terms of activity and experience rather than of facts to be stored' (GA, 1964).

The teaching of geography continued on this trajectory during the late 1960s and early 1970s, moving increasingly towards 'the use of models and the employment of a problem-solving or "hypothetical" mode of instruction' (Crisp, 1969, p.11). This gradual change in teaching methods represented a shift away from learning facts to learning how to learn and be a competent young geographer:

> Perhaps the most important of these factors are recent advances in geographical research, the precedent set by American curricular developments, a growing understanding of the nature of scientific inquiry, and a belief that, in our rapidly changing world, styles of learning are ultimately more important than facts.
>
> (Crisp, 1969, p.11)

Crisp (1969) goes on to explain how 'hypothetical' modes of teaching can help pupils to be involved in problem-solving and asking questions and that this can motivate the learner as '[they become] aware of alternative answers' (ibid., p.12). This method is in contrast to 'expository methods' which 'favor rote learning' (ibid., p.12) and the accumulation of geographical facts and concepts. Within the context of hypothetical modes of instruction, Crisp (ibid.) also describes how geographical 'models' can be either representative of the hypothesis itself, or, when considered alongside other models, can aid the development of new hypotheses or models. Models are generalisations and fundamental concepts: 'not meant to be ends in themselves but rather a means of understanding and memorizing generalities about the reality they represent' (ibid., p.13).

An example of a model is given as 'a land use pattern...[on] an imaginary farm [cocoa-producing village in Ghana], based on an idea by J. P. Cole' (ibid., p.13). Other examples from this series include; 'co-ordinates in a town', 'a detour around a creek', and 'relationships between crops and land' (Cole and Beynon,

1970). These models within this series are shown as illustrations and maps, with corresponding classroom-based activities.

The advantages of using hypothetical or problem-solving methods of teaching (which may include the use of models) are outlined in relation to the work of Bruner (Crisp, 1969). Firstly, Crisp argues that greater intellectual potency is achieved as children learn to use hypotheses or models to solve problems. They can progressively 'relate new instances to the framework of fundamental ideas' (ibid., p.13). He also argues that this method facilitates a shift from extrinsic to intrinsic rewards by giving the learner the opportunity to 'experience success and failure not as reward and punishment, but as information' (ibid., p.12). In other words, using this method helps children to develop confidence in their ability to learn, rather than them being overly concerned with what might be seen as correct or incorrect. The third advantage noted relates to conservation of memory and how 'discovery of things for oneself' (ibid., p.13) can lead to more personal and relevant storage of cognitive information; and that this in turn can facilitate ease of retrieval later.

Walford (1969) in his paper on 'operational games and geographical teaching', likens 'operational games' to the 'family of models and simulations which have recently been suggested as tools for the fruitful understanding of the subject in an increasingly complex environment' (Walford, 1969, p.34). Each 'game' comprises a generalisation (or model, hypothesis) and case study–specific detail; 'thus the "canvas" of the game serves both as study material in itself and as the basis for transfer of knowledge to use in other situations' (ibid., p.38). Walford claims that operational games help to make sense of increasingly complex data sets, enabling generalisations and hypotheses to be stated. Like many before, Walford emphasises the benefits of the problem-solving process in comparison to just learning the facts. Similarly to Crisp (1969), he relates his work to that of Bruner and argues that such teaching methods will increase motivation and engagement of young learners (Walford, 1969) whilst developing more advanced cognitive domains.

During the 1970s, emerging problems with the geography curriculum were identified, particularly in terms of '6th Form' geography. In response to this, Naish (1976) outlined a rationale and proposal for a new schools' curriculum development project in geography, which is now commonly known as the 16–19 Geography Project. It was thought that the problems with geography at 'Advanced Level' were due to innovation at Key Stage 3 and an increasing range of courses being offered. The constantly changing examination system, and increasing diversity within the pupil population in terms of ability, were also identified as key factors giving rise to these issues (Naish, 1976).

'One of the biggest impacts made by the curriculum development activities was in the area of pedagogy' (Rawling, 2001, p.38). Indeed, it was at this time that 'geographical enquiry' began to emerge as a pedagogical term within the context of the subject of geography. There were also a number of Schools Council geography projects at this time, many of which became associated with the enquiry approach; for example, Geography for the Young School Leaver Project (1970) , the 14–18 Geography Project (1970) and finally, the 16–19 Geography Project (1976).

The 16–19 Geography Project (Naish, 1976) set out to develop a clearer understanding of geography as a subject and to develop skills and techniques to help to make geography more 'scientific' in approach. The project was based at the London Institute and aimed to enlist the help of teachers, trainees and other professionals in examining the 16–19 curriculum and with the aim of developing and evaluating new curriculum resources. This shift towards a more scientific approach in geography became more formalised at this time through the work of the project, but also represented a natural development of earlier work which focused on the use of 'models', hypothesis testing and 'operational games' (Crisp, 1969; Cole and Beynon, 1970; Walford, 1969).

The curriculum framework which subsequently developed offered 'an integrative approach to the subject, a route for enquiry learning' (Naish, 1985, p.99), which was described as follows:

> students investigate the problems and issues in an active, enquiry-based style, clarifying questions, selecting, collecting and analysing appropriate data, producing and communicating their findings in a variety of ways... The approach recommended is that study should begin with the recognition and clarification of a question, or set of questions, issues or problems which arise from the interaction of people in their environment.
>
> (Naish, 1985, p.107)

This pedagogical approach was described as 'a distinctive approach to geography' (Naish, 1985, p.107) and was to be increasingly referred to as 'geographical enquiry' or 'enquiry-based learning' (Rawling, 2001). In essence, it is similar to earlier work (Crisp, 1969; Cole and Beyon, 1970; Walford, 1969), as the implication here is that learning is characterised by hypothesis testing and development in relation to a particular set of facts, rather than simply the acquisition of facts by rote.

In general, the following ideas about enquiry were introduced by the various Schools Council projects: that enquiry can be classroom-based as well as field-based; that enquiry represents an approach to learning and a process through which geographical concepts and content can be studied; that enquiry represents a shift from didactic methods to an approach which increases pupil participation and control; that enquiry should involve the use of a wide range of resources and skills (Roberts, 2003). The idea that pupils should start with a question or problem which is then researched and where findings are communicated is referred to and developed within subsequent National Curriculum documentation (DES, 1991; DfE, 1995; DfEE/QCA, 1999).

'Two necessary corollaries of a commitment to enquiry-based learning were changes in assessment and to the role of the teacher' (Rawling, 2001). Following on from the Schools Council projects, the DES (1986) published a discussion paper to explore teaching methods and assessment in relation to 'enquiry-based learning', the aims of which were seen as relating to the '[development] of a range of skills and competencies necessary to carry out geographical enquiry and to interpret geographical information' (DES, 1986, p.2). It should be noted, however, that methods in geography which could also be described as 'enquiry-based' date back to at least the early 1900s (Rooper, 1901), as discussed previously, and therefore the extent to which 'enquiry-based learning' represented an innovation in pedagogy at the time of the 16–19 Geography Project (Naish, 1976), for example, is questionable.

A useful discussion of 'geographical enquiry' as a teaching style is that by Roberts (1987). Using a framework based on the work of Barnes et al., Roberts (1987) identifies three styles of 'enquiry': closed, framed and negotiated, and explains the classification is based on 'the amount of control teachers maintain over subject content and activities' (Roberts, 1987, p.238). Roberts claims that this framework can be applied to geography in terms of raising questions, collecting and interpreting data and drawing conclusions, and goes on to illustrate each of the styles, with 'closed' representing the most teacher-controlled and led, where outcomes may be pre-determined by the teacher and not negotiated by the children. A 'framed' enquiry has more scope for pupils to raise their own questions and make decisions, but still with a reasonable steer from the teacher. This would seem an appropriate style for primary-aged children, as the teacher needs to ensure that the enquiry is sufficiently geographically focused within the context of time constraints and limited resources. A 'negotiated' enquiry can be developed within a broader topic of study chosen by the teacher, within which pupils can take increasing responsibility for specific research foci and methodologies. Within this approach both facts and skills are seen with arguably equal importance to enquiry-based research and learning.

As Roberts (1987) notes, the teaching styles within this framework ('the participation dimension') are in a constant state of flux and change, and the styles adopted by the teacher during any one lesson may shift along the continuum (of 'closed', 'framed' and 'negotiated') depending on learning objectives, resources being used, ability of individual children and other significant variables.

Historically, there has been a scarcity of research on enquiry in primary geography, but within the secondary phase, Roberts carried out several significant small research projects which focused on geographical enquiry at Key Stage 3 (1998a, 1999, 2003). The first of these was a focused study for QCA on the nature and extent of enquiry in secondary geography. This was later published (QCA, 1998) as non-statutory guidance for Key Stages 1 and 2, and represented the first discussion document of its kind. Findings from this project were also reported in 'Teaching Geography' (Roberts, 1998). Roberts' sample comprised six secondary schools across four authorities. Geography teachers were interviewed and schemes of work scrutinised. Roberts was interested in exploring teachers' understandings of the term 'geographical enquiry' and the sorts of classroom or field-based examples given. She found overall that there was an association of 'enquiry work' with 'work done outside of the classroom' (Roberts, 1998, p.164). Also, that across different categories, which were formulated based on the teachers' responses (fieldwork, surveys, library research, structured course-work and decision-making activities), 'each of the schools used some of the categories exemplified...but none of the schools used all of them' (Roberts, 1998, p.165). Basically, therefore, despite following the same statutory guidelines, interpretations of 'enquiry' were different. Whilst this is a relatively small-scale study, from which it is difficult to make significant generalisations, it does seem to suggest that perceptions and understandings of geographical enquiry may vary significantly within and across schools (primary and secondary) and authorities. This in turn also suggests that the respective emphasis on facts and skills may differ from one pedagogical context to another.

Enquiry and theories of learning

A consideration of how enquiry aligns with theories of learning is also of relevance to this debate, as it is generally perceived as being related to the seminal theories of constructivism and socio-constructivism (Roberts, 2003). The implication for the facts versus skills debate is that this means that enquiry is seen as a process through which pupils can 'learn about the world by actively making sense of it themselves', in contrast to models of learning where knowledge is seen as being 'transmitted to us ready-made' (Roberts, 2003, p.27). In terms of constructivism, learning is about constructing meaning in relation to what is already known. All learners understand the world in different ways due to varying social and cultural factors and contexts. Because of this phenomenon, new information has to be accommodated and assimilated within an individual's existing constructs, as opposed to be being 'bolted on' as ready-made knowledge (Barnes and Todd, 1995, cited in Roberts, 2003).

Similarly, Piaget makes the distinction between 'learning in the narrow sense' and 'learning in the specific sense' (Ginsburg and Opper, 1988):

> For example, in school geography, the child learns the names and locations of the states and their capitals. This kind of learning is obviously specific to particular cultural contexts...by contrast, learning in the broad sense, or development, involves the acquisition of general thought structures which apply to many situations. (Ginsburg and Opper, 1988, p.209)

Piaget's notions of 'learning in the specific sense' and 'learning in the broader sense' relate very clearly to discussions earlier which explore methods of teaching geography. For example, the use of 'models' in teaching geography (March, 1914; Crisp, 1969; Cole and Beynon, 1970; Walford, 1969) is clearly akin to 'learning in the broader sense'. The idea is that hypothetical or problem-solving methods in teaching and learning help pupils to develop, use and modify information and related generalisations, with a view to exploring geographical questions and issues. In contrast to this, and in line with Piaget's notion of 'learning in the specific sense', others see the teaching of geography as being centrally concerned with memorisation and the 'world-wide sweep and its encyclopaedic collection of place-names, race-names, facts and formulas' (Carpenter, 1918, p.234). In terms of recent and current geography curricula, both of these types of learning – acquisition of specific knowledge and the development of the processes of learning about geographical phenomena – are evident, although it could be argued that the emphasis varies (DfEE/QCA, 1999; DfE, 2013).

Bruner's ideas about learning are not dissimilar to those described above. He describes the 'act of learning' as involving 'three almost simultaneous processes' (Bruner, 1977, p.48). Firstly, 'acquisition' of new information (Bruner, 1977) can be equated with Piaget's 'specific learning', and secondly, 'transformation' of knowledge (Bruner, 1977) is similar in concept to Piaget's 'learning in the broader sense'. According to Bruner, transformation is about 'the process of manipulating knowledge to make it fit new tasks' (Bruner, 1977, p.48). This is interpreted as meaning the higher order application and development of existing knowledge and generalisations to make sense of new facts, problems and issues. Bruner goes on to identify the third process of learning as being 'evaluation', which essentially refers to the process of reflection on one's learning and the extent to which knowledge has been appropriately applied and manipulated; a process cited earlier, otherwise referred to as meta-cognition.

Social constructivism, of which Vygotsky is a key proponent, adds weight to this and emphasises the significance of others in helping us to understand the world. Vygotsky identifies the 'Zone of Proximal Development' as a model representing the level of achievement that can be reached unaided, compared with the higher levels of achievement facilitated through mediation by teacher or peers:

> the Zone of Proximal Development is...the distance between the actual developmental level as determined by independent problem solving and the level of potential development as determined through problem solving under adult guidance or in collaboration with more capable peers.
>
> (Vygotsky, 1978, p.86)

This assistance by others in pupils' learning is often referred to as 'scaffolding' (Daniels, 2001). The teacher (for example) can help 'a child or novice to solve a problem, carry out a task or achieve a goal which would (otherwise) be beyond his unassisted efforts' (Woods, 1976 cited in Daniels, 2001, p.107). 'Scaffolding' helps to simplify the role of the learner rather than the task, through structured help by more capable others.

The implications of constructivism for pupils, focusing on the work of Piaget, Bruner and Vygotsky, include the need to take prior learning into account and to provide pupils with the opportunity to construct and relate new knowledge to what is already known. In addition to this, the significance of others in helping to re-shape knowledge should also be taken into account. Within the context of primary geography, this means that pupils' prior knowledge should be explored and acknowledged, particularly as they are already operating as young geographers and navigating the places and spaces in which they live. This is the basis from which new geographical learning can be actively constructed and facilitated with help from more capable others such as the teacher, an additional adult or their peers. For example, some basic ideas about rivers can then be explored further in the field, where new experiences, observations and findings might be assimilated and accommodated within existing schema, resulting in a more sophisticated understanding of river systems and how these features present at different points in a river's course.

More recent pedagogical innovations within the geography curriculum have focused on 'thinking skills', a movement which really started to have an impact around the 1980s and links to the work of many important pioneers (Feuerstein, Rand, Hoffman and Miller, 1980; Lipman, 1980; do Bono, 1992; Leat, 1999). Both the notion of geographical enquiry and the thinking skills movement represented an ongoing and upward trajectory towards more progressive educational ideology (Rawling, 2001), as both aim to develop increased autonomy in learners, as learners, and with a reduced emphasis on facts to be stored and recited. This trend was perceived to plateau within the context of Cameron's government and Gove's proposals for a revised national Curriculum in 2013.

Summary

Since the 1960s, the story of the teaching and learning of history and geography in primary schools has reflected two quite different views of the subject – simplistically summarised as 'facts' versus 'skills'. This has been influenced by a number of factors which include the flux and change in the nature of the subjects, in addition to historical, political and pedagogical influences over time. For a very long period, these views were equally balanced in the compromise of the 1989 National Curriculum for history and geography. Since 2013, the balance has shifted away from compromise and the current National Curriculum appears as skewed towards a knowledge-based approach as the 'new' history and geography of the 1970s was skewed towards decontextualised skills. The development of an understanding of the methods of historical and geographical enquiry remains an underpinning aim of the current curriculum, however, and respect for evidence and sources is also central. The entirely factual content of the programme of study actually provides more freedom of choice in relation to teaching methods than the 1989 curriculum. Though this could mean a return to rote and Unstead's and Carpenter's narratives (1955; 1918), it could also give scope for enquiries which enable children to explore the evidence on which the 'facts' are based.

Questions for reflection

Reflect critically on the current National Curriculum requirements for primary history (DfE, 2013) and the balance between factual knowledge in the programmes of study and the skills of historical enquiry outlined in the Aims of the subject. To what extent does this balance reflect responses to Piagetian theory evident as far back as the Plowden Report of 1967?

Given your reflections and response to Question 1, is there any evidence of the compromise between 'facts and skills' that characterised the first National Curriculum for History in 1989?

Reflect critically on the current National Curriculum requirements for primary geography (DfE, 2013) and the implied balance between facts and skills. How prescriptive do you feel this curriculum is, and is there room for some flexibility?

Reflect critically on the concept of millennials, 'Generation Y', advancements in technology and a 21st-century society. How would you predict the future of geography in the primary school and, given the historical, political and pedagogical perspectives outlined above, what should the balance be in terms of facts versus skills?

Further reading and resources

Cooper, H. (2006) *History 3–11: A guide for Teachers*, Abingdon, United Kingdom: David Fulton Publishers/Taylor and Francis.

Hilary Cooper is Professor Emeritus of History and Pedagogy at the University of Cumbria. She has an international reputation for her work on the nature and pedagogy of primary school history. This is one of many books she has written about primary history teaching and learning. Though not her latest, it explores practice and underpinning theory across early years and primary phases. For Cooper, the process of enquiry is central to history at all levels.

Gillard, D. (2018) *Education in England: A History*. Available at: www .educationengland.org.uk/history.

Derek Gillard is a retired primary school headteacher from Oxford who has created this remarkable website which aims to chart the history of the school system in England from the arrival of the Romans to the present day, using original documents, reports and Acts of Parliament. It is particularly strong on the origins and development of the National Curriculum and the debates around content, including the balance of knowledge- and skills-based learning in subjects such as history and geography.

Pickford, T., Garner, W. & Jackson, E. (2013) *Primary Humanities: Learning Through Enquiry*, London: SAGE.

Providing a broad and balanced overview of the teaching of primary history and primary geography, this text is indispensable reading for all primary teacher education students wishing to develop their understanding of teaching humanities subjects.

Scoffham, S. (2017) *Teaching Geography Creatively* (2nd ed.), Abingdon, Oxon: Routledge.
This resource brings the National Curriculum 'to life' and clearly illustrates how the subject can be taught to engage young people; by instilling a sense of fun through the lens of purposeful enquiry. Of use to students and practitioners, the content of each chapter has been mapped across the current requirements of the National Curriculum.

References

Ballantyne, J. D. (1922) 'A scheme of geography in use in an elementary school, with notes on apparatus', *The Geographical Teacher*, 11(4): 214–217.

Bruner, J. (1977) *The Process of Education*, Cambridge, USA: Harvard University Press.

Carpenter, K. (1918) 'Geography in the middle school', *The Geographical Teacher*, 9(5): 233–235.

Catling, S. & Willy, T. (2018) *Teaching Primary Geography*, London: SAGE.

Central Advisory Council for Education (1967) *The Plowden Report, Children and Their Primary Schools*, London: HMSO.

Cole, J. & Beynon, N. (1970) *New Ways in Geography*, Oxford: Basil Blackwell.

Crisp, J. A. A. (1969) 'New approaches to teaching geography', *Geography*, 54(1): 11–17.

Cullis, O. M. (1919) 'An experiment in junior school work', *The Geographical Teacher*, 10(1): 27.

Daniels, H. (2001) *Vygotsky and Pedagogy*, London: RoutledgeFalmer.

De Bono, E. (1992). *Teaching Your Child to Think*. London: Penguin.

Department for Education (1995) *Geography in the National Curriculum* (England), London: HMSO.

Department for Education (2013) *National Curriculum in England: History Programmes of Study*. Available at: www.gov.uk/government/publications/natio nal-curriculum-inenglandhistory-programmes-ofstudy.

Department for Education and Employment/QCA (1999) *Geography – The National Curriculum for England*, London: HMSO.

Department of Education and Science (1986) *Geography from 5–16*, London: HMSO.

Department of Education and Science (1990) *National Curriculum, History Working Group: Final Report*, London: HMSO.

Department of Education and Science (1991) *Geography in the National Curriculum*, (England), London: HMSO.

Eliot Hurst, H. (1995) 'Geography has neither existence nor future'. In: Johnson, R. J. *The Future of Geography*, pp. 32–46, London: Blackwell.

Fairgrieve, J. (1936) 'Can we teach geography better?', *Geography*, 21(1): 1–17.

Feurestein, R., Rand, Y., Hoffman, M. B. & Miller, R. (1980) *Instrumental Enrichment: An Intervention Programme for Cognitive Modifiability*, Baltimore: University Park Press.

Furness, H. (2013) '"Don't sign up to Gove's insulting curriculum", Schama urges'. Available at: https://www.telegraph.co.uk/culture/hay-festival/10090287/Ha y-Festival-2013-Dont-sign-up-to-Goves-insulting-curriculum-Schama-urges.html (Accessed 24.01.20).

Geographical Association – Manchester Branch (1963) 'Geography in the junior school: Report of a one-day conference', *Geography*, 48(4): 420–421.

Geographical Association (1964) 'Geography teaching in primary education: A memorandum', *Geography*, 49(4): 410–415.

Geography Association (2019) Available at: https://www.geography.org.uk/Curriculum/What-is-geography

Gillard, D. (2018) *Education in England: A History*. Available at: www.educationengland.org.uk/history.

Ginsberg, H. P. & Opper, S. (1988) *Piaget's Theory of Intellectual Development*, New Jersey, USA: Prentice Hall.

Haddon, J. (1948). 'An experiment in teaching geography', *Geography*, 33(4), 190–193.

Jones, E. W. (1925) 'Results of experiments in teaching geography in elementary schools', *The Geographical Teacher*, 13(1), 64.

Leat, D. (1999) 'Thinking about thinking', *Primary Geographer*, 39: 14–15.

Lipman, M., Sharp, A., and Oscanyan, F. (1980). *Philosophy on the Classroom*. Princeton: Temple University Press.

March, M. C. (1914) 'The teaching of geography', *The Geographical Teacher*, 7(5): 297–300.

Naish, M. (1976) 'Geography 16–19', *Teaching Geography*, 1: 127–128.

Naish, M. (1985) 'Geography 16–19'. In: Boardman, D. (Ed.), *New Directions in Geographical Education*, pp. 99–115, Basingstoke: Falmer Press.

Ofsted (2011) *History for All*. Available at: www.ofsted.gov.uk/resources/history-for-all.

QCA (1998) *Geographical Enquiry at Key Stages 1–3*, London: QCA.

Rawling, E. (2001) *Changing the Subject*, Sheffield: Geographical Association.

Roberts, M. (1987) 'Teaching styles and strategies'. In: Kent, A. Lambert, D. Naish, M. & F. Slater (Eds.), *Viewpoints on Teaching and Learning: Geography in Education*, pp. 231–259, Cambridge: Cambridge University Press.

Roberts, M. (1998) 'The nature of geographical enquiry at key stage 3', *Teaching Geography*, 23(4): 164–167.

Roberts, M. (1999). Planning for progression in geographical enquiry (unpublished paper given at IGU conference, South Korea – see Appendix).

Roberts, M. (2003) *Learning through Enquiry*, Sheffield: Geographical Association.

Rooper, T. G. (1901) 'On methods of teaching geography', *The Geographical Teacher*, 1(1): 4–10.

Unstead, J. F. (1928) 'The primary school geography teacher: What should he know and be?', *Geography*, 14(4): 315–322.

Unstead, R. J. (1955) *Looking at History: From Cavemen to Present Day*, London: A & C Black Ltd.

Vygotsky, L. S. (1978) *Mind in Society*, Cambridge, USA: Harvard University Press.

Walford, R. (1969) 'Operational games and geography teaching', *Geography*, 54: 34–42.

Chapter 14

Using digital strategies for primary learning

Lee Hazeldine

Introduction

Using online digital media is increasingly the primary form through which young people will access information and entertainment – even at the age of 3 to 4 years of age, approximately half the children in the United Kingdom now have access to a tablet device to retrieve online content, whilst almost a quarter of 8 to 11 year olds have a social media profile (Ofcom, 2017). Digital online networks have altered much of society, enabling increased access to multimedia information, interactive content and communities on both a local and global scale.

When knowledge is increasingly seen as existing in networks, and learning as forming and navigating these networks, many existing aspects of education are perceived to be subject to change (Siemens, 2005; Mitra, 2006; Downes, 2012). It might be argued that the attributes of digital environments facilitate patterns of learning more appropriate for an information society that requires creativity, divergent thinking and lifelong learning, enabling an ability to adapt to the rapid changes that typify a post-industrial world (Florida, 2006; Robinson, 2010). Pupils' immersion in digital media and online networks means they inevitably expect education to be a participative, engaging, and active environment (Dede, 2005). Moreover, evidence suggests that pupils' motivation and attainment can be improved with the intervention of digital learning strategies (Underwood, 2009; Baytak, Tarman and Ayas, 2011; Mitra and Crawley, 2014; Education Endowment Foundation, 2018).

However, digital strategies for learning have been met with criticism and a cautious reception. It has been suggested that the use of digital strategies undermines the teaching profession, making the role of the teacher increasingly obsolete whilst reducing learners to passive receptacles of information, subject to instrumental targets and assessment, which fail to develop deeper levels of understanding (Bauerlein, 2009; Oppenheimer, 2004; Carr, 2011; Selwyn, 2014). Prominent theories of digital learning are contested for failing to provide a sufficient explanation of learning and the role of human agency within the process. Current debate therefore focuses on whether digital learning theories and environments enhance or limit pupils' learning and to what extent the role of the teacher is still important in learners' development.

Strategies of digital pedagogy within contemporary education

There are two main pedagogic models that incorporate the use of digital technologies within schools; online learning and blended learning. Online learning manifests itself in various ways, the most common of which is in the form of MOOCs (Massive Open Online Courses); this model can generally be defined as learning through engagement with resources that are exclusively online. In this model of digital learning, there is no requirement to engage with resources, students or tutors within traditional physical learning spaces. Online learning typically lacks geographical and temporal restraints – learners' engagement is often asynchronous and non-proximal. These courses normally consist of a variety of interactive digital media to support learning, including online games, forums, blogs, vlogs, collaborative spaces, electronic documents, interactive online assessments, virtual spaces, digital videos and audio files.

Blended learning is defined as a 'range of possibilities presented by combining Internet and digital media with established classroom forms that require the physical co-presence of teacher and students' (Friesen, 2012, p.1). Blended learning is typically a process whereby digital technology is integrated into learning activities to purposively differentiate, enhance and individualise learning for the benefit of pupil development. By providing opportunities for independent and differentiated engagement, blended learning has been championed as an effective means to free teachers from more traditional instructional or didactic forms of teaching, providing greater scope for individualised pupil learning support, formative assessment and focused target setting. There are a variety of models of blended learning that provide different opportunities for combining classroom and digital learning for the benefit of pupils' development. The influential *Clayton Christensen Institute* provides a taxonomy of different types of blended learning (Staker and Horn, 2012); the most popular models in the context of primary schools are the Station-Rotation Model and the Flipped Classroom Model.

The Station-Rotation model

The Station Rotation model allows pupils to rotate through learning stations on either a fixed or flexible schedule, where at least one of the stations is an online learning station (see Figure 14.1). This model is common in schools because teachers are already familiar with the use of carousel activities to support differentiation and learning. The online learning station is typically either a series of desktop computers within a classroom or a table of laptops or electronic tablets. The advantage of this model is that it allows teachers to focus their time on the pupils' application of knowledge, whilst also providing the means for pupils to forge individual learning pathways that develop their skills and understanding at a pace appropriate to themselves. It achieves this by allowing pupils to obtain skills and knowledge via online instructional training at one station, followed by the

The Station-Rotation Model

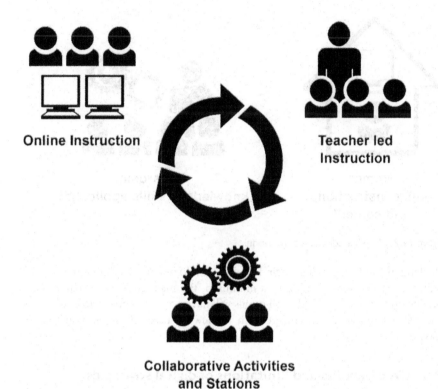

Online Instruction

Teacher led Instruction

Collaborative Activities and Stations

Figure 14.1 The Station-Rotation model.

application of this knowledge within the context of learning activities at another station. Because the majority of instructional activity is being performed online, the teacher is free to support and assess understanding, whilst providing differentiated guidance in which to enhance the learning and understanding of all.

The Flipped-Classroom model

The Flipped-Classroom model flips the traditional relationship between classroom teacher-led instruction and homework. Pupils learn content and skills at home via online homework, and teachers use class time for teacher-guided learning activities to challenge their understanding (see Figure 14.2). The perceived advantage of this model is that it enables teachers to use the whole of classroom time for learner knowledge/skill application, assessing pupil understanding and

The Flipped-Classroom Model

**Home:
online instructions
and content**

**Classroom:
knowledge / skills application**

Figure 14.2 The Flipped-Classroom model.

challenging and enhancing their learning development. Although this model reduces instructional teaching to a minimum, the main criticism is that it relies heavily on the assumption that all pupils will have access to appropriate resources and will be motivated to engage with homework tasks in preparation for the classroom.

Perceived benefits and limitations of digital strategies

There is evidence to suggest that digital education leads to enhanced learning outcomes and attainment levels for pupils. Recent national research concluded that a flipped learning approach to mathematics at Key Stage 2 generated attainment gains equivalent to one month's extra progress when compared to those control group schools that were not subject to a flipped learning intervention (Education Endowment Foundation, 2018). Underwood (2009) concluded that the use of digital technology in learning improved attainment in Science, English and Mathematics for pupils at Key Stage 2, as well as Science and English at Key Stage 1 for average to high attaining pupils (Underwood, 2009, p.3). Recent research conducted at St. Aidan's Church of England Primary School in Gateshead concluded that learning through online networks led to pupils being able to answer test questions significantly ahead of age-related expectations (in excess of seven years), whilst also obtaining acceptable test scores. The collaborative nature of the pupils' online learning led to individual retention of knowledge for up to three months after testing (Mitra and Crawley, 2014).

Digital learning strategies are perceived to benefit pupils by offering a learning experience which includes personalisation, agency and connectivity. Personalisation is the ability to provide 'unique learning pathways for individual[s]'; agency is the opportunity to allow pupils to 'participate in key decisions in their learning experience'; connectivity is the ability to give learners the opportunity to 'experience learning in collaboration with peers and [tutors both] locally and globally' (Green et al., 2017, p.6).

Personalisation within a digital environment not only differentiates pupils' learning by pace and level, it also provides scope for pupils to engage via a range of (or preferred) learning modalities. Multimodality is defined as communication that incorporates several modes, understood as 'socially and culturally shaped resource[s] for making meaning. Image, writing [...] speech, moving images are examples of different modes' (Kress, 2010, p.79). According to Peters (2000), multimodal digital spaces offer heteronomous learning opportunities that provide a rich 'cumulation, compression and intensification of presentation' (p.4). Such heteronomy is perceived to have the advantage of allowing the learner to continuously interact with multisensory forms which means that concepts 'can be repeated and understanding and comprehension strengthened and deepened' (ibid., p.5).

The connectivity associated with digital environments is deemed to provide pupils with both greater agency and the skills needed for lifelong learning within the 21st century. Current global technological advances are 'disrupting some jobs and occupations while creating others', which means that future economic security 'will not come from having a job for life but from having the ability to maintain and renew the right skills' (Government Office for Science, 2018, p.5–6). In this sense, the rapidly changing skills required in contemporary digital societies necessitates engagement with up-to-date, shared information to be found within networked learning environments, many of which no longer have the requirement for formal enrolment or accreditation. According to Resnick, to succeed in contemporary society 'students must learn to think creatively, plan systematically, analyse critically, work collaboratively, communicate clearly, design iteratively, and learn continuously' (Resnick, 2007, p.22). For Resnick, digital technologies 'have the potential, if properly designed and used, to help people develop as creative thinkers' (ibid., p.18). Online digital learning strategies have also been found to be effective for 'community-building and collaborative partnerships that will be essential in a 21st century participatory culture' (Coffey, 2012, p.400). Online spaces and digital devices empower pupils to share video, audio, text and image media, providing rich opportunities for pupils to 'think and design collaboratively and creatively within a community of practice [...] in open-ended engagements' (Mills, 2011, p.2); in this way, digital technology is perceived to facilitate the production of an inclusive and intensive learning environment which may increase pupils' motivation and enhance their independent learning. According to Baytak, Tarman and Ayas (2011, p.145), pupils 'feel an authority over their learning in classrooms with computers [...and] perceived that they cognitively feel more powerful [...] in their lessons'. By focusing on an intensity of connection, interaction, exploration and discovery, rather than the one-way transmission of information associated with traditional teaching, digital learning may facilitate independent learning spaces that provide the opportunity to 'get away from the *pedagogics of instruction* and create and implement *a pedagogics of enablement*' (Peters, 2000, p.16).

The potential for enablement and connectivity within digital learning strategies suggest a capacity to improve pupils' higher-level cognitive skills and critical capacities. Larson (2009, p.647) has demonstrated that online dialogues have provided pupils with 'equitable opportunities to share their thoughts and voice their opinions [...whilst allowing] for extra thinking time before formulating and posting responses'. This has had the effect of encouraging learners to 'respond deeply [...] and carefully consider multiple perspectives and thoughts' (ibid., p.646). By measuring increased use of meta-language in blended face-to-face and online collaboration, Simpson (2010, p.127) has demonstrated that a blended environment could support the development of students' critical awareness via a 'collaborative learning experience that could support students across a range of abilities'.

However, the capacity of digital learning strategies to enhance pupils' learning and understanding has been criticised and met with some caution. Critics have argued that the money spent on resources leading to modest blending learning gains would be better spent on 'knowledge-rich' classroom-based instruction, supported by relevant resources, training and assessment processes (Hazell, 2017, p.12). Rather than developing learners' cognitive potential, wisdom and creativity, digital learning can be viewed as being complicit with the development of surface, functional understanding that corresponds with a neoliberal focus upon flexible, instrumental utility within the workplace. For Selwyn (2014, p,126), the use of digital learning technology has clear links with the needs of contemporary labour, that is, the need for 'self-directing, self-disciplined and routinised workers who are comfortable working with (and within) informatics and algorithmic environments'. Such a view clearly negates the notion that digital learning strategies deepen learning and enable pupils to become more critical, creative thinkers. In this sense, digital learning is less about developing learners' wisdom and more about further imbuing education with 'market values of competitiveness, unregulated exchange [...] and the primacy of individual choice' (ibid., p.128). Such imbuing of market forces goes beyond learning practice and can be found within the consumption of education itself – once education can be achieved through the consumption of disparate online packages, learning becomes increasingly privatised into forms that are 'reducible, quantifiable and ultimately contractible to various actors outside of the educational community' (ibid., p.129). In this situation, limiting the role of the teacher within education in favour of digital learning has the effect of reducing education to a process of imparting information and assessing instrumental, measurable outcomes. Additionally, once education is perceived in terms of access to consumables, the prospect of inequality raises its head with those able to afford resources being at a clear advantage with regard to attainment, therefore pointing towards 'the role of technology in the perpetuation of accumulated advantage and the reproduction of inequalities in education' (Selwyn, 2014, p.138).

The consumption of digital education also has clear, somewhat ominous, implications for notions of lifelong learning when placed within the wider discourse of 'anytime, anyplace, any pace' that surrounds it. Lifelong learning can often be perceived as a process of prosumption (Ritzer, 2014) whereby the old division between consumption and production become blurred – it purports to offer a utopian vision in which the independent consumer of education is free to self-actualise, whereas reality dictates that such consumption is subject to the needs of production within the workplace, impelling each individual continually to invest in their value as a commodity; the lifelong learner thereby becomes 'responsible for their own lifelong financial well-being [...whilst] adding value for wider international competitivity of the nation [and] businesses' (Beighton, 2016, p.701). In this context, the affinity between the potential of digital education and lifelong learning becomes complicit with a neoliberal society that seeks to assimilate all relations to the dictates of market forces – for example, flipped learning provides resources to consume outside classroom time, which impinge on family relations, and which impart assessable skills that correspond to the needs of the contemporary workplace.

Furthermore, the abundant and ubiquitous nature of information within a digital society, and the form whereby we engage with it, can be perceived as being detrimental to developing a deeper understanding of the world. According to Carr (2011), digital networks increase our tendency to become distracted by surface details and irrelevancies which impair our capacity to develop deeper understandings; although the internet provides us with instant access to a 'library of information unprecedented in its size or scope [...what it diminishes is a] primary kind of knowledge: the ability to know, in depth, a subject for ourselves, to construct within our minds [...a] rich and idiosyncratic set of connections' (Carr, 2011, p.143).

In summary, debates about the effectiveness of digital education tend to revolve around the degree that digital technology is capable of developing substantial knowledge and understanding and the extent that it affects the role of the teacher for the benefit of learning. These debates are informed by developments in pedagogic theory which attempt to account for the role that technology plays in the development of learning and whether this process is both inevitable or beneficial; these developments in pedagogic theory also question the degree that a learner can ever be viewed as separate to technology.

Connectivism and technologically mediated learning

From Gutenberg to Zuckerberg. Arguably, each technology that transforms our mode of communication and representation also changes and mediates our relationship to knowledge, understanding and the generation of meaning. As McLuhan (1964, p.1) famously pointed out, the form of communication and interaction afforded by different technologies generates a 'change of scale or pace or pattern that it introduces into human affairs'. Recent neurological studies highlight our technologically mediated relationship to knowledge and meaning; Wolf (2008) describes how the established technology of writing literally rewired our brains, forging neuronal connections and patterns which transform our cognitive perception of the world. Carr (2011) makes a similar argument for digital technology: our brains are becoming more accustomed to the rapid location and categorisation of information that corresponds to the high-speed transfer of data in a computer.

According to Dewar (1998), our technological trajectory has moved us from Listeners to Readers to Users. Prior to print, learning and understanding primarily involved listening (to someone read a manuscript or give a lecture) – in such a mode, the spoken word and memorization of knowledge was paramount. In printed culture, people shifted from being listeners to being readers. Reading printed material signalled the abandonment of the principle that texts were derivative, corruptible representations of memorised spoken knowledge; mass-reproduced print allowed the preservation and dissemination of standardised texts which could be subject to scrutiny and subsequently revised, allowing for a rapid accumulation of advancing knowledge; as Eisenstein states, the 'closed sphere or single corpus passed down from generation to generation, was replaced by an open-ended investigatory process pressing against ever advancing frontiers' (Eisenstein, 1979, p.687). In such circumstances, the role of the mentor as the progenitor of knowledge began to be demoted as learning could be undergone increasingly without their presence, privately. Finally, the connected, decentred and less-sequential nature of online digital information requires that we become more interactive users of information and knowledge – in this digital environment, the learner can access information instantaneously and enter into dialogue with others who enhance understanding; learners can also revise and update information or link to further sources that extend their engagement. The form and properties of digital environments require that we interact with knowledge rather than passively consume information. As Siemens highlights:

> [w]e do not consume knowledge as a passive entity that remains unchanged as it moves through our world and our work. We dance and court the knowledge of others – in ways the original creators did not intend. We make it ours, and in so doing, diminish the prominence of the originator.
>
> (Siemens, 2006, p.7)

As Robinson (2010, p.230) pointed out, traditional schools were 'created in the image of industrialism [...based] on the principles of the assembly line and the efficient division of labour'. Traditional education is increasingly viewed as incongruous with the needs of contemporary society in which 'we are shifting from an economy based on physical inputs –land, capital, and labour – to an economy based on intellectual inputs, or human creativity' (Florida, 2006, p.22).

In the digital age there is the assumption that education's 'roots as "factory-school model" [...] are no longer capable of meeting the needs of today's society [...therefore, there is an] appeal to systemic change – from hierarchical control to flexible and adaptive networked models' (Siemens, 2008, p.8). The move towards a networked model of education has an affinity with Illich's (1971) critique of traditional institutionalised classrooms and mirrors his pre-digital utopian vision of education in which the 'search for new educational funnels must be reversed into the search for their institutional inverse: educational webs which heighten the opportunity for each one to transform each moment of his living into one of learning, sharing, and caring' (Illich, 1971, p.2).

For Dede (2005, p.7), millennial learners' immersion in digital media means they increasingly expect education to be a participative, engaging, and active environment. As a consequence, this expectation changes the learning experience due to it being 'based on seeking, sieving, and synthesizing, rather than on assimilating a single "validated" source of knowledge as from books, television, or [...] lecture'. In recent years, Siemens and Downes have promoted Connectivism as a theory of learning that highlights the potential of learning and understanding within the digital age. For Downes, connectivism is the thesis that knowledge is distributed across a network of connections characterised by 'diversity, autonomy, openness, and connectivity' (Downes, 2012, p.85). These characteristics constitute effective conditions for learning activity within a digital environment: connectivity allows connections to be made between participants and an abundance of information; diversity provides the widest possible spectrum of points of view; autonomy allows participants to recognise and generate new connections; openness allows perspectives to be entered into the system and engaged with by others. From the viewpoint of connectivism, knowledge acquisition in contemporary society is less about 'the acquisition of simple and durable 'truths' and more about [our] ability to 'manage complex and rapidly changing environment[s]' (ibid., p.93). Knowledge within digital environments is acquired by navigating a series of nodes, understood as points within an online network in which a plurality of information both intersects and branches out. Accordingly, users of digital communication can become 'nodes' themselves, equally capable of sharing their knowledge and expertise with other individuals (Kropf, 2013, p.13). In terms of learning within a digital environment, Downes (2012, pp.495–498) distinguishes between aggregating, which consists of accessing nodes distributed in the network; remixing, which consists of the learner keeping track of the nodes that they aggregate; and repurposing, which is the moment at which connective patterns (knowledge) emerge allowing the learner to use sets of connections in a new personal way.

Siemens has criticised previously established learning theories (Behaviourism, Cognitivism and Constructivism), suggesting connectivism offers a new theory that is more appropriate for an age in which understanding is largely mediated and facilitated through connections made within online digital networks. According to Siemens:

[a] central tenet of most learning theories is that learning occurs inside a person. Even social constructivist views, which hold that learning is a socially enacted process, promote the principality of the individual (and her/his physical presence – i.e. brain-based) in learning. These theories do not address learning that occurs outside of people (i.e. learning that is stored and manipulated by technology) [...] In a networked world, the very manner of information that we acquire is worth exploring.

(Siemens, 2005, p.5)

From this viewpoint, previous learning theories have failed to adequately consider how the intervention of technology affects the learning process which now surpasses the limits of physical presence and the connections made in the individual brain. Siemens asserts that, when underlying conditions have altered so significantly, the revision and evolution of previous learning theories becomes untenable and 'further modification is no longer sensible' (ibid.).

Arguably, the notion of learners as nodes themselves within a digital network continues the trajectory of the diminishing role of the traditional teacher, their centrality in the learning process being further undermined by learners' increasing capacity to actively make their own connections online without the intervention of an educator. From the viewpoint of connectivism, digital networks create exponentially developing knowledge and complexification within society that now require nonlinear models of learning in which concepts can be viewed like a mind map rather than a linear progression of ideas. Whereas the pre-digital age classroom positioned the teacher in the centre of a process of direct or guided instruction, the 21st century networked learning environment transforms the role of the educator into that of a curator. While curators are experts in their field, they do not adhere to traditional teacher-centric power structures. Instead of dispensing knowledge, they produce spaces in which knowledge can be created, explored, and connected (Siemens, 2008, p.17).

Mitra's 'Hole in the Wall' research appears to confirm the effectiveness of connectivism as a theory of knowledge acquisition in the 21st century, also suggesting the notion of the curator as a teaching model is an appropriate one for the future. In the 'Hole in the Wall' experiment (Mitra, 2000, 2006; Mitra & Rana 2001), computers with internet access were placed within walls in rural communities in India and left for local children to play with. In each location, the children managed to quickly teach themselves how to use the computer and were observed performing a range of online activities via websites. This experiment was followed by research to find out if a group of Tamil speaking 12-year-old children could teach themselves biotechnology in English on their own by just using the internet (Mitra and Dangwal, 2010). Within two months the children's test scores had gone from zero to 30%. The children had not only learned the complexities of biotechnology, some of them had taken on the roles of instructor and would help the other students learn. Following this, Mitra asked a person with no prior knowledge of biotechnology to engage with them through nothing more than curious questions and encouragement. Within another two months the children's test scores had gone up to 50% which matched those of children who had been afforded a formal education in New Delhi. Mitra's research suggests that children of the future will be able to learn effectively via an online network and make significant progress through curated learning dialogues and interactions. Mitra's research has now been expanded into an international community of schools and educational initiatives that are referred to as Self-Organizing Learning Environments, or SOLEs (School in the Cloud, 2019).

The success of Mitra's experiments seem to point to a future of education in which SOLEs can exist anywhere there is a networked computer and pupils who are ready to learn. Within SOLEs, pupils are given the freedom to learn collaboratively using the internet. An educator poses questions and pupils form groups to share information and find answers. SOLE sessions are characterised by discovery, sharing, spontaneity and limited teacher intervention, in which the educator assumes the role of curator.

Criticisms of connectivism as a new learning theory

Although connectivism purports to be a new theory for learning, such a claim has been criticised because the theory is perceived not to adequately account for the role of human agency in learning. Such an account is essential if we are to explain the role of both pupil and teacher within digital learning strategies, as well as how such strategies might effectively enhance and deepen learning. The focus on the use of technology as a resource to make connections in learning has led Verhagen (2006) to suggest that connectivism's critique of previous theories are based upon a categorical error in which the perceived deficiencies are observed at the level of the curriculum and not in the process of learning – on such a view, Siemens' premise for a new learning theory is perceived to rely on a failure to develop digital literacy skills at the level of the curriculum and not in learning in itself, thereby negating the need for a new theory of learning. According to Clara and Barbera (2013), connectivism cannot provide a new theory for learning because it fails to sufficiently address how we come to know something, as well as how we interact and develop as learners. Connectivism is perceived to fail to account for the Learning Paradox, a problem first outlined by Plato in which how we come to know something appears self-contradictory: on the one hand, if we do not know something, we cannot look for it, as we will not be unable to recognise it; on the other hand, if we are able to recognise something, it must be because we already had previous knowledge of it in some way. Different learning theories have different ways in which to account for this paradox: following a Kantian trajectory, Piaget solves the paradox via an account of learning based upon innate mechanisms, that of equilibration and decentring; in contrast, Vygotsky solves it by following a Hegelian path in which knowledge does not originally lie inside a person, but in the interaction with others within an environment. If, for connectivism, knowledge is perceived to be solely constituted through the recognition of connective patterns, then the paradox remains:

> How do you recognize a pattern if you do not already know that a specific configuration of connections is a pattern? When a pattern is connected for the first time, why are the nodes connected in that specific way, and why is that configuration seen as a pattern? It must be because, in some way, that pattern was already there [either] inside or outside the brain.
>
> (Clara and Barbera, 2013, p.201)

Connectivism's failure to adequately address how we come to know something has led many to suggest that much of the theory's underlying principles would be better drawn from traditional theories which are still considered fit for purpose (Verhagen, 2006; Kop and Hill, 2008; Clara and Barbera, 2013).

By perceiving interaction as essentially a relationship between connected nodes within a network, connectivism also falls short in accounting for how learning develops through our collaboration with others. In most educational theory, and in Siemens' notion of the educator as curator, the role of the other is that of an assistant to learning, not just an object within the process. In connective terms, the other as curator assists the learner to recognise a set of connections as a pattern; in such circumstances, the other is not just a 'node of the connective pattern [...but] fundamental to learning' (Clara and Barbera, 2013, p.202). Additionally, it can be suggested, interactivity with instructors is required to allow learners to effectively internalise concepts and apply them to real world circumstances (Duke, Harper and Johnston, 2013, p.8).

These perceived deficiencies within connectivism as a learning theory might be addressed with a supplementary consideration of the *virtual* within a rhizomatic learning pedagogy. Here, the virtual provides an account for the generation of meaning within a learning network, whilst delineating the role of interaction between teacher and pupil within the process – it does this without returning learning to the traditional classroom and the domain of the subject and the individualised brain.

Rhizomatic learning and the virtual

Rhizomatic learning is a pedagogy that has clear affinities with connectivism and is often associated with the theory (Cormier, 2008), as both provide nonlinear models of learning in which concepts can be viewed like a mind map rather than a linear progression of ideas. As with connectivism, rhizomatic learning occurs through creative connections without the prescribed trajectory that often defines a linear and hierarchical relationship to knowledge within the traditional classroom.

First popularised by Deleuze and Guattari in *A Thousand Plateaus* (2004), the rhizome is a botanical metaphor used to convey the decentred production of thought that can often occur beyond and across the boundaries of traditional knowledge. As a biological form, a rhizome constantly territorialises and de-territorialises without any established organising centre; as such it provides an effective metaphor for the decentred, networked generation of knowledge increasingly found within a digital society (see Figure 14.3). From a rhizomatic viewpoint, 'knowledge can only be negotiated, and the contextual, collaborative learning experience shared by [...] connectivist pedagogies is a social as well as a personal knowledge-creation process with mutable goals and constantly negotiated premises' (Cormier, 2008, p.3).

From the viewpoint of Deleuze, learning occurs when confronted with the virtual – the virtual is the potentiality that exists within a sign prior to it becoming a signified that can be understood (the virtual here is therefore not to be mistaken for the popular notion of simulations generated in digital representations). During the learning process, such virtual signs '"cause problems" through their disorientating shock, forcing thought to deal with experiences that disrupt the common coordinated functioning of the senses and faculties' (Bogue, 2004, p.337). From this perspective, learning is a disruptive encounter and not an act of recognition or recollection.

Given this perspective, rhizomatic learning can be considered to address the learning paradox by perceiving understanding to be the product of an encounter in which the learner interacts with the sign, considers it in a variety of different relations to their own experiences and memories until a general set of principles have been established for it – we therefore *move* with the sign through the world until we significantly understand its place therein. For Deleuze, our immersion

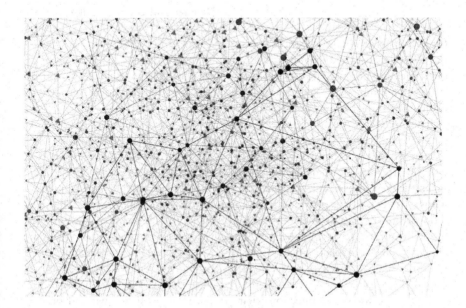

Figure 14.3 Nodes within a rhizomatic network.

amongst virtual signs allows us to 'make, remake and unmake [...our] concepts along a moving horizon, from an always decentered center, from an always displaced periphery which repeats and differentiates them.' (Deleuze, 1994, p.xx–xxi). In this sense, the diverse, heterogeneous signs within an online network may provide a rhizomatic virtual plane for a learner to generate new understandings when confronted with a learning problem; the network allows learners to forge new connections within their own assemblage of experiences, ideas, potentials and desires until the problem is understood and resolved within the context of their own world – learning is thus an encounter that both affects and transforms the learner in the process. Here the learner has not repeated or reproduced the actions of a teacher (such rote learning makes pupils into mere passive receptacles for information), instead, such an encounter extends their own ability to create in and with the world around them.

This conception of learning implies a specific notion of the subject and their position within the process, as well as the role played by interacting with others. For Deleuze and Guattari, the subject is an assemblage constituted by a series of intensities that are constantly subject to change and transformation – the term *haecceity* is used to indicate this individuated specificity:

> You are longitude and latitude, a set of speeds and slownesses between unformed particles, a set of nonsubjectified affects [...] It should not be thought that a haecceity consists simply of a décor or a backdrop that situates subjects [...] It is the entire assemblage in its individuated aggregate that is a haecceity.
>
> (Deleuze and Guattari, 2004, p.289)

From this perspective then, there is no such thing as the self-contained subject; the Cartesian *Cogito* does not exist. Rather, we are the sum of specific flows of intensities and potentialities always in flux – the subject is transformed by whichever specific rhizomatic assemblage it finds itself in within the world; the subject is therefore virtual and in a process of becoming.

The notion of the subject as an assemblage has clear implications for digital education – connectivism is correct to assume that the traditional didactic teacher is dead: the teacher is no longer a subject that knows, responsible for either bestowing knowledge onto a pupil or constructing their subjective reality. From the viewpoint of rhizomatic learning, both teacher and pupil are immersed within a networked society that affects the potentiality of both, rendering traditional hierarchal and linear relations to signs and subjectivities obsolete. As mutually intertwined assemblages within a learning space, the teacher and pupil are both afforded enhanced possibilities to develop deeper knowledge and understanding. When posed with a learning problem, the teacher as curator learns with the pupil with reference to technologically mediated signs that allow both teacher and pupil to discover connections that are pertinent to their own and other's lives – in this way, learning becomes a creative act in which new ideas are formed and understanding begins to synchronise between both pupil and teacher. Such a rhizomatic learning space therefore has an ethics of creativity which is committed to 'experimentation rather than the transmission of facts or inculcation of values' (May and Semetsky, 2008, p.143). In this spirit, 'the rigid classroom of old becomes a frenzied workshop of shared desires, and a playground of signs waiting to be discovered' (Drohan, 2013, pp.130–131).

Summary

The ways in which digital education is transforming the role of both teacher and pupil in learning is a highly contested topic; it can be perceived as either beneficial, detrimental or both. Education has always been a process whereby the form in which information is distributed and negotiated affects the ways in which learning happens; in this sense, the technologically mediated nature of learning is inevitable. However, danger arises once technology predetermines or limits the scale or type of learning that can occur; at which point, the process of substantial learning becomes distracted by superficial strategies that achieve little more than conveying information and measuring performance towards instrumental learning outcomes.

Evidence suggests that pupils' motivation and attainment can be improved by engaging in digital networks. However, the ways in which these online environments are designed need careful deliberation, if a digital pedagogy is to provide learning that is inclusive and challenging, whilst avoiding the pitfalls of superficiality. A diligent and critical consideration of the potential of digital learning needs to recognise (and accept) our technologically-mediated position within society and acknowledge the ways in which technology affects our interactivity with others and access to information which, in turn, both transforms our subjectivity and our understanding and place within the world.

Connectivism proclaims to offer a theoretical framework that explains how the diversity, openness, and connectivity associated with digital networks enables pupils to develop as active, autonomous learners. However, such a framework can only avoid the trap of superficiality if it clearly accounts for the development of deeper, substantial learning and the nature of collaboration within the learning process; to do this would be to endorse the theory as a path to liberation and creativity, rather than a road towards the shackles of utility. Armed with the insights of rhizomatic learning, the relationship between teacher and pupil within this framework becomes one of mutual learning in which the teacher as curator facilitates a non-hierarchical space conducive to the discovery of connections and ideas pertinent to pupils' own lives and understanding.

Questions for reflection

Given the prevalence of digital media within society, should pupils be encouraged to use its potential within the classroom, or does it provide an unnecessary distraction?

If we accept the premise that technology inevitably affects educational practice, to what extent should forms of traditional teaching be abandoned in favour of new models for a digital age?

To what extent, if any, are the classroom and teacher still needed when an abundance of information can be found online in locations outside the boundaries of school walls?

Further reading and resources

Downes, S. (2012) *Connectivism and Connective Knowledge: Essays on Meaning and Learning Networks*, Ontario: National Research Council Canada.

In this book, Stephen Downes gives a comprehensive account of connectivism and evaluates its significance as a learning theory for the digital age. The work will provide you with an understanding of the potential of digital technology for learning, as well as its benefits and limitations. The work is important for orientating you within the context of current debates about digital learning.

School in the Cloud https://www.theschoolinthecloud.org.

Launched by Sugata Mitra in partnership with Newcastle University, this website provides examples of contemporary research into self-organised learning environments (SOLEs). These examples provide theoretical and empirical accounts of digital learning in practice, demonstrating both the tangible benefits and limitations of digital strategies for the present and future.

Selwyn, N. (2014) *Distrusting Educational Technology: Critical Questions for Changing Times*, New York: Routledge.

In this book, Neil Selwyn draws upon a variety of theoretical and empirical perspectives, to provide a wide-ranging critique of digital technology and its role within education. The arguments given within this work will provide you with an antidote to the often exaggerated, utopian and inflated claims made on behalf of digital education.

References

Bauerlain, M. (2009) *The Dumbest Generation*, New York: Penguin.

Baytak, A., Tarman, B. & Ayas, C. (2011) 'Experiencing technology integration in education: Children's perceptions', *International Electronic Journal of Elementary Education*, 3(2): 139–151.

Beighton, C. (2016) 'Groundhog day? Nietzsche, Deleuze and the eternal return of prosumption in lifelong learning', *Journal of Consumer Culture*, 17(3): 695–712.

Bogue, R. (2004) 'Search, Swim and See: Deleuze's apprenticeship in signs and pedagogy of images', *Educational Philosophy and Theory*, 36(3): 327–342.

Carr, N. (2011) *The Shallows: What the Internet Is Doing to Our Brains*, New York: Norton and Company.

Clara, M. & Barbera, E. (2013) 'Three problems with the connectivist conception of learning', *Journal of Computer Assisted Learning*, 30(3): 197–206.

Coffey, G. (2012) 'Literacy and technology: Integrating technology with small group, peer-led discussions of literature', *International Electronic Journal of Elementary Education*, 4(2): 395–405.

Cormier, D. (2008) 'Rhizomatic education: Community as curriculum', *Innovate: Journal of Online Education*, 4: 5. Article 2.

Dede, C. (2005) 'Planning for neomillennial learning styles', *Educause Quarterly*, 28(1): 7–12.

Deleuze, G. (1994) *Difference and Repetition*, New York: Columbia University Press.

Deleuze, G. & Guattari, F. (2004) *A Thousand Plateaus: Capitalism and Schizophrenia*, London: Continuum.

Dewar, J. A. (1998) *The Information Age and the Printing Press: Looking Backward to See Ahead*, Santa Monica, CA: RAND.

Downes, S. (2012) *Connectivism and Connective Knowledge: Essays on Meaning and Learning Networks*, Ontario: National Research Council Canada.

Drohan, C. M. (2013) 'Deleuze and the virtual classroom'. In: Semetsky, I. & Masny, D. (Eds.), *Deleuze in Education*, Edinburgh: Edinburgh University Press.

Duke, B., Harper, G. & Johnston, M. (2013) 'Constructivism as a digital age learning theory', *The International HETL Review*, Special Issue: 4–13.

Educational Endowment Foundation (2018) *Flipped Learning*. Available at: https ://educationendowmentfoundation.org.uk/projects-and-evaluation/projects/fli pped-learning/ (Accessed 18.01.2019).

Eisenstein, E. L. (1979) *The Printing Press as an Agent of Change*, New York: Cambridge University Press.

Florida, R. (2006) 'The flight of the creative class: The new global competition for talent', *Liberal Education*, 92(3): 22–29.

Friesen, N. (2012) *Report: Defining Blended Learning*. Available at: https://www.scr ibd.com/document/213761016/Defining-Blended-Learning-2012 (Accessed 18.01.2019).

Government Office for Science (2017) Future Of Skills And Lifelong Learning, Available at: https://assets.publishing.service.gov.uk/government/uploads/syste m/uploads/attachment_data/file/727776/Foresight-future-of-skills-lifelong-l earning_V8.pdf (Accessed on 19th January 2019)

Green, T., Tucker, C. & Wycoff, T. (2017) *Blended Learning in Action: A Practical Guide Towards Sustainable Change*, London: SAGE.

Hazell, W. (2017) 'Why teachers need to pause before falling for flipped learning', *Times Educational Supplement*, 10 November, no. 5274: 10–13.

Illich, I. (1971) *Deschooling Society*. Available at: https://learning.media.mit.edu/ courses/mas713/readings/DESCHOOLING.pdf (Accessed 24.01.2019).

Kop, R. & Hill, A. (2008) 'Connectivism: Learning theory of the future or vestige of the past?' *International Review of Research in Open and Distance Learning*, 9(3): 1–13.

Kress, G (2010) *Multimodality: A Social Semiotic Approach to Contemporary Communication*. New York: Routledge.

Kropf, D. (2013). 'Connectivism: 21st century's new learning theory'. *European Journal of Open, Distance and E-Learning*, 16(2), 1324

Larson, L. (2009) 'Reader response meets new literacies: Empowering readers in online learning communities', *The Reading Teacher*, 62(8): 638–648.

May, T. & Semetsky, I. (2008) 'Deleuze, ethical education and the unconscious'. In: Semetsky, I. (Ed.), *Nomadic Education: Variations on a Theme by Deleuze and Guattari*, Rotterdam: Sense.

McLuhan, M. (1964) *Understanding Media: The Extensions of Man*, New York: Mentor.

Mills, K. A. (2011) *The Multiliteracies Classroom*, Bristol: Multilingual Matters.

Mitra, S. (2000) 'Minimally invasive education for mass computer literacy', *Paper Presented at the CRIDALA 2000 Conference*, Hong Kong. Available at: http://www.hole-in-the-wall.com/docs/Paper01.pdf (Accessed on 19.02.2019).

Mitra, S. (2006) *The Hole in the Wall: Self-Organising Systems in Education*, New York: Tata-McGraw-Hill.

Mitra, S. & Crawley, E. (2014) 'Effectiveness of self-organised learning by children: Gateshead experiments', *Journal of Education and Human Development*, 3(3): 79–88.

Mitra, S. & Dangwal, R. (2010) 'Limits to self-organising systems of learning – The Kalikuppam experiment', *British Journal of Educational Technology*, 41(5): 672–688.

Mitra, S. & Rana, V. (2001) 'Children and the Internet: Experiments with minimally invasive education in India', *The British Journal of Educational Technology*, 32(2): 221–232.

Ofcom (2017) *Children and Parents: Media Use and Attitudes Report*, London: Ofcom.

Oppenheimer, T. (2004) *The Flickering Mind: Saving Education from the False Promise of Technology*, New York, USA: Random House.

Peters, O. (2000) 'Digital learning environments: New possibilities and opportunities', *The International Review of Research in Open and Distributed Learning*, 1: 1.

Resnick, M. (2007) 'Sowing the seeds for a more creative society', *International Society for Technology in Education*, 35(4): 18–22.

Ritzer, G. (2014) 'Prosumption: Evolution, revolution, or eternal return of the same?' *Journal of Consumer Culture*, 14(1): 3–24.

Robinson, K. (2010) *The Element: How Finding Your Passion Changes Everything*, London: Penguin.

Selwyn, N. (2014) *Distrusting Educational Technology: Critical Questions for Changing Times*, New York: Routledge.

School in the Cloud (2019), *School in the Cloud*. Available at: https://www.theschoolinthecloud.org (Accessed 09.02.2019).

Siemens, G. (2005) 'Connectivism: A learning theory for a digital age', *International Journal of Instructional Technology and Distance Learning*, 2(1): 3–10.

Siemens, G. (2006) *Knowing knowledge*, Mountain View, CA: Creative Commons.

Siemens, G. (2008) *Learning and knowing in networks: Changing roles for educators and designers*. Available at: https://www.calvin.edu/~dsc8/documents/George SiemensPresentation-Jan2008.pdf (Accessed 04.01.2018).

Simpson, A. (2010) 'Integrating technology with literacy: Using teacher-guided collaborative online learning to encourage critical thinking'. *ALT-J: Research in Learning Technology*, 18(2): 119–131.

Staker, S. & Horn, M. B. (2012) *Classifying K-12 Blended Learning*, San Mateo, CA: Innosight Institute.

Underwood, J. (2009) *The Impact of Digital Technology: A Review of the Evidence of the Impact of Digital Technologies on Formal Education*, Coventry: Becta.

Verhagen, P. W. (2006) *Connectivism: A New Learning Theory?* Available at: http://elearning.surf.nl/e-learning/english/3793 (Accessed 18.01.2019).

Vygotsky, L. S. (1987) 'Thinking and speech'. (Minick, N. Trans). In: Reiber, R. W. & Carton, A. S. (Eds.), *The Collected Works of Lev Vygotsky, Vol. 1*, New York: Plenum Press.

Wolf, M (2008) *Proust and the Squid: The Story and Science of the Reading Brain.* Cambridge: Icon Books

Chapter 15

The teaching and learning of primary mathematics

Gina Donaldson

Introduction

Since 2016, a significant amount of Department for Education (DfE) funding has been allocated to developing a programme for primary mathematics which promotes a range of teaching approaches influenced by practices in areas of the world which perform well in international tests (Boylan et al., 2019). The locations where children scored the highest in these tests for the primary age group in 2015 tended to be in East Asia and include Singapore, Hong Kong, the republic of Korea, Chinese Taipei and Japan (Mullis et al., 2016). Successive governments in England have promoted a range of approaches to teaching mathematics which appear to be common to some of these locations, and the term 'teaching for mastery' has been used to describe these approaches.

Early evaluations of the impact of adopting a teaching for mastery approach were mixed. An evaluation of a programme based on practices in Singapore found a small positive effect on attainment in Key Stage 1 (Jerrim and Vignoles, 2016), whilst Boylan et al. (2019) identified a positive impact on Key Stage 1 attainment in some schools where teachers were directly involved in the teacher exchange programme with Shanghai and had implemented teaching for mastery for two years, but there was not yet evidence of impact at Key Stage 2. However, later evaluations have been much more promising (NCETM, 2019).

There is plenty of evidence of political use of benchmarks from international comparisons. For example, in 2011 the Department for Education published a paper titled 'Review of the National Curriculum in England: What can we learn from the English, mathematics and science curricula of high-performing jurisdictions?' However, the idea that policy and practice in England can be led by approaches which mirror those used elsewhere in the world has been questioned. Askew et al. (2010) argued that the success of primary mathematics teaching approaches abroad might be based on a range of cultural and language-based issues.

This chapter will not consider the broad and general issues of implementing policies and practices which are considered effective elsewhere in the world. It will instead focus on specific issues around the teaching approaches to primary mathematics being promoted. The discussion will be on particular approaches to teaching for mastery of mathematics, and will consider these key questions:

1. How does teaching for mastery challenge perceptions of what it is to understand primary mathematics?
2. What are the issues raised by the specific recommended approaches for teaching for mastery?
3. What are the implications of the teaching for mastery approaches for meeting individual needs of children?

How does teaching for mastery challenge perceptions of what it is to understand primary mathematics?

The National Centre for Excellence in Teaching Mathematics (NCETM) is funded by the DfE and is the main source of guidance for teaching mathematics in England. It aims to raise levels of achievement in mathematics and to increase appreciation of the power and wonder of mathematics. It has a large section of its site devoted to mastery and provides a set of guidance and teaching materials based on teaching for mastery approaches in the form of professional development materials (NCETM, https://www.ncetm.org.uk/). It defines mastery as a deep, long-term, secure and adaptable understanding of the subject and this is the definition used in this chapter.

Although the current National Curriculum for England (DfE) was written in 2013 and updated in 2014, when the government was promoting approaches used in high-performing jurisdictions and countries (DFE 2011), it did not mention the word 'mastery'. This might, at face value, seem to contradict the focus of policy. However, a close analysis of the aims of the National Curriculum demonstrates that the curriculum is very much in line with the mastery approach. The curriculum aims for all children to:

- become fluent in the fundamentals of mathematics, including through varied and frequent practice with increasingly complex problems over time, so that pupils develop conceptual understanding and the ability to recall and apply knowledge rapidly and accurately;
- reason mathematically by following a line of enquiry, conjecturing relationships and generalisations, and developing an argument, justification or proof using mathematical language;
- solve problems by applying their mathematics to a variety of routine and non-routine problems with increasing sophistication, including breaking down problems into a series of simpler steps and persevering in seeking solutions.

(DfE, 2014, p.3)

Without mentioning mastery itself, the aims can be seen to match the definition of mastery provided by the NCETM. It seems reasonable to argue that a deep, long-term, secure and adaptable understanding of mathematics would include fluency, conceptual understanding, reasoning and problem solving. Indeed, the teaching of mathematics in Shanghai is designed to develop conceptual understanding and procedural fluency (Boylan et al., 2019), linking well to the National Curriculum. The first aim of the National Curriculum in England states that children should develop conceptual understanding of mathematical ideas, and theories such as those of Skemp (1989) have helped to unpick models of understanding. Skemp defined two types of understanding: instrumental and relational. He defined instrumental understanding as knowing a rule but not the reason for the rule. For example, a child might know that when they add two odd numbers they get an even answer, without understanding why. Relational understanding, on the other hand, is knowing both what to do and why. In this case, a child might be able to understand *why* adding two odd numbers results in an even number. Understanding which is conceptual, rather than surface (or relational rather than instrumental, to use Skemp's terms) should be long-term and secure and therefore would correspond with mastery.

The result might be that teachers feel that all teaching of mathematics, whether it is described as teaching for mastery or not, would aim for the same sort of understanding of mathematics. On the surface, they might think that if they follow the aims of the National Curriculum, which they may have done throughout their teaching so far, then they will be teaching for mastery and there is no need to change their practice or philosophy. However, a deeper reflection on what mastery might mean reveals quite a different interpretation of the teaching and learning of mathematics.

For example, there has been an emphasis on progress in English primary education. The focus of school comparisons provided by the DfE are by progress in learning as well as by attainment against age-expected standards (DFE, https://www.gov.uk/school-performance-tables). It could be argued that a maths lesson ensures progress when a child has more understanding of a mathematical idea after the lesson than before. So it might be that a child can solve a mathematical problem, use a mathematical term, or make use of a mathematical procedure which they could not do before the lesson. However, if the aim is for mastery and therefore depth of understanding, would this be sufficient progress? In a mastery lesson it might be that a child begins the lesson already knowing an answer or able to use a term or procedure. The mastery lesson, however, deepens their learning, and more time might be spent on finding alternative ways of finding the answer or providing convincing arguments as to why the answer is correct. The answer is seen as the beginning of learning, rather than the end; finding the correct answer is not enough. For example, a teacher might teach a lesson on the four times table. If all the children can then recall the multiplication and division facts for multiples of four and use these to solve problems, they might feel ready to move on to a different area of mathematics in their next lesson. Or, in order to promote depth of understanding, they might decide to continue to explore with the children some of the facts in the four times table, looking, for example, at why all multiples of four are even, exploring the common multiples of two and four or investigating the link between multiplying by four and doubling.

There is also a tension, in the critical debate on what it is to understand mathematics, between learning and remembering. In terms of mastery, a deep, long-term, secure and adaptable understanding would certainly include rapid recall of number facts, but this alone would not be sufficient for mastery. It is possible to understand but not remember, or to remember but not understand. Mastery includes both understanding and memory. Clearly the two are linked. Skemp (1989) claimed that what is understood relationally is more likely to be remembered. This is reflected in the aims of the National Curriculum. The first aim of the National Curriculum focuses on children being fluent with mathematical ideas as well as developing conceptual understanding of them, placing value on both understanding and recalling. Russell (2000) identifies mathematical fluency itself as being more than rapid recall of facts and as including efficiency, accuracy and flexibility. For example, children should have rapid recall of facts, and also access to quick and accurate procedures for calculating. As they develop fluency they should also use procedures which are best suited to the calculation to be solved. They might recognise that they might use different methods to calculate 12×4, such as tackling this as 24×2, or calculating 10×4 and adding on 2×4.

As children develop fluency, they should also connect facts and operations. According to Russell (2000), the ability to make these sorts of connections is a significant part of fluency. The research by Askew et al. (1997) highlighted the role of connections in the learning of primary mathematics. In this way, connected understanding of one idea might be easier to recall as it is connected to other ideas.

So, knowing one fact, such as:

$$3 \times 4 = 12$$

enables learners also to have access to other facts such as:

$$4 \times 3 = 12$$
$$12 \div 4 = 3$$
$$40 \times 30 = 1200$$
$$0.4 \times 3 = 1.2$$

Teaching for mastery of mathematics therefore includes elements of establishing understanding and memory. Both are crucial. Understanding can be built by the use of manipulatives and visual images which represent the mathematical idea, and through skilful questioning and lesson design by the teacher. Memory of ideas might be promoted through opportunities to retrieve them and use them regularly.

Some approaches to teaching for mastery might at first sight look like rote learning. For example, there is often recitation in a mastery lesson, where children recite key facts and ideas together in order to help commit them to memory (Lai and Murray, 2012). Without time spent on understanding these ideas, reciting them would be less effective. Children need to have opportunities to understand and retrieve ideas (Karpicke and Blunt, 2011). The first aim of the National Curriculum suggests that understanding stems from fluency with ideas, so that remembering can precede understanding. A more traditional approach is that understanding comes first and is followed by recall.

The debate about understanding and memory is complicated further by the introduction of the multiplication tables check (DfE, https://www.gov.uk/g overnment/organisations/department-for-education). The multiplication check introduced by the DfE tests rapid recall of number facts only expressed as multiplication rather than as a connected division fact. The focus seems to be on rapid recall of a certain sort of fact, signalling its importance over a more connected understanding.

A critical debate, therefore, is about what is really meant by depth of mathematical understanding. This debate might emerge in a teacher's classroom. They may feel comfortable exploring depth of learning in their teaching, but inevitably external judgements will be made on their practice. Observations of a teacher's lessons and scrutiny of their children's books may reveal different interpretations of what it means to understand a mathematical idea. For example, anyone observing the lesson on deepening children's understanding of the four times table might note that the children seem to have already learned it, particularly if they have recited it accurately during the lesson. So where is the progression in their learning? In terms of mastery, a teacher might argue that this is in developing deep understanding, but there are tensions in the debate. For example, will there be time to cover the curriculum for the year group if the teacher devotes lessons to depth of understanding, when they could have moved on to a different or more complex idea? Or is time spent on depth of understanding providing a foundation for later learning, lessening the need for interventions when the children encounter more complex ideas?

The next section of this chapter will continue to reflect on this idea of depth of learning, analysing it from different angles by considering the specific teaching for mastery approaches.

What are the issues raised by the specific recommended approaches for teaching for mastery?

Teaching for mastery aims for children to have a deep, long-term, secure and adaptable understanding of mathematics. This section of the chapter will consider issues relating to two specific approaches to teaching for mastery which are being promoted by the DfE through the NCETM. The approaches discussed will be the use of representations of mathematical ideas, and the structure of sequences of teaching.

A key approach included in teaching for mastery relates to the representation of mathematical ideas. This is evident in the guidance and exemplar mastery lessons from the NCETM and will be considered now in more detail. In order to develop mastery of mathematics, teachers are guided towards choosing representations which expose the mathematical idea with which they want the children to engage (NCETM, https://www.ncetm.org.uk/). For example, teachers might choose place value cards to represent the way three-digit numbers are written and the use of zero as a place holder, but might choose Dienes apparatus to represent the idea of equivalence of ten ones for a ten and ten tens for a hundred in a three-digit number.

The practices appear to be based on Bruner's theory of representation. In 1966 Bruner articulated how ideas can be represented. Children might encounter an idea represented enactively where they actively manipulate objects; iconically, where children manipulate mental images which might be initially represented pictorially; and symbolically. In a mastery approach, this sequence of learning is sometimes denoted as CPA: Concrete, Pictorial and Abstract.

Approaches to teaching mastery have particularly focused on the use of specific models for supporting children's fluency. The 'part part whole model' has been encouraged to help children make connections between numbers and between operations, for example, linking addition and subtraction. This might be represented as a bar model. Representing numbers on a ten frame is promoted as a way of encouraging children to use facts to ten in addition and subtraction. Merttens (2012) argues that a typical mastery approach would involve pictures of items, often portrayed in textbooks, rather than experience with actual items.

The use of representations of mathematical ideas in the primary curriculum is not new. However, there has often been debate about how they are implemented in the classroom, and the call for mastery has reignited the debate. Bruner initially suggested that the stages of working with enactive, iconic and symbolic representations were loosely sequential, with learning building or translating from one to another, sparking a debate around when children should use the enactive representations of ideas. Should young children have access to concrete representations and then, as they become older, work with pictorial and then abstract ideas? In this case, children who are in the later stages of primary education might only access new ideas in a formal, symbolic and abstract representation. Alternatively, it might be suggested that it is children who find mathematics difficult who should have access to the concrete representations, even as they grow older. However, Haylock and Cockburn (2017) argue that learning is not sequential, and that constant connections need to be made between representations of ideas which are pictorial, concrete, language-based and symbolic. Therefore, all learners will need access to concrete representations of ideas, whether they are in the later or earlier stages of primary education, or if they find mathematics difficult or easy. It is not enough to use *any* manipulatives however; they must be carefully selected to physically represent the abstract idea the children are learning.

The call for teaching for mastery promotes the use of concrete, pictorial and abstract ideas for all children. Therefore, the youngest children should have real and meaningful experiences in which they learn mathematics and be supported in reaching some sort of abstract generalisation, for example about the meaning of odd and even numbers. Older children should encounter new ideas such as ratio in a concrete way as they too work towards general statements at their own level. This has re-opened the debate about the use of manipulatives in the primary curriculum, and also the ability of young children to work in an abstract way. Staff and children themselves need to be convinced that manipulatives are essential for the learning of all children in the primary school. This is difficult to argue for when the national testing in England for children aged seven does not allow children to use manipulatives in the written tests (DfE, https://www.gov.uk/government/organisations/department-for-education), potentially leading to the belief that their use should be avoided. Similarly, the use of manipulatives and images to support children who find learning mathematics difficult, allowing other children to feel that they no longer need to use them, promotes a view that learning mathematics is about moving quickly to the abstract and symbolic, rather than spending time exploring depth and mastery of these ideas. The manipulative needs to be acknowledged as a resource not only to scaffold learning until it can be removed but to enhance understanding. For example, children at the end of primary school might use manipulatives to develop and explain their understanding of a long division procedure. The other aspect of the debate is around the idea that all children are capable of considering abstract ideas if they are based on understanding. Young children can reach generalisations and formal understanding, if set in meaningful experiences, usually explored physically. For example, young children might explore the structure of odd and even numbers by creating them with counters or cubes arranged in twos, noticing that an even number is made from a group of twos and an odd number is made from a group of twos with one more. This is a powerful generalisation which will help them to understand other patterns with odd and even numbers later.

A further way to represent a mathematical idea to children is through the use of stem sentences. This is an approach particularly aimed to develop children's ability to reason mathematically. The key idea of the lesson is developed until the children reach an understanding of it, and then it is captured in a short sentence which the children repeat until they remember it. For example, in a lesson on comparing fractions, the stem sentence might be 'when comparing fractions with the same numerator, the larger the denominator, the smaller the fraction.' The idea is that children then call on these sentences as they reason and solve problems. As already noted, repetition of sentences like this might be reminiscent of rote learning, the subject of ongoing debate. However, the mastery approach is that children understand the idea captured in the stem sentence before they repeat it until it is memorised (Lai and Murray, 2012).

Finally, for this section, the way teachers structure their teaching will be considered. A review of the video exemplars on lessons on the NCETM site (NCETM, https://www.ncetm.org.uk/) shows that the structure of a mastery lesson is very different from the structure of lessons promoted by the National Numeracy Strategy in 1999 (DfEE, 1999) – the last detailed guidance provided by the government on primary mathematics lesson structure. In 1999, a clear message was that the lesson should begin with a mental and oral starter, include a whole-class direct teaching input from the teacher, then move into children's activities and finish with a plenary. A mastery lesson is structured quite differently, with a series of much shorter teaching inputs to the whole class, each followed by shorter whole-class activities throughout the lesson. The lesson is planned in coherent small steps, and the teacher takes the children through these steps gradually to ensure progression. Whereas in the traditional structure, the teacher may have covered a sequence of ideas in the teaching input, these shorter teaching sessions and interlaced children's activities in the mastery lesson are designed to ensure all children access each step. This throws the structure of lessons into question.

An analysis of lesson structure can be debated in terms of how it enables teachers to support progression in learning. For example, a lengthy teaching input can result in children becoming off-task as they struggle to concentrate for longer periods of time, or retain information. However, managing a series of shorter activities could result in holding some children back to wait until others are ready to move on to the next activity. The two approaches can also be analysed in terms of the way in which teachers view children as learners. Lengthy individual activities or group activities in the traditional structure emphasise the learning of individual children or children in groups. Moving the whole class together throughout the lesson through a series of shorter inputs and activities emphasises the learning of the class as a community. This will be discussed in more depth in the next section. Clearly the structure of a lesson can only be justified in terms of the teacher's aims. If the aim is mastery, the structure should promote opportunities to develop deep, long-term, secure and adaptable understanding.

Similarly, the structure of the long-term curriculum plans for mathematics can be debated. In the 1999 guidance for the National Numeracy Strategy, short topics of work were recommended, with each topic returned to regularly over a year. This use of a spiral curriculum dates back to Bruner's theories of learning (1996). A mastery approach, in its aim for depth of understanding, often takes the form of a different sort of curriculum planning. Longer topics are planned so that children develop a depth of understanding before moving on. Learning is seen to be clearly hierarchical, for example a year's curriculum plan might begin with place value, recognising that later learning of written methods for addition and subtraction will depend on secure and deep understanding of place value. Place value would then be covered in depth, to ensure all children understand it before moving on. So this aspect of the debate on mastery is on how best to structure children's learning over a year. Should children secure ideas first before moving on, but risk not covering all of the content of the curriculum? Alternatively, should children cover ideas at a quicker pace, with shorter topics which revisit ideas and recognise the need for a variety of topics in a term, but risk that they will understand very little? Another factor is the ability of children to recall and remember previous learning if the curriculum is arranged in long blocks and ideas are not revisited. An alternative view would be that the learning of particular areas of mathematics should be 'interleaved' so that ideas are regularly revisited, and connections made with other areas of mathematics and other areas of the curriculum.

Given a currently full curriculum, engagement with these debates is needed, enabling teachers to reflect critically and decide on their chosen approach so that they can justify it to themselves and those who hold them accountable. A key question for teachers is whether there is a balance between their teaching for understanding and memory, rather than coverage of content.

The final section of the chapter will consider the implications of teaching for mastery for meeting the needs of all children in the class.

What are the implications of the mastery approaches for meeting individual needs of children?

The teaching for mastery approaches promoted by the NCETM are for whole-class lessons where all children have access to the same mathematics. Teachers may feel that this should always be the case. However, do teachers really believe that all children will reach the learning intention of the lesson?

Mathematics lessons have traditionally included differentiation, often with groups of children working on different tasks, or having multiple learning intentions. There are many models of differentiation. We can provide children with different support to reach the same learning intention through the same activity, such as varying levels of adult support, or the use of different manipulatives. Alternatively, we can provide children with different activities to reach the same learning intention, such as asking some children to tackle calculations which have been modelled by the teacher and others to tackle new calculations. Or we can provide children with different learning intentions, even on the same theme, such as asking some children to order numbers to 20, others to order numbers to 1000 and some to order decimals...

The National Numeracy Strategy (1999) suggested that when children work on activities, teachers should 'control the degree of differentiation (for example, provide tasks on the same theme and usually at no more than three levels of difficulty)' (DfEE, 1999, p.14.). Although the guidance was clear about keeping the class together when possible, this use of a number of levels of difficulty has been popular. More recently teachers have allowed children to choose the level of their activity. However, careful differentiation by the teacher could in fact result in children not gaining access to the mathematics in the National Curriculum for their year group. Making the mathematics easier could have this effect. For example, allowing children in Year 3 to work with addition up to ten because they are not yet confident with their number bonds to ten, when others in the class are learning the formal column methods of adding numbers above 100, means that these children will miss the opportunity to learn this powerful calculation method. Confidence and fluency with number bonds to ten needs to be addressed, and meanwhile the children supported to access the written method with manipulatives to help them. In-class ability grouping or setting across classes could be very kindly meant but might have negative results based on low teacher expectations, and therefore widen the attainment gap between the children who find mathematics most and least difficult. Writers such as Boaler (2016) have suggested that this gap can then potentially widen as the children move through school. Both in-class and across-class grouping and differentiation by ability can restrict the opportunity for children to learn from others of differing ability, identified by key learning theories to be essential for learning, such as Vygotsky's notion of the more knowledge other (Vygotsky, 1978). Such an approach might also contradict the National Curriculum which states that: 'The expectation is that the majority of pupils will move through the programmes of study at broadly the same pace' (DfE, 2014, p.99).

Consider our use of language relating to ability and grouping. Teachers may refer to groups of children as 'least', or 'average' or 'more able' children. What is this judgement based on? It might be better to use the language of 'previously low attaining' or 'previously high attaining children'. Otherwise, the underlying belief is that mathematical ability is fixed. This belief has been challenged by Boaler (2016) who disputes the idea that some people are born with a 'maths brain' and others are not.

The use of whole-class lessons is again a reflection of practices in locations which perform well in international comparisons, such as Singapore and Shanghai. Children are taught together and there are high expectations of all. This should challenge our use of language and expectations of children. In a mastery lesson, the use of small and coherent steps and manipulatives and pictorial images is designed to ensure that as many children as possible can access the mathematics and develop deep, conceptual understanding and fluency. Stem sentences are designed to support their reasoning and ability to solve problems. The principle is that all children have a right to be taught the curriculum. When differentiation takes place in a mastery approach, it may be subtle and easy to miss on first observation. There may be questions asked throughout the lesson which offer increased challenge. For example, if the children are working with nine counters and looking at different ways of partitioning nine, children who work quickly might be asked to see if they can explain why, and they can list these ways systematically as a further challenge. The teacher would be flexible about who will be given this extra challenge, using assessment for learning practices during the lesson rather than pre-set ability judgements. Mastery lessons will include greater-depth questions, designed to increase depth of learning beyond what is expected for all children. These questions, however, are provided for all children to try. There are no preconceived expectations about who will find such questions too difficult.

In a teaching for mastery approach, children who find it difficult to reach the learning outcomes might receive an intervention during that same day, to help them to be included in the next day's lesson. This might open up questions about whether these children miss other areas of the curriculum whilst they are supported in the intervention. A broad and balanced curriculum is every child's right as part of the National Curriculum (DfE, 2014). However, it is often the children who are socially disadvantaged who underachieve in mathematics (Knowles, 2017) and teachers have a moral responsibility to tackle this pattern of underachievement. All children deserve to learn mathematics and be engaged with the subject. The continual feeling of failure in mathematics can cause anxiety, and there is a balance to be achieved between providing children with tasks they can succeed in whilst having high expectations for their ability to access what is expected for their age.

Narrowing the attainment gap inevitably has an impact on the children who find mathematics easy. At the early stages of introducing mastery into a school, this group of children may have previously been accelerated to the mathematics which appears in the curriculum for a later year group. They, and their parents, might have expectations about this, which will be challenged by the introduction of approaches to promote mastery of mathematics. Teaching the whole class together may result in periods of time when children are waiting for others to finish, or when the teacher has to continually provide deepening questions. The debate here is how teachers justify the fact that to narrow the attainment gap, these children might not make as much progress as in a traditional differentiated approach.

It is important to evaluate approaches to teaching mathematics, whether they be based on mastery or traditional approaches, against key issues. Will such approaches establish a love of learning which will ensure children will continue to want to engage with mathematics throughout their lives? Will the experiences offered in mathematics lessons contribute to or risk children's well-being and their understanding of themselves as learners of mathematics? Will there be the highest expectations for all children's learning?

Summary

This chapter has reflected on the current tensions in primary mathematics education, considering the call by recent governments for teachers to adopt approaches to teaching used in locations across the world who teach for mastery. In particular, the questions to be debated have rested on teachers' beliefs in what it is to learn and understand mathematics. The notion that children can understand mathematics at different levels, and that some of these levels might be considered deeper than others, underpins the debate. The ways in which this belief in the importance of depth of learning is manifested in how teachers represent ideas, structure lessons and curriculum plans and group children have been considered in this chapter.

Grappling with these debates is indicative of a commitment to the teacher's own learning, and their belief that this will enrich their practice and the learning of the children they teach, throughout their career. The introduction of mastery is an example of an imposed change on teaching, although many aspects have been largely welcomed. The teaching of mathematics may well be the subject of future change and teachers have a professional responsibility to reflect critically on developments as they take place. The author's perspectives on this particular change is that, although the copying of policy and practice from one country which performs well in a test to another may be faulty, the call for mastery of mathematics has to be welcomed with its focus on depth of mathematical understanding. A belief in establishing secure and deep understanding of mathematics in children will help a teacher to judge critically the implementation of other initiatives throughout their career.

Questions for reflection

What should a teacher aim for when they teach mathematics and how can this philosophy help them to critically evaluate the current and future changes called for in their career?

How important is it to be able to justify the approaches chosen to use in the teaching of mathematics?

Which aspects of the teaching for mastery of mathematics approaches can be fully justified and which are less convincing?

Further reading and resources

NCETM, https://www.ncetm.org.uk.
This site provides detailed guidance on teaching for mastery approaches. It offers specific support for teaching for mastery, and includes video clips of lessons.

Boylan, M., Maxwell, B., Wolstenholme, C. & Jay, T. (2019) *Longitudinal Evaluation of the Mathematics Teacher Exchange: China-England Third Interim Report*, Sheffield: Sheffield Hallam University.
This report evaluates the success of the exchange programme between teachers from Shanghai and England. It identifies ways in which teaching for mastery has been implemented.

Askew, M., Hodgen, J., Hossain, S. & Bretscher, N. (2010) *Values and Variables: Mathematics Education in High Performing Countries*, London: Nuffield Foundation.
This report questions the copying of practices and policies from other cultures.

References

Askew, M., Brown, M., Rhodes, V., William, D. & Johnson, D. (1997) *Effective Teachers of Numeracy: Report of a Study Carried Out for the Teacher Training Agency*, London: King's College, University of London.

Askew, M., Hodgen, J., Hossain, S. & Bretscher, N. (2010) *Values and Variables: Mathematics Education in High Performing Countries*, London: Nuffield Foundation.

Boaler, J. (2016) *Mathematical Mindsets*, San Francisco, CA: Jossey-Bass.

Boylan, M., Maxwell, B., Wolstenholme, C. & Jay, T. (2019) *Longitudinal Evaluation of the Mathematics Teacher Exchange: China-England Third Interim Report*, Sheffield: Sheffield Hallam University.

Bruner, J. (1966) *Toward a Theory of Instruction*, Cambridge, MA: Belknap Press.

Bruner, J. (1996) *The Culture of Education*, Cambridge, MA: Harvard University Press.

DfE (2011) *Review of the National Curriculum in England: What Can We Learn from the English, Mathematics and Science Curricula of High Performing Jurisdictions?*, London: DfE.

DfE (2014) *Mathematics Programmes of Study: Key Stages 1 and 2*, London: DfE.

DFE, https://www.gov.uk/school-performance-tables.

DfE, https://www.gov.uk/government/organisations/department-for-education.

DfEE (1999) *The National Numeracy Strategy*, Suffolk: Cambridge University Press.

Haylock, D. & Cockburn, A. (2017) *Understanding Mathematics for Young Children* (5th ed.), London: SAGE.

Jerrim, J. & Vignoles, A. (2016) The link between East Asian 'mastery' teaching methods and English children's mathematics skills, *Economics of Education Review*, 50: 29–44.

Karpicke, J. D. & Blunt, J. R. (2011) Retrieval practice produces more learning than elaborative studying with concept mapping, *Science*, 331(6018): 772–775.

Knowles, C. (2017) *Closing the Attainment Gap in Maths: A Study of Good Practice in Early Years and Primary Settings*, London: Fair Education Alliance.

Lai, M. & Murray, S. (2012) Teaching with procedural variation: A Chinese way of promoting deep understanding of mathematics, *International Journal for Mathematics Teaching and Learning*: 1–25.

Merttens, R. (2012). The 'Concrete-Pictorial-Abstract' heuristic. *Mathematics Teaching*, 228, 33–38.

Mullis, I., Martin, M., Foy, P. & Hooper, M. (2016) *TIMSS 2015 International Results in Mathematics*, Boston, MA : IEA.

NCETM, https://www.ncetm.org.uk.

NCETM (2019) *Teaching for Mastery*, Sheffield: NCETM.

Russell, S. (2000) Developing computational fluency with whole numbers in the elementary grades. In: Ferrucci, B. & Heid, K. (eds.) *Millennium Focus Issue: Perspectives on Principles and Standards*, The New England Math Journal, 32(2): 40–54.

Skemp, R. (1989) *Mathematics in the Primary School*, London: Routledge.

Vygotsky, L. S. (1978) *Mind in Society: The Development of Higher Psychological Processes*, Cambridge, MA: Harvard University Press.

Chapter 16

Debates in the teaching of primary physical education

Julia Lawrence

Introduction

Physical education is viewed by many as an essential subject within the primary school curricula across the world (Kirk, 2013; Harris, 2018; Ward and Griggs, 2018), and research suggests that its prominence within the curriculum has been stable for many years (Kirk, 2010). Its importance is further highlighted within the United Kingdom through a recent Association for Physical Education (AfPE) campaign championing it to become a core subject with parity with the current core subjects of English, Mathematics and Science (Harris, 2018). It has, however, long since been a debated subject within the primary curriculum in terms of the purpose of physical education, resulting in a range of 'interested parties' influencing the objectives, content and delivery. The subject itself is very much influenced by educationalists and outside agencies such as health, sport and culture, and additional funding through the Primary Physical Education and Sport Premium is testament to the status and importance of this subject.

Adding to the complexity of debate, definitions of physical education vary dependent on speaker and audience (Carse, Jess and Keay, 2018). The way the subject is defined is far more than just semantics, as how we define physical education influences how the subject is taught (Roberts, Newcombe and Davids, 2018).

This chapter seeks to review the current debates within the context of how physical education is defined, taking into account those who influence its content and delivery. Within this I will consider the purpose of physical education both as a discrete subject and also within a broader curriculum context. Central to the debate, therefore, will be the following questions:

- What is physical education?
- Why should we teach physical education?
- What should be taught in physical education and how should it be delivered?
- Who should be teaching physical education?

What is physical education?

So what does physical education mean to us? What would we say are the aims of physical education? Morgan and Hansen (2008, p.382) provide a simplistic viewpoint on physical education, identifying that it allows pupils to 'get outside and expend some energy'. I am sure few of us disagree that allowing pupils to expend energy is important, but most would argue that the subject encompasses wider factors and has the potential to promote development of the whole child.

An early viewpoint, from the Board of Education (1933, p.9), suggested that 'the object of Physical Education and Training is to help in the production and maintenance of health in body and mind'. In so doing, they provided a link between health, physicality (the body) and mental well-being (mind); a link that appears to have become embedded in how physical education is now viewed. Fast forward to the most recent iteration of the physical education curriculum in England (Department for Education [DfE], 2013, p.1) and we see a continuation of this health and well-being link with a focus around the social and emotional aspect of learning through the provision of 'opportunities for pupils to become physically confident in a way which supports health and fitness. Opportunities to compete in sport and other activities build character and help to embed values such as fairness and respect'.

What is clear is that both definitions suggest that physical education is more that just about physical activity. As Harris (2018, p.10) suggests, 'curriculum physical education is the most effective and inclusive means of providing all children with the skills, attitudes, values, knowledge and understanding for lifelong participation in physical activity'. In essence, she argues strongly that physical education makes a significant contribution to the development of the whole individual. This is in relation to physical development as well as development across the affective domain in terms of the social, mental, cultural and health aspects. This is a premise supported by Lawrence (2018, p.6) who proposes that 'physical education has and will probably continue to be defined not only as a single subject in its own right but also in relation to other aspects of physicality and how this manifests itself'.

In summary, we are looking at a curriculum subject that offers more that just knowledge development. It is seen as a subject that can influence health and well-being, attitudes towards physical activity as well as social and emotional development.

Whilst the term physical education can be traced back through the decades, more recent terminology, specifically physical literacy, has been developed to cover this more holistic viewpoint. Whitehead (2010, p.12) defines physical literacy as 'the motivation, confidence, physical competence, knowledge and understanding to maintain physical activity throughout the lifecourse.' Roberts, Newcombe and Davids (2019, p.164) consider physical literacy as multi-staged and working across domains of learning, supporting the premise that primary physical education is the start of a wider physical journey, acknowledging the impact early experiences may have on continuing development. They conclude that 'physical literacy is increasingly becoming the end goal of the means of physical education'.

Table 16.1 Concepts of physical education and physical literacy (Lawrence, 2018, p.10)

Board of Education (1933)	Bailey et al. (2006)	Whitehead (2010)	Almond (2015)
Healthy body	Physical development	Motivation	Health
Healthy mind	Social development	Confidence and competence	Purposeful
Emotional	Affective development	Self	Personal capital
• cheerful			
• joyous			
Cognitive	Cognitive development	Knowledge	Empowerment
• alertness			
• concentration			
		Understanding	
		Interaction with others	

Table 16.1 identifies some of the key characteristics in relation to how physical education and physical literacy have been defined over recent years. Looking at the core characteristics in such a way allows us to distinguish between the outcomes of the activity. Further, it allows us to consider what physical education can look like in practice and the ways in which lessons can be delivered.

If we examine what we do in physical education, we can argue that it is a subject that allows pupils to learn about their own physicality and how they can control themselves in contrasting situations. It allows us to provide opportunities for them to work together with different individuals, challenging themselves socially and at times emotionally. It might be concluded, therefore, that whilst physical education is a curriculum subject, the knowledge, skills and understanding it develops extend far wider. Indeed, its unique nature in developing the whole individual means that the subject has become a vehicle on which other disciplines travel to promote their own specific outcomes.

Why should physical education be taught?

We have already identified in Table 1 that physical education is not just about the physical. Physical education can also impact on the growth of the individual across domains of learning and development (Harris, 2018). Perhaps one of the key rationales for teaching physical education is the health agenda. There is a growing concern in relation to the physical activity levels of children and young adults (HM Government, 2015). Over the years, successive governments have looked to address these concerns through a range of strategies (Specialist Schools Programme circa 1990; School Sports Partnerships, 2011; Physical Education and Sports Premium, 2014; Active Sports, 2015), with much emphasis being placed on the delivery of physical education within the primary classroom (Domville,

Watson, Richardson and Fisher Grave, 2019). Such debate is not new, and reference to the definitions provided earlier in the chapter clearly show how physical education and health have been intertwined for many years.

However, in looking at physical education from a health and fitness perspective, are we not looking to gain some aspect of credibility for it? Studies (Department of Health, 2004; Biddle, Ciaccioni, Thomas and Vergeer, 2019) clearly show the benefits to the well-being of the individual afforded by regular participation in physical activity. Health guidelines identify minimum expected levels of activity as well as the types of activities that should be undertaken (Department of Health, 2004). But the extent to which physical education in primary schools can significantly contribute to this has not been convincingly proven, especially as curriculum constraints often limit the time afforded to the subject. It is clear, however, that there is an aspiration for the curriculum to provide 'opportunities for pupils to become physically confident in a way which supports health and fitness. Opportunities to compete in sport and other activities build character and help to embed values such as fairness and respect' (DfE, 2013, p.1). This leads to the question of what exactly should be taught in primary physical education and what pedagogies and practices might be utilised to ensure that the considerable benefits highlighted above are achieved. The next section explores these questions.

What should be taught in physical education and how should it be delivered?

If we look back at Whitehead's (2010) concept of physical literacy, an argument is made that we should be focusing on fundamental movement skills. Such skills become the foundations for other more recognised forms of activity, for example athletics, dance, gymnastics, games and so forth, evident within the national curricula around the world. However, the national curriculum in England and Wales (DfE, 2013) includes reference to swimming and outdoor- and adventure-based activities, which encourage pupils to engage in problem solving and team building activities. Within such curricula there is progression in the development and use of skills across more challenging and competitive situations. Whilst recent iterations of the national curriculum (DfE, 2013) appear less prescriptive (see, for example, Qualifications and Curriculum Authority, 2010) they clearly show that much of what we are teaching comes from directives issued by government. Such a premise is further supported in publications such as Foster and Roberts' (2019) briefing paper that reviews and details current physical education, physical activity and sport in schools initiatives. However, we are not alone in this. Backman and Larson (2016, p.186), looking at the Swedish Physical Education system, identify that much of what we teach is reflective of what has come before. Citing research spanning the last 30 years, they argue that the content delivered through physical education 'seems, in the end, to promote children who are already privileged in school and society'.

Consequently, what is taught depends on the experience of those teaching, not only in the activities they themselves have been exposed to, but also in how they have been trained. If we also look at the general facilities available within a primary school environment, these also limit or dictate to us the activities we can deliver. Whilst investment for equipment and training are more readily available (see the section looking at funding and accountability later in the chapter), funding for buildings and outdoor spaces are less accessible. Thus, our choice as teachers of physical education is limited. As with other subject areas, demands to meet set levels of achievement further limit the breadth of the activities we might offer. The narrowing of the curriculum becomes a realistic consequence, with pupils required to undertake activities that in many situations have little relevance to their interests. However, whilst Domville et al. (2019, p.214) argue that when pupils are asked about the type of activity they wish to participate in there is 'an increased sense of autonomy, through giving children a feeling that "everyone's opinion counts"' and that they were being listened to, giving pupils choice, particularly in primary schools, can be challenging.

But it is not only about what we teach. Consideration also needs to be given to how we teach. Kirk (2013) argues that the challenge in relation to the delivery of physical education is not necessarily relating to the content or specific subject matter, it is more the manner in which the activities are delivered, specifically the pedagogical approaches adopted, in particular ensuring that children are actively involved. This is reiterated by Roberts et al. (2019, p.166) who suggest that 'the learner must be offered/afforded the opportunity for interaction when engaging with their environment'; if we want pupils to develop competencies we need to provide opportunities for them to experience and practice them.

For those specialising in the teaching of physical education, knowledge of subject-specific pedagogical approaches will have been part of the wider training they received. However, in primary education training, whilst the core principles of teaching are common across subjects, models specific to the delivery of physical education are potentially less well known. For example, Mosston and Ashworth (1994) proposed a continuum of teaching styles which looked at the different roles undertaken by the teacher and the pupils within a teaching/learning episode (see Lawrence, 2018, Chapter 7 for more details). Starting with a purely teacher-directed approach and moving to a point where pupils take control of their own learning, the spectrum reflects the concept of reproductive pedagogy, where learning is first produced, to a productive pedagogy where new learning is created (Hayes, Mills, Christie and Lingard, 2006). Other models of instruction include those proposed by Metzler (2011) who links different approaches to core theories of learning and in particular argues that

> when looking at the planning and delivery of learning episodes... consideration needs to be given to where the learning is taking place (context), the

learners themselves, knowledge and application of theories, the domains in which learning is being encouraged, and the overall climate or environment required for learning to be achieved.

(cited in Lawrence, 2018, p.131)

Thus, how we deliver the subject must consider as central the needs of the pupils. It must reflect what we want the pupils to learn, alongside the most appropriate way in which the learning can take place. For example, if we are looking at developing competence in throwing and catching with a view of playing a game similar to netball, we can focus on practising the skill individually, with a partner and then in small groups. Maximising practice time (through working in small groups) allows pupils to make more rapid progress.

We also need to consider how this is reflected in our planning. To be most effective, our planning needs to provide an overview of what should be taught across the education journey of the pupils from when they arrive in the early years to when they transfer to secondary systems. Adopting this viewpoint allows us to understand how pupils should be encouraged to develop over time, as well as providing us with continuity and progression data ensuring that we consolidate and build on children's existing experiences, skills, knowledge and understanding.

Constraints around curriculum design and delivery appear to question and challenge *what* we should be teaching and, in many ways, *how* we teach physical education. Within such contexts, Ward and Griggs (2018, p.404) conclude that 'primary PE remains locked within an outmoded form of corporeal discourse which does not match evolutions in wider movement culture.'

Funding and accountability

The curriculum (its design and delivery) is of course influenced by both funding and accountability. Possibly one of the significant changes to the delivery of physical education in recent years is the introduction of the government-funded Physical Education and Sport Premium. Introduced in 2014, the funding is expected to ensure that '*all* pupils leaving primary school are physically literate and with the knowledge, skills and motivation necessary to equip them for a healthy, active lifestyle and lifelong participation in physical activity and sport' (Association for Physical Education (AfPE) and Youth Sport Trust, 2016, p.1).

Whilst previous governmental initiatives have been introduced over the past two decades, the significance of this scheme lies in where the funding goes (to the primary school) and the accountability (schools must report annually how the monies are spent). Funding equates to an average of approximately £9000 per school and is designed to provide resources to support teachers' continuing professional development as well as to purchase equipment to support curriculum delivery. Schools are accountable for the expenditure and are required to report to parents the activities they have undertaken in spending the funding as well as it being a focus within the current inspection regime. The premise, therefore, is that schools will use the funding to support improvements in physical education and sport within the school, specifically in relation to engagement, quality of teachers and teaching and range of opportunities provided (Lawrence, 2018).

Whilst additional funding for the subject is not being questioned, the manner in which the funding is used has raised concerns. Griggs (2018) is possibly the first person to review the impact of this funding within schools. His findings, whilst perhaps expected, identify a common use of the funding as the employment of sports coaches. This he sees as outsourcing of physical education and raises the question 'Who should teach physical education?'. The next section will examine the arguments around this contested area.

Who should teach physical education in schools?

In acknowledging the rise in the use of specialist coaches, researchers (Kirk, 2013; Griggs, 2018) identify that these might not be the most appropriate solution to the problem. For many years the difference between coaching and teaching within physical education has been debated. This situation has emerged as a result of successive policy implementations around physical education and school sport over the last 20 years (Griggs, 2018). Whilst these policies may not have been education-related, they have allowed a significant blurring of lines (Kirk, 2013; Griggs, 2018) between the teaching of physical education as part of the curriculum and the emergence of more sports-related activities.

However, there could be an argument that the 'blurred' lines have always been there in relation to physical education alongside sport. For example, prior to the Physical Education and Sport Premium, there were Sport Colleges and School Sport Partnerships. Schools have continually been encouraged to form partnerships with sports organisations to develop opportunities for pupils to participate in local sports clubs. National governing bodies such as the Football Association and the England and Wales Cricket Board promote school initiatives and teacher development programmes.

As such, the subject itself may have become somewhat politicised, with not just educationalists looking at engaging with the subject but the involvement of sporting and health bodies also promoting how they too can contribute. As Harris (2018) suggests in her informed rationale for physical education to become a core subject, there is evidence to suggest that previous policies have resulted in unintended consequences in the form of effectively outsourcing the teaching of the subject to private organisations and coaches.

So how has this significant change occurred? There is a general acceptance that the preparation of teachers during initial teacher training in the development of competence to deliver physical education is insufficient, with a decrease in the amount of time available to support knowledge development within the subject (Griggs and Randall, 2018; Harris, 2018; Kirk, 2013). It is also well researched that the confidence of a teacher in a specific subject impacts on their ability to teach it (Bradford, Gleddie and Millard, 2019; Morgan and Bourke, 2008). This lack of confidence can be due to a number of factors, not least one's personal experience of physical education and memories. As practitioners we need to understand that how we view physical education will have a significant impact on how and what we teach. Such values, beliefs and attitudes are built on the experiences we have had ourselves. For many this may have been positive, but for others memories of playing games in the cold and wet, running cross-country through the mud and having to perform sequences in front of others has resulted in a withdrawal from participation. I know that when I am working with pre-service teachers, my aim is to instil a sense of enjoyment and confidence in the subject so that they feel more positive about it and are then better equipped to teach it.

As a primary teacher, there is, of course, an expectation that you will teach across the curriculum. However, the value we assign to different subjects may well vary according to assessment practices and the pressures of testing. It is likely that more importance is assigned to subjects that are assessed and it is interesting to consider the position of certain subjects in the curriculum hierarchy. In terms of physical education, its position in the hierarchy is likely influenced by a number of factors including workload – changes to teaching timetables to release teachers to undertake planning, preparation and assessment have meant that physical education is generally seen as a subject that does not need to be delivered by the class teacher. Perhaps, therefore, this 'buying in' of specialist coaches is the solution. Or at least a short-term option. It is certainly a matter for debate.

Changes to the delivery of physical education are clearly highlighted in Sperka and Engright's (2018) scoping review, which focuses on the growth in outsourcing of health and physical education. From the literature reviewed, they clearly identify that expertise is a key factor in the process, with the continuing perception that being a coach is equivalent to being a teacher in the physical education context.

In looking at the outsourcing of physical education and the use of coaches to deliver the subject, the debate is not necessarily about *who* is delivering, but is more about *how* the subject is delivered. Domville et al. (2019, p.208) argue that a key area of consideration when using specialist coaches is the learning environment they create. Specifically, they identify that those delivering physical education 'are important in creating an environment that supports children's psychological needs for autonomy, competence and relatedness, which influence PE enjoyment'. The premise being that whilst they might be experts in their sport, their ability to deconstruct specific skills in a way that pupils can access learning, and their understanding of factors such as differentiation and behaviour management may not be as developed. Further, their knowledge across the requirements of the curriculum including different content areas and assessment may not be secure. Thus there is a need to consider how provision is quality assured.

Both Domville et al. (2019) and Kirk (2013) identify a specific link between quality teaching and the learning experience of pupils, acknowledging that primary experiences can impact on future health and well-being. Further support for this is found in *Sporting Future: A New Strategy for an Active Nation*

(HM Government, 2015, p.10) that suggests 'a person's attitude to sport is often shaped by their experience – or lack of experience – as a child, and many people drop out of sport before they even reach the age of 14'. Carse, Jess and Keay (2018) acknowledge that experience of physical education in the primary school has an influence on your levels of participation moving forward, and we can clearly see that as most children receive their first experience of physical education and potentially sport within the school curriculum, the pressure on those providing these experiences grows.

Taking much of this into account, Griggs and Randall (2018) conclude that whilst potentially unintended, government changes implemented in the 1990s to how teachers are trained and initiatives initially aimed at improving quality and opportunity have actually had a negative impact on the provision now being offered. The challenge, therefore, is to consider whether this trend can be reversed and in so doing, to consider what might be placed in jeopardy as a result. The development of primary physical education specialist training routes and potential changes to inspection frameworks with a greater emphasis on non-core subjects (i.e., not English, mathematics and science) may serve to start such a reversal.

Summary

This chapter has aimed to answer the following questions:

- What is physical education?
- Why should we teach physical education?
- What should be taught in physical education and how should it be delivered?
- Who should teach physical education?

In so doing, it has encouraged the reader to question their own understanding and teaching of the subject. It has questioned how physical education is viewed in education and beyond, demonstrating that physical education is somewhat unique in the number of influences that impact its design and delivery. What is clear is that physical education has not only the capacity to develop and consolidate pupils' learning about their ability to perform specific skills, but it can, if delivered by individuals who share positive values, attitudes and beliefs towards it, provide the building blocks for an active and healthy lifestyle.

What physical education is *not* is a tool to manage the health and well-being of pupils within the primary phases of education. The time allocated to it and the training provided to teachers are, in my opinion, insufficient for this to be an aim.

Perhaps, therefore, we need to ask ourselves the question whether physical education has become more of a political driver, influenced by a range of external organisations from health, sport and education, with a blurring of lines relating to who has the responsibility for its delivery and role. As a subject within the curriculum, do we need to reconsider what the aim of physical education is, and do we potentially need to remove it as a curriculum subject per se to become a stand-alone statutory subject which must take place, around which the main curriculum is delivered?

Have we as educators allowed our own perceptions of the subject to become 'blurred', resulting in the emergence of the void which has been filled by individuals that have seen an opportunity to promote their own agenda? Do we as a fraternity need to re-establish what we see physical education to be?

Questions for reflection

Having read this chapter, how has your attitude to physical education changed?
How well prepared do you feel to teach physical education?
How is physical education taught in your school? Do you agree with this?

Further reading and resources

Kirk, K. (2013) 'Future of Primary Physical Education', *Journal of Pedagogical Development*, 3(2), 38–44.
Available via pdf, this article considers the impact of recent changes on primary physical education. It questions the consistency of curriculum delivery as well as how primary teachers are trained to teach the subject.

Roberts, W. M., Newcombe, D. J., & Davids, K. (2019) 'Application of a Constraints-Led Approach to pedagogy in schools: embarking on a journey to nurture Physical Literacy in primary physical education', *Physical Education and Sport Pedagogy*, 24(2), 162–175.
This pedagogical-focused piece looks at the development and implementation of an innovative approach to the teaching of physical literacy. Through a link to its associated website, resources are available for you to use within your own teaching to challenge yourself in how you perceive and consequently plan for and deliver your physical education lessons.

Ward, G., & Griggs, G. (2018) 'Primary physical education: A memetic perspective', *European Physical Education Review*, 24(4), 400–417.
This highly insightful paper looks at how we view physical education and how those views are consolidated and repeated over time. It challenges us as educationalists to consider how we ourselves continue this common approach. Further, it highlights how the way we value the subject may be acting to perpetuate rather than challenge our attitudes, beliefs and delivery of the subject.

References

Almond, L. (2015) 'A change in focus for physical education', Physical Education Matters 10(1), 22–26.
Association for Physical Education (AfPE) and Youth Sport Trust (YST). (2016) *Evidencing the Impact of Primary PE and Sport Premium - Guidance and Template*. AfPE: Worcester. Available at: www.afpe.org.uk/physical-educa

tion/wp-content/uploads/Evidencing-the-Impact-Guidance-Impact-Resource -Web-Version.pdf

Backman, E. & Larsson, H. (2016) 'What should a physical education teacher know? An analysis of learning outcomes for future physical education in Sweden', *Physical Education and Sport Pedagogy*, 21(2): 185–200.

Bailey, R., Armour, K., Kirk, D., Jess, M., Pickup, I. and Sandford, R. (2006) *The Educational Benefits Claimed for Physical Education and School Sport: An Academic Review*. London: British Educational Research Association (BERA).

Biddle, S. J. H., Ciaccioni, S., Thomas, G. & Vergeer, I. (2019) 'Physical activity and mental health in children and adolescents: An updated review of reviews and an analysis of causality', *Psychology of Sport and Exercise*, 42: 146–155.

Board of Education (1933) *Syllabus of Physical Education Training for Schools*, London: HMSO.

Bradford, B., Gleddie, D. & Millard, C. (2019) 'The principal factor: A literature review juxtaposing the role of elementary school physical education teachers and principals', *Physical Education and Health Journal*, 84(4): 1–7.

Carse, N., Jess, M. & Keay, J. (2018) 'Primary physical education: Shifting perspectives to move forward', *European Physical Education Review*, 24(4): 487–502.

Department for Education (DfE) (2013) *The National Curriculum in England: Framework Document*, London: DfE.

Department of Health (DoH) (2004) *At Least Five a Week – Evidence of the Impact of Physical Activity and Its Relationship to Health*, London: HMSO.

Domville, M., Watson, P. M., Richardson, D. & Fisher Graves, L. E. (2019) 'Children's perceptions of factors that influence PE enjoyment: A qualitative investigation', *Physical Education and Sport Pedagogy*, 24(3): 207–219.

Foster, D. & Roberts, N. (2019) *Physical Education, Physical Activity and Sport in Schools – Briefing Paper Number 6836*, London: House of Commons Library Research Service.

Griggs, G. (2018) 'Investigating provision and impact of the primary physical education and sport premium: A West Midland case study', *Education 3–13*, 46(5): 517–524.

Griggs, G. & Randall, V. (2018) 'Primary physical education subject leadership: along the road from in-house solutions to outsourcing', *Education 3–13*, 47(6): 664–677.

Harris, J. (2018) 'The case for physical education becoming a core subject in the national curriculum', *Physical Education Matters*, Summer 2018: 9–12.

Hayes, D., Mills, M., Christie, P. & Lingard, B. (2006) *Teachers and Schooling Making a Difference: Productive Pedagogies, Assessment and Performance*, Crows Nest: Allen and Unwin.

HM Government (2015) *Sporting Future: A New Strategy for an Active Nation*, London: Cabinet Office.

Kirk, D. (2010) *Physical Education Futures*, London: Routledge.

Kirk, K. (2013) 'Future of primary physical education', *Journal of Pedagogical Development*, 3(2): 38–44.

Lawrence, J. (2018) *Teaching Primary Physical Education* (2nd ed.), London: SAGE.

Metzler, M. W. (2011) *Instructional Models for Physical Education* (3rd ed.), Scottsdale: AZ, Holcomb Hathaway Publishers.

Morgan, P. & Bourke, S. (2008) 'Non-specialist teachers' confidence to teach PE: The nature and influence of personal school experiences in PE', *Physical Education and Sport Pedagogy*, 13(1): 1–29.

Morgan, P. J. & Hansen, V. (2008) 'The relationship between PE biographies and PE teaching practices of classroom teachers', *Sport, Education and Society*, 13(4): 373–391.

Mosston, M. & Ashworth, S. (1994) *Teaching Physical Education* (4th ed.), New York: Macmillan College Publishing Company.

Qualifications and Curriculum Authority (2010) 'Schemes of work'. Available at: https://webarchive.nationalarchives.gov.uk/20100607215817/http://www.standards.dfes.gov.uk/schemes2/phe/?view=get (Accessed 24.01.2020).

Roberts, W. M., Newcombe, D. J. & Davids, K. (2018) 'Application of a constraints-led approach to pedagogy in schools: Embarking on a journey to nurture physical literacy in primary physical education', *Physical Education and Sport Pedagogy*, 24(2): 162–175.

Sperka, L. & Engright, E. (2018) 'The outsourcing of health and physical education: A scoping review', *European Physical Education Review*, 24(4): 349–371.

Ward, G. & Griggs, G. (2018) 'Primary physical education: A memetic perspective', *European Physical Education Review*, 24(4): 400–417.

Whitehead, M. (ed.) (2010) *Physical Literacy through the Lifecourse*, London: Routledge.

Chapter 17

Teachers as readers and writers

Teresa Cremin

Introduction

Since being able to read and write are critical skills in the 21st century, the teaching of English is always a matter of contention. Ways to teach phonics and grammar in particular are often hotly contested. Another longstanding debate, rather less to the forefront, is the notion that 'teachers of writing must write' and 'teachers of reading must be readers'. This purportedly common-sense view – that to be effective, teachers of literacy must be skilled role models – has long been deliberated. The notion that teachers must be readers is arguably presumed; the notion that teachers must be writers has received more attention, but both are debated, since teachers are expected to be literate role models in the classroom. The power of role models in education has been recognised since at least 1966 when Bruner described this as a 'day-to-day working model' to support children's learning.

The rationale underpinning such modelling is that through engaging reflexively as writers and readers within and beyond the classroom, teachers will be more authentic role models, with enriched understandings that may inform and shape their pedagogy, impacting upon their students' achievements (Gennrich and Janks, 2013). Teachers' attitudes to English and their assurance and self-esteem as readers and writers have been shown to influence their practice; research indicates that teachers' conceptions of literacy, their literate identities and pedagogic practice, frame, shape and often limit students' identities, both as writers (Ryan and Barton, 2014) and as readers (Hall, 2012). So, it is important to explore pre-service teachers' literate identities, to support positive dispositions and to enhance their awareness of the consequence of being a reading/writing role model in the classroom.

In this chapter, therefore, after exploring the relationship between literacy and identity, the focus turns to teachers' literate identities and the debate around the positioning of teachers as writers and readers. Following this, a more applied consideration of the ways in which teachers can choose to position themselves as readers and writers is offered and attention paid to the possible consequences of such positioning on children's literate identities. Through the chapter, a number of questions are addressed, including:

1. What does research indicate about the debate around teachers' roles as readers and writers in the classroom?
2. What are the benefits and challenges of teachers becoming role models as readers and writers for children?
3. What range of ways exist for teachers to reflect upon their literacy lives and practices and shape their practice in order to support children's development as literacy and language users?

Teachers' and children's literate identities

In recent years research into teachers' and children's identities has developed apace (Moje and Luke, 2009). Different notions of identity exist, but most coalesce around the conception that teachers are likely to be different at home from how they are at work, and in both contexts, will position and reposition themselves continually. In this way, identity is not something that one 'has', but is something one actively pursues; it involves ongoing work and is multiple and enacted in interaction (Moje and Luke, 2009). Underpinning this view of identity is an understanding that such identity positioning is fluid and relational. When teachers construct their literate identities in the classroom, they do so in relation to others – children, other teachers, head teachers, teaching assistants, volunteer helpers and parents for example. How teachers both perceive themselves and are perceived by others, (including children) as readers or writers is important since their literate engagement enables them to model the value, pleasure and satisfaction in leading a literate life, and induct children into leading their own literate lives (Kaufman, 2009).

Children's conceptualisations of what it means to be a reader or writer are constructed at an early age through their interactions with others at home and school (Bourne, 2002; Levy, 2009). They learn what counts as reading and writing and what it means to be a writer and reader in different contexts. Since literacy and identity are intertwined, classroom literacy practices have a direct bearing on the literate identities of children and create 'spaces for them to construct their identity as readers/writers and build their personal theories of literacy' (Seban and Tavsanli, 2015, p.220). Children quickly come to experience the consequences (both negative and positive) associated with the various literacy identities that are made available to them in the classroom.

Research suggests teachers may come to ascribe labels to children through applying narrow schooled definitions of reading and writing and using ability grouping based on these definitions. These tend to imply some children have 'below average' reader or writer capabilities and identities. Research also reveals the negative impact of such identity labelling. In Hall's (2012) study, for example, children were categorised as 'poor' readers, 'good' readers, or 'becoming good' readers which had consequences for the kinds of instruction and support they received. This was evident in a recent study of struggling boy readers where in one typical classroom, the reading group which spanned from Dickens (the top group) to Dahl (the bottom group) experienced significantly different opportunities to engage as readers (Hempel Jorgensen, Cremin, Harris and Chamberlain et al., 2018). The negative impacts of ascribing children 'below average' writer identities as a consequence of their perceived 'readiness' for school literacy learning has also been shown (Yoon, 2014). Whilst children can, in principle, accept or reject the identity positions made available to them, their classroom positions are difficult to challenge due to unequal power relations, so young people's literate identities are at least in part framed and shaped by teachers' conceptualisations of readers/reading and writers/writing and their pedagogy.

However, if teachers become more conscious of their own literate identities and diverse practices and preferences beyond the classroom, it is argued that this will prompt them to consider younger readers' identities, practices and preferences. In addition, they may come to consider the identity positions made available to children by their own classroom routines and seek to alter their practice. Scholars argue that if teachers see themselves as readers/writers this will impact positively on their practice (Andrews, 2008; Commeyras, Bisplinhoff and Olson, 2003).

But do teachers see themselves as readers/writers? Do they reflect upon their own practices and experience of reading/writing in order to nurture young learners? Is there evidence that their literate identities impact on those of the children they teach? It is to these issues that we now turn.

Teachers as writers

The notion that to be effective, teachers of writing must control the 'inseparable crafts' of both 'teaching and writing' (Graves, 1983, p.5) has been intensely debated over decades. Whilst the process approach that Graves and other colleagues advocated has been heavily criticised (Beard, 2000), his assertion that teachers of writing must be writers has remained the focus of research and professional discussion. Many scholars who were committed to the process approach to writing became advocates of this notion (Murray, 1985; Calkins, 1994). In addition, scholars who valued teachers' writing as practitioner researchers joined the 'teachers as writers' movement (Cochran-Smith and Lytle, 1993) and the US National Writing Project adopted the tenet that 'teachers of writing must write' (NWP and Nagin, 2006). In New Zealand a government funded NWP in 1987 also gave a central role to teachers as writers. Myriad researchers in these projects have made clear their support for this notion and have claimed, for example, that children benefit if teachers share their compositional difficulties (Root and Steinberg, 1996), and that young writers are highly motivated by teacher enthusiasm (Kaufman, 2002).

However, many scholars have argued against the positioning of teachers as writers (Jost, 1990; Robbins,1996; Gleeson and Prain, 1996). Some of these assert that if teachers write, this reduces the time for instruction and increases their susceptibility to being exposed as less-than-skilled writers (Gleeson and

Prain, 1996). Also, that teachers' perceptions of the importance of writing influences their efficacy far more than their involvement as writers in the classroom (Robbins, 1996). This early work comprised a series of claims and counter claims.

As a consequence, a systematic review of the literature of the field sought to lay this debate to rest (Cremin and Oliver, 2016). Encompassing the years 1990–2015 the review focused on teachers' identities and practices as writers in peer-reviewed empirical reports. Of the 439 papers identified, only 22 met the criteria applied since much of the early work was somewhat journalistic and anecdotal in nature. The review found a tendency towards negativity about writing amongst teachers and student teachers, and noted that considerable self-critique, doubt and discomfort was expressed (Cremin and Oliver, 2016). It showed that school and university experiences shaped teachers' attitudes in various ways with pedagogical consequences and ramifications for the dispositions and identities of younger writers. It also found that teachers have rather narrow conceptions of what counts as writing or what makes a 'writer'. They often associate 'writing' with 'creative writing' connected to literary print-based publications (McKinney and Giorgis, 2009; Woodard, 2015). Teachers' limited views of writing serve to reinforce a dichotomy between school and personal writing, which may limit their capacity to explore connections between real life writing and school writing.

The review also showed that whilst teachers and student teachers perceive there may be consequences if they position themselves as writers, few studies followed through to the classroom to examine if this is the case. Where teachers engaged in writing workshops at their own level, however, they perceived this enhanced their understanding of the writing process and their self-confidence as writers (Locke and Kato, 2012). After such workshops, teachers express their intentions to make classroom changes, including: creating more secure writing environments and offering more social/emotional support for writing and positive feedback (Morgan, 2010; Gardner, 2014).

Studies which do follow through to the classroom indicate that there are challenges for teachers who seek to be writing role models. They suggest that teachers often find demonstration writing an emotional struggle as they are both writer and teacher. Their desire to demonstrate agency as authentically engaged authors is complicated by their personal confidence, the subject matter, and their need to control the class (Cremin and Baker, 2010; Woodward, 2015). As teachers are expected to model writing and demonstrate their proficiency as writers, it is problematic if they lack confidence as writers, which will also influence their ability to respond flexibly to policy requirements and narrow skills-based writing models (Woodard, 2017). Other challenges include perceived discrepancies between curriculum policy and assessment priorities and teachers' own values and beliefs about writing (Cremin and Oliver, 2016).

Nonetheless, Yeo (2007) argues that teachers who develop their writing identities and become more assured writers, will transmit the benefits of this in their teaching of writing. So, despite the difficulties, it is arguably important for teachers to develop a richer sense of their own identities as writers, to engage in workshops and consider how they position themselves and their students in the writing classroom.

Teachers as readers

Studies focusing on teachers as readers are fewer overall, perhaps since writing is more commonly viewed as a challenging craft – an artistic act of production. Nonetheless, there are studies which highlight connections between teachers and children as engaged and self-motivated readers (Dreher, 2003). Some claim that teachers' lives and classroom practices are influenced by their pleasure in literature which nurtures both adults and children as readers (Rummel and Quintero, 1997). One study of teachers in the US coined the phrase 'Reading Teachers – teachers who read and readers who teach' to denote, with a capital R and a capital T, that these teachers are aware of their own reading passions and preferences and share these in the classroom (Commeyras et al., 2003). These US studies argue there is a link between a teacher's reader identity and their pedagogy. However, they rely almost exclusively on self-reports of classroom practice and none include observation or children's views on their teachers as readers.

The stance of being a Reading Teacher was examined within the OU/UK Literacy Association Teachers as Readers (TaRs) project which documented the difference made by Reading Teachers to children's reading identities and pleasure in reading (Cremin et al., 2014). Through considering their own reading lives and practices, some of the 43 TaRs practitioners transformed their understanding of the nature of reading and creatively adapted their pedagogy and classroom positioning as a result. They became highly interactive reading role models in the classroom.

However, the notion of being a Reading Teacher was not without challenge. Many project practitioners expressed reservations about taking time from teaching to share their reading lives and practices and remained unconvinced that adopting a more authentic and personally engaged stance as a reader would influence children's attitudes or attainment. For example:

> My work is to develop children as readers, not to share my reading life
> (Teacher, Suffolk)

> I have found this hard and don't get it yet – I'm still not sure it would really make a difference
> (Teacher, Medway).

Practitioners found the open-ended stance of a Reading Teacher created indecision and uncertainty. In a highly prescribed culture of teaching, they expressed concerns that no reading objectives were being 'covered' when they shared their experiences as readers. For example:

I'm not used to working without specific objectives

(Teacher, Birmingham)

I'm not sure I see the point of this, I mean I need to know them as readers, but do they need to know me?

(Teacher, Barking and Dagenham).

Some teachers were reticent to risk introducing this more individual dimension and initially felt that taking time from instruction and the curriculum was unjustified and might be 'exposing'. They were unsure if reflecting on their own reading histories and experiences and inviting the children to also reflect on theirs was of value and wanted assurance that this would result in raised reading standards. Yet, much depends upon the long-term goal – is this to achieve the 'expected standard' or to develop lifelong readers?

Other research has shown that there are negative consequences for young learners when their teachers lack passion for reading and that teachers who share their enthusiasm for reading help to motivate young readers (Commeyras et al., 2003; Kaufman, 2002). A number of the TaRs teachers reflected deeply on their habits as readers and began to teach 'from a reader's point of view'. By the close of the project a continuum of practice existed (Cremin et al., 2014). Significantly, the teachers who developed most fully as Reading Teachers positively influenced children's attitudes towards reading; frequency of reading for pleasure at home and school; teacher-child reader relationships; and children's knowledge and perception of their teachers as readers (Cremin et al., 2014). Reading became a more shared, sociable, relaxed experience in school and the young people developed reader relationships and reader networks.

Bruner's (1966) conception of practitioners as role models was someone with whom children would engage and interact with. As the TaRs research and recent classroom studies have shown, (Cremin, Thomson, Williams and Davies, 2018; Cremin, Williams and Denby, 2019), Reading Teachers engage in considerable informal conversational dialogue with children about reading which highlights diversity, authenticity and agency, enabling readers to make their own choices, state their own preferences and voice their own views. Nonetheless, challenges persist for teachers who wish to teach from a reader's point of view, especially in pressured contexts, where the assessment agenda drives the curriculum and reader relationships are backstage, whilst the standards agenda remains frontstage.

Exploring literate role models in the classroom

Having explored the research evidence and debate with regard to teachers as readers and writers in the classroom, we now consider the practical application of this stance. A continuum of literate identity positioning is offered (Figure 17.1). You may wish to decide whether and where to position yourself on this.

| Teachers who read/write and offer positive dispositions as literate role models. | Teachers who read/write, offer positive dispositions and reflect upon and share their reading/writing lives and practices as literate role models. They get to know the children as readers/writers and their everyday literacy practices beyond the classroom. | Teachers who read/write, offer positive dispositions and reflect upon and share their reading/writing lives and practices as literate role models. They get to know the children as readers/writers and their everyday literacy practices beyond the classroom. They also explore the possible pedagogical consequences of their experience and understanding of reading and writing in order to support children's identities and journeys as literate individuals. |

Figure 17.1 A continuum of teachers as reading/writing role models.

As the left of the continuum indicates, teachers who read and write and find some satisfaction in the process share their positive dispositions in school and make recommendations based on children's texts they enjoy. But is this enough? Your preferences for certain kinds of texts may constrain children's choices and if, as a writing role model, you select particular text types in response to curriculum requirements and only model composing these texts, this will also be limiting. As a literate role model, you may, inadvertently, be shaping children in your own making, not allowing them to be unique literacy learners with their own interests and preferences.

The midpoint on the continuum suggests that you can choose to offer more than a positive disposition; you can reflect on your literacy life and share your reading and writing practices beyond school, inviting children to share theirs also. You could create a 24-Hour Read/Write or Reading/Writing River. Such collages prompt consideration of the diversity of one's literacy life. The staff at Peover Superior primary in Cheshire created their own 24-Hour Reads and discussed these in a staff meeting. Some had read recipes, online and off, others had dipped into holiday brochures and other non-fiction texts, and emails, workload planning and road signs alongside some fiction, newspapers, junk mail and magazines. Differences were evident and areas of commonality too, offering opportunities for connections. In the process, the staff learnt much about diversity in reading and later about the children's reading practices and preferences beyond school.

Such strategies are also useful when considering writing practices. Joanna, an NQT, was surprised to find she wrote eleven different kinds of texts in one Sunday: a Mother's Day card, tweets, emails, texts to her children, a list, a shopping note, redirecting post, an ISA application, school marking, lesson planning and a draft of a haiku for the next day's demonstration writing. This highlighted that in her own words 'I do a lot of writing and I find some satisfaction in it, but it's all very quick often to get things sorted, pass messages on and such'. Her Writing River caused Jo to wonder if the writing she expected children in her class to do was 'schooled writing', writing for the system and not for themselves. As scholars have argued, such writing constrains children's engagement as writers, as it has almost no personal purpose or audience. Through recognising the diversity of your own writing life and sharing this, you model being a writer and demonstrate the everyday and real-world relevance of writing in all its modes and media.

The far point on the continuum suggests that if teachers offer a positive disposition and reflect upon the nature of their literacy lives, they frequently come to widen their understanding of the uses and value of reading and writing and notice their affective engagement in literacy. Significantly, this may prompt pedagogical changes to support the young on their journeys as readers and writers. Learning about children's practices beyond school may trigger the provision of a wider choice of texts for example and more child-led writing opportunities. In addition, through reflecting on your own reading/writing practices, for example skipping descriptive passages or giving up on a book, or what you do when faced with a blank page or lose your way as a writer, you may come, like Jo, to question what counts as reading and writing in school. In turn, this may prompt you to re-conceptualise literacy, consider children's rights as readers and writers and develop more authentic tasks which offer a higher than usual degree of congruence with writing in the real world.

Summary

The debate about the value of teachers being literate role models and assured readers and writers has long been the focus of professional examination. It is your choice how authentically you engage as a reader and writer in school, but it seems possible that if you choose to learn more about your practices and preferences, this will prompt you to widen your understanding of what counts as reading and writing in your classrooms with consequences for the teaching of reading and writing. This, some of the evidence suggests, has the potential to impact on young people's attitudes, motivations and their journeys as readers and writers, supporting them in developing positive identities as young literacy and language users.

Looking forward, more research is needed to offer nuanced accounts of the small but potentially significant insights developed by Reading and Writing Teachers as they seek to teach from a reader's and/or a writer's point of view. The pedagogical implications of these insights deserve to be closely documented, especially in the context of a dehumanising trend in education (Feilding, 2006). Additionally, since children's literate identities are laid down in the primary years and notoriously hard to alter, it is vital for the profession to consider the ways in which their routines and practices position and constrain or enable young readers and writers.

Questions for reflection

Looking back on your literacy history, what were in your view some of the
significant experiences or people that shaped the kind of reader and writer
you are?

To what extent do you conceive of yourself as an experienced and assured adult
reader or writer?

Recognising that you wish to develop lifelong readers and writers, to what extent
do you plan to position yourself explicitly as a Reading and/or Writing
Teacher in the classroom?

Further reading and resources

https://researchrichpedagogies.org/research/reading-for-pleasure.
This research-informed reading for pleasure website offers support materials for
teachers. It has sections on Reading Teachers and Developing Knowledge of Children
as Readers, and self-audits to support reflection, as well as classroom strategies for
developing as a Reading Teacher, videos and examples of teachers' research-informed
practice to inspire.

Cremin, T. Mottram, M. Powell, S, Collins, R. & Drury, R. (2015) *Researching
Literacy Lives: Building home School Communities*, London and NY: Routledge.
This won the 2016 UKLA Academic Book Award. It explores how re-positioning
teachers as researchers of children's home literacy lives challenged them to reflect on
their own literacy lives and re-consider what counts as literacy in school. The journey
enabled new understandings about children and families to develop, and different
literate identities to be enacted by teachers and children.

Gennrich, T. & Janks, H. (2013) 'Teachers' literate identities'. In: Hall, K. Cremin,
T. Comber, B. & Moll, L. (Eds.), *The Wiley Blackwell International Research
Handbook of Children's Literacy, Learning and Culture*, 456–468. Oxford: Wiley
Blackwell.
This chapter pays attention to the digital practices and identities of literacy teachers.
It offers a case study from the University of the Witwatersrand which explores how,
through teacher education, the complex literacy identities of future teachers born in
the digital era can be addressed.

References

Andrews, R. (2008) *The Case for a National Writing Project for Teachers*, Reading:
CfBT.
Beard, R. (2000) *Developing Writing 3–13*, London: Hodder and Stoughton.
Bourne, J. (2002) 'Oh what will miss say!' Constructing texts and identities in
the discursive processes of classroom writing, *Language and Education*, 16(4):
241–259.
Bruner, J. (1966) *Towards a Theory of Instruction*, London: Oxford University
Press.
Calkins, L. M. (1994) *The Art of Teaching Writing*, Portsmouth, NH: Heinemann.

Cochran-Smith, M. & Lytle, S. (1993) *Inside–Outside: Teacher Research and Knowledge*, New York: Teachers College Press.

Commeyras, M., Bisplinghoff, B. S. & Olson, J. (2003) *Teachers as Readers: Perspectives on the Importance of Reading in Teachers' Classrooms and Lives*, Newark: International Reading Association.

Cremin, T. & Baker, S. (2010) 'Exploring Teacher-Writer Identities in the Classroom: Conceptualising the Struggle', *English Teaching: Practice and Critique*, 9(3): 8–25.

Cremin, T., Mottram, M., Powell, S., Collins, R.. & Safford, K. (2014) *Building Communities of Engaged Readers: Reading for Pleasure*, London and New York : Routledge.

Cremin, T. & Oliver, L. (2016) 'Teachers as Writers: A Systematic Review', *Research Papers in Education*, 3(3): 269–295.

Cremin, T., Thomson, B., Williams, C. & Davies, S. (2018) 'Reading Teachers', *English: 4-11*, 62, Spring 2018: 4–8.

Cremin, T., Williams, C. & Denby, R. (2019) 'Reading Teachers: Exploring Non-fiction', *English: 4–11*, 68, Autumn 2019: 1–4.

Dreher, M. J. (2003) 'Motivating Teachers to Read', *The Reading Teacher*, 56(4): 338–340.

Fielding, M. (2006) 'Leadership, Radical Student Engagement and the Necessity of Person-Centred Education', *International Journal of Leadership in Education*, 9(4): 299–313.

Gardner, P. (2014) 'Becoming a Teacher of Writing: Primary Student Teachers Reviewing Their Relationship with Writing', *English in Education*, 48(2): 128–148.

Gennrich, T. & Janks, H. (2013) 'Teachers' Literate Identities'. In: Hall, K., Cremin, T., Comber, B. & Moll, L. (Eds.), *The Wiley Blackwell International Research Handbook of Children's Literacy, Learning and Culture*, 456–468, Oxford: Wiley Blackwell.

Gleeson, A. & Prain, V. (1996) 'Should Teachers of Writing Write Themselves? An Australian Contribution to the Debate', *The English Journal*, 85(6): 42–49.

Graves, D. (1983) *Writing: Teachers and Children at Work*, Portsmouth, NH: Heinemann.

Hall, L. A. (2012) 'Rewriting Identities: Creating Spaces for Students and Teachers to Challenge the Norms of What It Means to be a Reader in School', *Journal of Adolescent and Adult Literacy*, 55(5): 368–373.

Hempel-Jorgensen, A., Cremin, T., Harris D. and Chamberlain, L. (2018) Pedagogy for reading for pleasure in low socio-economic primary schools: beyond 'pedagogy of poverty'? Literacy 52 (2): 86–94

Jost, K. (1990) 'Rebuttal: Why High-School Writing Teachers Should Not Write', *The English Journal*, 79(3): 65–66.

Kaufman, D. (2002) 'Living a Literate Life, Revisited', *The English Journal*, 91(6): 51–57.

Kaufman, D. (2009) 'A Teacher Educator Writes and Shares', *Journal of Teacher Education*, 60(3): 338.

Levy, R. (2009) 'You Have to Understand Words…but Not Read Them', *Journal of Research in Reading*, 32(1): 75–91.

Locke, T. & Kato, H. (2012) 'Poetry for the Broken-Hearted', *English in Australia*, 17(1): 61–79.

McKinney, M. & Giorgis, C. (2009) 'Narrating and Performing Identity: Literacy Specialists' Writing Identities', *Journal of Literacy Research*, 41(1): 104–149.

Moje, E. B. &, Luke, A. (2009) 'Literacy and Identity: Examining the Metaphors in History and Contemporary Research', *Reading Research Quarterly*, 44(4): 415–437.

Morgan, D. N. (2010) 'Preservice Teachers as Writers', *Literacy Research and Instruction*, 49(4): 352–365.

Murray, D. (1985) *A Writer Teaches Writing: A Practical Method of Teaching Composition*, Boston, MA: Houghton Mifflin.

NWP (National Writing Project) & Nagin, C. (2006) *Because Writing Matters: Improving Student Writing in Our Schools*, San Francisco, CA: Jossey-Bass.

Robbins, B. W. (1996) 'Teachers as Writers: Tensions between Theory and Practice', *Journal of Teaching Writing*, 15(1): 107–128.

Root, R. L. & Steinberg, M. (Eds.) (1996) *Those Who Do, Can: Teachers Writing, Writers Teaching*, Urbana, IL: NCTE.

Rummel, M. K. & Quintero, P. (1997) *Teachers'/Reading Teachers' Lives*, Albany: State University of New York Press.

Ryan, M. & Barton, G. (2014) 'The Spatialized Practices of Teaching Writing in Elementary Schools', *Research in the Teaching of English*, 48(3): 303–328.

Seban, D. & Tavsanli, Ö. F. (2015) 'Children's Sense of Being a Writer', *International Electronic Journal of Elementary Education*, 7(2): 217–234.

Woodard, R. L. (2015) 'The Dialogic Interplay of Writing and Teaching Writing', *Research in the Teaching of English*, 50(1): 35–59.

Woodard, R. (2017) 'Working Towards 'I'm a Writer a Pretty Good Writer'. In: Steinberg, M. Cremin, T. & Locke, T. (Eds.), *Writer Identity and the Teaching and Learning of Writing*, 115–131, London and NZ, Routledge.

Yeo, M. (2007) 'New Literacies, Alternative Texts: Teachers' Conceptualisations of Composition and Literacy', *English Teaching: Practice and Critique*, 6(1): 113–131.

Yoon, H. S. (2014) 'Assessing Children in Kindergarten: The Narrowing of Language, Culture and Identity in the Testing Era', *Journal of Early Childhood Literacy*, 15(3): 364–393.

Chapter 18

Teaching poetry within an accountability culture

Andrew Lambirth

Introduction

The arts have always been the objects of persecution by governments when their economies are in crisis and austerity measures have been implemented. Despite the popular, but wrong-headed, myth that artists and poets thrive in an environment of oppression and poverty, I will argue in this chapter that there are specific positive conditions which are favourable for people to engage with poetry and the arts. I intend this chapter to contribute to the debate on whether teachers and children can explore poems in an atmosphere framed within the context of austerity and its consequences on education policy in England and the United Kingdom. These policy decisions, I want to argue, have systematically increased curricula regulation, control and made accountability measures a serious and damaging distraction for teachers.

If you think this is a gloomy subject for a chapter on poetry, please do not despair; my arguments will be informed by my experience of evaluating an inspirational professional development course for primary school teachers in England about poetry, taught mainly by published poets and writers. I shall describe the course and how the teachers, working within an accountability culture, responded professionally and personally to what the poets and the poems were 'telling them' about the arts and how to teach poetry. I will begin with the debate on current education policy and will introduce the notion of the 'culture of positivism' (Giroux, 1997) which I contend affects the climate for teaching the arts in schools. I will introduce the idea of aesthetic response as being a form of 'disinterested engagement' (Scruton, 1998), a notion that was, I believe, central to the message from the development course. I will conclude with some suggestions about how teachers can best approach the teaching of poetry in primary schools.

An accountability culture

Perryman, Ball, Maguire and Braun (2011) have argued that since the 1988 Education Reform Act, the professional work and status of teachers in England have been increasingly regulated and subsequently undermined by a number of key policy changes: namely the introduction of the National Curriculum, Statutory Assessment Tasks (SATs) and League Tables. It is within this policy context that the demand for accountability of teachers and headteachers has been the main drive. In arguing in the 1980s for more control over teachers' practice, Lord Donoghue stated:

> What had clearly become one of the great weaknesses of our system was its non- accountability. The secret garden had become a weed patch...you could no longer depend on the total dedication of the teaching force; it therefore needed more accountability.
>
> (cited in Chitty, 1989, p.67)

Those in business working alongside government policymakers, determined to produce a more flexible and arguably compliant workforce, were becoming increasingly concerned that state employed teachers had been working for too long in an environment that they found difficult to control. This perception by governments has led to what Perryman et al. (2011, p.181) call a 'low trust regime of increased accountability in education'. Consistent and determined monitoring of teachers' practice by increased surveillance and performance reporting was implemented to ensure what governments in England justified as a means to control the quality of teaching. Since 1989 successive governments in England, where this culture of accountability is probably at its most corrosive, have continued to introduce legislation which has tightened the control on teachers' practice. Much of this has been powered by mandatory use of objective quantitative measures to ensure all children in schools progress in a staged, linear trajectory, designed by external agencies for government. Furthermore, accountability has been measured by formal audits of student learning outcomes controlled by senior management, who themselves face scrutiny by their governors and the national inspection service. The evidence for pupil performance is measured by their outcomes and by classroom observation. In effect, school children have become objects and targets and the headteacher and senior management team made publicly accountable.

Lankshear and Knobel (2009) have argued that as a result of these changes schooling has lost its place as part of universal welfare rights, based on a social democratic model and has instead been transformed into a subsector of the economy as a whole. As Lyotard (1993) once explained, the knowledge provided in schools is no longer valued for what it offers in terms of universal truths about the human condition, the arts and the sciences, but instead its value is measured by what it offers in terms of exchange value and it is this that provides legitimacy for its transmission. It is worth quoting Lankshear and Knobel here fully:

> This is the principle of optimising the overall performance of social institutions (like schools) according to the criterion of efficiency. Specific institutions are legitimated by their contribution to maximising performance of the

state or corporate systems of which they are a part. In this way, enhanced demonstrable, measurable performance becomes its own end.

(Lankshear and Knobel, 2009, p.62)

To what extent can the arts and poetry find legitimacy in these environments? To further understand the difficulties faced by teachers in schools who want to encourage engagement with the arts, I want to introduce Giroux's epistemological and ideological positioning of modern contexts in schools.

A 'culture of positivism'

Giroux (1997), in a classic text, espoused the notion that a 'culture of positivism' dominates contemporary schooling in much of the world and has become more intense during periods of neo-liberal governance of education policy. Giroux (1997) describes the culture of positivism as being part of a legacy of general positivistic thought but makes an important distinction between the specific philosophical movement of positivism and, what he calls, forms of cultural hegemony. Major assumptions within this culture of positivism are drawn from the logic of the scientific methodology of the natural sciences. These include an emphasis on explanation, prediction and technical control. Giroux does not attack the philosophical basis of positivism and its contribution to science, but instead its proliferation into other aspects of our daily existence which can contribute to a deadening of the potential of the subjective experience and the unique form of knowledge it yields.

Giroux argues that the culture of positivism builds upon the notion of objectivity and the crucial separation of values from knowledge and forms of methodological inquiry. A 'fact' within a culture of positivism is by necessity objective and value free. Researchers in pursuit of these facts engage in inquiry that is itself thought to be value free. Importantly for the argument I am making in this chapter, this culture of positivism seeps into other domains beyond the methodology of the natural sciences:

The point here is that the culture of positivism is not just a set of ideas, disseminated by the culture industry; it is also a material force, a set of material practices that are embedded in the routine experiences of our daily lives.

(Giroux, 1997, p.12)

For Giroux, a positivistic mode of rationality fosters a mono-dimensional view of the world and divorces 'facts' from their social, historical contexts. Furthermore, important links between knowledge, imagination, will and creativity are lost within the positivistic reductionist tendency to perceive all phenomena as prisoners of the positivist empirical formulation.

Giroux (1997) argues that a culture of positivism applied to education is manifested in a search for reliability, consistency and quantitative predictions. The perception of knowledge becomes mediated through specific classroom method-ologies and is reduced to only what is countable, measurable and subsequently impersonal. Giroux contends that the result is the exclusion of values, feelings, subjectivity, 'possibility', questioning and a vision of 'what could be'. Instead, an adulation of 'facts' and a commitment to the politics of 'what is' dominates classrooms.

As you will see, expecting the arts and poetry to be embraced within this epis-temological and ideological environment creates serious challenges for the arts in many schools today. I intend to show that a satisfying, aesthetic engagement with the arts requires a radical shift in thinking and the intellectual tools used for perception, away from the normalised ontological and epistemological assump-tions towards the promotion of a heightened, transformed subjective experience that can act as a compass to an alternative way to 'know' the world.

Poetry in schools

Elsewhere, I have co-written about the long-time woeful neglect in schools of the enormous contribution poetry can make to young people's knowledge and intel-lectual development (Dymoke, Lambirth and Wilson, 2014). There have been a number of reports and studies over the years, for instance, that have shown that poetry is the least well taught part of English Curricula in the United Kingdom and abroad (Thompson, 1996; Ofsted, 2007; Locke, 2009). Moreover, due to the pressures that schools face, outlined above, poetry is disappearing from some schools altogether (Henry, 2001; Ofsted, 2007). We know that there are specific pedagogical challenges when it comes to teaching poetry, for both experienced and novice teachers, and that teachers' lack of confidence in teaching poetry is often one of the main reasons for some of the resulting teaching approaches(see Benton, 1984; Ray, 1999; Dymoke and Hughes, 2009; Lambirth et al., 2012). A culture of positivism in schools adds a further dimension to these already seri-ous challenges based on a normalised permissive discourse on the very nature of knowledge and perception. So, I was very pleased to be asked to take the role of a 'critical friend' and evaluate a high-profile poetry professional development course for primary school teachers being run by one of the United Kingdom's leading literacy Continuing Professional Development (CPD) providers.

The CPD

The course consisted of a programme of workshops for primary teachers. The workshops were co-delivered by a skilled and knowledgeable tutor from the CPD provider, and four poets and an anthologist who were described as the 'expert tutors'. It became clear to me that the role of the poets on the pro-gramme became pivotal in providing an important epistemological and conse-quently ideological bridge from the everyday culture of positivism operating in schools towards an understanding that knowledge can be discovered differently through the aesthetic lens of poetry and the arts. The course spanned two terms of an academic year, from February 2017–July 2017. Each poet involved worked with the CPD provider to develop and lead one of the days. Each session had a unique focus on an aspect of poetry. These sessions were based around the particular poet's inspirations, perspectives and passions and involved listening to, responding to, reading and writing poetry.

The course provided participating teachers with access to a number of resources. These included resources for their own professional and personal development about poetry and poets, as well as resources to support their teaching: poetry books by the poets involved; academic and professional work on teaching poetry; videos of poets performing their work; and teaching sequences related to the poets on the programme.

The five sessions focused on:

- Language and wordplay;
- Poetic forms and structures;
- Poetry across a range of cultures;
- Extended forms of poetry; verse novels, rhyming texts and lyrical language;
- The final session focussed on anthologies (led by a poetry anthologist).

My evaluation included observations of each session; two teacher surveys (beginning and end), interviews with participants, and the study of teachers' written 'case studies' of the poetry teaching they had been undertaking as well as their own reflections on attending the course.

Around 20 teachers participated in the programme. Only two of the participating teachers stated in their survey that they were already confident to teach poetry. The rest declared some form of unease about teaching it. In the initial survey the teachers were asked to name five poets. Most could do this. The five most cited being Rosen, McGough, Zephaniah, Ahlberg and Dahl. Two participants skipped this question and one could name only one. The majority of poets mentioned were poets who wrote for children.

In terms of their own personal interest in poems, most of the teachers stated that they only read poems 'Sometimes' or 'Never'. Out of those, most read poems (mainly written for children) for a combination of pleasure and for professional reasons. By the end of the programme this changed, with all of them stating that they now read poems for pleasure.

What the poets tell us

My observations of the sessions began to convince me that most of the poets, in introducing their sessions, needed to establish for the teachers a specific methodology for exploring poetry and the arts that appeared to have its own ontological and epistemological foundation. I want to call this aesthetic environment that was being created an 'arts bubble' that shielded the participating teachers from the normal discourses of school life. The poets wanted teachers to realise that the world around them can be engaged with and understood in ways with which they may be less consciously familiar. For me, this was something that everyone who wants to enjoy the arts might need to consider. I want to call it a form of 'aesthetic engagement' and, in this case, it was through the poems that the poets introduced which acted as a lens to this new kind of meaning-making about the world and human experience.

In the first two sessions each poet made a declaration to the group that they were not teachers but poets. By doing so, they gave notice that the discourses they brought were not those of current teaching accountability cultures. The first poet in session one informed the group that he was going to read many poems and that if what he said about the poems was found useful then 'all the better'. But his intention was to forefront the poems for their own sake. There were no specific objectives attached to the readings and the stated outcomes were refreshingly nebulous. Already the discourses of normal day-to-day exchanges and especially those associated with accountability cultures and the general culture of positivism were being challenged by his approach. A young female participating teacher I interviewed later told me she was at first sceptical and resistant to the way the poets in the first two sessions appeared to her to be simply reading their poems. She described the poets as 'going on a bit and I was ready to do something a bit more practical'. Yet as the sessions developed, she recognised that the poems could move her:

> I realised that there were poems that could really speak to me. One of the poems gave me goose-bumps on my arms.

The foregrounding of poems being read for their own sake by the poets highlighted how poems can create what Andrews (1991) has called 'margins of silence' and that poems may often provide 'hints and clues and silences' (Dias and Hayhoe, 1988, p.86) that legitimises and encourages a diverting of our normal means of understanding and interpreting the world and so lead to engagement in deep personal reflection. The poets in these sessions drew out the rich affordances of the poems and art in general. Implicit in their message to their audience was what I identified as a 'disinterested' (Scruton, 1998) aesthetic approach, which appeared to have great resonance with the participating teachers. 'Disinterested' does not have the same meaning in this context as one may think. 'Disinterested' engagement has its origins in the philosopher Kant's description of what an aesthetic experience can be for those who participate in the arts. This idea has been later championed by the neo-Kantian philosopher Roger Scruton (1998). Put simply, the pleasure that one can take from a poem or any work of art answers to no empirical interest; it is interest in the poem (or any work of art) for its own sake and that alone which is of most importance. The poem or work of art provides no direct interest in the normal representations, attentions, utilities and logic of our understanding of the world. In other words, the poem has no other purpose than to be a poem read by the reader – the experience of reading the poem does not happen in order to help the reader pass an exam, develop thinking skills, improve English or make any practical difference in the world. It is simply being read to be experienced as a poem. Indeed, as some of the poets pointed out, poetry and the arts can subvert 'meaning'. What we normally credit as being knowledge about the world which has specific functions and can be practically utilised is questioned or even made to appear strange and unusual.

I like to link this position on aesthetic engagement with Rosenblatt's (1978) differentiation between what she called 'aesthetic' and 'efferent' readings. According to Rosenblatt, these form the two poles of a continuum in the process and experience of reading. An aesthetic reading will adopt a reading stance which attends to the lived through experience during the reading of the poem (Rosenblatt, 1988). With this our attention is directed to the private and emotive elements of the meaning-making. In contrast to this, the attention given with efferent reading stances, is primarily what will remain after the reading (Rosenblatt, 1978). Instead of a more 'disinterested' stance, as with the aesthetic reading, there is an interest in what is explicitly provided by the text – sources of information, instruction and so on which have direct utility in the world. Rosenblatt was clear that any text can be read from either of these two stances and that most readings fall somewhere along the aesthetic/efferent continuum and readers can fluctuate as they read (Pantaleo, 2013). So, in order to encourage more aesthetic reading, teachers have a specific pedagogical challenge to overcome, particularly in environments which generally encourage reading approaches associated with a culture of positivism.

With a 'disinterested' aesthetic stance to the reading of poems, the reading experience is one which can include the justification for the legitimacy for subverted and distorted representations of our day-to-day understanding of the world and the experience of living within it. The poets in the course sessions demonstrated how poets and artists take advantage of the affordances which their art provides. One poet opened his session with a reading of Edwin Morgan's *The Loch Ness Monster's Song* to show how meanings can be made using the most unusual methods. After being introduced by the CPD tutor, without any initial commentary, the poet gave an animated reading of the poem. This poem consists entirely of what the readers must assume are the vocalisations of the Loch Ness monster, and strangely we found ourselves making meaning from what was being sung by this beast. For me, as the observer, and for the participating teachers, something unusual was happening; our normal means of attending to and representing the world were being interrupted and subverted. We were being encouraged to leave behind, temporarily, our standard means of engaging with the world and for some, as the teacher above testified, this was initially troubling. The poet went on to compound the challenge by introducing nonsense poems that equally demonstrated the way poems can subvert what we think we know about the world.

Another poet on a subsequent day presented an idea that drew on the work of the surrealist writer and poet Andre Breton. The participating teachers were asked to write, in what Breton called 'a stream of consciousness'; to 'let themselves go' for ten minutes, 'removing' as he said, 'that part of the brain that makes sense of things'. They were asked to write non-stop and not to think about what they were doing, allowing the words to come out spontaneously onto the page. Again, there was some initial scepticism from some of the teachers, but generally they appeared to enjoy the exercise. There was no planning of the writing, no editing and the work they produced had no specific function. Any normal 'interest', utility and logic in the production and content of the writing was suspended.

The teachers were asked to comment about what they had learned on these days about poems. One said poems can 'Play with readers' expectations and this is very clever'. Another said 'Poems provide different ways of conveying meaning. That it is about imagination not information'.

For me, these opening experiences introduced by the poets were establishing the methodological environment required to support the participating teachers to engage with the specific art of poetry. Embedded school cultures, their associated ideologies and discourses that normally define the legitimated knowledge and methodology of schooling in the classroom and staffroom – associated with a culture of positivism – were challenged and indeed smashed by the poets. The poets thoroughly understood the necessary cultural environment that was needed to secure a place for where their art could be fruitfully explored. By so doing, the poets introduced a model of methodology for a poetry pedagogy, one that the participating teachers could transfer to their own classrooms.

Teachers were very positive about the course and many comments in their case study notes demonstrated an increase in their confidence to teach poetry. A number of these comments emphasised how their own experience of engaging with poetry had influenced their teaching of poetry. One teacher reported:

> Since I have become more enthusiastic about it [poetry] the children are more interested. I have been reading a poem everyday with no work connected to it.

Another teacher spoke about her close observations of her children when she used one of the contributing poet's work:

> I really like watching the children mouthing the last word of the poem as they get the rhythm and pattern of the poem.

One teacher commented on the impact of the programme on her own feelings about poetry:

> Before I would think 'poetry schmoetry', now I'm bringing in poetry wherever I can, as I see it as being important.

There were some teachers who discussed the challenge of bringing poetry into their classrooms. Significantly, there were examples of teachers reporting that they found themselves needing to change their own professional attitudes and those of their colleagues to accept the place of poetry in their schools. One teacher wrote that: 'I had to take my ego out of the lessons. I had to step back a bit'. This teacher had introduced poetry journals to the children in her class in response to one of the suggestions provided on the course. Poetry journals are books where children can write poems whenever they feel inclined. The introduction of these journals made the teacher accept work from the children that was not necessarily linked to any learning objective. Finding the time and place for poetry was a challenging task for many of the teachers and many understood the need to release engagement with poetry from many of the formal strictures associated with school 'work'. Another teacher wrote:

> Exposure to a range of poetry was necessary. It was important, then, that I developed a habit, myself, of reading poems to the children without any expectation of a formal response. They found this strange at first, but I could tell they relaxed once they realised there was no written task involved! I had to overcome some of my own hang-ups too; SATs were looming and reading poetry just didn't seem to be the best way of getting evidence for that writing checklist...but I went ahead and focused on animal poems for fun and, eventually, we used these as part of our topic on endangered species.

Summary and ways forward with 'bubbles'

In times when education policy is attempting to reduce state schooling to being only about maximising the performance of the state and corporate systems of which they are a part, the arts can be considered as superfluous. This is compounded when teachers are held to account for their commitment and focus on reaching these ends. At these times, poetry and the arts need to be protected and given what I want to call 'bubbles' of intellectual and aesthetic space in schools, which can shield children from the pervasive and damaging effects of the culture of positivism, which in turn can affect their willingness to engage with the arts. In the absence of a government determined to fundamentally change the present form of education policy, teachers may wish to consider ways to at least create temporary arts 'bubbles' where poetry can begin to be nurtured to thrive in schools.

These arts bubbles are formed by teachers carefully introducing ways of representing the world aesthetically that can challenge a culture of positivism – an epistemological and consequently an ideological approach that children may well have just undergone in their previous classroom sessions. For poetry, this is undertaken by reading poems and asking children to read and perform poems suspended from the normal pedagogical discourses of schooling. This was modelled well by the poets' approach discussed earlier in this chapter. As I have already reported, the poets gently introduced poems in ways that encouraged the teachers to study the 'silences' and spaces left by the poems and to begin to open up the ways the poems explore and represent the world. The power of the poems themselves support this kind of aesthetic reading. Within this 'bubble' teachers can create a 'safe' environment for the children to experience the arts through poems. There are many approaches and ideas to assist children in engaging with poetry. The list of book recommendations at the end of this chapter will support these experiences. But the 'bubble' needs to be formed right from the start.

3 × 10 poetry planning

A few years ago, I had the great privilege of working alongside my then-colleague, the teacher and poet Susanna Steele, on a project that was similar to the course discussed in this chapter. We devised a plan to ensure poetry has 3 x 10 minutes of space in a day. It was a way to inflate the 'arts bubble' that I have been discussing in this chapter.

The 3 × 10 plan suggests that teachers choose 12 poems – three to be read every day from Monday through to Thursday. Teachers can collect poems in threes which have a theme – food, weather, animals, the sea etc. There needs to be enough copies of the poems for children to choose one and to take it away with them. Teachers then choose three 10-minute periods in the school day when they can read one poem each time. For example: one first thing in the morning/before break time, just before or after lunch and just before home time. After the reading of each poem the plan suggests that teachers ask the children to talk about their responses to the poem as a whole group, with the teacher leading the discussion and sharing their own personal responses too. The 3 x 10 plan is intended to have a light touch with a focus on enjoyment and aesthetic engagement and so teachers need to encourage personal responses before anything else. With younger children the poem could be projected on the interactive whiteboard, whilst older children may want a copy to read for themselves.

At the end of the last reading of the day, the teacher asks the class which of the three poems they would like to take home. The children are asked to read the poem they have chosen to another member of their family and to try and remember the relative's response. For younger/less experienced children the parents can be asked to read it to the child. The intention is for the teacher to get some feedback the next day. Some children may not wish to take a poem home, or they might not like any of the poems, or they may be unsure about reading poetry. As the week progresses teachers will need to be aware of any changes in responses. As this is about the pleasures of poetry, it is important to make taking a poem home a choice not an obligation. On Friday the teacher can ask the children to choose their favourite poems from all 12 they have heard in the week. The children can then form small groups to plan a reading of a poem chosen from the 12.

30 minutes a day can create arts bubbles based on poetry. The poems lead the discussions amongst the group and hopefully will open up opportunities for children to begin to grasp aesthetic engagement and free them and the teachers from the everyday imposed school discourses and to enable a 'disinterested' relationship with the art form.

Summary

Poetry and the arts cannot coexist well in schools operating within an accountability regime that feeds off a culture of positivism. Governments responsible for policies that lead to these cultures must be removed from office; teachers have an important political role to play in this mission. But when policies like these persist, or when the arts are forced into the background for other reasons, then teachers may wish to find ways to nurture engagement with the arts by introducing these art 'bubbles' that can float free, even temporarily, from the day-to-day pervasive discourses. Good luck.

Questions for reflection

What effects does the accountability culture have in the schools you know?
What role do poems have in your personal life?
If you are a primary school teacher, do you feel confident that poetry is enjoyed by children in your class?

Further reading and resources

Rosen, M. (2016) *What is Poetry? The Essential Guide to Reading and Writing Poems*, London: Walker Books.
This is a very accessible handbook for teachers or children who want an introduction to what poetry is all about. It explains what poetry can be and what one can do with it and goes on to talk about how one can write poems too.

Furniss, T. & Bath, M. (1996) *Reading Poetry: An Introduction*, Hemel Hempstead: Prentice Hall Europe.
There are many books that provide a more academic introduction to poetry. This is the book I used to improve my understanding of how best to read and enjoy poems. I still refer to it regularly.

Dymoke, S. Lambirth, A. & Wilson, A. (Eds.) (2015) *Making Poetry Matter: International Research on Poetry Pedagogy*, London: Bloomsbury.
Dymoke, S. Lambirth, A. & Wilson, A. (Eds.) (2014) *Making Poetry Happen: Transforming the Poetry Classroom*, London: Bloomsbury.

Two books for which I was partly responsible. These books were the result of a high-profile seminar series on poetry that brought together academics, teachers and poets to talk about giving poetry a higher profile in primary and secondary schools. The *Matters* book contains research about poetry in schools and the *Happen* book contains practical ideas for poetry in schools.

References

Andrews, R. (1991) *The Problem with Poetry*, Milton Keynes: Open University Press.

Benton, M. (1984) 'Teaching poetry: The rhetoric and the reality', *Oxford Review of Education*, 1(3): 19–27.

Chitty, C. (1989) *Towards a New Education System. The Victory of the New Right?* London: Falmer.

Dias, P. & Hayhoe, M. (1988) *Developing Response to Poetry*, Buckingham: Open University Press.

Dymoke, S. & Hughes, J. (2009) 'Using a poetry wiki: How can the medium support pre-service teachers of English in their professional learning about writing poetry and teaching poetry writing in a digital age?' *English Teaching: Practice and Critique*, 8(3): 91–106.

Dymoke, S., Lambirth, A. & Wilson, A. (eds.) (2014) *Making Poetry Happen: Transforming the Poetry Classroom*, London: Bloomsbury.

Dymoke, S., Lambirth, A. & Wilson, A. (eds.) (2015) *Making Poetry Matter: International Research on Poetry Pedagogy*, London: Bloomsbury.

Furniss, T. & Bath, M. (1996) *Reading Poetry: An Introduction*, Hemel Hempstead: Prentice Hall Europe.

Giroux, H. (1997). *Pedagogy and the politics of hope: Theory, culture, and schooling.* Boulder, CO: Westview

Henry, J. (2001) 'Warning to cool the frenzy', *Times Educational Supplement*, November 2nd No. 4453, 8.

Lambirth, A., Smith, S. & Steele, S. (2012) '"Poetry is happening but I don't exactly know how" Literacy Subject Leaders' perceptions of poetry in their primary schools', *Literacy*, 46(2): 73–80.

Lankshear, C. & Knobel, M. (2009) 'More than words: Chris Searle's approach to critical literacy as cultural action', *Race and Class*, 51(2): 59–78.

Locke, T. (2009) 'The disappearance of enjoyment: How literature went wandering in the literacy woods and got lost'. In: Manuel, J., Brock, P., Carter, D. & Sawyer, W. (eds.), *Imagination, Innovation, Creativity: Re-Visioning English in Education*, pp. 123–138, Putney, NSW: Phoenix Education.

Lyotard, J. F. (1993) *The Postmodern Condition: A Report on Knowledge*, Minneapolis, MN: University of Minnesota Press.

Morgan, E. *The Lochness Monster's Song.* Available at: http://www.scottishpoetrylibra ry.org.uk/poem/loch-ness-monsters-song/ (Accessed on 15.04.2019).

Ofsted (2007) *Poetry in Schools A Survey of Practice 2006/7*, London: Ofsted.

Pantaleo, S. (2013) 'Revisiting Rosenblatt's aesthetic response through 'the Arrival'', *Australian Journal of Language and Literacy*, 36(3): 125–134.

Perryman, J., Ball, S., Maguire, M. & Braun, A. (2011) 'Life in the pressure cooker – School league tables and English and mathematics teachers' responses to accountability in a results-driven era', *British Journal of Educational Studies*, 59(2): 179–195.

Ray, R. (1999) 'The diversity of poetry: How trainees teachers' perceptions affect their attitude to poetry teaching', *The Curriculum Journal*, 10(3): 403–418.

Rosenblatt, L. (1978) *The Reader, the Text, the Poem: The Transactional Theory of the Literary Work*, Carbondale, IL: Southern Illinois University Press.

Rosenblatt, L. (1988) 'The literary transaction'. In: Demers, P. (ed.), *The Creating Word*, pp. 66–85, Edmonton, AB: University of Alberta Press.

Scruton, R. (1998) *An Intelligent Person's Guide to Modern Culture*, London: Gerald Duckworth.

Thompson, L. (1996) *The Teaching of Poetry: European Perspectives*, London: Cassell.

Chapter 19

'The needs of the many outweigh the needs of the few'

Support for children with SEND in times of austerity

Andy Bloor

Introduction

After the financial crash in 2010 we began to hear more and more about a term we had only ever heard in passing before: 'austerity'. Irrespective of what your political, economic or ideological views of the term are, the inescapable truth was less money was flowing into the public sector than it had before. So, when, in 2011 the government first fielded the need for a significant review of the support given to children with a Special Educational Need / Disability (SEND), some believed that it was an attempt to redraw lines of accountability and duty. This chapter will consider some of the moral and theoretical perspectives around the debate about the allocation of resources in schools at the start of the 21st century. It will consider if there are any moral imperatives around the debates on how we fund education for all children, but particularly those with a Special Educational Need and Disability (SEND). It will finally consider what responses we can and should make when faced with difficult choices around funding and what current theory and debates can do to support us in making considered, proactive, positive and empowering choices. I do not for one minute presume to offer any answers; indeed, I do not think there are any easy answers to such a morally difficult question, but if this chapter can at least trigger a reasoned and grounded debate, I will consider it to have been successful.

Historical context

After a recent visit to the US, I cracked my head open and had to go to the Emergency Room. On entering, the first thing I was asked was 'Who are you insured with?' Coming from the UK, a country where I grew up with a National Health Service (NHS), this came as a bit of a culture shock. In Accident & Emergency in the UK, the only concerns are 'what is wrong with you and how urgent is your need?' An American friend of mine was recently taken ill in the UK. He is diabetic and is used to paying for his insulin and needles. He was startled that the main concern was for his wellbeing. He kept expecting charges to be levied upon him, but throughout his whole stay in Accident & Emergency whilst he expected someone to come and explain how he would be billed, the only people who spoke to him were nurses and doctors. That night I saw our NHS through an outsider's eyes, and I was even more grateful that we have universal healthcare in the UK.

As has been observed, the NHS was set up because:

> Illness is neither an indulgence for which people have to pay, nor an offence for which they should be penalised, but a misfortune the cost of which should be shared by the community.
>
> (Attrib. T.H. Marshall, although also often to Bevan)

Indeed, the 'Father of the NHS' Aneurin Bevan stated that:

> Their entrance into the scheme, and their having a free doctor and a free hospital service, is emancipation for many... There is nothing that destroys the family budget of the professional worker more than heavy hospital bills and doctors' bills.
>
> (Bevan, 1948)

Growing up in the 1970s and 80s, I remember my grandparents talking about a time when you had to pay to see a doctor and often had to think twice about it, no matter how ill you were. This was often followed by a short lecture about the importance of the NHS and how much we should value it.

In 1970, the Education Act (Handicapped Children) moved the responsibility of education of handicapped children (who we now refer to as those with a Special Educational Need / Disability or SEND) from the medical profession to the Local Education Authority. The result was that for almost the first time, settings had to consider the education of some of the most severely disabled in society. Initially the response was a categorisation of needs, which included the term 'ineducable', describing those children who it was felt could not benefit from education in the 'normal sense'. This was challenged and reframed in 1978 by the Report of the Committee of Enquiry into the Education of Handicapped Children and Young People (known as the Warnock Report) which saw education as:

> a good, and a specifically human good, to which all human beings are entitled. There exists, therefore, a clear obligation to educate the most severely disabled for no other reason than that they are human.
>
> (1.7, DfES, 1978)

In the 21st century we have come to understand the term 'good' to be a consumable commodity. In the UK this could be traced back to the 1988 Education Act. This act created a sense of the parent as consumer, school as provider of a service and children as educational units to be maximised. I believe, however, that Warnock meant it to mean a 'good thing' – a wholesome thing – to which all children are entitled, simply by the fact they are human.

A term often used in relation to Special Educational Needs is 'one-in-five' or '20 percent'. This concept came originally from the Warnock Report, where it was stated one in five children may need a SEND provision at some point in their life, but Warnock was clear to point out that this did not mean 'one in five' would need it persistently throughout their schooling. Instead, it was posited that whilst there would be a core group of children with persistent needs, the majority would have short-term needs that could be met with short-term support.

This often used term 'one in five' is most commonly attributed to the Warnock report, but as we have already noted, the concept of SEND expressed in the report (and the subsequent Education Act 1981 that followed it), was radically different from our current concept. Today, whilst we have absorbed the 'familial and social' difficulties a child may encounter in their lives into the general support any child can expect from their teacher, the 'one in five' now relates to a core of children with long-term pervasive difficulties. Further though, whilst the report made it clear that children should ideally be educated in their local mainstream school, they could be educated in a special school or attached unit if it was the right place for them. This is not, however, how the report is often character-ised. This led in 2005 to the rather odd spectacle of Warnock pointing out that inclusion was not being enacted as her committee had seen it and being roundly mocked for saying this. Warnock summed up her position as: 'Inclusion is not a matter of where you are geographically, but of where you feel you belong' (cited in Murray and Lawson, 2006, p.41–2). This view opens up the possibility for 'inclusion' to mean a specialist school placement where the child feels a sense of belonging.

It is a sign of how far we have come when Warnock cited the potential needs as 'familial or social' (DfES, 1978, 1.2). Today many teachers would consider it an everyday core part of their professional activity. The support of children with social or familial needs – familial separation/breakup, poverty and a home envi-ronment of criminal or offending behaviour – has become so much a part of the professional role that as teacher educators we routinely talk to our trainees about it as naturally as we would planning and assessment. Yet still the one in five / 20 percent figure persists.

In 2010 the education inspectorate in the UK, the Office for Standards in Education (OFSTED) published the report 'The Special Educational Needs and Disability Review: A Statement is not Enough.' In it they again reiterated the one in five figure, but here there was a different understanding; SEND as a concept had shifted so now the 'familial and social' is taken as read – a normal part of a teacher's role – and the 'one in five' now relates to children with pervasive and long-term SEND. The reason for this increase in a specific part of the SEND population is manifold. Two examples are that children being born with complex medical disabilities are now surviving when even just two decades ago they would have died in infancy; and there is a recognition of conditions (Autism/Asperger's

Syndrome, ADHD) that whilst emergent would probably not have been recognised as requiring specialist educational input in 1978. This is generally seen as a positive thing; children are now getting the support they need to make the best educational progress possible. Children that previously may have been seen as ineducable are now seen as warranting education; indeed, in the case of children with 'locked in syndrome' and cerebral palsy, we are now in a position to recognise that cognitively there may be no impairment at all.

No longer then is 'looking after' a child potentially in an institutional setting such as an asylum for the mentally ill, acceptable. We can draw a direct line from the 1970 Handicapped Children Act, through Warnock, to the Children and Families Act (2010) showing how education for children with SEND has moved from being perceived as a medical issue and instead an issue that, whilst it may be grounded in a medical aetiology, is addressed in the educational sphere. With rising complexity of need though, comes the requirement to fund even more complex input.

What then of the funding? Where does it come from and how is it distributed? The next section will move on to consider the imperatives – moral and economic – behind the decisions being made regarding the funding of children with SEND.

Moral and economic imperatives

In October 2019 the Social Affairs editor of *The Times*, Greg Hurst, wrote an article entitled 'Pupils lose out as £400m schools funding diverted to special needs'. Before one even reads this article there are immediate problems with the premise of it. The idea that 'special needs' is benefitting anyone other than children is ludicrous, but there is a darker subtext here. Hurst goes on to make this even clearer:

> Children have been losing out because millions of pounds earmarked for their education has been siphoned off to pay for special needs education.

The othering of children with SEND – the idea that they are not part of the 'children' mentioned in the quote – is insidious and deeply concerning. It has been observed and documented that children with SEND are all too often disproportionately represented as victims of bullying, with media stories still telling of situations where children have been placed in difficult situations that have exacerbated bullying (Chatzitheochari, Parsons and Platt, 2014; Education Policy Institute, 2018; Jayanetti, 2019).

One idea I will keep returning to is the moral imperative for a headteacher in a school. Let us imagine that this fictitious headteacher has been given funding to support the individual needs of one child. This amount of money, however, will also fix the hole in the roof above the school hall. At the moment a bucket is constantly having to be used and carefully monitored in rainy weather. Should the headteacher fix the hole in the roof – which is disadvantaging all children – and thus ensure the needs of all children are supported, or use the funding as it was intended, for the child with SEND? I realise this is a vast over-simplification of a complex matter and does not address issues around the legality of any potentially ring-fenced money, but the dilemma itself is one that works at both a micro- and macro-level. Do the needs of the many outweigh the needs of the few?

In discussing this theory, we are looking at the ethical theory of Utilitarianism. Utilitarianism considers what the final utility of an action is; what action will cause the greatest good and the least ill? In this matter, we consider the difference between Hume's 'is' and 'ought' as expressed by Bentham (Williams, 2011; Brown and Morris, 2012; Baujard, 2010). Hume acknowledges the gap between what ought to be and what is – a moral gap that we seek to narrow and even remove in a utopian society. When we consider this with Bentham's Utilitarianism theory, we commoditise the idea of people feeling good about doing the 'right thing'; of narrowing the gap between 'ought' and 'is'. There are echoes here of Russell's statements regarding the desires that drive mankind to do the right thing:

> all the important human relations, socially desirable acts, towards which there is an instinct not strong enough to be always compelling, are enforced by social ethics.
>
> (Russell, 2009, p.13)

All these may be summated then by the maxim that man should acknowledge that all he does is ultimately driven by his own desires. There may be a direct effect or simply the good feeling of having 'done the right thing', but whatever we do, we do because we want to, not because we perceive it in itself as intrinsically 'right'.

Let us then come back to the headteacher and the hole in the roof. The headteacher feels an ambivalence to the situation. The child with SEND deserves the right to a good education and common orthodoxy says that good inclusive practice means a child should be educated in their local mainstream school, with suitable adaptations made to ensure that they can access the curriculum in as meaningful a way as possible and as comparably close to their peers as is possible. At this point, it would be useful to bring in the legal imperative to the act. In the UK, an Education Health & Care Plan (EHCP) usually carries with it funding attached to whatever provision is necessary. Currently, each school receives funding either directly from central government or via the Local Authority (LA) for children with additional needs that are not severe enough to require a specialist EHCP. For those children that *do* require an EHCP, the additional finance is allocated via top-up funding from the LA. For those children with an EHCP, a place in a special(ist) school setting is often an outcome of the plan. Where the dilemma comes (especially for our fictional headteacher) is the funding that comes as part of the generalist school budget for those children under the threshold for a statutory assessment.

The Children & Families Act in the UK is enacted through the Code of Practice (2015), which, regarding funding, states that:

> Schools have an amount identified within their overall budget, called the notional SEN budget. This is not a ring-fenced amount, and it is for the school to provide high quality appropriate support from the whole of its budget.

(6.96, DfE / DOH, 2015)

In most cases, budget decisions fall on the headteacher and yet it would seem more useful to involve other members of the school team in these discussions. It has always been surprising to me that whilst a school's Special Educational Needs Coordinator (SENCo) should ideally be a member of the Senior Leadership Team in a school, how rarely they know what the notional budget is and, in some cases, that it even exists. Despite this, the above paragraph makes it clear that the school should only be using this to supplement high quality support for all its children.

So, let us return to our fictitious headteacher: they have exemplified best practice and told their SENCo about the notional budget. With the SENCo they have carefully planned what needs to be spent to ensure best practice, but there remains the dilemma that since the money is not ring-fenced, they can do as they wish with it. There could be another scenario though; one where the budget is insufficient, and needs cannot be met. Now we are in the territory of the dilemma we explored at the beginning: what happens when the notional budget does not cover the need?

It is likely that, as is often the case, any cuts will come in what might appear to be small, almost imperceptible ways. An example of this is an article from the Stoke-on-Trent daily newspaper *The Sentinel*, where it was observed that Staffordshire County Council felt the need to cut their budget on residential care for children with severe needs (McInnes, 2019). The number of families impacted by this decision may be relatively low, reflecting the number of children with the most severe needs, but the nature of that impact on those families would be profound. So, was the council's decision correct? And what might the headteacher in my ongoing scenario do?

'The body politic'

Austerity can be described as a movement which focuses on social engineering of the population; where austerity is a response to an economic crisis (McRuer, 2018). This in itself is a compelling narrative; is austerity a myth aimed at suppressing people; a way of pushing through an agenda where funding to those groups that are not deemed necessary are underfunded in a sanctioned manner? In discussing the contentious term 'Crip' from which he draws the term 'Crip Theory', McRuer claims that austerity is in fact crippling disabled people. Far from allowing them autonomy and empowered lives, austerity is limiting and, in some extreme cases, cutting short lives. This then is political policy as a form of social engineering. It would be easy to dismiss this as hyperbole, but this is exactly the political situation that existed in the late 1930s Germany; indeed, it is worth remembering that the first phase of the Holocaust targeted the disabled (Russell, 2019).

It has also been argued that the way we use 'the body' as an object is in itself an act of marginalisation. This is particularly the case where others are making a decision about an individual's body. When examining the concept of disability, there are several different models that can help us to understand it on a theoretical basis. Of them, the two most prevalent are the Social Model and the Medical Model. The Medical Model considers a disability to be housed with the individual; it is their physical or mental impairment that disables them. Thus, to support them best we need to support them as individuals. The Social Model argues that the disability rests with society; that it is society that disables a person not they themselves. An example is a person who uses a wheelchair accessing an entrance to a building. The entrance to the building is four feet above street level. Society can either put in a ramp (that everyone can use) or stairs (that only able-bodied people can use). If we subscribe to the Medical Model, then the problem lies with the fact that the person uses a wheelchair: we need to consider how we support them in overcoming this barrier. If we see disability through the Social Model, then the decision is wholly down to society: will we put in a ramp or stairs? The choice about which is used will determine if the person wanting to enter the building is disabled or not. This leads to an idea that how disabled someone is lies in the gift of society. This of course has darker overtones when we consider the power of the individual who makes decisions about another's body. In some cases, we are not only not enabled by society, but sometimes actively debilitated by it. The Right to Maim considers the idea from the US that it is seen as preferable for arresting police officers, when faced with a hostile situation, to maim someone rather than to kill them; that even though this is debilitating them, it is still a preferable alternative to killing them (Puar, 2017). This approach sanctions the debilitation of a person's body as a preferable to its elimination, but in allowing this to happen, society sanctions the maiming. In the case of funding for a child with SEND, are we giving authorities the right to disable as a preference to no funding at all?

Returning to our child in the school: the headteacher may decide to fill in the hole in the roof at the cost of some (or possibly all) the provision for the child with SEND. Maybe this means that the child does not get access to the full curriculum; maybe there are times when they are integrated into the space but are not able to be fully included. The hearing-impaired child who has sign language lessons when the other children have music or the child who uses a wheelchair who is always the referee/scorer in all Physical Education lessons. The child is debilitated by the choices that the school has made about how they may or may not access the curriculum. This is the perfect example of where the Medical Model of disability incorrectly places the onus on the individual to address the social situation in which they find themselves. The decision, whilst ostensibly benign, has in fact limited the child's capabilities – when in reality the child could have been able to access the curriculum fully. The decision is presented as a 'lesser evil' and thus sanctioned on this basis. However, this does not allow any dissent to the orthodoxy that this is 'the right approach' and when used in conjunction with a prevalent narrative of austerity it becomes an almost unassailable argument.

Who gets funding in the first place is also an issue. A child in England, for example, will only get direct funding after an exhaustive assessment and a resultant individual EHCP is created for them. Up to this point the assessment and support of a child's needs is left to the gift of the school. This is congruent with approaches taken in other parts of the world (such as Bulgaria) where disability is seen as something that must be assessed and 'awarded' as a status to someone (Mladenov, 2015). This is distinctly at odds, however, with the English definition in the Equality Act 2010, where whilst disability is framed, it is entirely self-defining for the individual themselves and need have no input from a clinician or an assessment process.

But what are the long-term implications of this? It can easily be argued that by denying a child with a disability an effective education you are limiting their ability to both take a productive role in society, as well as flourish economically in future life. In the case of countries like the US for example, where one of the highest reasons for bankruptcy is an inability to pay for medical bills, then a reduction in the economic capacity of the individual to care for their most basic needs creates a significant inequality on a basic human rights level (Puar, 2017).

The economist Amartya Sen gives us another angle on poverty though that bears consideration: poverty as capability deprivation (Sen, 2009) (see also Chapter 1 for a discussion on this). Predominantly, poverty is described in purely economic terms, but once we consider what the impact on the person is, it is natural to consider the impact on the wellbeing of individuals. In 2019 the New Zealand government declared that it was to undertake a 'wellbeing budget' (Ainge Roy, 2019). New Zealand claimed that whilst other countries measured wellbeing by economic growth and wealth, they wanted to focus more on mental health as a measure of wellbeing; essentially, how the economy can make you happy. This rejects the common marker of 'growth' as the measure of economic success and instead focusses on how successful the economy is in making its residents feel mentally well. This ties in with Sen's concept of wealth and poverty and leads us onto the question 'How do we best use our wealth/capital for the greatest wellbeing of the population?'

By returning to utilitarianism we may find a way through this argument. If we accept that we are a society as a whole and reject Hurst's (2019) inferred othering and segregation of children with SEND, then we are considering the wellbeing of all the children in a school. Given this, we need to consider if a bucket in the hall catching the rain is preferable to even one child being denied access to education. Could it be that the price of all children being genuinely included is a slight inconvenience (even a reduction in quality) to all? If we consider the utility to be education of all in a school, then this becomes a compelling argument.

What this does not consider, however, is that there are some very difficult decisions being made in schools today. When you have 'trimmed the fat' in a situation by reducing waste and rationalising the resources you have, when further cuts are necessary, you start 'cutting into the flesh' of provision. Here the temptation is to look at the resources that are creating the greatest demand and see if these can be eliminated from the system. I would argue that tempting as this may be, when we do this by denying some children the right to an education, it is too high a price to pay.

Summary

We must avoid the 'othering' of children with SEND at all costs; if we fail, it will be too easy to exclude them from education. Instead, we need to consider what the utility or 'outcome' of education is. How do children with SEND fit in to this narrative and how do we use this view to inform the decisions we make when funding is reduced? If we are successful in the ideological aspect of inclusion then the practical aspects of protecting disabled children's human rights and, in particular, their right to live a life not blighted by either economic poverty or social/ life-choice poverty are more likely to be attainable, even in times of austerity.

This in itself brings us to the most critical aspect of all funding for children with a disability: how, if at all, we are helping the children of today to self-actualise themselves into the successful and productive adults of tomorrow? Poverty of any description, including economic and social poverty will blight any individual's opportunities. At a time when the government are talking about special educational needs covering children from 0 to 25 years of age, the only acceptable reality is for their education to prepare them successfully for the future that they, and we as their fellow members of society deserve; for only when we accept that the disabled child's utility is the same as the utility of the wider society will it truly become the inclusive society that aspire to.

Questions for reflection

When we are faced with austerity measures, what are acceptable and unacceptable cuts?

How can we protect against the 'othering' of any group of children in our schools, but especially children with SEND?

What is the 'utility' in your school? How do you – indeed do you at all – articulate the purpose of your school? How precise is this utility? Is this utility measurable?

Further reading and resources

Cohen, S. (2011) *Folk Devils and Moral Panics*, London: Routledge.
This text considers how demonisation of groups and their subsequent 'othering' is something that has a historical basis and historical answers to the dilemmas of difference. This is a seminal text in understanding how people are made 'other' and how society creates narratives around people that it views as outside the norm.

Lander, V. & Knowles, G. (2011) *Diversity, Equality and Achievement in Education*, London: Sage.
This work considers the othering of children, seen through the lens of critical race theory. It asks us to question the inherent prejudices we have in education and how we tackle them. This is a text that keeps rewarding the reader with thought-provoking ideas and questions to enable us all to critically reflect on our own practice.

Luxon, N. (ed.) (2019) *Archives of Power. Foucault on State Power in the Lives of Ordinary People*, Minneapolis: University of Minnesota Press.
This work looks at one of the seminal thinkers on the subject of power. Foucault is a controversial figure, mainly due to the provocative nature of his thinking, but despite the challenge of his writing, it is nonetheless worth the effort of engaging with his work.

References

Ainge Roy, E. (2019) New Zealand's world-first 'wellbeing' budget to focus on poverty and mental health. *The Guardian* (Online) 14 May 2019. Available at: https ://www.theguardian.com/world/2019/may/14/new-zealands-world-first-well being-budget-to-focus-on-poverty-and-mental-health (Accessed: 20.01.2020).

Baujard, A. (2010) Collective interest vs. individual interest in Bentham's Felicific Calculus. Questioning welfarism and fairness. *European Journal of the History of Economic Thought*, 17(4), 607–634.

Bevan, A. (1948) National health service. *Hansard: House of Commons Debate.* February 1948, Vol. 447, Column 48. Available at: https://hansard.parliamen t.uk/Commons/1948-02-09/debates/4c6dfcf8-0c50-45f8-9538-0622bdd22 8cc/NationalHealthService (Accessed: 27.09.2019).

Brown, C. R. & Morris, W. E. (2012) *Starting with Hume*, London: Continuum.

Chatzitheochari, S., Parsons, S. & Platt, L. (2014) *Bullying Experiences Among Disabled Children and Young People in England: Evidence from Two Longitudinal Studies*, Department of Quantitative Social Science, IoE. Available at: http://rep ec.ioe.ac.uk/REPEc/pdf/qsswp1411.pdf (Accessed: 12.12.2019).

Department for Education and Science (DfES) (1978) *Special Educational Needs. Report of the Committee of Enquiry into the Education of Handicapped Children and Young People*, London: HMSO, Available at: http://www.educationengland .org.uk/documents/warnock/warnock1978.html (Accessed 27.09.2019).

DfE / DoH (2015) *Special Educational Needs and Disability Code of Practice: 0 to 25 Years. Statutory Guidance for Organisations Who Work with and Support Children and Young People with Special Educational Needs and Disabilities.* Available at: https://assets.publishing.service.gov.uk/government/uploads/syste m/uploads/attachment_data/file/398815/SEND_Code_of_Practice_January _2015.pdf (Accessed: 27.09.19).

Education Policy Institute (2018) *Bullying: A Review of the Evidence.* Available at: https://epi.org.uk/publications-and-research/bullying-a-review-of-the-evide nce/ (Accessed: 12.12.2019).

Hurst, G. (2019) 'Pupils lose out as £400m schools funding diverted to special needs'. *The Times* 14 October 2019.

Jayanetti, C. (2019) Teachers 'forced special needs child to make a list of his faults'. *The Guardian*, 28 July 2019. Available at: https://www.theguardian.com/ed ucation/2019/jul/28/derby-primary-school-boy-with-special-needs-blamed -for-being-bullied (Accessed: 12.12.2019).

McInnes, K. (2019) 'We feel like our heart is being ripped out' – Government urged to step in as five special schools face losing all their residential care funding.

McRuer, R. (2018) *Crip Times. Disability, Globalization, and Resistance*, New York: New York University Press.

Mladenov, T. (2015) *Critical Theory and Disability. A Phenomenological Approach*, London: Bloomsbury.

Murray, D. & Lawson, W. (2006) Inclusion through technology for autistic children. In: Cigman, R. (eds.), *Included or Excluded?: The Challenge of the Mainstream for Some SEN Children*. Available at: http://ebookcentral.proquest.com/lib/derby/ detail.action?docID=425420 (Accessed 29.09.19).

National Archives (2010) *Equality Act 2010*. Available at: http://www.legislation.go v.uk/ukpga/2010/15/contents (Accessed 01.02.19).

Ofsted (2010) *The Special Educational Needs and Disability Review: A Statement Is Not Enough*, Nottingham: HMSO.

Puar, J. K. (2017) *The Right to Maim. Debility, Capacity, Disability*, Durham, NC: Duke University Press.

Russell, B. (2009) *Marriage and Morals*, Abingdon: Routledge.

Russell, M. (2019) *Capitalism & Disability. Selected Writings by Martha Russell*, ed. Rosenthal, K., Chicago, IL: Haymarket Press.

Sen, A. (2009) *The Idea of Justice*, London: Penguin.

Stoke-On-TrentLive / The Sentinel, 16 September 2019. Available at: https://ww w.stokesentinel.co.uk/news/stoke-on-trent-news/we-feel-like-heart-being-331 3811 (Accessed 10.01.2020).

Warnock, M. (2005) *Impact 11: Special Educational Needs: A New Look*, London: Philosophy of Education Society of Great Britain.

Williams, B. (2011) *Ethics and the Limits of Philosophy*, London: Routledge.

Chapter 20

Leading the way

Catherine Carden

Introduction

Leadership in primary education, and of primary schools, is regularly debated, be it through Ofsted reports, an article in the local newspaper about a headteacher, a report on the crisis around recruiting leaders for our primary schools or tweets about primary leaders marching against the lack of school funding.

There is no doubt that there are challenges facing the leadership of primary education in England. The National Governance Association (NGA) reports that governors are struggling to recruit headteachers and senior leaders, particularly in deprived areas (NGA, 2015; Weale, 2016) with 26% of the 261 primary schools advertising for headships in January 2013 having to re-advertise within two months (The Future Leaders Trust, 2016). At the time of writing (October, 2018) there were 55 live advertisements on the Times Education Supplement (TES) for primary headteachers. It is not only recruitment that is the challenge but also attrition. A Mayor of London Report in 2016 identified that 50% of the headteachers in London were aged 50 years or over and nearing retirement, with The Future Leadership Trust Survey (2016) identifying that out of the 268 headteachers they interviewed, 28% plan to leave headship within five years and half did not expect to be a headteacher in ten years time (The Future Leadership Trust, 2016).

Whilst this is of serious concern, as headteachers are indeed the significant leaders in schools, this chapter will debate the idea that we are *all* leaders. Through developing such a mindset, I would argue that there exists great potential to establish a robust and sustainable primary education system based upon effective and strong contemporary leadership. The barriers to achieving such strength and sustainability within primary leadership will be identified by exploring the challenges, arguments and questions that arise when applying concepts and ideas to the 'real life' of the school and classroom.

The chapter will begin by presenting a debate relating to the differences between leadership and management, before going on to discuss who might be leaders. I will then go on to explore what is key to great leadership and how this can be upheld even when times get tough. The chapter then finishes with some suggestions as to the way forward for leadership in educational settings.

What does leadership mean?

Leadership is a common term in education parlance, yet 'if put on the spot and asked to define leadership it is a struggle' (Carden, 2019, p.69). Some will put forward a simple, clean definition of the term such as 'the activity of leading a group of people or an organisation or the ability to do this' (Business Dictionary, n.d.) whilst others argue that leadership is a far more complex notion that has a variety of definitions (Kotterman, 2006; Bogenschneider, 2016; University of Cambridge, 2017). Such complexity often leads to definitions of leadership becoming a list of skills and attributes of effective leaders, which in itself is not a definition of leadership but a theoretical perspective of effective leadership as the possession of key traits.

Rather than perceiving leadership as a simple term to be defined, it would be better to understand it as a multi-layered, complex concept. Four key theories, adapted from the work of Eddy and Van der Linden (2006) are summarised in Table 20.1.

Management, on the other hand, is much easier to define and centres on the process of attaining organisational objectives through co-ordination of resources and business activity and directing a group of people through the hierarchy structure (Katz, 1955 cited in Algahtani, 2014; Shead, 2019).

Often the terms management and leadership are used interchangably with persons referring to themselves as 'part of the management team' or as 'a manager' whilst others reference a 'leadership team' and being 'a leader'. The difference in the choice of vocabulary used in this context is confusing and demonstrates a distinct lack of understanding between these two functions (Kotterman, 2006; Kotter, 2013). The words utilised also change the emphasis of the role, with those referring to themselves and their team as managers more likely to be adopting a much more managerial, top-down approach than those who are referencing leadership and perceive themselves as leaders.

Leadership and management are not the same thing and should not be conflated (Kotter, 2013). In order to lead an organisation or team effectively these terms must be clearly defined and understood, highlighting the absolute differences between the two. Figure 20.1 summarises how leadership and management are different, highlighting the importance of strong leadership and the drawbacks of being trapped in a managerial approach. It must be assumed that most leaders will aspire to be on the right-hand side of the diagram but may notice that the daily tasks taking up the majority of their time, sit to the left-hand side. It can be difficult to see a way to move from left to right and Crowley (2011) suggests that this might be attributable to the fact that leaders are trapped in an industrial management mode. A move from left to right requires a clear understanding of what it is to lead, an investment of time and focus as well as the courage to make difficult and bold decisions with regards to changes in practice and process.

It must also be acknowledged that management and leadership can at times overlap (Kotterman, 2006). As a leader, there are parts of the role description and expectations that are managerial tasks and cannot be avoided or ignored. Tasks

Table 20.1 Leadership theories adapted from Eddy and Vander Linden (2006)

Leadership Theory Category	Summary	Example Theories
Trait Theories	Suggests that effective leaders all share similar personality and characteristic traits –which they are born with – and links personal traits to specific behaviours. Traits of effective leaders might include: trustworthiness, decisiveness, people skills, competency, creativity, assertiveness, empathy and intelligence (Cherry, 2018).	Trait Theory Great Man Theory
Power & Influence Theories	Based on how the leader chooses to utilise the power and influence they have in order to achieve what they need to achieve. Power can be used both positively and negatively with positional power through hierarchy playing a key role.	Transactional Leadership Transformational Leadership
Behavioural Theories	Focused on what successful leaders do and how they behave rather than the innate qualities of leaders. For example, do leaders involve their team in decision making or simply tell their team what to do? This theory suggests that leadership skills can be learned rather than being based upon our personality traits. Behavioural theories are linked to the leadership styles of autocratic, democratic and laissez faire identified by Lewin in the 1930s. It is now commonly understood that the best leaders can use a mix of styles.	Transactional Leadership French and Raven's Five Forms of Power Transformational Leadership
Contingency Theories	This theory acknowledges that there is no ideal type of leader or leadership style but that approaches to leadership must adapt to suit the situation. This theory also acknowledges that the same leader can, and indeed should, behave differently in different situations being able to match the correct style to the circumstance.	Situational leadership theory Path-Goal Theory Fielder's Contingency Model

such as completion of the budget, submission of data, the writing of reports and the signing off on actions are all managerial tasks rather than leadership activity but are a necessary requirement of a leader. Leading does not preclude someone from undertaking such tasks; what is important is that leaders must be consciously aware of when they are leading and when they are managing.

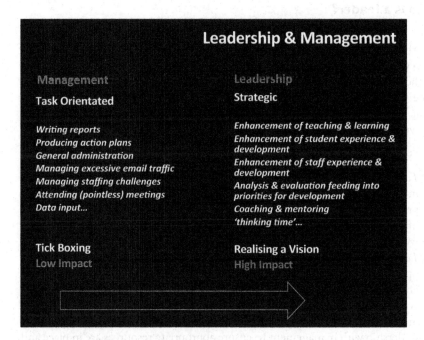

Figure 20.1 The difference between leadership and management.

Whilst there exists a significant body of work exploring the differences between leadership and management there is an alternative view that highlights a lack of scientific evidence that these terms are in fact different (Azad, Anderson, Brooks et al., 2017). Azad, Anderson, Brooks et al. (ibid.) go on to say that exploring these concepts as individual functions has the potential to do organisations more harm than good. Instead, they argue that leadership and management are not just complementary but are in essence the same concept on a continuum that forms the 'framework for skills and abilities that are necessary for an individual to drive team success' (ibid., p.102). Acknowledging this continuum might enable people to identify when they are managing and when they are leading, and perhaps consider the appropriateness of when to use each approach.

At times, managerialism overshadows investment in leadership because of the need, desire, and pressure to achieve quick results (Carden, 2019). However, it is long-term, sustainable results that should be desired, rather than quick fixes, and investment in strong leadership brings such results. This in turn leads to a more stable and motivated workforce and creates a culture where leaders are able to find solutions and a way to steer through the challenges and pressures they face with clarity and purpose, taking the organisation into a better future (Kotter, 2013).

The remainder of this chapter will focus on leadership as opposed to management. It might be timely at this point to consider whether you perceive leadership and management as very different concepts or favour the idea of a continuum.

Who is a leader?

When we talk of leaders we often think of the person at the top of the hierarchy; the Headteacher in a school, or simply put, the most 'important' person. However, leading, and being a leader should not be identified solely with becoming the Headteacher, the 'boss' or the person 'in charge' (Kotter, 2013); I would argue that we should all see ourselves as leaders. Being a leader is much more about how you present and conduct yourself, and the behaviours you exhibit, than your place in the hierarchy. It is therefore helpful to see leadership in three ways:

- *Leading ourselves*: This refers to how we behave as a professional and contribute to useful and relevant change. This involves engagement with continuing professional development, contributions to the wider school community and interactions with others. Here, management skills need to be called upon with regards to time management and prioritisation of work;
- *Leading learning*: This refers to how we work within our settings to ensure optimum learning takes place. Consider how you work with others as you engage children in their learning and create intrigue and interest that offers you the opportunity to challenge and stretch yourself and others. This might include successfully working with other adults in the classroom; combining leadership with management to ensure appropriate resources are in place and that the classroom is managed in the most appropriate manner;
- *Leading others*: As we progress within our careers it is normal to take on responsibility for others. As a teacher you are often leading others from an early stage. If there is a Teaching Assistant (TA) in the classroom it is the responsibility of the class teacher to lead this person, to support their development and enable them to support you in establishing change and to lead learning effectively. The same could be applied to student teachers or volunteer readers. Changing perspective to that of leading rather than managing other personnel can change your ethos and approach.

So, I would argue that leadership involves all personnel in a setting, and this includes the governors. In order for the SLT to develop into strong leaders who are able to make difficult decisions and be brave, the school must accumulate a strong and informed governing body. Governance is a key element of the leadership and management of a school and influences inspection outcomes (James, 2015). Governors must offer robust challenges to the Headteacher but at the same time offer relevant support. A strong governing body will fully understand the context of the school, its challenges and aspirations and be prepared to support and challenge the Headteacher in addressing and realising these (NGA, 2017).

The combination of a strong leadership team and strong governing body enables the school to robustly face challenges, create space for creativity and innovation and move the school forward. Here is a brief example of this approach in practice:

St John's Primary School had a first-time, new-to-post Headteacher. The school was the result of an amalgamation of two schools. When the school was inspected in February 2014 it was placed into special measures in all categories. The introduction of a skilled Interim Executive Board and the commitment and vision of the Headteacher saw the school removed from measures in March 2016. Further leadership development, the refusal to academise, providing evidence to the DfE that despite the school meeting their 'coasting' definition, progress was being made and the development of a strong governing body enabled the school to move forward gaining a grading of 'good' in September 2018. This was only possible as a result of strong and courageous leadership and governance.

It may seem a simple equation: strong Headteacher and leadership team plus skilled and informed governing body equals strong school leadership that affords the school space to be innovative, creative and to stick to their vision and values. The formula is not foolproof, however. Governance is a voluntary role with significant responsibility, and staff mobility in many schools is fluid for a number of reasons. It falls upon the Headteacher to ensure that there is excellent succession planning and capacity building whilst creating an environment whereby staff want to remain at the school and offering a structure that creates career progression. At the same time the chair of the governing body must ensure a thoughtful and balanced governance, which in itself requires them to be informed, skilled, knowledgeable and a strong leader in their own right (DfE, 2014).

Recognising these different types of leadership, and discussing the implications within educational settings, is vital for several reasons. Practitioners need to have a strong awareness of the part they play in the setting; if there are too many leaders co-ordinating activities and focusing on their own goals and priorities, useful results can be side-lined by the perceived need for each leader to influence others (Markman, 2016). In such a situation, each leader wishes their way of working to be the influence. This can lead to organisational paralysis and internal conflict.

Additionally, considering everyone to have the potential to be a leader can lead to a perceived de-valuing of leadership resulting in too many leaders and no followers. Not everybody wants to lead or has the capacity to do so. Aspiring to be a leader is not enough (Myatt, 2013); self-reflection and evaluation as a professional is key in order to be realistic apropos your capacity to develop as a leader and which category of leader that might be.

What is key to great leadership?

Highly effective leadership is needed within our schools for three key reasons:

- Education is a constantly changing, increasingly competitive and dynamic environment (Kairys, 2018);

- Teaching, in England, is a chaotic and challenging career prone to intense political interference, the regular movement of goalposts and subject to a rigorous testing and inspection regime;
- Teacher recruitment and retention is a significant challenge which is being directly linked to teacher wellbeing and workload (House of Commons Education Committee, 2017).

Many of the challenges outlined above are magnified by a lack of strong and effective leadership at all levels from policy-making decisions through to school leadership. Knee-jerk reactions to new initiatives and changing policy results in both school leaders and teachers having to change their approach and focus on a regular basis. Headteachers feel significant pressure to ensure their school performs at a high level against varying benchmarks, inspection regimes as well as national and international league tables (More Than a Score, 2019). This pressure filters to staff and then the children. Often, as a result of such pressures, Headteachers and wider leadership teams implement initiative after initiative fearing the consequences of non-compliance. Yet, the real consequences of such an approach are teachers choosing to leave the profession, staff sickness and a negative impact on the school community and the educational experience for the children.

Navigating a way through challenges of teacher retention, workload, finance and the accountability agenda is not an easy task. Having the strength to step back and do what is right for the school is a key requirement for any leader.

Leadership experts (Hargreaves, Boyle and Harris, 2014; Bak-Maier, 2018; Wiseman, 2010; Crowley, 2011) suggest varying requirements and behaviours of effective leadership which can be collated into four areas:

- Have vision and a clear set of values;
- Look after people;
- Create an effective team;
- Be brave, have courage, be happy and slow down.

I shall now discuss each of these in turn.

Have vision and a clear set of values

Having a clear vision is key: a vision for life, work and the team. In order to establish this vision, career direction, aspirations and goals need to be considered. A vision does not need to remain fixed and may change as you move through your career. A vision cannot be achieved independently; the support and commitment of others is key in the achievement of any vision and, as such, a vision should be shared. Establishing personal and professional values can be a complex exercise but it is one that is vitally important for any strong leader. To establish a clear set of values, a leader must consider what they believe in, what their moral purpose is and what actions and aspects of behaviour are tolerable and which are not. Personal values form the foundation upon which actions are taken and decisions made: who you choose to work with, and for, and the way you present yourself. Personal values should be referenced and checked back on regularly as part of the process of self-reflection (see Chapter 2 by Jonathan Barnes for further discussion on values).

Creating a personal vision and set of values is an important first step to undertake as a leader yet it does not stop here. A strong leader will work with their team in order to establish a co-constructed vision and set of values for the team. An example of a set of co-created values can be seen in Figure 20.2. These values were developed by the Primary Initial Teacher Education Team at Canterbury Christ Church University and underpin their work with student teachers and partnership schools, as well as within the team.

Whilst many believe in the importance of establishing a vision statement and set of values for a school (Gupta, 2017; Monteith, 2018), some challenge the value of these, suggesting that vision statements are often comprised of

VALUES IN THE PRIMARY PHASE OF THE SCHOOL OF TEACHER EDUCATION AND DEVELOPMENT AT CANTERBURY CHRIST CHURCH UNIVERSITY

We believe that our work as individuals and as a community of educators needs to be set within a framework of clearly articulated values. Values are deeply held beliefs that act as 'guides to action' at every level of our lives. Values provide every one of us with direction and define the destination of our actions. When we discuss our values it helps to clarify what drives us.

Sometimes we find that our personal values conflict with those of the place where we work or study. Recognising these disagreements helps to stop us feeling unhappy, misunderstood or compromised. It is unlikely that we will agree on everything but conversations about what is most meaningful and important to each of us builds our understanding of ourselves and others and enhances our professional identity.

We highlight the following themes as providing a potential focus for a values discussion:

- **Community**: *We recognise the importance of learning from each other through conversation, co-operation, collaboration and building quality relationships*
- **Respect**: *We know that learning can flourish in environments where people feel trusted, nurtured, loved and supported in becoming autonomous*
- **Knowledge**: *We believe in the importance of developing the expertise of all learners in all disciplines*
- **Evidence**: *We affirm that all educational activity needs to be underpinned by research, debate and the opportunity for critical reflection*
- **Innovation**: *We seek to support each other to move beyond compliance by taking risks, being creative and thinking globally*

Figure 20.2 Co-constructed team values in Primary ITE at Canterbury Christ Church University.

meaningless marketing jargon that may look impressive but have very little impact on how a school operates (Allen and Kern, 2018). It is argued that establishing a vision statement will not be the cure for a school in challenging circumstances (Martin, 2012).

Look after people

People are important: employees, employers, colleagues, pupils, parents and mentors. It is vital to get to know them, look after them and consider their welfare. A priority for any leader must be to create a safe environment that enables people to flourish, make mistakes and learn.

Areas for professional development and next steps are often the focus for learning conversations and post lesson observation debriefs. This is of course important to enable progress and improvement, yet at the same time it is important to take time to celebrate and cheer colleagues' successes, as everyone needs cheering from time to time (Bak-Maier, 2018). This celebration can be undertaken privately, publicly, or indeed both. A good leader, who knows their people, will know how their team would prefer their successes to be recognised; more importantly, the recognition must be genuine, specific and sincere (Crowley, 2011).

Working in education is all about working effectively with people. School life can be frenetic, and all too often teaching staff and leaders become embroiled in endless task completion, which can result in staff becoming isolated in their own offices and classrooms. Connecting with people is crucial but is often the first thing that stops when the pressure is on. A good leader reminds people to prioritise connecting with others and being more visible (Bak-Maier, 2018; Hargreaves, Boyle and Harris 2014).

Creating an environment of trust is vital when working with people (Hargreaves, Boyle and Harris, 2014). In order to gain trust a person must themselves trust others rather than be skeptical of them. A leader must believe in, and trust, the people that work with and for them as people will not often, and rarely intentionally, let their leader down (Bak-Maier, 2018).

It is important for any leader to support and empower those who work for them. Empowering people is reliant on allowing others to have autonomy and voice, as well as the opportunity to have the final say on matters that are under their control. Wiseman (2010) suggests giving those reporting directly to you 51% of the vote. Whilst this sounds a daunting prospect, it in fact creates decision makers and increases accountability whilst at the same time opens the door to different approaches and ideas. Handing over decision-making powers is not easy for a leader, but failing to do so has significant long-term consequences; staff become disillusioned, demotivated and will, over time, cease making suggestions or sharing ideas. A leader must acknowledge that not all the decisions made by staff will be successful or indeed correct but it is their role to afford people the opportunity to fail (Wiseman, 2010) and then learn. Creating an environment whereby staff are empowered to grow and succeed is something all effective leaders need to aspire to. It is important that when staff do grow and succeed that the leader does not begin to feel threatened (Hargreaves, Boyle and Harris, 2014). A good leader will constantly aim to push others to the fore, identifying talent and supporting those who are talented to become smarter than the leader (Wiseman, 2010). This is a key measure of a good leader.

Create an effective team

Creating results with and for other people is what leadership is all about (Bak-Maier, 2018). To do this you must create an effective team as no one can achieve great things alone. After all, 'there is no "I" in team'. This, in one sense is true, however, to lead an effective team, a leader must look after and invest in themselves, ensuring they have access to opportunity and reward just as much as their team do. If a leader fails to look after themselves, it is the team that ultimately suffers. Bak-Maier (2018) sums this up by suggesting that whilst there is no 'I' in team, 'there is also no we without an I'.

Whilst many may chase leadership positions for status, leadership has little to do with a position in a hierarchy, organisation or team (Bak-Maier, 2018). Position and job title are merely a by-product of becoming a leader. People in pursuit of promotion for the place in the hierarchy and the job title – those leaders who believe that things and people are beneath them now that they have 'made it' – are not, in my view, true leaders. Leaders who give orders to their team instead of asking questions need to critically reflect upon the impact that their approach is having upon their team and their credibility (Wiseman, 2010). It is vital that a leader stays grounded and works alongside their team to achieve a shared vision. Nothing should be beneath you as a leader (Hargreaves, Boyle and Harris, 2014).

To establish an effective team, a leader must know exactly what talent is required and, at the same time, always seek ways to improve and strengthen their team (Crowley, 2011). Professional development for all staff is therefore key. A leader must, firstly, identify potential within their team and, secondly, ensure that the appropriate development opportunities are made available. This may include offering opportunities and experiences that are beyond the staff member's current role – for example observing, or contributing to, a senior leadership team meeting. This affords staff the opportunity to have a glimpse of working in a different context and opens their eyes to new, and future opportunities. When identifying talent, it is important that a leader is not simply drawn to the extroverts but seeks potential in the quieter members of staff too (Hargreaves, Boyle and Harris, 2014).

Be brave, have courage, be happy and slow down

Being an effective leader is not easy and, at times, can be lonely but these four suggestions may help:

Be brave: As a leader it is important to be your unique self rather than feeling obliged to always conform and follow convention. It is important that a leader takes risks, is bold and seizes opportunities that leave them feeling both excited yet slightly afraid (Bak-Maier, 2018; Barsh and Cranston, 2009). It is such acts that inspire others;

Have courage: A leader needs to address poor performance and team members who do not effectively contribute to the team; they cannot ignore behaviours that challenge the core values of the team. A leader has to 'have a team that will walk through a hail of bullets with [them]. And [they] have to be willing to do it [for their team]' (Barsh and Cranston, 2009, p.118);

Be happy: A leader should focus on being happy. Happiness is motivating and happier leaders are generally more effective (Joseph, Dhanani, Shen et al., 2015). A leader should also focus on creating a happy environment and staff as happier teams are more creative. Being happy also improves our physical health and stamina (Barsh and Cranston, 2009). Ways to achieve this can be by simply smiling more often and greeting everyone as you go by with a smile and positive greeting. There are also ways in which you can work to develop your own happiness such as practising mindfulness, ensuring you are being proactive in managing your wellbeing and taking time to reflect on achievements. Different approaches will work for different people;

Slow down: Slowing down and taking time to think gives a leader greater authority and wisdom to make better decisions. Leaders are effective when they achieve wise results over and above quick results. Poor decisions are often made when a leader allows herself to be rushed (Bak-Maier, 2018). Part of this is striving for a work–life balance, to ensure that mentally you are in a good place to make decisions in a measured and timely way. Achieving a work-life balance is a hot topic within education, with the workload surveys, guidance and toolkit emerging from the DfE (2014, 2019 2017, 2018). Barsh and Cranston (2009) challenge the idea of leaders being able to achieve a work–life balance and suggest that they should stop chasing this unattainable ideal but instead adapt to a life of 'managed disequilibrium'. A managed disequilibrium acknowledges that there are times when work will be the priority and 'take over' but highlights the importance of balancing this with other times when greater time is created for friends and family (Barsh and Cranston, 2009).

This section has championed a leadership approach that is developmental and supportive; one offering opportunity, autonomy and empowerment. However, an effective leader must have a hard edge and expect a lot (Wiseman, 2010). A leader must address issues, challenge people, create belief in the impossible and hold people to account (Bak-Maier, 2018). A leader must address concerns regarding performance, tackle team members who are blocking progress, who are difficult or exhibiting 'prima donna' style behaviours (Wiseman, 2010). These difficult conversations must result in a clear message being conveyed whilst at the same time be conducted with dignity. It is vital to avoid a poisonous culture developing, and that a leader does not burn bridges or harbour grudges as a result of these conversations (Hargreaves, Boyle and Harris 2014).

An effective leader also needs to know how to cope when times get tough and the next section will examine this.

What happens when times are tough?

Being a leader in education is a privilege, yet at times it can be extremely challenging with significant demands and pressure. It is during these more difficult times that it is important to remember the privilege of working with, and leading, children and colleagues. Allow yourself to fall in love with your job and the people with whom you work every day. Even the most challenging of children and colleagues have endearing characteristics! Allow yourself to embrace the emotions that come with leadership. Laugh a lot, cry if needed, let off steam appropriately and most importantly take time to be creative, have fun and remain enthusiastic (Bak-Maier, 2018).

Leadership requires resilience and the path to leadership and the daily life of a leader can be tough. There are many challenges that a leader must face that require difficult decisions to be made and at such times leadership can be lonely (Carden, 2019). It is vital that during such times a leader seeks support and asks for help; having people who will listen and are able to offer practical and realistic advice that helps a leader to find their way (Hargreaves, Boyle and Harris, 2014). Investing time in developing strong support networks of mentors, coaches and supporters who may consist of colleagues, line managers and friends is important (Bak-Mairer 2018, Barsh and Cranston, 2009). Never be afraid to approach people who would be ideal mentors. The worst that can happen is that they politely decline!

Each of these supporting roles are different and can also be complementary:

- A coach – will work to enable you to find the answers and come to decisions through skillful questioning;
- A mentor – usually a more experienced person or someone for whom you have a lot of respect or see as a role model. Mentors listen and will work with you to develop your career, offering advice and guidance;
- A supporter – someone who will champion you and push you forward for things. The person who will make a suggestion to the 'boss' that you would make an excellent candidate for a forthcoming post or someone who will publicly applaud your work (Barsh and Cranston, 2009).

When the pressures of leadership result in working long hours to complete an ever increasing to do list, a leader might find it difficult to justify to themselves, or their teams, the time to network or be mentored or coached; or indeed allocate time within their packed calendars just to think and read. The mere suggestion of engaging in a mentoring and coaching process might add additional pressure to a leader but I would argue that, without attention to a leader's own needs, the whole team will suffer.

A way forward

There is unlikely to be a sudden interest in and applications for leadership posts, especially with the DfE encouraging the development of career pathways outside of movement into a leadership role (DfE, 2019) (which is a positive offer for teachers and is good for the profession). However, other positive solutions need to be explored to compensate for the lack of strong, effective leaders. I would like to offer three possible solutions:

A 'what works' approach: Could inexperienced leaders be supported by a clear blueprint for effective school leadership? Perhaps a leadership toolkit that offers a 'what works' menu of solutions and approaches to support their leadership decisions? Toolkits are championed by the DfE with the workload toolkit being recently introduced (July, 2018). This could take away the pressure to appoint excellent leaders.

Further expansion of Multi-Academy Trusts and Federations: If there are too few strong and effective school leaders and governors, an immediate solution would be to further expand the academy and/or federation model whereby Headteachers are no longer required in the same volume and are replaced by fewer CEOs or Executive Heads. This model perceives the strategic work lying with the CEO or Executive Head who oversee and lead at least two, but often many more, schools. Each individual school then only requires a Head of School (essentially a competent deputy) rather than a Headteacher. These have a much more operational role immediately reducing the need to find each school an effective leader. The same applies to governing bodies with an MAT needing far fewer strategic, informed and knowledgeable people to sit as Directors or Trustees. This is not how all MATs or Federations operate but it could be a very pragmatic and potentially effective solution.

Schemes and pre-prepared resources: Through the teacher workload review, teaching schemes and pre-prepared resources are being increasingly advocated as a way of reducing unnecessary workload (Independent Teacher Workload Review Group, 2016; DfE, 2018). Alongside this, the introduction of schemes for certain curriculum areas could reduce the requirement for effective subject leadership moving more to subject co-ordination.

Summary

There is no blueprint for leadership success and no way of predicting what challenges will confront a leader on any given day. Despite this complexity, leaders are often quickly criticised. Most leaders work extremely hard in order to do what is best or to minimise the impact of an issue or problem, often spending nights awake thinking things over and making extremely difficult decisions that affect the lives of people (Bak-Maier, 2018). To support leaders, staff can refrain from shallow cynicism, not be too quick to judge their leader, support and help their leader and respect the decisions of the leader despite not always agreeing with them (Bak-Maier, 2018). If leaders access support through the establishment of networks and can create a culture of transparency and respect, leadership is an exciting and rewarding role.

There are many factors that will affect a child's educational experience, but a key factor is the effective leadership within and across schools – where every member of staff views themselves as a leader; of learning, of others and of themselves. Those who have significant leadership responsibilities need to be trusted, supported and respected by their teams and in turn leaders must be transparent, create autonomy, invest in their team and see themselves as lifelong learners. This involves setting aside time for their own development through mentoring and coaching as well as taking time to think and read without feeling guilt. Further, they must support their team in doing the same.

Leadership needs to be invested in and understood as a discipline. Schools need to be well led and, as professionals, we need to know when to lead and when to be led. Focusing efforts on effective leadership will offer the opportunity to achieve long-term, sustainable impact which is positive for both staff, children and the wider community. Without strong, knowledgeable leadership our schools will not realise the vision of educational excellence for all.

Questions for reflection

After reading this chapter can you identify areas of your practice or role where you are a leader?

Can you think of a leader who has inspired, supported or developed you; what specific behaviours did they exhibit and how did these behaviours have an impact on you?

What values do you hold, and how are these evident within your leadership practice be that leading yourself, leading learning or leading others?

Further reading and resources

www.womened.org
'#WomenEd is a grassroots movement which connects existing and aspiring leaders in education'. The movement was established by those working in education and has grown into a national network. They have an active Twitter feed, blog and a recently published book called *10% Braver: Inspiring Women to Lead Education.*

Crowley, M. (2011) *Lead from the Heart: Transformational Leadership for the 21st Century*, Bloomington: Balboa Press.
In this book, Mark Crowley debunks the notion that management and leadership are adversely affected if they involve emotion. He advocates the power of leading from the heart in order to achieve increased staff motivation and productivity.

Sinek, S. (2014) *Why Good Leaders Make You Feel Safe* (Ted Talk), https://www.ted .com/talks/simon_sinek_why_good_leaders_make_you_feel_safe?language=en.
In this talk, Simon Sinek explores why leaders who make their employees feel secure are the best leaders. At the same time, he acknowledges that this is not something easily achieved. The talk is inspiring and thought-provoking.

References

Algahtani, A. (2014) 'Are leadership and management different? A review', *The Journal of Management Policies and Practices*, 2(3): 71–82.

Allen, K. & Kern, P. (2018) 'School vision and mission statements should not be dismissed as empty words', *The Conversation*, 14 June 2018, Available at: http://theconversation.com/school-vision-and-mission-statements-should-not-be-dismissed-as-empty-words-97375 (Accessed on 11.05.2019).

Azad, N. H., Anderson Jr, G., Brooks, A., Garza, O., O'Neil, C., Stutz, M. M. & Sobotka, J. L. (2017) 'Leadership and management are one and the same', *American Journal of Pharmaceutical Education*, 81: 6, Article 102.

Bak-Maier, M. (2018) *Keynote Lecture at Senior Leadership Conference*, Canterbury: Canterbury Christ Church University, March 2018.

Barsh, J. & Cranston, S. (2009) *How Remarkable Women Lead*, New York: McKinsey & Company Inc.

Bogenschneider, B. (2016) 'Leadership epistemology', *Creighton Journal of Interdisciplinary Leadership*, 2(2): 3–16.

Business Dictionary (n.d.) *Leadership*. Available at: http://www.businessdictionary.com/definition/leadership.html (Accessed on 17.04.2019).

Carden, C. (2019) 'Are you a manager or a leader?' *Primary School Management*, 3, 69–70.

Carden, C. (2019) 'Leadership can be lonely', *Primary School Management*, 3(2): 73.

Cherry, K. (2018) *Understanding the Trait Theory of Leadership*. Available at https://www.verywellmind.com/what-is-the-trait-theory-of-leadership-2795322 (Accessed on 17.04.2019).

Crowley, M. (2011) *Lead from the Heart*, Bloomington: Balboa Press.

DfE (2014) *Leading Governors: The Role of the Chair of Governors in Schools and Academies*. Available at: https://assets.publishing.service.gov.uk/government/uploads/system/uploads/attachment_data/file/323830/leading-governors-the-role-of-the-chair-of-governors-in-schools-and-academies.pdf (Accessed on 01.05.2019).

DfE (2018) *Ways to Reduce Workload in Your School(s): Tips and Case Studies from School Leaders, Teachers and Sector Experts*. Available at: https://www.gov.uk/government/publications/ways-to-reduce-workload-in-your-school-tips-from-school-leaders (Accessed on 01.05.2019).

DfE (2019) *Teacher Recruitment and Retention Strategy*. Available at: https://assets.publishing.service.gov.uk/government/uploads/system/uploads/attachment

_data/file/786856/DFE_Teacher_Retention_Strategy_Report.pdf (Accessed on 17.04.2019).

Eddy, P. & VenDerLinden, K. (2006) 'Emerging definitions of leadership in higher education: New visions of leadership or same old 'hero' leader?' *Community College Review*, 34(1): 5–26.

Gupta, P. (2017) 'Co-creating a school vision: Steps to follow', *EdTeach Review*, 08 May 2017. Available at: http://ftp.edtechreview.in/trends-insights/insights /2774-co-creating-school-vision (Accessed on 11.05.2019).

Hargreves, A., Boyle, A. & Harris A. (2014) *Uplifting Leadership: How Organisations, Teams and Communities Raise Performance*, San Fransisco: Jossey-Bass.

House of Commons Education Committee (2017) *Recruitment and Retention of Teachers: Fifth Report of Session*, 2016–17.

James, H. (2015) *Effective Relationships with Your Governors*. Headteacher Update, 10 June 2015. Available at http://www.headteacher-update.com/best-practi ce-article/effective-relationships-with-your-governors/86105/   (Accessed 17.04.2019).

Joseph, D., Dhanani, L., Shen, W., McHugh, B. C. & McCord, M. A. (2015) 'Is a happy leader a good leader? A meta-analytic investigation of a leader trait affect and leadership', *The Leadership Quarterly*, 26(4): 557–576.

Kairys, M. (2018) 'The influence of gender on leadership in education management', *International Journal of Education Management*, 32(5): 931–941.

Katz, R. L. (1955). Skills of an effective administrator. *Harvard Business Review*, 33(1), 33–42.

Kotter, J. (2013) 'Management is (still) not leadership', *Harvard Business Review*. Available at: https://hbr.org/2013/01/management-is-still-not-leadership (Accessed on 18.04.2019).

Kotterman, J. (2006) 'Leadership versus management: What's the difference?' *The Journal for Quality and Participation*, 29(2): 13–17.

Markman, A. (2016) 'Too many leaders spoil the group', *Psychology Today*. Available at: https://www.psychologytoday.com/gb/blog/ulterior-motives/201602/too -many-leaders-spoil-the-group (Accessed on 18.04.2019).

Martin, K. (2012) *The Outstanding Organization*, New York: McGraw-Hill Education.

Monteith, A. (2018) *5 Tips on Communicating Your Values and Vision*, Ambition Institute, Available at: https://www.ambition.org.uk/blog/5-tips-communicat ing-your-vision-and-values/ (Accessed on 11.05.2019).

More Than A Score (2019) *Primary School Leaders Deliver Damning Verdict on High-Pressure Testing*. Available at: https://www.morethanascore.org.uk/2019/03 /18/primary-school-leaders-deliver-damning-verdict-on-high-pressure-testing/ (Accessed on 01.05.2019).

Myatt, M. (2013) *Why You're not A leader*, Forbes Available at: https://www.for bes.com/sites/mikemyatt/2013/01/23/why-youre-not-a-leader/#2fbcfa336fb 8 (Accessed on 18.04.2019).

NGA (2015) *NGA Comments on the Findings from the Biggest Governance Survey of the Year*, 4 September 2015. Available at: https://www.nga.org.uk/News/NG A-News/Pre-2016/NGA-comments-on-the-findings-from-the-biggest-gove.asp x (Accessed on 19.10.2018).

NGA (2017) *What Governing Boards Should Expect from Schools Leaders and What School Leaders Should Expect from Governing Boards*. Available at: https://www

.nga.org.uk/getattachment/a15a49f8-609b-47bf-a37e-80d95b8c0653/What-we-expect-2017-Final.pdf (Accessed on 17.04.2019).

Shead, M. (2019) *The Definition of Management*, Leadership 501. Available at: http://www.leadership501.com/definition-of-management/21/ (Accessed on 18.04.2019).

Sinek, S. (2014) *Why Good Leaders Make You Feel Safe*. Available at: https://www.ted.com/talks/simon_sinek_why_good_leaders_make_you_feel_safe (Accessed 21.05.2019).

The Future Leaders Trust (2016) *The Headteacher Shortage in England*, 26 January 2016. Available at: https://www.ambitionschoolleadership.org.uk/blog/englands-headteacher-shortage/ (Accessed on 18.10.2018).

The Independent Teacher Workload Review Group (2016) *Eliminating Unnecessary Workload Around Planning and Teaching Resources*. Available at: https://assets.publishing.service.gov.uk/government/uploads/system/uploads/attachment_data/file/511257/Eliminating-unnecessary-workload-around-planning-and-teaching-resources.pdf (Accessed on 01.05.2019).

University of Cambridge Institute for Sustainable Leadership (CISL) A Report Commissioned by the British Council (2017) *Global Definitions of Leadership and Theories of Leadership Development: Literature Review*, Cambridge, UK, June 2017.

Weale, S. (2016) 'English schools struggling to recruit headteachers, report finds', *The Guardian*, 26 January 2016. Available at: https://www.theguardian.com/education/2016/jan/26/english-schools-struggling-to-recruit-headteachers-research-finds (Accessed on 19.10.2018).

Wiseman, L. (2010) *Multipliers: How the Best Leaders Make Everyone Smarter*, New York: Harper Collins.

WomenEd (n.d.) Available at: www.womened.org (Accessed on 20.05.2019).

Index